The World Chess Championship

The World
Chess Championship

S. GLIGORIĆ. R. G. WADE.

PART ONE TRANSLATED BY LOVETT F. EDWARDS

B. T. Batsford Limited *London*

First published 1972
© S. Gligoric and R. G. Wade, 1972

7134 0358 6

Printed and Bound in Great Britain by
C. Tinling & Co. Ltd, London and Prescot
for the Publishers

B. T. Batsford Ltd
4 Fitzhardinge Street, Portman Square, London W1

Contents

Acknowledgments

Svetozar Gligoric wrote the introduction and Part I in Serbo-Croat and looked over the English translation. Except for the last three pages of Part I the translation was made by Lovett F. Edwards. The cooperation of John Keable at this stage is gratefully acknowledged. The last section of Part I was kindly translated by Drazen Marovic.

The games and abbreviated annotations of Part II were organised by the editor, but the work was carried out as follows:

1948 Tournament	James B. Adams
1951 Match	Kevin J. O'Connell
1954 Match	Leslie S. Blackstock
1957 Match	Leonard M. Pickett
1958 Match	George S. Botterill
1960 Match	Leonard M. Pickett
1961 Match	John L. Moles
1963 Match	Anthony K. Swift
1966 Match	Leslie S. Blackstock
1969 Match	James B. Adams

Part I has been proof-read by Mr. Gligoric and the editor; a considerable portion of the manuscript and proofs of Part II were checked by Daniel Castello to whom the whole team is deeply indebted. In addition thanks are due to Gordon Botley and Kevin Wicker for preparing diagrams and checking proofs.

Books referred to include Keres, *Match Tournament for the World Chess Championship, Hague-Moscow 1948;* Golombek, *World Chess Championship 1948;* Winter and Wade, *World Chess Championship 1951;* Golombek, *World Chess Championship 1954;* Botvinnik, *Match Botvinnik-Smyslov;* Golombek, *World Chess Championship 1957;* Mohaupt and Machatscheck, *Weltmeisterschaftsturnier 1957 Botvinnik-Smyslow* Tal, *Match Tal-Botvinnik 1960;* Alfred Kalnajs and Son, *Tal-Botvinnik II Match;* Wade, *World Chess Championship 1963;* Boleslavsky and Bondarevsky, *Petrosian-Spassky 1969;* O'Kelly, *Campeonato del Mundo 1969*, and various bulletins from the USSR.

R. G. Wade
Editor

Symbols

+	Check
+ +	Double check
±	Some advantage for White
∓	Some advantage for Black
±	Clear advantage for White
∓	Clear advantage for Black
=	Balanced position
!	Good move
!!	Super move
! ?	Interesting move
? !	Doubtful move

W or *B* by the side of each diagram indicates which side is to move. In the text, a number in brackets refers to the number of a diagram of the particular position.

1–0	Black resigned
$\frac{1}{2}$–$\frac{1}{2}$	Draw agreed
0–1	White resigned

Within brackets alternative variations are separated by a semi-colon.

Introduction: After Alekhine

The moment of death has the power to stress in a single move the achievement or the futility of a life.

The death of Alekhine contains a paradox. If he had sought happiness, he found something different; if he had wanted fame, his name will live as long as chess is played. When this solitary man was found dead in his hotel at Estoril near Lisbon, his head drooping to one side, a chessboard in front of him, someone took a snapshot of the scene and thus left us a photograph to serve as a symbol of the journey through life of an unusual personality. Throughout his life he had sold his soul to the god of chess and only thus was he able to scale the heights. Those who might have marvelled at him while he was still alive, loved his creativeness after he was dead. When he was young it disturbed him to have a homeland, for he wanted to be independent, able to go wherever he wished at the summons of a tournament. He had no friends, for he was too self-centred. He had no need of women, for it was with chess alone that he was in love. He married women older than himself. He who passed his whole life in hotels wanted a wife who would not make any demands of her own, but would protect him – the solitary. His predecessor, Capablanca, who owed everything to his genius and nothing to his southern sloth, seemed, in his match against Alekhine 1927, an unarmed Epicurean, to whom pleasure was more precious than ambition, faced by a warrior of iron will and armed to the teeth.

As the human brain and nerves cannot endure twenty-four hours of meditation in abstract spheres in no way similar to life, Alekhine filled in the intervals with alcohol. But alcohol was never more needful to him than chess. When he was burning to recover his lost title he drank only milk. He was superstitious and wore a jersey with a black cat embroidered on it all through his match with Euwe.

Morphy, perhaps, had a more brilliant and meteoric career, Lasker a longer one, Capablanca a more convincing one, but such a fanatic as Alekhine the world had never seen before.

PART I THE CONTESTANTS

1 Botvinnik-Bronstein-Smyslov 1948–1959

1948: Botvinnik ascends the vacant throne

This, then, was the man Mikhail Botvinnik was destined to succeed. Botvinnik was similar to Alekhine in his tremendous energy and his will to win. In every other way Botvinnik developed in different circumstances. For the first time the state gave material support to the development of chess and considered that it added to the prestige of the social system. The schoolboy from Leningrad in patched trousers had plenty of encouragement to devote himself to the game he loved. Till that time the leading chess players of the world had been cosmopolitan in their way of life and had looked after their own interests. Botvinnik, on the other hand, travelled little and introduced the innovation of an enormous preparation for competition. His successes were assured beforehand by work at home. He spent far more time in analysis and in the verification of efficient lines of play than he spent in the actual game in which his new ideas were introduced. Such methods were also characteristic of Alekhine, but never on so grandiose a scale. Above all, Alekhine's personal life was not, nor could it have been, regular. For Botvinnik, however, everything was ordered and calculated to obtain the maximum effect.

His assault on the highest title was planned for years. In order to preserve his form during the war Botvinnik took part in several national tournaments, spiritually undisturbed in his aspirations even by the threat of Hitler at the gates of Moscow.

After the war the death of the physically failing and psychologically depressed Alekhine meant the cancellation of the match for which preliminary discussions had already begun. The others – Smyslov, Reshevsky, Keres, Euwe, or at the championship tournament the absent Fine – were not dangerous to Botvinnik. This was his moment. More than all the others, Botvinnik was ready for the great leap forward.

When he had achieved his life's dream, Botvinnik isolated himself for several years as world champion, lulled by the thought of his own superiority. If his ambition was equal to Alekhine's, his devotion to chess was not. Botvinnik was a sober man, who, parallel with his chess career, chose the less known but more secure profession of electrotechnical engineer. While Bronstein and Smyslov grew stronger and stronger in tournament practice, Botvinnik made no move. His new aim was to achieve the degree of Doctor of Technical Science. In the Soviet Union this means much. Not only the reputation but the salary and fees, legally fixed, are much greater. Alekhine too had the distinction of Doctor of Law at the Paris Sorbonne, but that was more for social prestige as he flitted around the world playing chess, whereas with Botvinnik it was for practical ends. To Alekhine his distinction was necessary because of chess, whereas to Botvinnik it was necessary in case one day he gave up chess. To both one and the other, however, chess was his life's work.

Botvinnik defends himself against his first challenger

Dr Botvinnik played with less assurance than Mr Botvinnik. When the time came to defend his title against David Bronstein in 1951 he had not played in a tournament for three years. But his serious approach to his task remained the same. Botvinnik took a good six months' leave of absence – to prepare himself. This time, however, he was facing a dedicated artist who knew nothing of 'spare time' and devoted himself to chess more than any other of Botvinnik's rivals. Days of analysis and nights of 'unprofitable' play had made Bronstein a formidable exponent. In other words, Bronstein, winner of the first Candidates' Tournament, was the better prepared.

Bronstein was in no way pleasing to Botvinnik. In many ways they had very different natures. Botvinnik rarely appeared in public and always prepared himself in the peace of his own home. Bronstein enjoyed the turmoil of a chess club, playing lightning chess every evening. One was serious and concentrated, the other all nerves and fiery imagination. The outward manifestations of Bronstein's vivacity were displeasing to the tranquil Botvinnik – Bronstein's habit of standing and watching the board after every move he made, quite unconscious of the apparent condescension of his position far from the board, even the manner in which Bronstein drank his tea, holding his cup in both hands. Photos of the match show that at difficult moments Botvinnik frequently shaded his eyes with his hands so as not to see his opponent on the other side of the table, lest his appearance or behaviour disturb his concentration.

Bronstein was a very correct player, as was also Botvinnik. But he also had his weaknesses; he loved to argue. Botvinnik, a very suspicious man (did the times in which his career began make him such?) proposed an innovation before the match started; namely that whenever the game was adjourned the secret move should be sealed in two separate envelopes, instead of one as was the custom. The second envelope should be handed to the assistant referee in order to prevent any dishonesty should the referee be a partisan of either one of the rivals (what an idea!) and should open the envelope, thus making it possible for the player to alter his move should he find by analysis that he had not sealed the best one.

Botvinnik considered that his request was a simple and happy solution in view of the importance of the match; and Bronstein was pleased that he had found a subject for argument. Botvinnik did not know Bronstein's weakness and it irritated him that the matter was discussed for a whole month during the negotiations before the match. Bronstein painstakingly analyzed every possible consequence and rejoiced if he found defects in Botvinnik's proposal. Every day brought a fresh comment from Bronstein and Botvinnik became more and more irritated. What if the move written in the two envelopes was not identical? Botvinnik replied angrily and curtly: 'Then the person concerned loses the game by default!' Finally Bronstein agreed to Botvinnik's demands. But after what protracted negotiations!

Still untouched by adversity, Botvinnik underestimated the danger of his meeting with Bronstein. In fact, he had facing him an exceptionally experienced player and a daring psychologist. David Bronstein had aroused the enthusiasm of the chess world by his astonishingly rapid rise and the tirelessness of his creative imagination. An uneasy spirit faced a calm and profound logician! Their behaviour too was very different, and in accord with their temperaments. The younger man irritated the older one. Bronstein never had enough of chess. Even when standing and drinking tea, his eyes were on the chessboard. Botvinnik, annoyed, remarked: 'Here one plays chess and there', pointing to the next room, 'one drinks tea!'

What interested Bronstein above all was the tactical value of the moves. He enjoyed a fiery contest, the exploitation of his opponent's weaknesses and the daring of his own imagination. In his match with Botvinnik, who had long been without practice, Bronstein found a rich field for his psychological tactics, such as had not been seen from the time of Alekhine's match against Capablanca in 1927. He played the openings which Botvinnik himself played, so that the world champion was placed in a difficult psychological position: how should he play against himself? Furthermore, as a man of great experience in lightning chess, Bronstein at first intentionally made moderately strong moves and began with threats only after the thirtieth move when both contestants were suffering from lack of time. He fished continually in muddied waters. The match was transformed into an intensely complex struggle. Botvinnik had an iron will and great energy. He used his colossal experience and subtle strategy as well as he could, but none the less these unforeseen complications greatly exhausted him. The time-trouble, in which Bronstein was like a fish in water, and the psychological tactics, in which Botvinnik was faced with systems he himself used, brought him to the brink of catastrophe. But Bronstein showed a certain levity and played poorly in the endgames, which cost him important points. By a supreme effort Botvinnik equalized the score with an endgame of genius in which he sacrificed a pawn without obvious purpose in order that much later – when a draw hovered over his head like the sword of Damocles – he could prove the advantage of his pair of bishops over his opponent's knights. Only thus did he succeed in preserving his title.

The personality of David Bronstein and his later fate

There are men who make a religion of their profession. Their devotion to their calling resembles the service of a deity which they have themselves created. Chess is not everywhere recognized as a vocation but if this noble game has its priests, then Bronstein was a priest of the spirit of chess.

Bronstein's approach to a game was like entering into a trance. He often did not make the first move for a long time and the spectators were forced to go on looking at the demonstration board still in the initial position. Perhaps the game had not yet begun? But Bronstein's clock had been ticking away, spilling out time which could later prove precious to him. There must have been some singular beauty, some kind of enchantment, which the dance of the pieces evoked in the bowed head of this bald young man. In truth, he never repeated his record of watching the two motionless rows of pieces for fifty minutes, as in one match-game against Boleslavsky. Had he lost his sense of reality and practicality? Finally, he 'remembered' where he was and began to play.

Time-trouble came. Bronstein looked vaguely about him, as if distant in spirit. But then a miracle occurred. To every one of his opponent's moves came a reply in which was concealed a spark of inspiration. The secret was revealed. Whatever he did, his thoughts were continually on the board. Others in his position, while looking at the board, think of

B

the clock. Bronstein, not thinking of the clock, thought of the board. Victory ensued.

In a modest manner, head bent slightly to the right, he explained to his opponent all that he had seen during the game. He wanted to foresee every move which the pieces could make. He was filled with a thirst to attain the unattainable.

What was the critical moment for Bronstein? Much later, at Portorož, in 1958 – after which he was never again able to reach the Candidates' Tournament. Everyone will say: 'The Filipino Cardoso in the last round.' It was not. The decision had already been reached in the penultimate twentieth round, in Bronstein's game with the six-foot-six Czechoslovak grandmaster, Filip. Young Bronstein, who was as full of ideas as a pomegranate is of pips, jealously preserved the secret of his 'innovation' for the most important occasion. Many had already played that variation of the Nimzo-Indian Defence, believing that they had found the solution to the eternal tournament problem, 'Black plays and draws.' It was clear that Filip too would not avoid this temptation. Perhaps Bronstein would have postponed the revelation of his 'discovery' for the Candidates' Tournament, but now it was a question of his very qualification. After the first twenty-seven moves Bronstein was one pawn up and – which was for him a marvel – had plenty of time to think. Everything seemed clear: Bronstein would qualify and surely there was no one who anticipated anything different.

Everyone believed that. Only Bronstein, approaching the finishing-post, wavered. Filip had succeeded in extending the game to forty-one moves. Bronstein had to adjourn the game and find a way to realize his advantage. But no. Bronstein no longer had the patience to live in uncertainty and played the first move that pleased him. He blundered the pawn away and the game was a draw. What happened with Cardoso was only a consequence of the result with Filip. Bronstein's nerve had gone. He wanted to forget. This must be the explanation of the 'suicidal' incident in which he spent long hours playing lightning games with Tal on the day before the final decision. Had he beaten the Czechoslovak and thus made his position secure, he would probably have beaten the Filipino also. Then he would have been much better placed and no one would have noticed that he was in the throes of a crisis.

We saw him a year later at Kiev, at the Soviet Union – Yugoslavia match. Modest, reserved and always incredibly courteous – even though he was going through a difficult period – he remained the same as in the days of his greatest fame. Then they had written books about him and called him 'the genius of modern chess'. But now, when genius was no longer the prerogative of any single grandmaster, the title of 'the romantic of modern chess' would have suited him better.

After a year as a bachelor, he was once again married when we met him in Kiev. His wife, this time, was not a chess-player, but there was in that something which his friends and sympathizers regarded as a good sign. Far be it for me to say that chess marriages are undesirable – there are so many happy examples – but in Bronstein's specific case it may be that his life was better balanced. For a man so enamoured of his art, this should have been a good sign and for that very reason it is hard to discover the cause of his shortcomings.

The graph of his success is enigmatic. In 1948 he shone unexpectedly at the First Interzonal Tournament and by so doing he reached Botvinnik. In the 1951 duel the title of world champion escaped him 'by a hair's breadth'. For years afterwards he was at the summit of world chess, but then Smyslov's era commenced and Bronstein no longer managed to dominate as in 1950. At that time Smyslov wanted to become an opera singer, but neither then nor later did Bronstein have any ambitions outside chess.

Only now did he realize how precious his moment of glory had been and regretted the lost opportunity, but he did not give up hope – until Portorož. The sensational outcome of his game with Cardoso he still regarded as an unfortunate incident, but it was hard for him to have to wait another three years for his next chance. The continual necessity to qualify was really exhausting and dragged down everybody – except the holder of the world title. David, however, had fresh misfortunes. He suffered at the Soviet championship at Tiflis, and then to some extent corrected the impression by his triple tie with Smyslov and Spassky at the lesser international tournament at Moscow. But then followed – Kiev.

On the eve of the match with Yugoslavia there were arguments about the third board. Taimanov laid claim to it, citing the more recent results, but Bronstein's reputation was such that, at the secret ballot, all the Soviet grandmasters supported David. Thus the finger of fate decreed that he meet Fuderer, who had his own reasons for being well disposed.

Fuderer, who by his university career had acquired inner calm, gladly involved himself in the preliminary complications, for he felt secure in his calculations. Bronstein, however, who never failed to be intrigued that one could play either in this way or in that and was almost overjoyed because his beloved game was so rich in possibilities, was not in a state to decide which line was best in the limited time allowed for thought. The insoluble riddles which were continually placed before him in the course of a game provided an inexhaustible field for investigation.

Perhaps within him, the creator, there sometimes appeared the worm of doubt and now he was happy that there was no reason to be disillusioned with his art, that chess surpassed the capacity of his mind to arrange everything, to classify and discover the solution in advance. In that there was beauty. Every grandmaster seeks through chess to find some truth of his own, and for Bronstein truth was in beauty.

Bronstein was constantly tormented by an almost painful longing to create something new, to reveal something hitherto unknown; perhaps one could play in this way, or perhaps it could be done in some other way. In that nostalgia for the undiscovered he sometimes defied all established rules.

His fantasy was a torrent which could not be dammed. I remember our games and the analysis afterwards. I regarded with disbelief the variations which Bronstein considered during play. It was a fantastic world into which my cold reason, even had I been able, would never have entered. It always angered me a little that Bronstein, despite everything that he saw, always played against me those normal moves that I myself would have played had I been in his place.

Could it have been that this sense, which before had always brought him back to reality, had begun to weaken? Could he still withdraw before his imaginative forays led him into dangerous paths in which he 'died for beauty'?

The slight catastrophe with Fuderer only partially affected Bronstein's inner calm. At Kiev, Bronstein had accompanied our players to the airport, courteous and good-humoured. The philosopher and aesthete in Bronstein remained enthusiastic for chess, but the spirit of the competition fighter wavered within him. After a 1–3 result David said to me: 'As far as I am concerned, competitive chess is not for me.'

Had Bronstein found a higher relationship with chess, or was all that the expression of a temporary crisis? The answer is not clear; it is a matter of personal taste. The fact remains that his games, by the wealth of their content and individuality, have aroused enthusiasm for more than two decades. He had bad luck in that the rule limiting the number of Soviet participants (it is no longer in force) deprived him of his well-earned right to take part in the Candidates' Tournament after the Interzonal Tournament at Amsterdam in 1964, where he was placed among the first six.

Botvinnik and his rival for many years—Smyslov

Long before he became world champion Mikhail Botvinnik had been the chess ruler of the Soviet Union. The world had not yet come to its senses after the devastation of the war when it became clear that a great power in chess had arisen whose absolute domination had no equal in the international tournament practice of the time. In the meantime the great men of chess – Lasker, Capablanca, Alekhine – had gone from the land of the living.

Thenceforward the world championship became more or less the monopoly of a single country; only a few of his younger colleagues from his own city contested the world throne with Botvinnik. Botvinnik's hegemony on his home ground already dated from the period between the two wars, so the zeal of his new rivals to topple him from his pedestal was comprehensible. They travelled, played, fretted and fumed at competitions abroad, while Botvinnik sat at home in Moscow.

When the moment came, through the newly founded FIDE competition to choose for the first time a challenger to the world champion, everyone expected that it would be Vasily Smyslov. From 1941, when he was in his twentieth year, Vasily was invariably regarded as the second chess-player of the Soviet Union. Almost all the championships revolved around the rivalry of these two – Botvinnik and the ten years' younger Smyslov. Smyslov was second in the match-tournament of 1948 at which engineer Botvinnik achieved his life's aim of becoming the foremost chess-player in the world.

Meanwhile the formerly little known name of David Bronstein shone forth like a meteor (and also Boleslavsky, though his ambition was rapidly quenched after his unfortunately lost elimination match with Bronstein on the road towards Botvinnik). At the Candidates' Tournament in 1950 Smyslov was third, but he felt that he was last. He was disillusioned to such an extent that he wanted to give up chess and become an opera singer. He entered the short list of candidates for the Bolshoi Theatre, but suddenly recalled that he was, first and foremost, a great chess player. Vasily pulled himself together and waited for his chance, which was to come three years later.

Smyslov dominated the next two tournaments by his infallibility. Whether in attack or in defence, Smyslov was always right! During those six years he had three matches with Botvinnik!

Smyslov was of quite different temperament from Bronstein. When the triviality about the double sealing of moves came up again he did not consider it worth an argument. He at once agreed with the suspicious Botvinnik, who attached so much importance to it. Compared with Bronstein, Smyslov was less impulsive and less of a fanatic. Bronstein always talked only about chess, and this preoccupation of his recalled Alekhine. Smyslov, in his quiet, orderly manner, was equally devoted to music and to other things. What interested Smyslov in chess was its objective values. Thus he had a better technique, better treatment of the endgame, and a greater assurance in his many systems than Bronstein, but he paid less attention to psychology and perhaps had fewer original ideas.

Smyslov set himself the task, consonant with his character, of surpassing Botvinnik not in the psychological and tactical field but on the creative level. With that intention he carried out the enormous task of writing out some eight hundred of Botvinnik's more important games with comments about his play in the various phases. In order to prepare himself thoroughly Smyslov wanted the match to begin as late as possible, but Botvinnik did not want to have to play the end of the match during the hot season in Moscow. Finally they agreed that the match should begin a month earlier than Smyslov had wanted.

System and methodical play are inseparable features of Botvinnik's character. The importance which he attributed to his preparations is shown by one example. Before the match Botvinnik was resting in his summer villa near Moscow and every day at noon would walk for two hours. One day a camera crew came from Moscow and, as is often the case, the preparation of the equipment was somewhat delayed. When the time came for his walk and deep-breathing exercises, Botvinnik became impatient. He looked at his watch and told the crowd of journalists and cameramen that he would have to leave them. He always went the same way, counting his breaths. He paid no attention to the crew, who had wasted their day's work and had been left twiddling their thumbs.

Botvinnik appeared to trust no one, not even his second. After his first match with Smyslov he wrote, prudently concealing his exasperation, that Smyslov had made 'further progress in his method of preparation' for he had three times refuted Botvinnik's secret analyses, playing without hesitation. Botvinnik then made a subtle proposal that Smyslov should share his analytical preparations with other players in a series of lectures throughout the country, to further Soviet chess. The proposal was a clever one, but Botvinnik's innocent assistant, Kan, a very straightforward man as everyone admitted, was more than somewhat unhappy because of the hidden allusion.

Botvinnik, who never went far from Moscow so as not to break his daily routine, certainly considered that he owed much to his planned exploitation of working energy. This is reflected both in the strong and in the weak facets of his style of play. In positional play, which can be reduced to a system, Botvinnik was an incomparable virtuoso and tournament contestant. In positions of indeterminate character, on the other hand, he did not feel himself secure. Smyslov revealed this weakness in the twentieth game of the match, when he created pawn tension in the centre and on both wings. Botvinnik was not in a weaker position, but he could not bear the thought that he did not know what might arise out of this situation and hastened to introduce clarity into the pawn structure and to establish it. This was to his disadvantage and was the main reason for his defeat in this game.

The world champion did not win his first two matches against his challengers – Bronstein (1951) and Smyslov (1954) – but retained his title by a drawn result. Thus all three players had some reason to claim a moral victory. However, Botvinnik, who could not forget the glorious days of his supremacy, longed for further moral proofs and complained of the rules of FIDE which favoured him, since in the event of a draw he retained his title of world champion. At the same time he took advantage of the rules. In the last game of the first match, when Botvinnik was in the stronger position, Smyslov offered a draw and Botvinnik replied: 'Your offer is so attractive that it is impossible for me to refuse it.' Was this to justify himself, or did he mean something else?

Though they had no special attraction for one another, none the less Botvinnik and Smyslov were in many ways similar – in their reserved behaviour, and their tendency to choose objective continuations. Each held to his own ideas in accordance with his chess taste, and in the following two matches victory went to whomever played better.

More about Smyslov—in the role of ex-champion

If a man may be summed up by a single characteristic, then the most suitable one for Smyslov as a chess player would be – assurance. Not only in his method of play but also in his movements Smyslov gives this impression. Tall and strongly built, he walks firmly and steadily, his speech is quiet, but not condescending, his movements slow and dignified. In whatever he says there is always a tincture of delicate irony. It is not pomposity but good humour, which perhaps stems from Smyslov's belief that he is above petty human weaknesses.

Smyslov's humour is without malice and springs from his own feeling of impartiality. If he is an artist in chess, he is also a scientist. He has never been interested in psychological tricks, only in objective values. It is characteristic that, perhaps from prejudice, Smyslov for a long time regarded the King's Indian Defence as a half-correct system in which Black does not pay enough heed to space. While almost all Soviet grandmasters have owed many of their successes to this system of play, Smyslov remained true to himself and resisted the general fashion for several years, even though it afforded obvious advantages to his rivals. For a long time others took first place, but Smyslov obstinately continued to go his own way. It was as if he believed: what I create neither time nor fresh analyses will erase. When the vogue for fixed systems passed, Smyslov's moment had come.

Smyslov makes his moves as coldly as if his thoughts were unaccompanied by any sort of emotion. None the less, he is not an automaton but a man. When his opponents try to make things awkward for him, he begins involuntarily to set down his pieces with greater emphasis. Is he angry at something in his opponent or in himself?

That he never loses his head was shown at a banquet in Switzerland. Smyslov was asked to sing, as music was his lifelong interest apart from chess. He was accompanied by an amateur choir of Swiss provincial officials, which had striven as a surprise to learn for the occasion a Russian song. Smyslov, unworried, sang 'Stenka Razin' in his strong baritone voice, as if unaware of the strident sounds which assailed him. He assiduously carried out his part as soloist, leaving the 'choir of Swiss Cossacks' to do as it liked, and then once more patiently took over the melody. Though the grandmaster was the high spot of the evening, those present eagerly awaited the close. Not for a moment did Smyslov become confused. He calmly accepted his share of the applause and sat down once more at his table.

In what state of mind did Smyslov appear at his third Candidates' Tournament in 1959 in Yugoslavia, now as former world champion? Alone among the participants Smyslov had no happy illusions. He had had to step down in order to give himself the chance of returning to his former position. Within himself he was probably irritated with Botvinnik, who had contrived his right to a return match and had forced it through the disinterested FIDE Congress, just at the time when his first deposition from the throne was imminent in 1957. If the results of both their matches, in 1957 and in 1958 (when Botvinnik recovered his title) were collated, Smyslov still had one more game to his credit.

What sort of situation had arisen? Botvinnik, sitting inviolate at

Moscow, still had his rights, while Smyslov, the ex-world champion, was levelled with the others and had to wander through the world, once more enduring the fiercest competition from other grandmasters before he could create the possibility of revenge, which Botvinnik had obtained so simply and easily. It was very exhausting. As Smyslov said in public at Kiev, he must this time destroy the law of probability and for the third time running be victorious in the Candidates' Tournament, which was a 'pretty difficult task'.

Two photos, found by chance in some leaflet, arouse thoughts of the impermanence of fame. In one of them Smyslov, burdened with a 'symbolic' but enormous laurel wreath about his shoulders, stands frowning and exceedingly dignified, looking straight ahead of him as if gazing at the accomplishment of his dreams, as if conscious that the world championship was his by right. He had achieved so much in one decade and his efforts had been crowned with success after his second attempt in six years. In the other photo Smyslov is seen emerging, smiling and excited, into the street as the new world champion, surrounded by an admiring crowd. Nothing but success gives a face such an expression of satisfaction and serenity.

All this was quickly lost in a moment of natural and inescapable relaxation. Tacit indignation at the injustice of his position could avail him nothing. For many years to come he would not succeed in obtaining his unrecognized rights.

'It is very difficult to win first place in the Candidates' Tournament even once,' someone said before Amsterdam in 1956, 'and twice is impossible.' Smyslov accomplished the 'impossible'. When a man like this is in question, one who sits at a chessboard like an immovable rock, the law of probability loses value – but only once.

For six years he wrestled stoically with his rivals and with Botvinnik, till at last, in 1957, he wrested the title from him in the ninth year of Botvinnik's reign. That the whole of that superhuman effort should be swept away after only a year was a blow which could discourage anyone.

After the lost match Vasily appeared for the first time abroad at the Munich Olympiad in 1958. The inquisitive expected some change in the thirty-seven-year-old ex-champion, who had till recently dominated the international scene. Smyslov's sovereign calm, however, appeared unruffled. His reaction was more like one of wonder that the lost opportunity could have occurred. He did not blame his form so much as his health during the return match. That was a sign that he still had not lost the will, that like Sisyphus he would once more push the same rock up the same hill, and that, if need be, he would still play a fourth, or a fifth, match with Botvinnik. Time, however, swept all that away.

By 1960 Smyslov was waiting in the wings, for the first time surpassed by others. He had needed two victories at the Candidates' Tournament, two matches with Botvinnik (that is to say twice as many as his rivals) to become world champion. And then – his laurels had remained green for only a year.

But for the return match he would have had a year's rest, fame and social satisfaction, filled with hospitality on both sides of the ocean. Smyslov had had to renounce all that and to think constantly – and unwillingly – of his great rival. It seemed that Smyslov, in the logical order of things, had initiated a fresh epoch. Unexpectedly, even for Smyslov himself, the healthy Botvinnik arose from his too precipitately dug grave, and restored the old order once again.

Smyslov had to take a step back, to the spot where he had been earlier – the Candidates' Tournament. The mischievous tactics of Tal dealt the supremacy of Smyslov's style an even heavier blow. Two more steps back – to the very beginning! After a long time Smyslov would again appear in the Soviet championships. Only after that would come the Interzonal Tournament, then the Candidates' Tournament. How terribly distant, all of a sudden, were Botvinnik and Tal!

They asked Smyslov:

'Who is your most dangerous opponent?'

'In chess, as in life, a man is his own most dangerous opponent.'

'To what extent does chess play a role in your life?'

'Fifty per cent.' (The other fifty per cent was probably opera singing.)

'What is your greatest ambition?'

'Nothing. I have abandoned all my ambitions.'

Through chess he expressed his thoughts; through singing, his emotions. He had had to forsake singing because of chess, and chess meant a road entangled by thorns, far longer than ever before.

At the concluding ceremony of the Leipzig Olympiad in 1960 both rivals won cups. Botvinnik was serene; he had the best result on the second board which he regarded as an encouraging sign before his return match with Tal. Smyslov's face betrayed the opposite reaction. He also returned from the dais with a cup for the best score as – first reserve! His expression spoke volumes.

I never saw Smyslov so reserved as at that Olympiad. But his step was full of energy, clearly that of a man burning with impatience to restore things to their proper place.

He seldom talked; as if every word spoken meant a watering down of his resolution. His road was a long one. He must begin literally at the beginning. . . .
But he did not give the impression that his resolve had weakened. We in Europe did not often meet Smyslov in the following years. For two chess seasons he wandered a good deal in Latin America, taking first prize wherever he appeared – in Argentina, Chile and Cuba. In the meantime he lost, astonishingly easily, his match in the first round of the challengers' matches, as if he wanted to free himself from official matches as soon as possible. He was expected to play Botvinnik. But Botvinnik announced his withdrawal at the last moment and, instead of 'old Misha', Jefim Geller, probably Smyslov's most difficult opponent, appeared. For Geller had beaten him in a match for the Soviet Championship (five draws and one win) and that many years before when Smyslov was at the height of his powers and had seemed almost invincible.

Geller was small of stature but physically extremely robust (he was an excellent basket-ball player) and Smyslov chose a strange method of preparation before meeting him at the chessboard; the tall and quiet Smyslov took boxing lessons. But, as we know, it was all in vain.

Among the great players there are some completely devoted to chess and to chess alone, whereas others have other interests or at least hobbies. Smyslov certainly belongs to the second group. One gets the impression that he wanted to become an opera singer more than anything else, but his exceptional gifts transformed him into a chess champion. He had no other profession than chess. None the less, he always remained divided within himself.

There is something strange in Smyslov's personality. He is ready to make a quick draw, even with White, as for example with Reshevsky at Mar del Plata or with me at Monte Carlo. At other times he wins by making his usual simple moves (are they really so simple?) when he feels that the moment is ripe. It might be thought that he is lazy by nature; nevertheless, among contemporary masters, it is he who has invented the greatest number of basic new ideas in the Ruy Lopez, French Defence, Caro-Kann, Queen's Gambit accepted, Slav Defence, the Nimzo-Indian, the Grünfeld Defence, the English Opening, and even in irregular systems. He has an intuitive genius for maintaining the balance or taking the initiative. He also has an exceptional talent for the endgame, but he has no love for the patient memorizing of variations, as modern competitive chess more and more requires.

2 Botvinnik-Tal 1959–1961

Tal appears on the scene

In 1959 there came to Yugoslavia a dark twenty-three-year-old youth of incandescent gaze, whose meteoric career vividly recalls that of Bronstein in the period 1948–1950. He came with the idea that everyone must be treated alike – be it Benkö, Olafsson and the young Fischer or even Smyslov and Keres.

Mikhail (Tal) was very intelligent and had passed all his school examinations three years before the normal time. None the less, pitiless analysts are still seeking an explanation of the phenomenon that someone even in the twentieth century could win tournaments as if famous names mattered not a jot. The analysts malevolently cut Tal's combinations to pieces and victoriously pounced upon an occasional 'hole'. Tal was fond of an ironic play on words, and answered wittily: 'They compare me with Lasker, which is an exaggerated honour. Lasker made mistakes in every game and I only in every second one!'

In ancient Sparta, before leaving for war, a mother said to her son on handing him his shield: 'Either with it or upon it!' This merciless slogan might also have been adopted by the grandmasters ever since Tal appeared in tournaments. Someone wants to be first? Then let him forsake all his habits and breathlessly pursue – Tal.

For six years the infallible Smyslov ruled the international arena and certain codes of 'good behaviour' had become established. The grandmasters mutually respected one another. Impenetrability with Black and a certain efficiency when one had the initiative with White were the keys to success in the most powerful competitions. The percentage of points which the victor obtained was not very high nor were the other contestants his hapless victims.

Then appeared Tal, younger by fifteen years. He 'sinned' greatly, but was rarely admonished, and imposed a fierce rate of scoring. Among the other competitors reigned a feeling of 'bloodymindedness'. The customary number of draws suddenly lessened and discussion about whether chess was dying spontaneously disappeared. The others, chasing Tal, excelled themselves and won more games than ever, assuring their success – in second place.

Unfortunate Keres! The tournament in Yugoslavia was the climax of his life's work. With those eighteen and a half points out of a possible twenty-eight he would have been first at all the three preceding competitions of this type – at Budapest in 1950, at Zurich in 1953 and at Amsterdam in 1956. Not even this time, in his forty-third year, was he to achieve his dreamed-of match against Botvinnik.

The following comparison shows how much Keres had improved on his second place at Amsterdam three years before; discounting draws, he had one loss and three wins. Now, in Yugoslavia, six losses, but fifteen wins, that is, instead of two, nine 'pluses'! What use was that when Tal was there with his twenty points!

Bobby Fischer was furious. At the banquet he said to me: 'In four games I had the winning position and lost them all to Tal!' Analysis, in fact, sometimes shows a lack of consistency in Tal's games. When he won the Soviet championship for the first time, everyone croaked: 'He had a hell of a lot of luck!' The embittered Taimanov even threatened to give up chess if Tal should once more become Soviet champion. When that happened, Taimanov conveniently forgot his threat.

Was Tal lucky? His style made him so. What, for example, happened at the Candidates' Tournament in his game with Smyslov? Smyslov had outplayed him strategically. Tal went on to complicate the play. Smyslov won a piece. Tal continued to complicate the game. Smyslov, finally, slipped into time-trouble, made a mistake and from two games gained only half a point.

Many will think that now is the time to mention some of Tal's brilliant victories. As an example of Tal's cool nerve at dangerous junctures, consider his game against Olafsson in the eighteenth round of the Interzonal Tournament at Portorož in 1958. Tal was menaced by defeat. Haggard from repeated time-trouble, the thin ascetic face of the fair-haired Icelander seemed made up entirely of eyes. There was, in fact, still enough energy in that tall, exaggeratedly slender youth but, lacking time for thought, he made a slip which gave the young Soviet champion a chance to continue his resistance to the next day.

Tal could not afford to lose, since it would threaten his winning margin of points. It was interesting to watch him in his new role. He had always passed his examinations in the subjects 'attack', 'combination' or 'sacrifice' with success, but now he had patiently to write his essay on the theme 'how to save a draw' in a difficult position against Olafsson.

For the twenty-two-year-old student from Riga, this unpleasant examination consisted of two parts. First – analysis of the adjourned game. This showed that Black lost in all variants. There remained one more straw for the drowning man – the psychology of the chessboard. He had to choose a continuation which, taking into consideration the character of his opponent, would be the greatest surprise and the natural replies of White would be just those moves which were wrong.

Examination of a defence was painful for the aggressive Tal, but he passed brilliantly. He knew that after eight correct moves by Olafsson further struggle would be useless, but he behaved as though he were indifferent, played quickly and, as always, walked about among the other tables. The third move of the lively Tal came as a surprise to Olafsson and threw him off balance. To Black's fourth move, Olafsson replied 'naturally' but incorrectly and the 'black-avised uneasy one' scored the precious half point by rapid and confident moves.

A twofold effort was always necessary to get Tal on his back on the mat. His second, Averbakh, wittily compared him to a wrestler who fought vigorously, wrestled, made a bridge and then suddenly twisted and lo! – his opponent, who had been putting pressure on him all the time, was now beneath him. I remember my own encounter with Tal at Zurich. I had never won against him and I did then only because I guessed the best possible move at a moment when I no longer had time to think.

That 'luck' was not accidental. It was the fruit of Tal's inexhaustible facility for finding unexpected answers. To this must be added his strong fighting spirit. Our fourth meeting was at the Candidates' Tournament; I had found a saving combination which Tal overlooked. What did he do? He avoided the normal combination, for that would have given me a clear line of action. He took a risk and exchanged his queen for two rooks. He might even have lost, but he reckoned daringly on my extreme lack of time for thought. Quite right! I soon made a catastrophic blunder.

How was it possible to destroy the existing norms? How could the accumulated experience of more than a hundred years of international tournament practice be suddenly forgotten and all the enormously increased defence technique be wiped out? All of that remained. What Tal did was to reveal the age-old truth that grandmasters are not chess encyclopaedias but living men.

These 'revelations' are not so much a matter of Tal's understanding or of some rarified psychological reasoning as the product of his temperament. Tal cannot play if he thinks his opponent feels serene. Therefore it is not important to Tal if he is a pawn or a piece up or down. It is essential that his opponent be confronted by new problems which must be solved *ab initio*.

His opponent has countered all Tal's threats. What must be done? Tal has another shot in his locker; he sacrifices a piece. He does it by intuition, not reckoning the consequences. Is Tal convinced at that moment of the correctness of his adventurous idea? Perhaps he is (he was astonished when his proposed combination against Fischer did not achieve a brilliant result, unaware that his sacrifice contained a 'hole'). But that is not important. His aim is to disconcert his opponent; whenever he steers clear of one reef, he must be confronted by another. Only then does Tal feel himself safe; if his chance thought is not fully justified, then his opponent's fatigue or lack of time for thought will serve his purpose.

I remember Tal's admission to me at Zurich. It threw him out of his stride when I rejected his offer of a draw after the opening. His opponent's security meant his insecurity. The inaccessibility of my position irritated him. Though I was unable to do anything against him, he was unaware of it. He did not have the patience to wait and instead sacrificed a pawn. That gave me my opportunity.

So never offer Tal a draw! You will reveal your momentary weakness to him, for which he has been eagerly waiting. Consider his encounters with Keres in the Candidates' Tournament of 1959. On three occasions Keres consolidated his position. Tal cannot bear closed positions in which his opponent feels secure and each time he sacrificed a knight. Three unnecessary defeats! In one game only did Keres make the mistake of offering a draw. Tal was in no better a position, perhaps even in a worse one, but despite his bad experience he refused the offer. His opponent was at last hesitant. That day Tal won.

That was the decisive turning-point in his struggle for first place. After the first half, played at Bled, Keres seemed gloomy, even though he was leading the tournament, as if he guessed that an advantage of half a point was a ridiculously small obstacle for Tal. Tal took the lead at Zagreb from the very start.

Tal fought all out. He let Fischer, Benkö and Olafsson know that he intended to annihilate them 4–0. They lost their level-headedness when they played with him. That was what Tal wanted. Every movement of his got on their nerves, his continual walking about the table, his standing behind their backs. When he played Tal, Benkö put on dark glasses to show symbolically that he did not want to see his opponent. Tal loved humour (at university his subject was satire) and he too put on dark glasses of grotesque shape. Benkö's 'protest' became transformed into a comedy which aroused general laughter in the hall.

At Belgrade Keres did his best to catch up with Tal. But he was beaten by Smyslov who, the previous day, had failed to do the same against Tal. Both belonged to another generation, another style, and the reserved Keres remarked in jest to Smyslov: 'You, Vasily, are on Tal's side.'

At the finish Keres did the impossible. Tal, already losing, contrived a cunning checkmate trap. The methodical Paul was on the watch and saw it all. He beat Tal with Black, but it was not enough. However, two rounds before the end a crisis arose when Tal played Fischer. For the first time Tal looked anxious. But Fischer failed to rise to the occasion. Everything ended as had been expected.

It seemed that the others had prepared themselves badly. They had studied systems, instead of the men with whom they were competing. Another age had begun. The standard-bearer of that age was Tal. Perhaps history was repeating itself. In his own times Lasker had been underestimated too. He had no pupils and had not added much to chess theory. None the less, he was the greatest tournament player of all time and world champion for twenty-seven years.

They asked Tal whose follower he was; he replied 'Bronstein's'. In truth, by his style and the wealth of his imagination, he recalled Bronstein more than anyone else. But Tal was in love with the contest and its sporting result and Bronstein with the creative heritage which the struggle bequeathed. Thus it came to the paradoxical situation that Bronstein the teacher rejected his over-successful pupil – Tal.

What was it that Bronstein did not like about Tal? Above all his lightning play in the opening. The unusual, almost contemptuous speed with which Tal made his opening moves was a part of his combat technique, teasing, provoking and outsmarting his opponent. To Bronstein this was an unpardonable superficiality, a lack of striving for the creative spark. Bronstein was by nature prudent and limited himself to the remark that Tal had his own reason for his behaviour. In an actual game David often lacked time to solve all his problems in its critical phases. None the less, he did not agree with the pragmatic attitude of reserving his energy until later.

Why was Tal at this time the most successful tournament fighter in the world? Like Lasker, he saw very much and, like Bronstein, he had a more lively imagination than the other grandmasters.

Though the opposite of Smyslov, Tal by his tournament successes was Smyslov's direct successor. By his style and character Tal was the opposite of Botvinnik. Would he succeed him?

On the eve of the Botvinnik–Tal match

A match is different from a tournament. Considering Tal's objective weaknesses, Bronstein, on the eve of the first Botvinnik-Tal match, foresaw that the new challenger must change his style for that occasion. In Yugoslavia Tal had gained points from 'the lower house' and not against his peers.

Many doubted if Tal would be able to develop his qualities to their full extent when held back by Botvinnik's iron strategy. Were they wrong? Tal was extraordinarily experienced and at the lightning tournament at Belgrade, for example, recalled the god Shiva. While his adversary was groping for the clock with his hand, Tal had already moved and pressed his button so that his opponent did not manage, generally speaking, to set his clock going during a crisis in the game.

One must recall the Botvinnik-Bronstein match ten years before, to which the forthcoming match for the world championship was as like as one egg to another. Had not the tactical ideas of Bronstein tired Botvinnik out and almost brought him to the edge of the abyss? In one game Botvinnik even was a rook up (doesn't this situation created by Bronstein remind one of Tal?) and only drew. How many breakneck combinations would Tal be able to think up?

It had seemed that the titanic duel between Botvinnik and Smyslov would go on for a long time yet until the older man, in the natural order of things, gave way. Suddenly a third party had intervened – Mikhail Tal. Who says that history does not repeat itself? Everything hung by a thread, as when Bronstein had appeared. The same speed, the same firsts – Riga, Moscow, Portorož, Zurich, Belgrade! The world had not yet recovered from its astonishment and Tal had already reached Botvinnik. But this time the challenger was twenty-five years younger.

Would Botvinnik, now ten years older than when he had played Bronstein, be able to endure once more the pressure to which Bronstein had subjected him? The Soviet grandmasters for a wonder, despite the human inclination of always longing for a change, were united in their forecast against Tal. What was it about him that they did not like? Tal had surpassed them all, almost as if in jest. At the same time he had not sufficiently proved his superiority over his Soviet rivals in individual encounters. Perhaps they did not like Tal's temperament which forced him to play in a speculative manner, by intuition. Every one of them was concerned about what the coming generation would think of their creativeness, but Tal seemed as if he were not interested in the value of the

c

content but only in the result of the contest. Whence their desire that someone should at last teach Tal a lesson – that man was Botvinnik.

For the first time the challenger was not from Moscow. This introduced a considerable change in the cosy domestic atmosphere. The young man, only twenty-three years old, was already a town councillor and Riga was ready to put up a statue to him. A building had been donated as a chess centre and a state chess newspaper was promoted. It was not enough for it to appear monthly, but twice monthly in contrast to that of Moscow. During the tournament in Yugoslavia the main street in Riga was crammed with people and Tal's every move was reported by telephone. Nothing of the sort had ever happened in Moscow!

There is no doubt that Tal was both glad and eager to play Botvinnik. There is a story that at one time when Botvinnik was on holiday in Latvia Tal, then a boy, arrived at Botvinnik's summer home with a chessboard in his hand and asked Botvinnik for a game. He was told that the champion was sleeping and could not be disturbed. The boy's long-cherished ambition had now come true (till now they had never met across a chessboard).

Those who knew Botvinnik reckoned that if the world champion did not succeed in creating a solid advantage by his greater knowledge of the game in the first half of the match Tal would gain the upper hand at the finish. It was recalled that in the second part of his return match with Smyslov, Botvinnik, immersed in analysis and somewhat fatigued, had forgotten the clock and overstepped the time limit when in a winning position. Such a blow could be fatal if Botvinnik did not already have several points advantage.

Or – let us quote his first match with Smyslov in which Botvinnik had a tremendous start but only managed to draw. Though he was in excellent physical condition and seemed younger than in fact he was, Botvinnik was the one who would probably tire first in this, his fifth, match for the world title. Therefore the champion must behave from the start like a squirrel at the approach of winter – or so it was then thought. . . .

It had always been a mystery how this technical engineer who appeared in public as a chess-player once every two years had never experienced any loss of 'form'. How was it possible that he was always in such good practice, more so than anyone else, despite the long intervals which no other grandmaster allowed himself?

How was it that the laws which affected others did not affect him? He did not appear at the chessboard for ten, twenty, months and yet from his first game in public was fully integrated into the new atmosphere, did not become affected by time difficulties and usually played very accurately.

The world champion did not hide his secret – or at least a part of it. He obtained four months' leave. He prepared, studied his opponent's opening theory. He intensified his physical training. His step was firm, a striking proof of his strict régime.

It seemed a miracle. But the 'miracle' was the tremendous preparatory work which Botvinnik carried out and his dedication to his chosen task. Only Botvinnik was capable, for months, day after day, of playing exhausting private matches from which he gained no obvious advantage and of which the world would never know. Sometimes one of these games might be repeated in a real tournament as, for example, Botvinnik's famous victory over Spielmann in Moscow in 1935 in only eleven moves, or some of his victories in the match-tournament of 1948 when he became world champion. On these occasions Botvinnik's opponents seemed unarmed contestants against a champion armed to the teeth.

Who was Botvinnik's sparring-partner (or partners)? Not even his closest friends knew. It is supposed that at one time it was Ragozin, then Averbakh, now perhaps his official trainer – Goldberg. Or perhaps he chose his partners according to circumstances; this time Bronstein or Geller – as the most like Tal? Were there many, or only one?

Everything is wrapped in the veil of mystery. Botvinnik, very cautious by nature, did not confide in even his closest colleagues, and his trainer or trainers were as if bound by a vow of silence and, insofar as there may have been several of them, probably did not even know one another. The inborn suspicion of Botvinnik also had its logical reason; if anyone betrayed the content of Botvinnik's preparations the world champion would have found himself, to a considerable degree, disarmed before his challenger.

There was an intrinsic disparity between his training methods and his need for security. He could not renounce co-operation with others during his preparation for that would have meant that later, in the course of the contest, much would have to be left to chance and Botvinnik's conscientiousness would never forgive the acceptance of any system which he had not secretly tried out and tested thoroughly. At the same time, Botvinnik could not help being plagued by doubts.

In the preface to the book about his first match with Smyslov in 1954 Botvinnik could not refrain from evident allusions. For reasons of tact, he says nothing directly. He only quotes three examples from the match where he introduced new moves to which Smyslov, to Botvinnik's consternation, found the best answers almost without reflection.

Botvinnik then (and with what irony!) adds that Smyslov revealed new methods of preparation in his openings. Formerly, preparations were made against one's opponent's known repertoire but Smyslov had gone 'a step further' and prepared also for what his opponent intended to play! What did Botvinnik mean by this 'step further'? Perhaps at one time he meant Kann and then, perhaps, Simagin! Simagin had once been Botvinnik's second and later had trained Smyslov. The disconsolate Simagin complained to all Botvinnik's friends that he had been unjustly attacked, and that Botvinnik had been misled. Simagin felt, if not because of his personal honour then at least because of the time which had elapsed between the two matches, that his personal knowledge was outdated.

What was Botvinnik's training method? He was incomparable in analysis and very probably he himself had laid out the programme and divided the work into sections. It may be assumed that after the training-game had been played, Botvinnik did not exchange impressions with his sparring-partner but kept his precious conclusions to himself.

How did Tal prepare to meet such an adversary? He took part in a tournament! Were the two months of the Candidates' Tournament in Yugoslavia not enough for him? Perhaps not. The next tournament was at Riga. Thus he fulfilled his obligation to his native city which treated him as its 'favourite son'.

Tal even suffered defeats. Perhaps that hurt him, now that everyone expected him to be first. Perhaps it meant little to him. It was important that Botvinnik should not be able to avoid him and that the match he dreamed about as a boy should really come true.

How did Tal, still only twenty-three, react to temporary setbacks? Like a cat, which always lands on its feet wherever it may be thrown. A minor personal catastrophe at the Soviet Spartakiad did not prevent him, a little later, from achieving his greatest triumph at the Candidates' Tournament in Yugoslavia. In Riga he did moderately, considering that he was the favourite. However, with his usual buoyancy, this had no adverse psychological effect on him in his match with Botvinnik.

But one thing is clear; Botvinnik began to think about Tal much earlier than Tal began to think about Botvinnik. There are some who will say that Botvinnik was a serious man and Tal an incurable optimist but it would be more correct to say that there was a great gulf between them in years, temperament, style and intellectual understanding.

Tal was young. He had not had to tread the thorny path of Smyslov. Everything had come easily to him, and at once. Why should he think of hardships and that, perhaps, he would have to play two matches with

Botvinnik in the next two years? It was quite possible that he, as Smyslov, somewhat underestimated Botvinnik. This was not a bad thing for the beginning, but it could be bad for the end. The world champion believed, and not quite without reason, that he was the stronger and he had an iron intention to prove it, no matter what happened in the course of the struggle. . . .

Tal—world champion

Few experts could foresee such a style and such an outcome at the beginning of the first Botvinnik-Tal match in 1960. A draw was enough for the world champion to retain his title and it would have been reasonable to see Botvinnik cautiously keeping the balance with Black and with White seeking out the weak points in Tal's somewhat doubtful repertoire.

What, however, happened? Already in the first game, though Black, Botvinnik played vigorously for a win from the first move. Defying the laws of chess logic that the initiative must lie with the player who has the white pieces, Botvinnik played as though he wished to wipe Tal off the face of the board even before the first blows were exchanged.

Why such impatience? Had Botvinnik become infected with the condescending attitude which many Soviet grandmasters had towards Tal because of his breakneck career, his 'flighty' play, his optimistic belief in his 'lucky star'? Or did Botvinnik have doubts about his own endurance based on his experience in earlier matches and wanted to pile up a great advantage at the start and thus assure a sufficient reserve for the second part of the match when his much younger opponent might have the initiative?

However that might be, these aggressive tactics ended in the complete defeat of Botvinnik in the first game. Perhaps Tal's play could be criticized for its lack of abstract philosophical principles, but Botvinnik should never have dared to underestimate Tal's enormous speculative talent and his unsurpassed capacity to penetrate the real nature of complicated positions of unknown type and to find the most suitable solutions with incredible rapidity and ease. Perhaps even more unpleasant for Botvinnik than the nought itself was that Tal found an hour and a half sufficient time for thought and had despatched him summarily in thirty-two moves. Tal's achievement in demolishing Botvinnik's conceptions and outplaying him on the board is worthy of all respect, even though old Mikhail had tested his theoretical innovations in long analyses at home before the game.

Many regarded the loss of the first game as a chance tactical error by Botvinnik. Maybe they were right; in the next four games Botvinnik kept the initiative.

But the psychological wound suffered by Botvinnik would not heal so easily. Tal, in any case, did not need to gain self-confidence and his triumph at his first encounter with Botvinnik was just what he needed most of all at that moment. From then on, Tal took the lead and never lost it.

Strangely enough Tal's early three-point lead seemed to have less significance than his later two-point lead. The 5–2 result might be regarded as a crisis – of hitherto unkown dimensions, but transitory – for Botvinnik. In confirmation of that came two Botvinnik victories. Then, at the moment of Botvinnik's triumph, Tal unexpectedly took the initiative and again increased his lead. If the first act of the drama could be regarded as chance, the third act could not. In that lay the psychological pressure of Tal's lead which in the next phase weighed with doubled force on Botvinnik.

After the eleventh game in which Botvinnik, depressed by his passive role throughout the whole of that game, let slip a chance to save a 'measly' half point, the world champion felt exhausted. He exercised his right to postpone the next encounter for three days, so that he might recover from his great efforts and the unfortunate result, and once more collect his strength to repeat his exploit of the eighth and ninth games.

After the postponement came the twelfth game. It is hard to say if it was the greatest drama or the greatest comedy of this hard-fought match.

Botvinnik, visibly refreshed by his three-day rest, sat down at the board with the determination of a man fighting in the last ditch. His mood could have been a secret to no one, least of all to Tal. True to his tactics of facing his opponent on every occasion with the type of play most likely to make him nervous, Tal's first aim was to disconcert Botvinnik's aggressive intentions – nothing more – and thus lessen the newly aroused and bellicose enthusiasm of the menaced world champion.

What happened? Both great contestants took up classical positions, Botvinnik because he had reason to believe that therein lay his advantage over his younger and less experienced challenger, and Tal because, despite his usual custom, he did not want to take the slightest risk. Only his still powerful will led the exhausted Botvinnik to believe that he must destroy the fortress of his now barricaded opponent.

So the twelfth game ceased to be a normal contest in which clear laws governed the result and was transformed into a psychological duel between the two men in differing moods. Botvinnik believed that this was the moment when he must catch up with Tal and Tal was convinced that if he managed to give this game a calm and peaceful character his efforts would most easily be crowned with success. Each was immersed in his psychological aims and neither any longer saw the real position on the board. Each was intent only on his own desires. The twelfth game was thus transformed into a tragicomedy of two exhausted rivals.

Botvinnik induced some weak points in Black centre and Tal took king-side chances. In fact, Botvinnik, who believed in the lasting value of his strategic outposts, was the one who attacked, and Tal, who was forced to prepare an attack on the white king, really only wished to defend himself, trying by counter-play to even his chances and establish a dynamic balance on the board.

Each influenced by his chosen role, neither saw the real truth. Botvinnik played unconvincingly and did not make the most of his chances after Tal's imprecise opening play. Nevertheless, he continued to regard the initiative as his. Tal, in his usual manner, as soon as the game was becoming involved, recovered himself and quickly corrected his initial mistakes. But he was not aware that he already had the advantage and with only one desire in his heart – offered a draw.

Botvinnik, naturally (!?), refused. There was nothing left to him, if he wanted to win, but to take an undefended pawn on the queen side. He took it and as a result withdrew his queen from the centre of the struggle. Tal was angry at the obstinacy of his opponent and played fast. The first move was excellent. Botvinnik had his 'answer' ready. Now Tal could sacrifice a rook and drive the unprotected white king into a mating net. In any lightning game he would have seen it. The combination was very simple, much below the level of those which Tal usually composed at the board. But Tal was blinded by his new defensive role in the match. He was not thinking of victory but of the shortest way to a draw. He played quickly, to prove to his opponent that he could not win. Tal did not see – to the great astonishment of all – the simple rook sacrifice. And that from the greatest international player of the time! Tal hastened to sail into a calm haven and overlooked his opponent's answers. Botvinnik remained with a pawn up but did not seal the best move and, after the adjournment, Tal saved the draw. Both had made such mistakes that the epilogue was perhaps a just one.

Exhausted by analysis and all that had taken place in the previous game, Tal and Botvinnik in the thirteenth game made their first 'grandmaster's draw'. After sixteen moves and eighteen minutes Tal proposed a draw.

The position was such that the disappointed Botvinnik had no reason to refuse. He did not succeed in recovering himself before the end of the match, and lost the title. Suddenly, to the surprise of the chess world, Tal was champion!

Botvinnik was in a difficult position while the world waited for his decision about a return match. Only in one match for the world championship had the difference in age between the two competitors been even greater. In 1894 Steinitz had been thirty-two years older than Lasker and he had never recovered his title. Botvinnik was, however, still at the height of his powers and one should not dare to make an analogy. But the danger was there. It was called – Tal.

As world champion Tal remained just as he had been before – the darling of the public. After Botvinnik's hegemony, full of dignity and respect, Tal somehow or other diminished the institution of world champion and came closer to ordinary chess lovers; anyone who cared could play cafe chess with the world champion until late at night. When had there been anything of this sort? At the Leipzig Olympiad Botvinnik, as if he had changed his habits under Tal's influence, often remained until the small hours in the lounge of his hotel. The more experienced said that it was because of his age; in later life it is harder to go to sleep early.

Everyone thought that Tal's title had not gone to his head. He was popular for he had not changed. Hadn't he? Tal had made his way up, ignoring everyone and everything. Now there was no one left to ignore. How could he adapt himself to his new position?

The return match

'He is the greatest optimist in the world', one of his friends once said to me of Botvinnik. Neither his friends nor his enemies, however, believed that he would be able to win back the title taken from him by the ebullient Tal.

None the less, at the banquet at Leipzig, Botvinnik's face beamed from the table where the Soviet team was sitting; he had just received the cup for the best score on the second board. Actually, it was the first time in his life that he had played second board in the Soviet team. But nevertheless he radiated joy. He wanted tangible proof of his belief in his own powers. Now he had it.

An American once wrote a book called *Life begins at forty*. Botvinnik might have added, 'No, at fifty!' He would be that in March when he would once again sit opposite Tal. No one believed in Botvinnik – except Botvinnik. One should have known him better, felt as he did....

In April 1961 it became clear that the young world champion wanted to give the return match the character of a continuation of the second half of his previous match with Botvinnik. Then Tal had been ahead on points and did not allow Botvinnik the chance for in-fighting.

Despite the fact that the course of this new match did not conform to this plan and that Botvinnik was in the lead after the first four games, Tal made up his mind to persevere with his tactics. To a certain extent that meant withdrawal into defence and a lack of will to take risks.

There is no doubt that this sort of play, in which positions arose with clearly defined characteristics, suited Botvinnik excellently. His logic was crystal clear and his strategy was more forthright than Tal's wandering imagination.

Why did Tal stick so obstinately to the Nimzo-Indian, the weapon of solid citizens, inadequate for his piratical style? He lost the first game (as Black). Tal considered that the opening was not to blame. However, he lost the third game also. Tal reconsidered; the opening must be put right. He must play more precisely. He believed that Botvinnik as White would persist in his well-beaten path. So Tal would confront Botvinnik with his improvement and thus check Botvinnik's confidence that he could achieve something with White. Tal would come into his own and sooner or later be able to correct the difference in points.

The psychological 'wearing down' method, however, failed to work. Botvinnik played much the same – or just a little differently – and it was always Tal who found himself faced with fresh problems. Tal was unwilling to concede that these positions suited Botvinnik's style better. However, Tal managed to save the draw a pawn down and was satisfied. Next time the barricade would be raised still higher.

In the sixth game Tal, as White, began with high hopes. In the fourth game he had succeeded for the first time in enlivening and complicating the play – even though then he had not been able to achieve much – and this time he believed that he would have better luck. It was, he considered, a great thing that he had succeeded in making his adversary stray from his familiar path.

But – disillusion! Though Tal had much that was new to say, Botvinnik built up an impenetrable position. Once more the white pieces were 'wasted' but Tal believed that in the end they would still be of greater value to him than to Botvinnik.

In the seventh game – surprise! The older challenger, even though he had a superiority in points, was the one still ready to take a risk and forced a hot pace on his opponent. Aiming at further increasing the difference and thus creating a reserve for the finish when the endurance of the older man might be put to the test, Botvinnik showed daring and a still greater capacity to serve up some unpleasantness to his rival.

Once more the Nimzo-Indian Defence, but Botvinnik as White abandoned his previous variation which Tal now knew well, and instead played the double-edged Saemisch. Botvinnik had also played it in the first match, with little success, but – a blow is a blow. This time Tal had not expected it. Had Botvinnik something up his sleeve? A further difficulty for Tal was that now a draw was hardly sufficient. The young champion decided on another, less recognized, continuation.

Botvinnik was in his element. Tal had compromised his position and was weak on both sides. Faced with growing difficulties, Tal decided to take an offered pawn, but that only hastened the end. Botvinnik struck like a hammer. In a bad situation Tal was unable to offer even a minimal resistance. His worst defeat – and Botvinnik's shortest victory.

At the moment when it seemed that Tal would not have the strength to recover from this twofold shock, when he was playing superficially and was behind on points, something unusual occurred – Tal won his first victory. For some strange reason Botvinnik allowed his Caro-Kann to be transformed into the French Defence a move behind. Therefore he was defeated in the eighth game just as briefly as he had defeated Tal two days before.

The excitement grew. Tal too felt that the moment had come to strike. In the ninth game, for the first time, Tal played vigorously as Black.

What did that mean? Was it an underestimation of his older opponent or the laws which reigned on the board, or merely a desperate bluff? Tal went pawn hunting and neglected his development. It was not hard for Botvinnik to refute so naive a conception. At the end it was Tal who remained a pawn down. He still had chances of a draw but defended himself weakly. This was not the Tal of the year before.

The initiative was once again with Botvinnik. In the tenth game Tal still nourished the hope of repeating his exploit of the eighth game and thus creating the missing atmosphere of tension. But Botvinnik had drawn the moral. He no longer insisted on his prearranged ideas but kept to the conventional line. Tal once more employed the bluff of a pawn onslaught and – for a world champion – misjudged the position. His bishop wandered to the wrong side and Botvinnik's logic, as always in such a situation, was inexorable.

It was the brink of catastrophe. Would Tal accept it? It was expected that he would choose one of the weapons with which he could strike at

Botvinnik's weak points. But – Tal forgot them, or could not find any. In the eleventh game he appeared demoralized and played tamely for a draw, at a moment when he was three points behind! For Botvinnik the match had become a pleasant entertainment. It was not sensible for Tal to play a symmetrical position with *a tempo* down in which he had no threat. Not even bishops of opposite colours could save him.

The match was not over. But it was clear that Botvinnik would return to his throne and that meant the end of the most sudden fame in post-war chess. Nevertheless it was hard to believe that this was the same man who had won so easily in so many tournaments and had beaten even Botvinnik himself in a match. Perhaps Tal was obsessed by his own shortcomings, even as Botvinnik had been when he had lost. Only – whence this lack of understanding of certain essential principles of the sixty-four squares?

The real sovereign—Mikhail Botvinnik

Alekhine's exploit had been surpassed. Botvinnik, in his fiftieth year, had succeeded for the second time in winning back his lost title. Alekhine had abbreviated the 'highest title' to 'his title'. After he had taken it from Euwe he used to say:

'I have got my title back.' It was not in Botvinnik's nature to say that. But he showed it by his actions.

Only a man of tremendous will who had never ceased and would never cease to believe in himself could have defeated an adversary after he himself had been defeated by him a year before.

In truth, everything had been against Botvinnik. Not even Smyslov had inflicted such a defeat on him. The fact that after the ninth game of the first match with Tal he could not win a single game gave one the impression of a real personal catastrophe.

In such a situation would he even want to try to get his revenge on his rival, who had also the irrevocable advantage of being only half his age? Botvinnik did not comment. Once before, in a similar situation against Smyslov, he had postponed his reply to the last possible moment. That had annoyed Smyslov, as did also Botvinnik's further explanation that he would play 'at the insistence of his friends'.

This time Botvinnik parried inquisitive questions with the statement that he wanted first of all to study his games with Tal and if, as a result, he still felt that he had a reasonable chance in a return match he would send a challenge. He took care to behave modestly in public and not to show bitterness at the moment of his downfall. He did not want to appear as an ageing prima donna who had lost all sense of judgement and was not ready to accept the fact that 'his time was over'. But the ominous truth was clear to Botvinnik that he lost most frequently because of serious mistakes in the fifth hour of play when tiredness supervened. In reality the decision had been made when Botvinnik, with head bowed and looking at the floor in an apparently humbled frame of mind, congratulated Tal on his victory. Tal, on the contrary, smiled ecstatically while the camera recorded the picture.

The camera was mistaken. Was Mikhail Botvinnik to retire before a newcomer whom the chess world perhaps recognized but not his old colleagues at home, whose leader Botvinnik had been for three decades? Revenge – that was inevitable.

He must try everything while he had breath in his body. From the time of his fateful match with Smyslov to the present, Botvinnik had become considerably greyer, but his health still served him well, a reward for the faithful observance of a strict regime which admitted no waverings or minor human weaknesses. He was the first example among the grand-masters, from the time when they still wore beards, to whom physical training and monotonous walks meant a part of a carefully considered tournament system worked out in every detail.

His philosophy of chess was no secret. He wrote that if acoustics were a science which informed the world about sounds, music was an art which revealed the beauty of that world, and if logic were a science which revealed the laws of thought, then chess was an art which illustrated the beauty of logic. Therefore he valued above all the integrity of chess creation and could not abide errors which, however inevitable they might be, spoiled the beauty of the game.

With all his longing Botvinnik, in spite of the shock of his defeat a year earlier, could not deny his chess faith, his life's work and all that was dear to him. It is not very likely that Tal was aware of what sort of man he had to confront at their second meeting.

On the basis of the first match Tal had every reason to underestimate the danger. Not only that, but the new champion had responded to every request and paid no heed to the passing of time or to the demands on his health, always somewhat suspect. Probably he would have behaved thus even if he had not been carefree by nature, carried away by the joy of his youth in which everything had fallen so easily into his hands.

By contrast with the first match, there were now some doubting Thomases who did not bet on the younger man. It had become clear that there would be seated at the chessboard on one side a great improviser and on the other the real world champion, even though at the moment he did not hold the title.

What a fantastic metamorphosis in Botvinnik in the course of only one year! Those preparations, that training in secret, must have been tremendous since they had changed roles to such an extent. Botvinnik suddenly appeared at the height of his powers whereas Tal, the best lightning player in the world, fell into time-trouble.

Many unjustifiably accused Tal of levity. This time he simply had no chance against a personality who attached such enormous importance to the content of chess creation and the title of world champion.

What, then, were the reasons for such oscillations in Botvinnik's form in his matches over a single decade? Botvinnik himself gives some explanation in his short autobiography, in which he says: 'I, therefore, have two vocations: chess and engineering. If I played chess only, I believe that my successes would not have been significantly greater. I can play chess well only when I have fully convalesced from chess and when the "hunger for chess" once more awakens within me.'

Those who know Botvinnik intimately say that chess is Botvinnik's real life, whether he admits it or not. Which are the moments Botvinnik considers worthy of mention in his meagre description of his life? The death of his brother during the siege of Leningrad; the birth of his daughter; then, much earlier, in 1935, when the great chess slogan was 'catch up with the West' and as a prize for his first great international success he received a motor car from Ordzonikidze; and long before that when his mother specially bought for him a new Russian shirt when as a schoolboy he gained his simultaneous victory at Leningrad against Capablanca.

Nevertheless, from the two short pages of the autobiography included in his collection of games, a whole paragraph deals with the daughter who followed in her father's footsteps and studied electrical engineering. The reason for Botvinnik's dual nature must perhaps be sought for in his youth; his parents were opposed to his passion for chess. His father was a dental technician and his mother a dentist, and it was understood that he would follow their example.

The headmaster of his school took up the defence of his star pupil: 'Don't stand in the boy's way. Leave him to his inclinations; he is a real bookworm!' His parents soon divorced and that was the first blow in Misha's life. He turned even more to books and chess, and never afterwards left them.

I have seen the self-controlled Botvinnik many times. But there were other occasions: when he cracked his fingers because of a terrible blunder against Pachman at the Moscow tournament of 1947 and his wife calmed him down as he was putting on his coat; and nine years later when he produced an analysis of genius of his adjourned game with Najdorf and accompanied every one of his moves with the childish exclamation: 'Pam!' I also remember how, with exaggeratedly brisk steps, he hurried up to me in the street at Munich, wishing to share his good humour with someone, for a few moments before he had had his revenge on Dückstein for his only defeat in the semi-final of the Olympiad.

Because of his taciturnity and reserve he has been compared to a machine in human form. He appeared thus even when he was thirteen and, thanks to his thick spectacles, made out that he was older than he was in order to become a member of the city chess club.

Many regretted Tal's defeat, for the young man had made the institution of world champion more democratic and had associated with ordinary chess-lovers, playing with anyone at any time of the day or night. They were afraid lest Botvinnik should once more withdraw into his regal dignity.

But in one thing they were mistaken – to think that Botvinnik was not as modest as Tal. I have seen him acting as scrupulous scorekeeper of an unimportant game of cards for his colleagues of the Soviet team. There was no pose about Botvinnik.

Tal as ex-champion

There was a tremendous hullabaloo about Tal at the chess Olympiad at Leipzig in 1960, but not at Havana in 1966. Why was that? The public loves to be impressed. Tal not only had ceased to be world champion, but he no longer impressed as the one-time magician of the chessboard who could do marvels and turn every position to his own advantage. Tal continued to win many tournaments, but his admirers, because of his incomparable imagination in the history of chess, wanted him to win all the tournaments.

Tal, however, could not do it again. He now had young competitors who met him on equal terms, and his bad health further affected his form from time to time. None the less, in the comparatively tranquil atmosphere of the third board at the Havana Olympiad, Tal achieved the highest percentage with an impressive 92.31 per cent with eleven victories and only two draws out of thirteen games.

If no longer unique, Tal continued to rank among the best. What was he now capable of? That remained to be seen in the next elimination matches of the Candidates' Tournament of 1965, for which only Spassky and Tal had the uncontested right to take part.

One of those who interrupted Tal's flight to the stars was Botvinnik. Though heavily defeated in their match in 1960 Botvinnik had had a unique revenge the following year. One of his main weapons was the Caro-Kann. In two long matches with Botvinnik and many, many games using the Caro-Kann, Tal, though from time to time worried about his repertoire, never attempted the Panov variation which Botvinnik himself, as a lover of closed systems, would also have preferred for White.

These two met again five years later on the first board in the team championship of the Soviet Union. On the eve of that meeting Botvinnik had been showing his best form, defeating Smyslov, Keres and Spassky; and against Tal again made use of his favourite Caro-Kann. For the first time against his great rival Tal replied with the Panov variation. And he achieved an astonishingly easy victory. There were some who thought with melancholy: he should have done that long before. . . .

3 Botvinnik-Petrosian-Spassky 1962-

An unexpected champion—Petrosian!

Tigran Petrosian was born in 1929. But he treated the ancient game as if he had acquired the wisdom of a centenarian over whose head wars and floods had passed without harm. Everything seemed to pass – only Petrosian would remain! He had long ago moved to Moscow, but he had not forgotten the teaching of his Armenian background. Let us avoid unnecessary agitation; thus we will live longer, play longer in chess tournaments! Even before he began to rise to the summit Tigran did not hide his secret from his rivals, for he was good hearted.

The example of Bronstein seemed to justify him. David had wasted his energies mercilessly, burnt himself out, till at last his nerves betrayed him and, even before Cardoso, he had whispered that he was fed up with the necessity to be forever qualifying. He was like a tempest which swayed even the firmly rooted Botvinnik but now the storm had blown itself out.

Petrosian, however, went on tranquilly like water dripping on a stone. In the course of years it will wear the stone away. They criticized him at home because of his many draws and few victories, but Tigran went on – not losing.

After Petrosian's colossal exploit at the Soviet-Hungarian match on the eve of the Candidates' Tournament at Amsterdam in 1956, the late Dr Asztalos remarked that he could recognize a future champion in this Soviet grandmaster. In truth, Petrosian was the moral victor of the tournament. He was very far-sighted and never once found himself in a bad position. What is more, in at least half his games he outplayed his opponents and had excellent winning chances. Then mistake followed mistake. The young Tigran was not yet accustomed to playing for first place. His motto was: 'Always upward, never first', and then he found himself in circumstances which were not in accord with his belief in taking his time.

He made a similar excursion into uncertainty at a Soviet championship, to show his critics that he was capable of it. Then he once more withdrew into his philosophical calm with one more lesson learnt; Candidates' Tournaments should be his only exception. After Portorož he admitted that he would play for the first place in Yugoslavia in 1959 since in order to knock at Botvinnik's door no other place had any significance. In this regard Petrosian was right. He had come to Yugoslavia in 1959 with high hopes, for he had never been in such good form and he remembered the chances which he had let slip three years before in Holland, but which he would not let slip a second time. Tigran took the lead at the start. But Tal had once more started a series of victories which could not be halted. Petrosian, the Soviet champion, lost his impetus. Furthermore, all the signs showed that he had concluded a non-aggression pact with Tal, which gave Tal four free days and the possibility of attacking the others with even greater energy. Perhaps Petrosian lost interest and wanted to go home again as quickly as possible with a respectable score.

His moment came on the island of Curaçao three years later. Five rounds before the end the tension was at its height; Keres, Geller and Petrosian were leading with the same score. At this red-hot moment Petrosian made a cold-blooded forecast – as if his own fate were not in question – that whoever did not lose a single game until the end of the tournament would win.

While everyone was expecting a stormy finish to the struggle, Petrosian true to his word, made five draws and confirmed himself as the greatest realist in world chess for all time, for thereby he won first place and at the same time showed his ability most accurately to sum up the strong and weak points of his own play and that of his rivals. Keres and Geller burnt themselves out in the struggle and lost points at the most critical moment. Keres' last chance, over a period of twenty-five years, vanished; he remained the eternal second!

Botvinnik was probably pleased that he had so tame an opponent to contest his title in 1963. Petrosian was overawed at their first meeting and lost the first game of the match, though playing with White. Botvinnik was in good humour, prepared to wipe out his 'not dangerous' rival. Petrosian at once pulled himself together, realizing that awe had been the cause of his initial defeat, and employed the tactics of a genius. He began to tire out the aggressive world champion by a series of dry draws and when Botvinnik began to lose patience, Petrosian began to strike in positions of simple type. General astonishment! The title passed quite smoothly and definitely into the hands of the younger man. Only Petrosian, grown terribly thin in the course of those two months, knew what it had cost him. It was as if Providence had told him when to choose

D

his time. For just on the eve of the match a West German proposal was passed at the FIDE Congress which cancelled Botvinnik's 'holy right' to a return match.

Botvinnik finally retires!

There is no doubt that among living grandmasters Botvinnik is the one who has achieved the greatest results in world chess. With the exception of two one-year interludes when Smyslov and Tal ruled, Botvinnik had held the position of world champion for fifteen years!

Since he was not yet fifty-five, it was an astonishment to many when he withdrew from official competitions and did not take advantage of his right to play in the Candidates' Tournament of 1965. It seemed as if Botvinnik had changed and had lost his former ambition. So Tolush thought when, after a long interval, he had to meet Botvinnik for the first time in a Leningrad-Moscow match. Tolush asked his friend Korchnoi in jest:

'Should I frighten him?'

'Better not,' replied Korchnoi, 'he could frighten you.'

How well Korchnoi knew the former world champion can be seen from the fact that Botvinnik beat Tolush in both games.

In the second team competition Botvinnik outplayed Stein, opening with the king's pawn, which he rarely did. Stein could not breathe in the constricted position. But Botvinnik's years took their toll. Sometimes Botvinnik had not the strength to reckon all the complicated tactical possibilities. So it was here; he lost unluckily to his younger opponent.

Botvinnik suffered when he lost. Today, as earlier, he still loves a struggle on the chessboard. His method of play has not changed; he has always been able to win against no matter whom among the strongest, as he has proved continually in the club championships in the Soviet Union. His colleagues are filled with respect and whisper more than ever among themselves: that is a real world champion!

The true explanation why Botvinnik withdrew is that the oldest of world champions felt that he was no longer able to endure the series of several matches that the present system demands. He will certainly never cease to be irritated at the FIDE which, without consulting him, took away his right to a return match, even though he had proved a justification for this, having won every one of them. Many believe that he would not have refused to play a return match with Petrosian had he been given the right to do so.

Spassky fails

Although before he had not had so great a reputation, when he took his seat on the throne it was prophesied that Petrosian would have a long reign. In his cautious approach to competitive chess, Petrosian was perhaps not so impressive; but he was very impressive in his incomparable ability to foresee danger on the board and to avoid every risk of defeat. After his match with Botvinnik, Petrosian seemed almost invincible. Even Botvinnik, despite his iron will and energy, was exhausted by the endurance of his younger rival. For Petrosian was able, whenever it was necessary to assure his safety, to dry up the position on the board and to make sure that Botvinnik's attempts never reached fruition.

It would, however, be false to regard Petrosian as a player with a predominantly passive style. No one would be able to become world champion if he were not able to win many, many games. Petrosian's aggressiveness took the form of positional masterpieces, in which with exemplary patience he revealed the weak points of his opponent's camp and took advantage of them with exceptional skill and determination.

None the less a fuller explanation is needed to understand the rarity of Petrosian's defeats. No one routed him, for he foresaw very much. It is strange, but like his stylistic antithesis Tal, Petrosian could see a vast number of tactical possibilities in a few seconds. It is thus clear that Petrosian, alongside Tal, is one of the strongest lightning players in the world.

The world champion was a very modest man. He accepted the responsibility of his title with an ease unkown in Botvinnik's time. Immediately after his match with Botvinnik when he set out for Los Angeles he did not show that he felt the burden of his new obligations on his shoulders. He shared first place at the first tournament for the Piatigorsky cup in 1963 and then also in Argentina, each time with Keres.

Everything seemed to run smoothly until 1965. The abolition of the right to a return match by Botvinnik made it possible for Petrosian to remain tranquil and undisturbed and he undertook a tour of the Soviet Union and West Germany. Since he is an Armenian he was welcomed in Erevan as a national hero. Another year passed quickly. Tigran was always ready to accept any attractive offer. But in Zagreb he only came third. A new tournament was arranged at Erevan to strengthen the champion's reputation, but this time Korchnoi took first place.

Before his match with his first challenger (Spassky) in 1966 matters seemed much less clear. There were many challengers because of the post-war competition system of FIDE, but Spassky was something new. Because of the very recent transformation of the candidates' tournament into a system of individual elimination three-round matches, Spassky had cleared the way for himself by winning matches, not a tournament. This was a very advantageous experience for a final contest which also took the form of a match.

In fact, of all the contestants Spassky had the hardest programme. None the less, he succeeded in eliminating his most powerful opponents in fewer games than might have been expected, taking into consideration the enormous reputation of those whom he defeated.

Something strange happened to all Spassky's rivals. Whether they were in excellent form before that or not, all of them – Keres, Geller and Tal – were obviously not up to their usual standard when they met the twenty-eight year old Boris.

The explanation must, it seems, lie in Spassky himself. Even though he was not always at his best in all the games of these duels, all three of his adversaries behaved as if they were discouraged, without self-confidence to develop, even with White, a significant initiative. The secret strength of Spassky lay in his colossal skill in adapting himself to the different styles of his opponents and thus countering them most efficiently. Only Alekhine, and perhaps Lasker, had previously shown such adaptability.

Spassky had many faces. In his matches he revealed three. He could play gambits, could attack or defend, according to circumstances. He was not perfect – nobody is – but he had very good health and nerves and a strong will to make a decision at any given moment. A fairly heavy smoker, he gave up this bad habit during play.

He acknowledges that he felt depressed after a series of five draws in his match with Tal. At the same time, he says, during the breathing space before a new game he realized that so aggressive a fighter as Tal must feel even more tired of this continual fractioning of points. Spassky at once felt better. The continuation justified his psychological approach to the contest, for Tal lost the next three games and the match.

Spassky knew that everything had so far gone far too smoothly and that he would have a far more difficult task with Petrosian. In an interview on the British radio, Spassky announced that his many years of personal friendship with Tal and his deep knowledge of his adversary at the board had helped him very much in choosing the right tactics. As far as Petrosian was concerned, the world champion was to Spassky, in his own words, 'a dark horse' and after Hastings he had only three months to get to know him better. . . .

In the two years previous to the match for the world championship Spassky had a more solid list of successes than Petrosian. However, the match for the primacy of the world in 1966 developed for a long time without major excitement. In a way the character of the game seemed ordered as if by a tacitly understood mutual agreement between the contestants, Tigran Petrosian the champion and Boris Spassky the challenger, that risk must not be regarded as a suitable weapon of good tactics in a match of such importance.

In consequence the players aimed at establishing solid positions as Black and attempted to profit by the smallest superiority as White. In this atmosphere, to all outward appearance calm but filled with nervous tension, both rivals made mistakes in technique unusual for them and this failed to transform better positions into a win.

In the seventh game, however, Spassky, who had begun badly, felt encouraged because of his initiative in the last few games and began to force in a position in which he had nothing to his advantage. The result was that he revealed a weakness in the centre and gave Petrosian a marvellous opportunity for a masterpiece of technical skill.

Though behind in points, the challenger twice tried to maintain his cautious approach to the match as the champion had always done. But nothing happened and there was no change for the better.

Then Spassky made up his mind to make a change in the general climate of the match from the tenth game onward. He once again lost against the more experienced Petrosian. But the temperature of the great struggle rose sharply. That 'change of weather' could be to the advantage of the challenger who no longer had any reason to keep cool.

Later in the course of the match Spassky sometimes made use of unreliable systems in order to complicate the game and tire out his opponent who was leading. Petrosian had a temporary crisis but did not let the leadership pass out of his hands. When Spassky almost overhauled him and when it seemed that the world champion was menaced, Spassky suddenly chose a bad variation and definitely lost the twentieth game.

Surprisingly, the challenger was still optimistic; in the course of the match Spassky gained seven kilogrammes and Petrosian grew thinner by the same amount. In fact, Petrosian expended more energy in order to save the title. Spassky reduced the score and won a fine game just when Petrosian had already decided the general encounter in his favour. The following year Spassky beat Petrosian in a club championship competition, but everything suggested that it was due to a lost opportunity. For later results showed that Spassky was in best form and that it was a real achievement for the momentarily tired Petrosian to have won two matches for the world championship against the strongest of his opponents – Botvinnik and Spassky.

Spassky and Petrosian on the eve of the second match

I witnessed an interesting scene at Palma de Majorca in December 1968. Petrosian and Spassky behaved as inseparable friends. In Botvinnik's time anything of that sort would have been impossible. Only chilly business contact could have existed at the time of signing an agreement for a forthcoming match. Botvinnik's attitude was logical; at such a moment his opponent represented a mortal enemy, since he was aiming at taking from him what was dearest to him – his title. Botvinnik, in fact, only began to associate with Smyslov at tournaments when many years had passed and both had stepped down from the dais of fame and renounced their struggle for the official primacy of the world.

A man of open nature and a lover of company, Petrosian had no secrets and explained his motives for coming to Palma de Majorca. In his wife Rona, who herself sometimes played in women's tournaments, he had found a trusty helper and adviser. In Moscow she had said to him: 'Tigran, if Boris goes to Spain to play, why shouldn't you go too?'

It was not the same thing. Spassky liked travelling and in the course of his recent travels had overcome all his main antagonists. For the holder of the title, however, it was a different matter. He urgently needed an inner re-appraisal and the opportunity to convince himself that he could again excel among his peers.

A new, sharp note appeared in Petrosian's play. Though quiet and unpretentious the stories current about him, that he did not produce results worthy of a world champion, irritated him. He strove with all his forces to win more often and was courageous in his newly-born ambition, but none the less he could not keep in step with the professional efficiency of 'tournament wolves' like Korchnoi, Larsen or Spassky.

Spassky regarded him with a lively curiosity. Something in the whole affair deeply intrigued him, but there was one thing which I was never able to explain to myself; from his whole behaviour it seemed that Spassky sincerely desired Petrosian's success! To me it would have seemed logical if Spassky should wish Petrosian to become morally depressed at this international tournament on the Spanish island and that the world champion should lose the last traces of self-confidence. Therefore I watched their meeting with special interest, Spassky playing

White. But unfortunately there was only a little smoke, without fire! The first, sharper, attempt cost Petrosian a fresh loss of time but Spassky quickly steadied the intentionally created symmetrical position and a draw was agreed. I could not avoid the impression that I had been watching a game of blind man's bluff.

I sought for an explanation, turning over in my mind the careers of the two men. Who had the challenger beaten in this cycle? Keres, Geller, Tal, Larsen, Korchnoi – and with such ease! All the most imposing names which caused far greater fear and trembling at international tournaments than he who sat on the official throne. Spassky's achievement was really fantastic. How then could he have lost the first match against the 'tame' Petrosian in 1966?

There must be a clue somewhere! Good looking, young and healthy, Spassky had no reason to complain of a life which had allowed him to live as at a perpetual banquet. Good natured towards all men, he made friends readily and was willing for friendship's sake to waste his time on trifles. Perhaps he was most satisfied when he was able to do someone a good turn. His spirit, little subject to social disciplines, found its kingdom in chess.

Whence that streak of ruthlessness in his style of play? At an interview he admitted that the hidden tension of his muscles which he felt when sitting at the chessboard filled him with a pleasant, psychological confidence. With so great a gift for infallibly summing up every position he had within him a terrifying inner calm. Chess afforded him a personal independence which many strive for in vain. In such a situation what can the most aggressive of opponents expect, no matter how great he may be? Inexorable punishment for every error! After Spassky's victory in Spain, Korchnoi in a statement revealed with irritation and a concealed longing for revenge the secret of his unlucky match: 'Spassky taught me not to expose my pawns too much!'

Yes, there lay the explanation of that balance of forces, at first sight so unusual, between the world champion and his challenger! Petrosian was a character completely different from all the others whom Spassky had met. Somewhat older and less attractive in appearance than Spassky, with a gift for music but handicapped by a slight tendency to deafness, Petrosian had from a child developed an incomparable sense of accepting reality exactly as it was and that quality, combined with his very lively intelligence, was Petrosian's most murderous weapon in chess. For what others knew he too could know, what others understood he too could understand.

Life had taught him not to expect too much and that he must face every danger himself. In chess he would always assure his position in time and would never take vain risks like a Larsen or a Korchnoi. With no less talent than others for that strange rich game, he was in his time the only rival comparable to the fiery genius of Tal in lightning competitions. He reacted exceptionally swiftly and was also very strong in other fast-moving games, such as table tennis.

Though he had perhaps dreamed less about it than others, fate had awarded him the role of world champion. He found himself in the position of a man who has to prove more than he wants or can. But even as he did not underestimate others, neither did he underestimate himself. He would know how to defend his title even more tenaciously than the aggressive Botvinnik himself. None the less, sensitive to continual criticism, he wanted to prove his worth before the world. Spassky felt this and was pleased. Such an opponent would be simpler for him. That could be an interpretation of the somewhat inexplicable attitude of Spassky at Majorca.

They were often together there, like men whom the common fate of a gladiatorial combat has drawn together. Others, distant from world leadership, discussed their petty personal reckonings while Petrosian and Spassky awaited the inevitable, that when the moment came one of those two must die. Then, perhaps, this inopportune friendship would come to an end.

Petrosian was forty and if he stepped down from the throne he would step down probably for ever. Spassky was at the height of his powers and must try to profit from a chance which life rarely offers three times. There was no mercy for either.

In their first match, in 1966, Spassky had probably underestimated Petrosian, for he believed that he would win the match even after his carriage had begun to slide downhill. However, a considerable gloom hung over Petrosian's private celebration at home, to which Spassky too was invited, for that day he had well and truly lost the last game of the match and thereby dulled the brilliance of his triumph.

Then, they had not known one another. The match had been their first direct contact. Now, in 1969, they knew one another. The new match started badly for Spassky, who was this time, on paper, the favourite. Petrosian had some difficulties in the first game and spent much time in thought, but in Spassky's place he would have felt earlier that things should not be pushed and that perhaps he might not lose.

However, all that did not mean anything final and conclusive. Petrosian had lost the first game of his match with Botvinnik because of apprehension and Spassky because of lack of it. At Moscow, it was the show of the year.

Spassky victorious

A feeling of duty towards their friends brought both of them to the traditional international match in Yugoslavia and it was a pleasant surprise that the two tired duellists had agreed so quickly to appear again before the public – and the Yugoslav public at that. They kept silent about their match, but beneath this taciturnity there seemed a hidden smouldering tension. Still unfamiliar with their new roles, they seemed to us to have changed and that this change implied a deep division. They behaved normally, but at Skopje, spontaneously, they were much less together.

The scene on the Spanish island, six months before, had been different. Both open-hearted and friendly, Petrosian and his challenger for the second time, almost ten years younger, had seemed almost inseparable in the streets of Palma de Majorca. It didn't seem to worry them that Korchnoi, always envious of others, was blazing his trail towards the first prize; the world champion and Spassky looked on the international tournament as an occasion offered by chance as a dress rehearsal for the far more important performance at Moscow.

Their mutual good humour was not, however, a mask to conceal the subtle nuances of their actions. In essence, Petrosian was glowing with a secret satisfaction that he was still champion, and Spassky because he had a fresh chance, ripened by a three-year-old patina. Open by nature, there was nothing in their private lives with which to reproach one another. The time had not yet come for their paths to divide.

Had the older Botvinnik been present he would have looked with astonishment at the friendship of the two rivals and would probably have felt suspicious. Petrosian and Spassky, however, were products of post-war development. Though the situation could have become tense with intolerance, it did not set them against one another, even though fate like a Roman emperor had assigned them the trappings of two gladiators about to take part in a combat in which one of them would have to die.

In chess this is a figurative expression, but none the less the drama must have told with intolerable pressure on the nerves of the two rivals. Before the duel Spassky had let it be known that, if he failed, he had no intention of taking part for a third time in the exhausting qualifying matches; and

Petrosian, during the match, said that if he were defeated he did not see much sense in trying to tread the thorny path to an eventual revenge. Time and the laws of existence were bound to change such moods. But whatever might happen a tacit accord of this nature spoke of the momentary, terrifying consciousness that within two and a half months they would be fighting to the death.

All that took place in that marathon encounter contributed to the atmosphere of Armageddon. To some extent the regular course of their first match three years before had by now given place to sudden changes which 'raised the hair on the heads' of their respective fans. The outcome could not be foreseen for in the first two-thirds of the match the rivals had stood no less than twice on the knife edge between triumph and despair. To recover from such unexpected blows, each of them took the fullest advantage of their right to postpone an individual game and thus obtain a breathing space.

Generally speaking, it was Petrosian who had to struggle to keep the score level, but for the holder of the title that was equivalent to winning. He complained about the Moscow climate and the continual changes of pressure and humidity in the spring, and also about the difficult conditions of play, whereas Spassky regretted his lack of foresight in living outside the city 'in the fresh air' so that for every round of the first and longer part of the match he had to endure more than an hour's journey to the tournament building. In the car he felt excellent but as soon as he entered the hall he felt that 'this isn't it'.

Then came the seventeenth game. The situation was more or less what it had been at the beginning, so now the holder of the throne of chess had to be decided in the shortened match of at the most eight games. This was the phase upon which Spassky had also placed his hopes, in truth in vain, in the first match in 1966. This time Petrosian succeeded in building up a firm position, but after twenty moves he made a mistake, then another, then a third and the challenger, now less unexpectedly, for the third time took the lead.

Suddenly Petrosian felt less sure of himself. Continual oversights in the game itself threatened tragic consequences. As world champion he said tranquilly that, like his predecessors, he was at peace with the thought that he too would have to lose the title one day or another, but an elegant phrase is one thing and a battle without quarter is another.

Faced with the imminence of a great change, the always realist Petrosian lost his legendary capacity for cold evaluation. In the finish he continually made mistakes in his choice of system with the black pieces. He considered, wrongly, that when Spassky was in the lead he would try to withdraw into his fortress and preserve what he had won, but instead he met with a fiery opponent who was tired of uncertainty and who was resolved never again to let slip any life chance that once more might be offered. To Petrosian's taking of risks in the nineteenth game, Spassky replied by a direct attack on the king. The game was his.

Petrosian's fine victory in the twentieth game was an illustration of his great intelligence and the swan-song of the then world champion. In the next games, Tigran again wavered in his tactics. In the last, the twenty-third, game Spassky with a pacific offer extorted the last, necessary half-point 'with a pistol at his opponent's heart', for in the adjourned position, after desperate, heroic forcing, Petrosian was faced with a fresh defeat.

Later, in Belgrade and Skopje, the new champion and the new ex-champion kept silent about what was most important as they chatted amiably with the journalists and, indeed, seemed far away in spirit. Spassky knew that he was the holder of the highest title but had not yet realized it fully, while Petrosian had bitterly to recapitulate all that he had failed to do.

I got the impression that Spassky was waiting to be alone in order the better to understand where he now stood, and that Petrosian also was longing for rest so that somewhere within himself he could find the true aim of his future activities. In his simultaneous exhibitions it could be seen that Spassky felt increased concern about his results. It seemed that the young chess champion would work still harder in order to prove that the crown was rightfully his and that Petrosian, despite his announcement, would be among the participants in the candidates' matches for the world championship within the next two or three years.

The American challenge – Bobby Fischer

We live in the age of computers. An American computer's prognosis for the 1971 Candidates' matches was almost correct in the case of the quarter-final winners, having forecast 5.7–4.3 in favour of Petrosian against Hübner (final result 4–3 to the ex-world champion), 5.4–4.6 for Korchnoi against Geller (final score $5\frac{1}{2}$–$2\frac{1}{2}$) and 6.1–3.9 for Larsen versus Uhlmann (match finished $5\frac{1}{2}$–$3\frac{1}{2}$). We must forgive the mechanical brain if it failed to predict the sudden collapse of Geller's resistance and Hübner's essentially human reaction which led to the sudden stopping of his fight in Seville; otherwise the predictions corresponded with what happened in these matches. But the estimate of probability missed out completely in

Vancouver where Fischer and Taimanov met; the calculated relative strengths had been 5.8–3.1 with the deduction that only nine games would be needed to reach a decision in favour of Fischer. Taimanov had to live through an absolute catastrophe in the first half of that match.

Though in our age machines frequently discover better methods than thinking beings, the present author was called to give his opinion in writing about the Taimanov-Fischer encounter which was the only match the electronic mind failed to explain in advance.

A Soviet colleague of Grandmaster Taimanov described him humorously as 'the first line of defence'. After a quarter of a century's dominance by one country of world chess, the chess throne is being threatened for the first time from outside. Much more than from Bent Larsen, the danger is 28-year-old Robert J. Fischer whose first hurdle on the way to World Champion Spassky was 44-year-old Grandmaster Mark Taimanov of Leningrad.

That Fischer is a much more dangerous rival to Spassky than any of the Soviet grandmasters derives not only from his youth; in spite of his personal negative score with Spassky the American grandmaster has much better percentile successes than the world champion himself on the rating lists. In this situation, even if he were not the incurable optimist that they say he is, it was not so surprising that Taimanov stuck to his Sisyphean task, even when the score was 5–0 to his opponent, and did not surrender.

Taimanov flew towards the Pacific coast of Canada in high spirits, calming himself with the nice thought that in the match against Fischer he could only win and had nothing to lose. Behind this serenity was masked a theoretical preparation and a secret desire to cause a surprise, by destroying all the other side's hopes that a new moment in the world championship had dawned.

Against the outwardly calm Taimanov was pitted the nervous lonely Fischer who could not accept even the companionship of his friend, grandmaster Larry Evans as his second. He had dreamed about this day for more than a decade – the day when he would take part in an equal fight for the greatest title and when his argument from Curaçao in 1962, that the Soviet grandmasters were in a majority and could act as a team, no longer had any basis; it was a chest-to-chest fight, one against one. It is in that context that we should read Fischer's statement that he had been preparing for this match all his life.

In the intervening period he had, in 1967, thrown away the same chance by withdrawing (for insignificant reasons) from the Interzonal Tournament when he was leading. His faith in himself, in his strength and in his knowledge, based on his enormous love for the game, had always been disturbed by a passion for perfection that was not fully realised, by a secret doubt that his 'innate superiority' would not achieve full expression because of the proliferation of analysed schemes and the growing experience and professional work of others. To that was added suspicion. When Taimanov drew the envelope allotting him the white pieces in the first game Fischer checked the other envelope. Sometimes with reason and sometimes seemingly without he made a series of additions to the terms under which he was prepared to play, from indirect strong lighting from the ceiling and absolute silence to that his Sabbath be respected (the Bible is his favourite literature) and that the players' seconds and camp followers be seated no further forward than the ninth row in the hall. He resurrected the forgotten tradition of extra honoraria which drew attention to the greater need for organisers to appreciate the time and energy invested in chess by the players. Hotel rooms too often failed to satisfy him and he frequently changed them. He is even ready to accept an airless closet in order to achieve ideal isolation from the noise which chases him everywhere. When during the second Piatigorsky Cup tournament at Santa Monica, California, in 1966 he was not seen in the light of day because he was seeking a new room every day, Spassky, who gets on well with him, told him to stop it and start to behave normally like the other participants. Unexpectedly Fischer accepted that the advice was friendly, stayed where he was and joined his colleagues in the hotel lounge every morning; immediately his play improved and if the tournament had lasted just a little longer he would have threatened Spassky's first place.

In Vancouver Taimanov stated something similar – that he had prepared for the match with Fischer for a long time. He did not phrase it so, but he was referring to his sixteen years' absence from the official competition and the opportunity it gave him after such a long time to try to crush legend and achieve his greatest success. Looking young for his years, successful in society in many a sense, Taimanov plays easily, making up his mind quickly and yet finding inventive solutions. In the very first game he chose a new and ultra-sharp line in a wide-open battle.

In fact, the fight began before they even sat down. If Fischer liked a quiet small hall without public this did not mean that Taimanov was ready to acquiese in the terms of the younger player, and agree to a hall which would have had a depressing effect on him. While they were trying to find a hall suitable for both sides it seemed as if the match might never start. But knowing of the troublesome experiences of Tunisia, from which Fischer withdrew in 1967, the executive director of the American Chess Federation stayed constantly at Fischer's side just as at Palma de Mallorca Interzonal Tournament in 1970. There, although director of a large organisation the retired air force colonel, Ed Edmondson, did not consider it below his dignity to act as doorkeeper, keeping the door closed and noise out while Fischer was thinking over his next move. The attitude behind Edmondson's self-sacrifice was disclosed when, in answering a provocative question put by a correspondent of *The New York Times* as to whether it paid to play chess when other activities are monetarily more rewarding, he replied, 'Fischer is a genius. Nobody, will remember our millionaires when they die.'

Fischer's whims could have caused difficulties in Vancouver and therefore Edmondson took on his own shoulders all the talks about the venue. During these Bobby was quiet and did not fuss. Once he privately admitted that he was conscious of his 'debt to American chess'. In time both contenders became fed up with this diplomatic wrangling. Fischer said, 'Let's get going', and the new hall, that neither had seen before the first game, was accepted.

Conscious of his intelligence and many-sided talent, Taimanov was not afraid to take risks. He appeared balanced and calm while Fischer could not keep his hands or legs still. When Fischer demanded of the Yugoslav referee, Kazic, that he forbid Taimanov to walk behind his back, Kazic had to pacify Fischer while insisting that there was no relevant rule.

Anyway the result was completely contrary to first impressions. Beneath Taimanov's attractive style is a note of superficiality hard to detect. Fischer, with his excellent orientation in every position, was always compelling him to find the best move through five, seven or even nine hours of play. Taimanov is just a human and although he rarely missed his way an expert will appreciate that the match became, not a fight of cat and mouse, but an inescapable catastrophe.

In the 1971 Candidates' semi-finals Fischer beat Larsen also 6–0 while Petrosian overcame Korchnoi $5\frac{1}{2}$–$4\frac{1}{2}$ (one win and nine draws). In the final played at Buenos Aires, Fischer beat Petrosian $6\frac{1}{2}$–$2\frac{1}{2}$ – and was due to meet Spassky during 1972 to contest the world crown.

PART II   THE GAMES

PART II THE GAMES

1 World Championship Tournament

First 10 rounds, The Hague 2–25 March 1948
Remaining 15 rounds, Moscow 11 April–17 May 1948

	Botvinnik	Smyslov	Keres	Reshevsky	Euwe	
Botvinnik	—	½½1½½	11110	1½011	1½1½½	14
Smyslov	½½0½½	—	00½1½	½½1½½	11011	11
Keres	00001	11½0½	—	0½10½	1½111	10½
Reshevsky	0½100	½½0½½	1½01½	—	1½½11	10½
Euwe	0½0½½	00100	0½000	0½½00	—	4

Round 1: Euwe–Keres 0–1
Smyslov–Reshevsky ½–½
1) **Euwe–Keres,** Ruy Lopez 1 P–K4 P–
K4 2 N–KB3 N–QB3 3 B–N5 P–QR3
4 B–R4 P–Q3 5 P–B3 B–Q2 6 P–Q4
KN–K2 7 B–N3 P–R3 8 QN–Q2 N–
N3 9 N–B4 B–K2 10 0–0 0–0 11 N–K3
B–B3 12 N–Q5 P×P 13 N×QP R–K1
14 N×B+ Q×N 15 P–B3 N–B5
(threatens 16 . . . N×N 17 P×N Q×
QP+) 16 N×N B×N (16 . . . P×N!
and 17 . . . P–QB4) 17 B–K3 QR–Q1 18
Q–Q2 N–N3 19 B–Q4 Q–K2 20 QR–
K1 (20 P–QB4! followed by Q–B3, QR–
K1 and P–B4; not 20 P–KB4 Q×P 21 P–
B5 Q–K7!) 20 . . . Q–Q2 21 P–QB4 B–
R5 22 B×B Q×B 23 Q–B3 P–KB3 24
P–B4? (24 B×P P×B 25 Q×P N–B1 26
P–QN3 Q×RP 27 P–K5 R–Q2 28 R–
K4 R–N2 29 R–N4!) 24 . . . K–R2 25
P–QN3 Q–Q2 26 Q–B3 P–N4 27 Q–
Q3 P×P 28 Q×P? (28 P×P) 28 . . .
R×P! 29 R×R P–Q4 30 Q×RP P×
R 31 B–K3 Q–N5! 32 Q–B4 R–Q6!
33 B–B1 (33 Q×KP? Q–K7) (1)
33 . . . N–R5! 34 Q×P+ P–B4 35
Q–N7 P–B3 36 Q×P R–QB6 37 Q–Q5
R–B4! 38 Q–Q2 R×B! 39 P–KR3 Q–
N6? (39 . . . N–B6+!) 40 Q–K2 Q×BP
41 R×R Q×R+ 42 K–R2 Q–B5+
43 K–N1 N–N3 44 Q–QB2 N–K2 45

P–QR4 Q–Q5+ 46 K–R2 Q–K4+ 47
K–N1 N–Q4 48 Q–Q1 N–B6 49 Q–B2
K–N3 50 K–R1 Q–K8+ 51 K–R2 N–
K7 52 Q–B6+ K–R2 53 Q–B5 N–N6
54 Q–Q6 N–B8+ 55 K–N1 P–R4 56
Q–B4 0–1 on time (56 . . . N–K6+ 57
K–R2 P–R5!)

2) **Smyslov–Reshevsky,** Ruy Lopez
1 P–K4 P–K4 2 N–KB3 N–QB3 3 B–
N5 P–QR3 4 B–R4 N–B3 5 0–0 B–K2
6 R–K1 P–QN4 7 B–N3 0–0 8 P–B3
P–Q3 9 P–KR3 N–QR4 10 B–B2 P–
B4 11 P–Q4 Q–B2 12 QN–Q2 BP×P
13 P×P N–B3 14 N–N3 P–QR4 15
B–K3 P–R5 16 QN–Q2 B–Q2 17 R–
QB1 KR–B1 18 B–N1 Q–N1 19 N–B1
N–QR4 20 R×R B×R 21 B–N5 P–
R3 22 B–R4 N–B3 23 N–K3 N×QP?

(23 ... Q–N2 24 P×P P×P 25 N–Q5
B–K3) 24 N×N P×N (2)

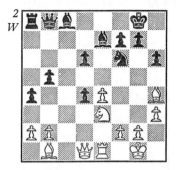

25 Q×QP(?) (25 N–Q5! N×N 26 P×
N B–B1 27 Q–B2! P–N3 28 R–K8 Q–
N2 29 Q–B6!) 25 ... Q–R2 26 Q–Q3
(threatens 27 B×N B×B 28 P–K5 P×P
29 Q–R7+ K–B1 30 N–Q5) 26 ... B–
K3! (so if 27 Q×NP R–N1 28 Q–K2 Q–
Q5!) 27 B–N3? (27 R–QB1!) 27 ... Q–
B4 28 N–Q5? (28 R–Q1) B×N! 29
P×B R–R2 30 R–Q1 R–B2 31 B–R4
P–N3 32 P–R3 Q×QP (32 ... N–R4!)
33 B×N (33 Q×Q N×Q 34 R×N B×
B 35 R×P? R–B8+) 33 ... Q×Q 34
B×Q B×B 35 B×QNP B×P 36 R–
Q3 R–B4 37 B×P R–QR4 38 B–N3
B×P 39 R–KB3 P–Q4 (39 ... R–R2
40 B×P+) 40 B×P R×B 41 R×B ½–½
Round 2: Keres–Smyslov 1–0
        Botvinnik–Euwe 1–0

3) Keres–Smyslov, Slav 1 P–QB4 N–
KB3 2 N–KB3 P–B3 3 N–B3 P–Q4 4
P–K3 P–KN3 5 P–Q4 B–N2 6 P×P
N×P 7 B–B4 0–0 8 0–0 P–N3? (8 ...
N–N3) 9 Q–N3 N×N 10 P×N B–
QR3 11 B–R3 B×B 12 Q×B R–K1
13 P–K4 P–QN4 14 Q–N3 N–Q2 15
P–B4 R–N1? (15 ... P–QB4) 16 QR–
Q1 Q–R4 17 P–B5! P–N5 18 B–N2
P–K4 19 N–N5! R–K2 (19 ... R–KB1
20 P–B4 P×QP 21 P–B5 Q×BP 22 N×
BP!) 20 P–B4! P×QP 21 P–B5 (3)
21 ... N×P? (21 ... Q×BP! 22 N×
BP – 22 P×P? Q×N – 22 ... P–Q6+

23 K–R1 Q–QB7! 24 N–R6+ K–R1 25
Q×Q P×Q 26 R×N P–B8(Q)!; 25 P–
B6 N×P 26 R×N Q×Q 27 P×Q R×
P 28 QR–KB1 R/5–K1 is unclear) 22 Q–
KR3 P–R4 (22 ... P–KR3 23 P–B6 B×
P 24 R×B P×N 25 B×P) 23 P–B6 B–
R3 24 P×R B×N 25 Q–KB3! P–B3
(25 ... Q×P 26 Q–KN3 B–K6+ 27
Q×B P×Q 28 R–Q8+ wins) 26 B×P
N–Q2 27 P–KR4! (27 ... B×P 28 Q–
B4; 27 ... B–R3 28 Q–KN3) 1–0

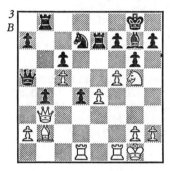

4) Botvinnik–Euwe, Slav 1 P–Q4 P–
Q4 2 P–QB4 P–K3 3 N–KB3 N–KB3
4 N–B3 P–B3 5 P–K3 QN–Q2 6 B–Q3
B–N5 7 P–QR3 B–R4 8 Q–B2 Q–K2
9 B–Q2 P×P 10 B×BP P–K4 11 0–0
0–0 12 QR–K1 B–N2 13 N–K4 N×N
14 Q×N P–QR4 15 B–R2 N–B3 16
Q–R4 P–K5 (4)

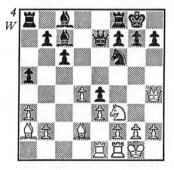

17 N–K5! B×N (17 ... B–K3 18 B–N1
B–Q4 19 B–B3 KR–K1 20 P–B3 B×N
21 P×B N–Q2) 18 P×B Q×KP 19 B–

B3 Q–K2 20 P–B3 N–Q4 (20 . . . P×P
21 B–N1 P–R3 22 R×P N–Q4 23 R–
N3!) 21 Q×Q N×Q 22 P×P P–QN3?
(22 . . . B–N5 23 R–B4 B–R4 24 P–
KN4 B–N3 25 R–Q1 QR–Q1 26 R×R
R×R 27 B×RP R–Q8+ 28 K–B2 R–
QB8 offers better chances) 23 R–Q1
(threatens 24 R×P) 23 . . . N–N3 24 R–
Q6 B–R3 25 R–B2 B–N4 26 P–K5 N–
K2 27 P–K4 P–B4 28 P–K6 P–B3 29
R×NP B–B3? 30 R×B! N×R 31 P–
K7+ R–B2 32 B–Q5! (32 . . . R–QB1
33 P–K8(Q)+ R×Q 34 B×N and 35 B–
Q5) 1–0
Round 3: Smyslov-Botvinnik ½–½
Reshevsky-Keres 1–0

5) Smyslov-Botvinnik, Grünfeld 1
P–Q4 N–KB3 2 P–QB4 P–KN3 3 N–
QB3 P–Q4 4 N–B3 B–N2 5 Q–N3
P–B3 6 P×P N×P 7 P–K4 N–N3 8 B–
K3 B–K3 9 Q–B2 B–B5 10 B–K2 N–
R3 11 0–0 0–0 12 KR–Q1 Q–Q3 13 P–
QN3 B×B 14 N×B QR–B1 15 B–B4
Q–K3 16 B–K5 P–B3 17 B–N3 Q–B2
18 N–B4 B–R3 19 N–Q3 P–KB4 20
N–B5? (20 P×P Q×BP 21 R–K1 N–Q4
22 R–K5 and 23 QR–K1) 20 . . . P×P
21 Q×P (21 N–K5 Q–Q4 22 N×QNP
P–B4!=) 21 . . . N×N 22 P×N N–Q4
23 R–K1 QR–K1 24 B–K5 B–B5 25
B–N2 Q–B4 26 Q–B4 P–K4 27 R–K4?
(27 R–K2 P–K5 28 QR–K1) 27 . . . Q–
B2 28 QR–K1 N–B3! 29 Q×Q+
(29 N×P? Q×Q 30 R×Q N–N5!)
29 . . . R×Q 30 R/4–K2 N–Q2 31
P–QN4 P–QR4 32 P–QR3 P×P 33
P×P R2–K2! 34 P–N3 B–R3 35 N×P
(5)
35 . . . B–N2! 36 P–B4 N–B3 37 K–B2
N–Q4 38 R–K4 N–B3 39 R/4–K3
N–Q4 40 R–N3 P–KN4! 41 K–B3
R–KB1 42 R–K4 N–B3 43 R–K2 N–Q4
44 R–K4 N–B3 ½–½

6) Reshevsky-Keres, King's Indian 1
N–KB3 N–KB3 2 P–B4 P–QN3 3
P–Q3 P–N3 4 P–K4 P–Q3 5 N–B3
B–KN2 6 P–Q4 0–0 7 B–K2 B–N2 8

Q–B2 P–K4 9 P×P P×P 10 B–K3
R–K1 11 0–0 QN–Q2 12 KR–Q1
P–B3 13 P–QN4 Q–K2? (13 . . . Q–B2)

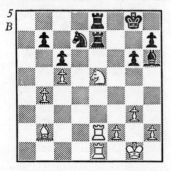

14 QR–N1 N–B1 15 P–QR4 Q–B2 16
P–N5 KR–Q1 17 R×R R×R 18 P–R5!
N–N5 (18 . . . NP×P 19 P–N6!) 19
P×NP RP×P 20 B–N5 P–B3? (20 . . .
B–B3 21 B–Q2 B–K2 and 22 . . . B–B4)
21 P×P B×P 22 B–Q2 P–B4 (22 . . . N–
K3 23 Q–N3) 23 B–N5 (23 P×P?
P–K5) 23 . . . R–K1 24 P–R3 P×P 25
N.QB3×P B×N 26 Q×B N–B3 27 Q–
K3 N/1–Q2 28 Q–N3 R–N1 29 B–K3
N–B4 30 Q–B2 R–R1 31 N–N5 R–K1
32 P–R4 P–K5 33 N–R3 R–Q1?
(33 . . . B–B1 34 N–B4 B–Q3) 34 N–
B4 R–Q3 35 P–R5 P–KN4 (35 . . .
P×P) 36 N–Q5 N×N 37 P×N P–R3
38 B×N *(6)*

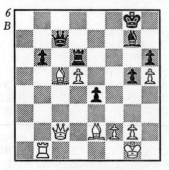

38 . . . P×B? (38 . . . Q×B 40 Q×P
R–KB3) 39 Q×KP B–Q5? 40 Q–K8+
K–N2 41 R–N8 1–0

Round 4: Botvinnik–Reshevsky 1–0
Euwe–Smyslov 0–1

7) Botvinnik-Reshevsky, Nimzo-Indian 1 P–Q4 N–KB3 2 P–QB4 P–K3 3 N–QB3 B–N5 4 P–K3 P–Q4 5 P–QR3 B–K2 6 N–B3 0–0 7 P–QN4 QN–Q2 8 B–N2 P–B3 9 B–Q3 P×P 10 B×BP B–Q3 11 N–K2? (11 0–0 P–K4 12 Q–B2) 11 . . . P–QR4! 12 P–N5 N–N3 13 B–Q3 P×P 14 B×NP B–Q2 15 Q–N3 P–R5 16 Q–Q3 R–R4 17 N–B3 (17 B×B Q×B 18 B–B3 Q–N4 19 Q–N1 Q×Q+ 20 R×Q R–R3 with a good ending for Black) 17 . . . Q–K1 18 B×B Q×B 19 0–0 R–B1 20 P–K4? (20 KR–N1 N–B5 21 B–B1) 20 . . . N–B5 21 B–B1 P–K4! 22 R–Q1 P×P 23 Q×P Q–K3 24 R–R2 P–R3 25 P–R3 R–R3 (threatens 26 . . . N–K4!) 26 N–Q5! N×KP 27 R–K2 P–B4 28 P–N4 (7)

7
B

28 . . . B–B4? (28 . . . N–N4! 29 R×Q N×N+ 30 K–N2 N×Q 31 R×N P×P; 29 Q–Q3 N×N+ 30 Q×N P×P; 29 N×N Q×R 30 N–B6+ P×N 31 Q–Q5+ K–R1 32 N–B7+ K–R2 33 N–N5+ P×N 34 Q–B7+ K–R1 35 Q–B6+ K–N1 36 Q–N6+ K–B1!) 29 P×P Q×P? (29 . . . B×Q 30 P×Q B×P+ 31 R×B N×R 32 K×N R×P) 30 Q×N/K4 (not 30 Q×B? R×Q 31 N–K7+ K–R2 32 N×Q N–B6) 30 . . . Q×P 31 N–R2 R1–B3 32 N–B4 1–0 on time

8) Euwe–Smyslov, Ruy Lopez 1 P–K4 P–K4 2 N–KB3 N–QB3 3 B–N5 P–QR3 4 B–R4 N–B3 5 0–0 B–K2 6 R–K1 P–QN4 7 B–N3 0–0 8 P–B3 P–Q3 9 P–KR3 N–QR4 10 B–B2 P–B4 11 P–Q4 Q–B2 12 QN–Q2 N–B3 13 P×BP P×P 14 N–B1 B–K3 15 N–K3 QR–Q1 16 Q–K2 P–N3 17 N–N5 B–B1 18 B–Q2 K–N2 19 QR–Q1 P–R3 (19 . . . N–Q5? 20 P×N BP×P 21 N–B1 Q×B 22 N–K6+!) 20 N–B3 B–K3 21 P–QR4 Q–N1 22 B–B1 R×R? (22 . . . KR–K1 and 23 . . . P–B5) 23 R×R R–Q1 24 R×R B×R 25 P×P P×P 26 N–Q5! N–N1 (26 . . . N×N? 27 P×N B×QP 28 B×RP+; 26 . . . B×N? 27 P×B N×P 28 B–K4!) 27 B–K3 P–B5 28 P–QN3! N–R4? 29 N×P! P×P 30 B–N1 Q–N2 31 B–Q4 K–R2 32 N–KB4 B–B5 (8)

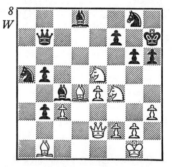

8
W

33 N/5×NP! P×N (33 . . . B×Q 34 N–B8 mate!) 34 N×P? (34 Q–N4! Q–KB2 35 P–K5 N–K2 36 P–K6 Q–K1 37 N–R5!; 34 . . . B–KB2 35 P–K5 B–N4 36 P–K6 B–K1 37 N×P B×N 38 Q–B5! Q–N2 39 Q–B7! Q×Q 40 P×Q B×B 41 P–B8(N) mate – Euwe; 34 . . . N–K2 35 P–K5 B–KB2 36 P–R4 N/4–B3 37 P–R5 N×B 38 P×P+ B×P 39 B×B+ N×B 40 Q×N+ K–R1 41 P×N with a winning position) 34 . . . K×N 35 P–K5+ (35 Q–B3! N–KB3 36 P–K5+ K–B2 37 Q–B5! Q–B3 38 Q–N6+ K–K2 39 Q–N7+ K–K3 40 P×N; 35 . . . B–K3 36 Q–B8!) 35 . . . K–B2 36 Q–R5+ K–B1

37 P–B4 B–N3 38 Q–B5+ K–K2 39 Q–R7+ K–Q1 40 B×B+ Q×B+ 41 K–R2 Q–K6 42 Q–B5 N–QB3 0–1
Round 5: Reshevsky-Euwe 1–0
Keres–Botvinnik 0–1

9) Reshevsky-Euwe, Slav 1 P–Q4 P–Q4 2 P–QB4 P–K3 3 N–KB3 N–KB3 4 N–B3 P–B3 5 P–K3 QN–Q2 6 B–Q3 B–N5 7 P–QR3 B–R4 8 Q–B2 Q–K2 9 B–Q2 P×P 10 B×BP P–K4 11 0–0 0–0 12 P–Q5 P–B4? (12 . . . B×N; 12 . . . N–N3; 12 . . . B–B2) 13 P–Q6! Q–Q1 (13 . . . Q×P? 14 N–QN5 Q–N3 15 P–QN4 wins) 14 QR–Q1 R–N1 15 N–Q5 N×N 16 B×B Q×B (16 . . . N×P 17 P×N Q×B 18 N–N5!) 17 R×N P–K5 18 N–N5 P–N4 19 B–R2 Q–N3 20 N×KP (20 R–B5! P–B5 - 20 . . . N–B3 21 R×P Q×P 22 N×BP! – 21 Q×KP Q×P 22 R×NP N–B3 23 Q×P B–R3 24 Q×BP+! R×Q 25 N×R Q–B2 26 R×R+ Q×R 27 R–Q1!) 20 . . . B–N2 21 R–Q2 (21 N×P!) 21 . . . P–B5 22 B–N1 P–N3 23 Q–B3 KR–K1 (better 23 . . . Q–B3 or 23 . . . B×N) 24 N–B6+ N×N 25 Q×N Q–B3 26 P–K4? (26 Q–N5) 26 . . . R–K3 27 Q–B4 R–Q1 28 KR–Q1 P–QR4 29 P–KR4 P–R4 30 P–Q7? (30 R–Q4 with Q–Q2, P–B4 and P–K5) 30 . . . R–K2 31 P–KN4 R2×QP 32 P×P R×R 33 R×R R×R 34 Q×R P×P? (34 . . . Q–B3) 35 Q–N5+ (*9*)

35 . . . Q–N3? (35 . . . K–B1 36 Q×RP Q–Q3!) 36 Q×Q+ P×Q 37 P–B4 P–N5 38 P×P P×P 39 K–B2 P–B6 40 P–N3 K–B2 41 K–K3 B–B1 (s) 1–0

10) Keres-Botvinnik, English 1 P–QB4 P–K3 2 P–KN3 P–Q4 3 B–N2 P–Q5 4 P–QN4 P–QB4 5 P–N5 P–K4 6 P–Q3 B–Q3 7 P–K4 Q–B2 8 N–K2 P–KR4 9 P–KR4 (9 P–B4 P–B3 10 P–B5! 9 . . . B–N5 10 P–KR3 B×N 11 Q×B P×P 12 P–K5!) 9 . . . N–KR3 10 0–0 B–N5 11 P–B3 B–K3 12 P–B4 B–N5 13 P–B5 (13 P×P B×P 14 B–B4) 13 . . . N–Q2 14 N–Q2 P–KN3 15 P× P P×P 16 N–KB3 B–K2 (16 . . . 0–0–0 17 N–N5) 17 R–B2 Q–Q3 18 B×N? (better 18 B–Q2 and 19 Q–QB1) 18 . . . R×B 19 Q–Q2 R–R1 20 N–N5 N–B3 21 R–K1 (threatens 22 N–B4!) 21 . . . Q–N3 22 N–KB3 N–Q2 23 N–N5 R–KB1 24 R×R+ B×R 25 P–R4? (25 N–B3 0–0–0 26 N–R2 B–K3 27 R–KB1 B–N2 28 Q–N5) 25 . . . B–R3 26 P–R5 Q–KB3 27 N–B1 0–0–0 28 N–N3 R–B1 29 R–R1? (29 R–KB1 Q–K2 30 Q–B1) 29 . . . Q–K2 30 Q–B1 K–N1 31 R–R2 R–B2 32 Q–R3 B×N 33 P×B B–Q8! 34 Q–B1 B×N 35 R–N2 B–Q8 36 Q×B Q×P 37 Q–K1 N–B1 38 K–R2 Q–B3 39 B–R3 N–R2 40 Q–Q1 N–N4 41 P–N6 P–R5! 42 Q–N4 (42 KNP×P Q–B5+ 43 K–N2 N×B 44 K×N R–R2) 42 . . . KRP×P+ 43 K×P R–B1 44 P×P+ K×P 45 P–R6 (*10*)

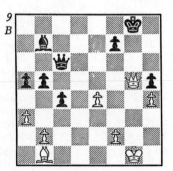

45 ... N×B! (45 ... K×P 46 R–R2+
K–N3 47 R–N2+ K–R2 48 R×P+
K×R 49 Q–Q7+=) 46 Q×N (46
R×P+ K×P; 46 K×N Q–B8+)
46 ... Q–B5+ 47 K–N2 Q–B8+
48 K–R2 R–B7+ 49 R×R Q×R+
50 K–R1 Q–K8+ 51 K–N2 Q–K7+
52 K–N1 Q–K6+ 53 Q×Q P×Q
54 P×P K×P 55 K–N2 K–N3 56 K–B3
K–R4 57 K×P K–N5 58 K–Q2 P–N4
0–1

Round 6: Keres-Euwe ½–½
Reshevsky-Smyslov ½–½

11) Keres-Euwe, Ruy Lopez 1 P–K4
P–K4 2 N–KB3 N–QB3 3 B–N5
P–QR3 4 B–R4 N–B3 5 0–0 B–K2
6 Q–K2 P–QN4 7 B–N3 0–0 8 P–B3
P–Q4 9 P–Q3 P–Q5 10 P×P N×QP
11 N×N Q×N 12 B–K3 Q–Q3
13 N–B3 B–K3 14 B×B? (14 B–B2)
14 ... P×B! 15 P–B4? P×P 16 B×P
P–K4 17 B–N3 QR–Q1 18 QR–Q1
Q–K3 19 R–B5 B–B4+ 20 K–R1 B–Q5
21 B–R4 R–Q2 22 R–QB1? (22 R/1–
KB1) 22 ... QR–B2 23 P–QR3 B×N?
(23 ... P–N3) 24 P×B (24 R×B?
N–Q4!) 24 ... N–Q2 25 R×R R×R
26 B–N3? (26 Q–QB2) 26 ... Q–N6
27 P–Q4 Q×RP 28 Q–Q1 N–B3
29 R–R1 (29 P×P N×P 30 P–K6 R–B1
31 R–R1) *(11)*

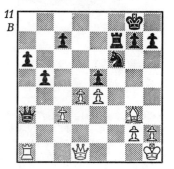

29 ... Q–B1 (29 ... Q×P? 30 P×P
N×P 31 P–K6 R–B3 32 Q–Q8+
R–B1 33 R–Q1!) 30 P×P N×P 31 Q–

Q3 (31 P–R3? R–B8+!) 31 ... N–B4
(31 ... N×P? 32 P–K6; 31 ... R–B4!)
32 Q–K2 N–K3 33 P–R3 Q–B1
34 Q–R2 ½–½

12) Reshevsky-Smyslov, Slav 1 P–
QB4 N–KB3 2 N–QB3 P–Q4 3 P–Q4
P–B3 4 N–B3 P×P 5 P–QR4 B–B4
6 N–K5 P–K3 7 P–B3 B–QN5 8 P–K4
B×P 9 P×B N×P 10 B–Q2 Q×P
11 N×N Q×N+ 12 Q–K2 B×B+
13 K×B Q–Q4+ 14 K–B2 N–R3
15 R–Q1 (15 N×P/4 0–0–0 16 Q–K5)
15 ... Q–R4 16 N×P/4 Q×P+ 17 P–
N3 *(12)*

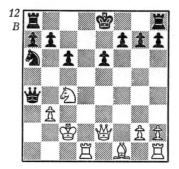

17 ... Q–R7+? (17 ... N–N5+ 18
K–B3 N–Q4+ 19 K–N2 - 19 R×N?
Q–R8+ - 19 ... Q–N5) 18 K–B3
Q×Q 19 B×Q K–K2 20 N–R5 (20
N–Q6! P–QN4 21 B–B3 QR–Q1 22
N–N7) 20 ... N–B4 (threatens 21 ...
N–K5+ and 22 ... N–B7) 21 B–B3
KR–QB1 22 P–QN4 N–R3 23 K–N3?
(23 N×NP? N×P! 23 R–R1 QR–N1
24 N×P+!) 23 ... QR–N1 24 R–R1
P–KB4? (24 ... N–B2 25 B×P! 24 ...
R–B2 25 ... R/1–QB1 and 26 ...
N–N1) 25 KR–QB1? (25 KR–K1
K–B3 26 N×BP P×N 27 R×N)
25 ... K–B3 26 N×BP P×N 27 R×N
P–B4 28 R–B4 R×P+ 29 R×R P×R
30 R×RP P–R3 31 R–R6 K–K4 32
K×P P–N4 33 R–B6 R×R 34 B×R
K–Q5! 35 B–Q7 K–K6 36 B×P K–B7
37 B–Q5 P–N5 38 K–B5 K–N8 39

K–Q4 K×P 40 K–K5 K–N6 41 K×P
P–R4 42 K–N5 P–R5 43 B–B6 P–R6
44 P×P P×P 45 B–N7 ½–½
Round 7: Smyslov–Keres 0–1
        Euwe–Botvinnik ½–½

13) **Smyslov–Keres,** Catalan 1 P–Q4
N–KB3 2 P–QB4 P–K3 3 P–KN3
P–Q4 4 B–N2 P×P 5 Q–R4+ B–Q2
6 Q×BP B–B3 7 N–KB3 QN–Q2
8 N–B3 N–N3 9 Q–Q3 B–N5 10 0–0
0–0 11 R–Q1 P–KR3 12 B–Q2 Q–K2
13 P–QR3 B×N 14 Q×B KR–Q1
15 B–K1 QR–B1 16 B–B1 B–Q4
17 P–QN4 QN–Q2 18 N–R4 N–K5
19 Q–B2 N–Q3 20 P–B3 P–KN4
21 N–N2 P–KB4 22 B–B2 N–B3 23 N–
K1 P–QR4 24 N–Q3 R–R1 25 B–N2
R–R2 26 R–K1 Q–R2 27 P–N5?
(27 P×P R×P 28 KR–B1 followed by
B–K1–N4) 27 . . . N×P 28 Q–B5 P–B3
29 P–QR4 N–Q2! 30 Q–B2 N–Q3
31 N–K5? (better 31 N–B5 P–B5?
32 Q×Q+ K×Q 33 P×P P×P 34
B–R4! 31 . . . N–B3 32 P–K4 P×P
33 P×P P–N3!) 31 . . . N–B3 32 QR–
B1 R/2–R1 33 N–Q3 QR–N1 34 N–B5
P–N3 35 P–K4 P×P 36 N×P/4
(36 P×P P×N 37 P×B Q×Q 38 R×Q
KP×P 39 R×P N/Q–K5 40 R×BP
QR–B1!) 36 . . . Q–N3 37 Q–K2
R–N2 38 N–B3 B–B5 39 Q–N2 P–N4
40 P×P P×P 41 N–K4 (threatens
42 N×N.Q6 R×N 43 R×B) 41 . . .
N/Q3×N 42 P×N N–N5 (*13*)

43 R×B Q–R4! (43 . . . N×B 44 R–B3!
– 44 K×N R–B2+; 44 Q×N P×R –
44 . . . N–N5 45 P–R3!) 44 R–B2?
(44 P–R4! N×B 45 R–KB1 N–Q8
46 Q–N3 P×R 47 Q×R N–K6 is
unclear) 44 . . . Q×P+ 45 K–B1
R–KB2 46 R/1–K2 Q×P 47 Q–B3
(47 R–B3 Q–Q3!) 47 . . . Q×Q (also
47 . . . N×B wins) 48 R×Q R/1–KB1
49 R/3–B2 N×B 50 R×N R×R+
51 R×R R×R+ 52 K×R P–R5!
53 B–R3 K–B2 54 P–Q5 P×P (54 . . .
P–R6!) 55 B–Q7 K–B3 56 B–B6 P×P
57 B×NP P–R6 0–1

14) **Euwe–Botvinnik,** French 1 P–K4
P–K3 2 P–Q4 P–Q4 3 N–Q2 P–QB4
4 KP×P KP×P 5 B–N5+ N–B3 6 Q–
K2+ Q–K2 7 P×P Q×P+ 8 N×Q
B×P 9 N–QN3 B–N3 10 B–Q2 N–K2
11 B–N4 P–QR3 12 B–B5! B–B2
13 B×N+ N×B 14 0–0–0 B–K3 15
N/2–Q4 0–0–0 16 N×N P×N 17 R–
Q4 K–Q2 18 P–N3 P–B3 19 R–QR4
R–R1 20 R–K1 KR–K1 21 B–K3 B–Q3
22 B–B4 B–B1 23 B–K3 B–KB4 24
R–Q1 K–B2 25 R/1–Q4 B–K5 (*14*)

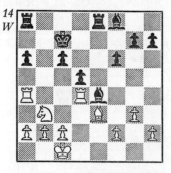

14
W

26 R–R5 (26 B–B4+ K–N3? 27
R/Q4–N4+!; 26 . . . K–N2 27 N–R5+
K–N3 28 R/Q4–N4+ B×R 29
R×B+ K×N 30 R–N7! 26 . . . B–Q3
27 B×B+ K×B 28 R–R5! 26 . . .
K–B1!) 26 . . . B–N7! 27 N–B5 B–B8
(27 . . . K–N3? 28 R–N4+! K×R
29 N–N7) 28 N–Q3 (28 R/4–QR4?

13
W

B–N4 29 N×P+ K–N2 30 N–B5+
B×N 31 R×R B×B+) 28 . . . R–K5
29 R/4–R4 R×R 30 R×R B×N 31 P×B
P–QB4 32 P–N3 P–Q5 33 B–Q2 K–N3
34 K–Q1 R–K1 35 P–QR3 K–N4 36 R–
R5+ K–N3 37 P–QN4 R–K4 38 P×
P+ B×P 39 P–B4 R–K1 (39 . . . R–K6?
40 R×B K×R 41 B×R P×B 42 K–K2
K–Q5 43 P–N4! wins) 40 R–R4
K–N4 ½–½
Round 8: Botvinnik-Smyslov ½–½
Keres-Reshevsky ½–½

15) Botvinnik-Smyslov, Grünfeld 1
P–Q4 N–KB3 2 P–QB4 P–KN3 3 N–
QB3 P–Q4 4 N–B3 B–N2 5 Q–N3
P×P 6 Q×BP 0–0 7 P–K4 B–N5 8 B–
K3 N/3–Q2 9 N–Q2 N–N3 10 Q–
Q3 P–QB3 (10 . . . P–KB4 11 P–B3
P×P!) 11 P–B3 B–K3 12 R–Q1 N–R3
13 P–QR3 Q–Q2 14 Q–B2 N–B2
(14 . . . B×P 15 B×B Q×B 16 N–B4
Q–B3 17 N–R5) 15 N–N3 B–B5
16 B–K2 B×B 17 Q×B QR–Q1
18 0–0 Q–K3 19 N–B5 (19 N–R5!)
19 . . . Q–B1 20 K–R1 N–Q2 21 N–N3
P–N3 22 Q–B4 Q–N2 23 P–B4 P–K3
24 R–B1 N–B3 (24 . . . P–KB4!?) 25 B–
N1 R–B1 26 R–QB2 KR–Q1 27 Q–
K2 N–N4 28 P–K5! (28 N×N P×N
29 R×R R×R 30 P–K5 N–Q4 31 Q×P
R–B7!) 28 . . . N×N 29 NP×N N–Q4
30 P–B4 N–K2 31 N–Q2 N–B4 32 N–
K4 N×P (32 . . . R×P 33 B×R N×B
34 N–Q6!) 33 B×N R×B 34 N–Q6
R×N 35 P×R P–QB4 36 R–Q2 R–Q1
37 Q–B3 Q×Q? (37 . . . Q–Q2) 38
R×Q B–Q5 39 P–N3 R×P 40 K–N2
P–B4? (40 . . . P–KR4) 41 P–QR4
K–B2 42 R–N3 K–B3 43 R–R2?
(43 P–R5 P×P 44 R–R3 R–N3 45 R–Q
B2!) 43 . . . P–QR4! 44 R–Q2 K–K2 45
K–B3 K–Q2? (45 . . . P–R4! 46 P–R3
K–K1 47 P–N4 P–R5!) 46 P–N4 P–R3
47 R–KN2 (47 P×P KP×P 48 R–K2!)
K–K2 48 R–Q3 K–B2 (*15*)
49 P–R4? (49 R–N2 K–K2 50 R–N1
K–Q2 51 P–R3 K–Q1 52 K–K2 K–Q2

53 R3–QN3 K–B2 54 R–KN3 K–Q2
55 P–R4! and 56 P–R5) 49 . . . P×P+
50 R×P P–R4 51 R–N2 R–Q1 52 R/2–
Q2 K–K1 53 R–KN2 K–B2 54 R/2–Q2
K–K1 55 K–K2 (55 K–K4 B–B3 56 R–
Q6 B–K2 57 R×R+ B×R 58 K–K5
K–K2 59 R×B? K×R 60 K×P P–QN4!
wins) 55 . . . K–K2 (55 . . . B–B3 56 R–

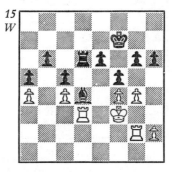

15
W

Q6) 56 R–Q1 R–KB1! 57 R–KB1 B–
B3 58 R–QN3 B×P 59 R×P B–N6
60 R–N7+ K–B3 (60 . . . K–Q3 61 R–
Q1+ K–B3 62 R1–QN1 mates) 61
R–N5 (61 K–B3 P–R5 62 K–N4
R–Q1 63 R–N5 R–Q5 64 R×BP
R–K5!) 61 . . . K–B4? (61 . . . K–N2
62 R×BP B×P 63 R×P P–R5!) 62
R×BP+ K–K5 63 R–K5+ K–Q5 64
R–Q1+ K×P 65 R–K4+ K–B4 66 K–
B3 P–R5 67 R–QN1 K–Q3 68 R–N6+
K–Q2 69 K–N4 (69 R/N6×P R×P+!)
69 . . . R–B4 70 R–Q4+? (70 R–R6!)
70 . . . K–K2 71 R–N7+ K–B3 72 R–
N5 P–K4! 73 R–Q6+ K–N2 74
R×RP (74 P×P R–B5+ 75 K–R3
R×P=) 74 . . . R×P+ 75 K–R3 K–R3
76 R/5–R6 K–R4 77 R×P R×P 78 R–
R6+ K–N4 79 KR/R6–N6+ K–R4 ½–½

16) Keres-Reshevsky, Ruy Lopez 1
P–K4 P–K4 2 N–KB3 N–QB3 3 B–
N5 P–QR3 4 B–R4 P–Q3 5 P–B4
B–N5 6 N–B3 N–K2 7 P–KR3 B×N
8 Q×B N–N3 9 N–Q5! R–QN1
10 N–N4 (10 P–QN4 P–N4 11 P×P
P×P 12 Q–B3 N–Q5!) 10 . . . N–K2

11 N–B2 Q–Q2 12 P–Q3? (12 P–QN4) 12 ... N–B1 13 B–Q2 B–K2 14 Q–N3 B–B3 15 R–QB1? (P–QN4) 15 ... N–N3! 16 B–N3? Q–Q1! 17 0–0 N–Q2 18 P–R3 N–B4 19 B–R2 0–0 20 P–N4 N–K3 21 B–K3 (*16*)

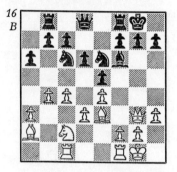

21 ... N–B5! 22 Q–B3 (22 B×N P×B 23 Q×P B–N4; 23 Q–B3 N–K4 24 Q–Q1 P–B4!) 22 ... N×QP 23 R–N1 N–B5 24 P–N5 ½–½

Round 9: Reshevsky-Botvinnik ½–½
Smyslov-Euwe 1–0

17) Reshevsky-Botvinnik, Dutch 1 P–Q4 P–K3 2 P–QB4 P–KB4 3 P–KN3 N–KB3 4 B–N2 B–K2 5 N–KR3 0–0 6 0–0 P–Q3 7 N–B3 Q–K1 8 P–K4 P×P 9 N–B4 (9 N×P P–K4!) 9 ... P–B3 10 N×P/K4 N×N 11 B×N P–K4 12 N–N2 (12 P×P P×P 13 N–Q3) 12 ... N–Q2 13 N–K3 P×P! 14 Q×P N–K4 15 P–B4 N–N5 16 N×N B×N 17 R–K1 B–B3 18 Q–Q3 (18 Q×QP? R–Q1 19 B×P+ K×B 20 R×Q KR×R wins) 18 ... Q–R4 19 B–Q2 KR–K1 20 QR–N1? (20 R–K3) (*17*) 20 ... R–K2? (20 ... R–K3 21 R–K3 QR–K1 22 QR–K1 B×P 23 R–N1 R×B! 24 R×R R R×R 25 Q×R B–B4 26 Q–K1 B–Q5+ wins) 21 B–N4 QR–K1 22 B×QP R–K3 (22 ... R×B 23 R×R R×R 24 Q×R B–B4 25 Q–K3!) 23 R–K3 R×B/Q3 (23 ... B–B4 24 B–K5) 24 Q×R R–Q1 25 Q–B7 Q–QB4?

(25 ... R–Q2 26 Q–B8+ R–Q1 27 Q×NP? B–Q5 28 Q–N3 B–Q8! 29 Q–Q3 B–B7!) 26 QR–K1 R–QB1 (26 ... R–Q8? 27 B–Q5+) 27 Q×QNP B–Q5 28 K–B2? (28 Q–N3!) 28 ... B×R+ 29 R×B Q–Q5? (29 ... R–Q1

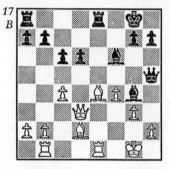

30 Q–N3 R–Q7+=) 30 Q–N3? (30 B–B3! R–K1 31 Q–N3) 30 ... Q–Q7+ 31 K–N1 Q–B8+ 32 K–B2 Q–Q7+ 33 K–N1 Q–B8+ ½–½ (33 ... B–K7 34 P–KR4; 33 ... R–Q1 34 B–B3)

18) Smyslov-Euwe, Ruy Lopez 1 P–K4 P–K4 2 N–KB3 N–QB3 3 B–N5 P–QR3 4 B–R4 N–B3 5 0–0 B–K2 6 R–K1 P–QN4 7 B–N3 P–Q3 8 P–B3 N–QR4 9 B–B2 P–B4 10 P–Q4 Q–B2 11 QN–Q2 B–N2 12 N–B1 BP×P 13 P×P QR–B1 14 R–K2 0–0 15 N–N3 KR–K1 16 P–N3 B–B1 17 B–N2 P–N3 18 Q–Q2 B–N2 19 R–QB1 N–Q2 20 R/2–K1 N–QB3 21 B–N1 Q–N3 22 P–Q5 N–K2 23 B–B3! B–QR1 24 P–KR4 P–KR4 25 B–R5! Q–N1 26 N–B1 26 ... R×R 27 R×R R–QB1 28 N–K1 N–QB4 29 Q–N5 K–B1 30 Q–K3 N–N1 31 Q–R3 B–R3 32 R–B3 N–K2 33 B–B2 N–N2 34 R×R+ Q×R 35 Q×Q+ N×Q 36 B–B3 N–B4 37 B–N4 K–K2 38 P–B3 K–Q2? (38 ... N–N3–Q2) 39 N–Q3 N×N 40 B×N N–K2 (*18*) 41 P–N4! P×P? (41 ... B–B5) 42 P×P B–B8! (42 ... P–B3 43 P–N5! P×P

44 B–Q2; 42 ... P–B4 43 P–N5; 42 ...
B–B5 43 P–N5 N–N1 44 P–R4 P×P
45 P×P B–N2 46 N–Q2 P–B3 47 N–
B4!) 43 P–N5! B–N2 44 K–B2 N–B1
(44 ... N–N1 45 N–N3! P–B3 46
N–K2) 45 N–K3 K–K2 46 B–R5!
B–R6 47 K–N3 B–B4 48 B–Q2 K–B1
(48 ... N–N3 49 P–R5!) 49 N–B2
K–K2 (49 ... N–K2 50 B–R5 B–B1 -
50 ... N–N1 51 N–N4 - 51 P–N4 and
52 B–B7) 50 B–K2 N–R2? (better
50 ... N–N3 then 51 P–R5) 51 B–QR5!
N–B1 (51 ... B–B1 52 P–N4 B–N8

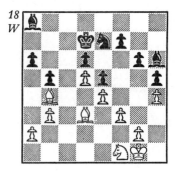

18
W

53 K–N2 B–Q5 54 N×B P×N 55 B–
N6!) 52 B–KN4! P–B3 (52 ... K–K1
53 B–B7 K–K2 54 K–N2! zugszwang)
53 B–K6 P×P 54 P×P N–N3 (54 ...
K–K1 55 B–B7 K–K2 56 K–B3!)
55 P–N4 N–B5 (55 ... B–N8 56 K–
N2) 56 P×B N×B 57 P×P+ K×P
58 B–B7 N–B5 59 B×P P–R4 60 K–N4
P–N5 61 B–B5 K–K2 62 B–K6 N–Q3
63 N–K3! N×P (63 ... P–R5 64 N–
B5+!) 64 K–B5 N–Q3+ 65 K×P
N–B2+ 66 K–B4 N–Q1 67 N–B5+
K–B1 68 P–N6 N×B+ 69 P×N P–
R5 70 K–K5 1–0
Round 10: Euwe-Reshevsky ½–½
Botvinnik-Keres 1–0

19) Euwe-Reshevsky, Ruy Lopez 1
P–K4 P–K4 2 N–KB3 N–QB3 3 B–
N5 P–QR3 4 B–R4 P–Q3 5 P–B3
B–Q2 6 P–Q4 KN–K2 7 P–R4 P–R3
8 B–K3 P×P 9 P×P P–Q4 10 P–K5

P–QN4 11 B–B2 N–R4 (11 ... N–N5
12 QN–Q2!) 12 N–B3 B–N5 13 P–R4
P–QB3 14 Q–Q3 B–B4 15 Q–K2
P–N5 16 N–Q1 Q–Q2 17 R–QB1
B×B 18 Q×B N–B4 19 P–N4?
N–K2! 20 N–Q2 Q×P 21 Q–B5 N–
N2 22 Q×NP N–Q1 23 P–B3 Q–N7
24 R–KN1 Q–R6 25 B–B2 Q–B1
26 Q–B3 N–B4 27 N–K3 R–QN1?
28 N×P Q–Q2 (28 ... Q–N2 29 N–
K3!) 29 N–KB4 B–N5 30 Q–Q3 0–0
31 K–B1? (31 R–B2) 31 ... B×N
32 Q×B N–K3 33 N–R5 K–R1 34
R–N4 R–N6? (34 ... Q–Q4!) 35 R–B3
R–N5? (35 KR–QN1) 36 P–Q5! P–R4
37 Q–Q3 (37 R×R P×R 38 R×P
R–Q1!) 37 ... Q×P 38 Q×N R×NP
39 R–Q3? (39 B–K1!) 39 ... Q–R7
40 B–K1 R–R7 (19)

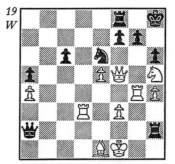

19
W

41 R–K3 (41 K–N1!) 41 ... R–R8+
42 R–N1 Q–R7 43 Q–N4 P–N3 44
R–K2? (44 N–B6 N–B5 45 N–K4!)
44 ... R×R+ 45 Q×R Q×Q+ 46
K×P P×N 47 R–K4 K–R2 (47 ...
R–QR1 48 P–B4!) 48 B×P R–QN1
49 R–QN4 R–QR1 50 B–N6 K–N3 51
P–R5 K–B4 52 R–K4 R–R3 53 K–B2
N–B5 54 R–B4 P–B4 55 K–N3 N–Q4
56 B–Q8 R–R1 57 B–N6 ½–½

20) Botvinnik-Keres, Nimzo-Indian
1 P–Q4 N–KB3 2 P–QB4 P–K3 3 N–
QB3 B–N5 4 P–K3 0–0 5 P–QR3
B×N+ 6 P×B R–K1 7 N–K2 P–K4
8 N–N3 P–Q3 9 B–K2 QN–Q2

10 0–0 P–B4 11 P–B3 BP×P? (11 . . . N–B1 12 P–K4 N–K3) 12 BP×P N–N3? (12 . . . N–B1 or 12 . . . P–QN3) 13 B–N2 P×P 14 P–K4! (14 P×P or 14 B×P P–Q4; 14 Q×P N–R5) 14 . . . B–K3 15 R–B1 R–K2? (15 . . . R–QB1 16 Q×P N–R5 17 B–R1 N–B4) 16 Q×P Q–B2? (16 . . . N–R5–B4) 17 P–B5! P×P 18 R×P Q–B5? (18 . . . Q–Q1) 19 B–B1 Q–N1 (19 . . . R–Q2 20 Q–N4) 20 R–KN5 QN–Q2 (20 . . . N–K1 21 N–R5) (20)

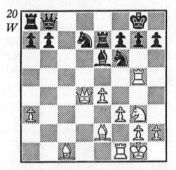

21 R×P+ K×R (21 . . . K–B1 22 R× RP!; 21 . . . K–R1 22 N–R5) 22 N–R5+ K–N3 (22 . . . K–R1 23 B–KN5; 22 . . . K–B1 23 N×N N×N 24 Q×N K–K1 25 B–N5+ R–Q2 26 B–N5) 23 Q–K3 1–0

Round 11: Euwe–Keres 0–1
Smyslov–Reshevsky 1–0

21) Euwe–Keres, Ruy Lopez 1 P–K4 P–K4 2 N–KB3 N–QB3 3 B–N5 P–QR3 4 B–R4 P–Q3 5 P–B3 P–B4 6 P×P B×P 7 P–Q4 P–K5 8 N–N5 P–Q4 (8 . . . P–R3 9 Q–N3!) 9 P–B3 P–K6! (9 . . . P×P 10 0–0; 9 . . . P–R3 10 P×P) 10 P–KB4 B–Q3 11 Q–B3 (11 Q–R5+ P–N3 12 Q–B3) 11 . . . Q–B3 12 Q×P+ N–K2 13 B×N+? (13 0–0 0–0 14 N–B3) 13 . . . P×B 14 0–0 0–0 15 N–Q2? (better 15 N–B3 but 15 . . . B×N 16 R×B Q–N3 17 B–Q2 R×P) 15 . . . N–N3 16 P–KN3 QR–K1! 17 Q–B2 (17 Q–B3 P–

R3) 17 . . . B–Q6 18 R–K1 R×R+ 19 Q×R (21)
19 . . . B×P! 20 P×B (20 Q–K6+ Q×Q

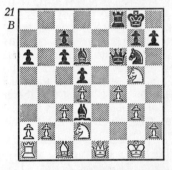

21 N×Q B–K6+) 20 . . . N×P 21 QN–B3 (21 KN–B3 Q–N3+; 21 Q–R4 N–K7+ 22 K–N2 B–K5+) 21 . . . N–K7+ 22 K–N2 P–R3! 23 Q–Q2 Q–B4 24 Q–K3 P×N 25 B–Q2 B–K5 0–1

22) Smyslov–Reshevsky, Ruy Lopez 1 P–K4 P–K4 2 N–KB3 N–QB3 3 B–N5 P–QR3 4 B–R4 P–Q3 5 P–B3 N–K2 6 P–Q4 B–Q2 7 B–N3 P–R3 8 QN–Q2 N–N3 9 N–B4 B–K2 10 0–0 0–0 11 N–K3 B–B3 12 N–Q5 R–K1 13 P×P! B×P (13 . . . P×P 14 N×B+; 13 . . . N/N3×P 14 N×N N×N 15 P–KB4 N–B3 16 P–K5!) 14 N×B P×N 15 Q–B3 B–K3 16 R–Q1 B×N 17 R×B Q–K2 18 Q–B5! N–B1 (18 . . . QR–Q1 19 B×P!) 19 B–K3 N–K3 20 QR–Q1 KR–Q1 21 P–N3 R–Q3 22 R×R P×R 23 Q–N4 K–R1 (23 . . . K–B1 24 B–N6 N–B2 25 Q–B5!) 24 B–N6! N–N1 (24 . . . N–B2 25 Q–B3 R–KB1 26 Q–Q3 N–K1 27 B–R4!; 24 . . . R–QB1 25 R–Q2 N–N1 26 Q–Q1 R–B3 27 B–R7 N–Q2 28 B–Q5 R–B2 29 B×N Q×B 30 R×P) 25 B×N P×B (22)
26 Q–R4! Q–Q2 (26 . . . Q×Q 27 P×Q wins the QP) 27 Q–Q8+ Q×Q 28 B×Q N–Q2 29 B–B7 N–B4 30 R×P R–QB1 (30 . . . N×P 31 R×KP) 31 B–N6 N–R5 32 R×P N×NP 33 R×KP

N–B5 (33 . . . R×P 34 B–Q4!) 34 R–K6
N×B 35 R×N R×P 36 R×NP R–B7
37 P–KR4 R×RP 38 K–N2 P–QR4
39 P–R5 P–R5 40 R–R7 K–N1 41 P–N4
P–R6 42 K–N3 R–K7 43 K–B3 R–R7
44 K–K3 K–B1 45 P–B3 R–R8 46 K–B4

N1 Q–Q8+ 37 K–N2 Q–Q4+ 38 P–
B3 Q–N4 39 Q–Q4 Q–K7+ 40 Q–B2
Q×Q+ 41 K×Q K–B2 42 K–K3 K–K3
½–½

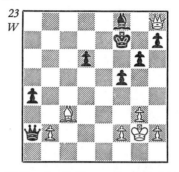

24) **Botvinnik-Euwe,** Slav 1 P–Q4 P–
Q4 2 N–KB3 N–KB3 3 P–B4 P–K3
4 N–B3 P–B3 5 P–K3 QN–Q2 6 B–Q3
P×P 7 B×BP P–QN4 8 B–Q3 P–QR3
9 P–K4 P–B4 10 P–K5 P×P 11 N×NP
P×N (11 . . . N×P!) 12 P×N Q–N3
13 P×P B×P 14 0–0 N–B4 15 B–KB4
B–N2 16 R–K1 R–Q1? (16 . . . N×B
17 Q×N B×N 18 Q×B 0–0 19 Q–
KN3 P–B3,) 17 R–B1! R–Q4 (17 . . .
B×N 18 Q×B 0–0 19 B×P+!) 18
B–K5! B×B 19 R×B R×R (19 . . . R–
N1 20 R×R B×R 21 B×RP R–N2
22 Q×P) 20 N×R N×B (20 . . . R–N1
21 B–B1) 21 Q×N P–B3 (21 . . . R–N1
22 Q×RP!; 21 . . . 0–0 22 N–Q7) (24)

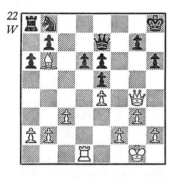

P–R7 47 P–K5 K–N1 48 K–B5 R–KB8
49 R×RP R×P+ 50 K–N6 K–B1 51 R–
R8+ K–K2 52 R–R7+ 1–0
Round 12: Keres-Smyslow ½–½
       Botvinnik-Euwe 1–0

23) **Keres-Smyslov,** Grünfeld 1 P–Q4
N–KB3 2 P–QB4 P–KN3 3 N–QB3
P–Q4 4 N–B3 B–N2 5 Q–N3 P×P
6 Q×BP 0–0 7 P–K4 B–N5 8 B–K3
N/3-Q2 9 Q–N3 N–N3 10 R–Q1
P–K4 11 P×P (11 B–K2!) 11 . . . QN–
Q2 12 B–K2 Q–K2 13 B–KN5? (13 P–
KR3 or N–Q4) 13 . . . Q–K1 14 0–0
N×P 15 N–Q5 N/3×N 16 P×N N×
N+ 17 B×N B×B 18 Q×B Q–Q2
(18 . . . Q–R5 19 Q–B4) 19 R–Q2 KR–
K1 20 R–B1 B–K4 21 P–KN3 P–QR4
22 K–N2 P–R5 23 R–K2 B–Q3 24
R/1–K1 R×R 25 R×R R–K1 26 R×
R+ Q×R 27 B–B6 B–B1 28 P–Q6
P×P 29 Q×P Q–K3 30 B–B3 Q×P
31 Q–K4 P–B4 (31 . . . B–N2 32 Q–
R8+ B–B1 33 B–Q2) 32 Q–Q4 K–B2
33 Q–R8 (23)
33 . . . K–K1? (33 . . . P–R3! 34 Q–
R7+ K–K1 35 Q×P+ Q–B2=) 34
Q×P (34 B–N7 Q–B2 35 B–R6!)
34 . . . Q–B2 35 Q–R4 Q–Q4+ 36 K–

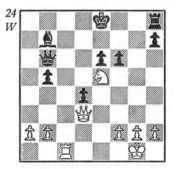

22 Q–KN3! P×N 23 Q–N7 R–B1 24
R–B7 Q×R (24 . . . Q–Q3 25 R×B

P–Q6 26 R–R7 Q–Q1 27 Q×RP)
25 Q×Q B–Q4 26 Q×KP P–Q6 27 Q–
K3 B–B5 28 P–QN3 R–B2 29 P–B3
R–Q2 30 Q–Q2 P–K4 31 P×B P×P 32
K–B2 K–B2 (32 . . . P–B6 33 Q×BP
P–Q7 34 Q–B8+ K–K2 35 Q×R+!)
33 K–K3 K–K3 34 Q–N4 R–QB2 35
K–Q2 R–B3 36 P–QR4 1–0

Round 13: Smyslov–Botvinnik 0–1
Reshevsky–Keres 0–1

25) Smyslov–Botvinnik, Sicilian 1 P–
K4 P–QB4 2 N–KB3 N–QB3 3 P–Q4
P×P 4 N×P N–B3 5 N–QB3 P–Q3
6 B–KN5 P–K3 7 B–K2 B–K2 8 0–0
0–0 9 N/4–N5 P–QR3 10 B×N P×B?
11 N–Q4 K–R1 12 K–R1 R–KN1 13
P–B4 B–Q2 14 B–B3? (14 P–B5! N–K4
15 B–R5 and QN–K2–B4) 14...R–
QB1 15 N×N? P×N 16 N–K2 P–Q4
17 P–B5? (17 P–B4) 17 . . . Q–B2 18
P–B4 P×QBP 19 Q–Q4 P–B4 20
Q×P/B4 B–Q3 21 P–KN3 B–N4 22
Q–B2 P×P! 23 P×P (23 P–QR4 B–B3
24 P×P QR–K1) 23 . . . QR–K1 24
R–B2 R–K6 25 B–N2 (25 N–B3 B–B3
26 B–N2 B×P!) 25 . . . Q–K2 26 N–
N1 B–Q6 27 Q–Q2 P–B5 28 R–B3
R–K1 29 R–Q1 (29 R×R Q×R 30
Q×Q R×Q and 31 . . . B–K4) 29 . . .
B–B4 30 P–N3 (*25*)

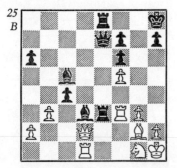

30 . . . R–K8! (threatens 31 . . . B×N)
31 P×B B×QBP 32 B–B1 R×R 33
Q×R R–Q1 34 Q–B2 (34 Q×R+ Q×Q
35 B×B Q–Q5!) 34 . . . B–Q4 35 Q–B3

B–Q5 36 Q–Q3 Q–K6 37 Q×Q B×Q
38 B–N2 B×R 39 B×B R–Q7 40 N–K2
R×P 41 K–N2 0–1

26) Reshevsky–Keres, Slav 1 P–Q4
P–Q4 2 P–QB4 P–QB3 3 N–KB3
N–B3 4 N–B3 P–K3 5 P–K3 P–QR3
6 P–B5 QN–Q2 7 P–QN4 P–QR4
8 P–N5 P–K4 9 Q–R4! Q–B2 10 B–R3
P–K5 11 N–Q2 B–K2 12 B–K2 P–R4
13 P–N6 (13 0–0 N–N5) 13 . . . Q–Q1
14 P–R3 (14 P–B3!) 14 . . . N–B1
0–0–0– N–K3? (15 . . . N–N3) (*26*)

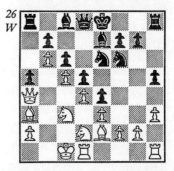

16 N/2×P N×N (16 . . . P×N 17 P–Q5)
17 N×N P–R5 (17 . . . P×N 18 P–Q5
B×P 19 P×P! B×B+ 20 K–B2 Q×P
21 P×P+; 20 . . . B–Q3 21 P–B7+
Q–Q2 22 B–N5) 18 N–Q2 0–0 19
KR–N1 R–K1 20 B–Q3 B–B1 21 B–N2
N–N4 22 Q–B2 P–R5 23 P–R3 Q–K2
24 QR–K1 N–K5 25 N–B1 Q–N4 26
P–B3 N–B3 27 K–N1 N–R4 28 B–B3
B–Q2 29 P–B4 Q–R3 30 Q–B2 Q–B3
31 K–N2 B–B4 32 Q–B2 (32 B–K2!;
32 B×B Q×B 33 Q×P Q–Q6!? 34
34 Q×N B×P! 35 P×B P–Q5 is unclear)
32 . . . B–K5 33 P–N4 P×P ep 34 N×P
N×N 35 R×N B×B 36 Q×B R–K5
37 R/1–KN1 QR–K1 38 R–KB1 Q–R5
39 R/1–KN1 R/1–K3 40 Q–Q2 P–B4
(40 . . . R–N3!) 41 Q–Q3 (41 Q–N2
Q–K2 42 B–Q2 R×BP!) 41 . . . Q–R4!
42 B–Q2 P–N3 43 R–N5 Q×P 44 R/1–
N3 Q–R7 45 R×P+ R×R 46 R×R+
K–B2 47 R–N5? (47 R×P! P×R 48

P–N7 R–K1 49 Q×P+=) 47 . . .
B–K2! 48 R×P+ B–B3! 49 K–B3
Q–R6 50 R×B+ K×R 51 Q–B2 Q–
B8! (51 . . . R×BP 52 Q×P; 51 . . .
R×P+=) 52 Q×P Q–R8+ 53 K–B2
R–K1 54 Q–N3 R–QR1 55 B–B1 (55
Q–N2 Q×P 56 Q×Q R×Q 57 P–K4!?
R–R7+ 58 K–B3 P×P 59 P–Q5 P×P
60 P–B6 P–Q5+!; 58 K–Q1 R–R1!)
55 . . . R–R1 56 P–K4? (56 B–Q2)
56 . . . R–R8 57 P–K5+ K–K2 58 Q–
K3 Q–R7+ 59 K–B3 R–R7 60 Q–Q3
Q–R8+ 61 K–N3 Q×B 62 P–B5
Q–N7+ 63 K–R4 R–R1 0–1
Round 14: Botvinnik-Reshevsky 0–1
Euwe-Smyslov 1–0

27) Botvinnik-Reshevsky, Nimzo-
Indian 1 P–Q4 N–KB3 2 P–QB4 P–K3
3 N–QB3 B–N5 4 P–K3 P–B4 5 P–QR3
B×N+ 6 P×B N–B3 7 B–Q3 0–0
8 N–K2 P–QN3 9 P–K4 N–K1! 10 B–
K3 P–Q3 11 0–0 N–R4 12 N–N3
B–R3 13 Q–K2 Q–Q2 14 P–B4? (14 P–
K5!) 14 . . . P–B4 15 QR–K1 P–N3
16 R–Q1 Q–KB2 (16 . . . Q–R5 17
P–Q5!) 17 P–K5 R–B1 18 KR–K1
QP×P! (18 . . . P×QP 19 B×QP B×P
20 P×P N×P 21 Q–K5!) 19 QP×KP
KN–N2 20 N–B1 KR–Q1 21 B–KB2
N–R4! 22 B–N3 Q–K1 23 N–K3 Q–
R5 24 Q–R2 N×B 25 P×N P–R4 (25
. . . Q–N6!) (27)

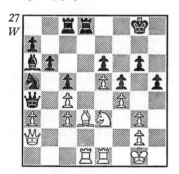

27
W

26 B–K2? (26 B–B2! B×P 27 B×Q
B×Q 28 B–Q7 R–N1 29 P–QB4!;

26 . . . Q–B3 27 P–R4) 26 . . . K–B2
27 K–B2 Q–N6! 28 Q×Q N×Q 29 B–
Q3 K–K2 30 K–K2 N–R4 31 R–Q2
R–B2? (31 . . . K–B2) 32 P–N4! R/2–Q2
(32 . . . RP×P 33 R–KR1) 33 P×BP
NP×P 34 R/1–Q1? (34 R/2–Q1 and
35 R–KR1) 34 . . . P–R5 35 K–K1 (35
R–KR1 B×P!) 35 . . . N–N6 36 N–
Q5+ P×N 37 B×P N×R 38 R×N
P×P 39 B×R R×B 40 R–KB2 K–K3
41 R–B3 R–Q6 42 K–K2 0–1

28) Euwe-Smyslov, Grünfeld 1 P–Q4
N–KB3 2 P–QB4 P–KN3 3 N–QB3
P–Q4 4 N–B3 B–N2 5 Q–N3 P×P
6 Q×BP 0–0 7 P–K4 B–N5 8 B–K3
KN–Q2 9 Q–N3 N–N3 10 P–QR4
P–QR4 11 P–Q5 N–R3? (11 . . . B×N
and 12 . . . Q–Q3) 12 B–K2 P–K3
13 P–R3 B×KN 14 B×B P×P 15 P×P
Q–R5? (15 . . . Q–Q3–N5) 16 N–K4!
(threatens 17 B–N5) 16 . . . QR–K1
17 P–N3 Q–Q1 (17 . . . Q–K2 18 P–
Q6) 18 P–Q6 N–B1 (better 18 . . .
N–N5) 19 P×P Q×P 20 0–0 R–K3
21 QR–B1 Q–K4 (21 . . . Q–K2 22 N–
N5) 22 Q×P N–K2 (22 . . . Q×P 23
Q×N/B8!) 23 N–N5! R–KB3 24 B–B4
R×B 25 P×R Q×BP (25 . . . Q–B3
26 KR–K1 N–B4 27 R–B6) 26 Q×N/
K7 B–B3 (26 . . . B–R3 27 N×BP!)
(28)

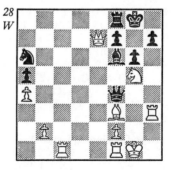

28
W

27 Q–K3? (27 Q×P+! R×Q 28 R–
B8+ B–Q1 29 R×B+ R–B1 30 N–
K6) 27 . . . Q×Q 28 P×Q B×N 29

R–B3 P–B4 30 R–Q1 N–B4 31 P–N3
R–K1 32 R–Q5 B×P+ 33 K–N2
N–R3 34 R–Q7 B–B5 35 R–R7 N–N5
36 R×QRP K–N2 37 R–N5 B–Q7
38 R–B7+ K–B3 39 R–Q7 B–K8
40 R–N6+ K–N4 41 P–R4+ K–B5
42 R×N+ 1–0
Round 15: Reshevsky-Euwe ½–½
Keres-Botvinnik 0–1

29) Reshevsky-Euwe, English 1 P–
QB4 P–K3 2 N–KB3 P–Q4 3 P–KN3
P–Q5 4 P–K3 N–QB3 5 P×P N×P
6 B–N2 N–R3 7 0–0 KN–B4 8 P–Q3
B–K2 9 N×N N×N 10 N–Q2 0–0
11 N–B3 B–B3 12 N×N B×N 13
R–N1 P–K4 14 P–QN4 B–KB4 (14 . . .
R–N1 or 14 . . . P–QR4) 15 B×P (*29*)

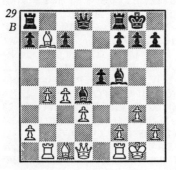

15 . . . B×QP 16 B×R (16 Q×B
B×P+) 16 . . . B×KR (16 . . . B×QR
17 B–Q5 P–B3 18 B×P B–Q6 19 B–
KN5 Q–Q3 20 B–K7=) 17 Q×B/B1
(17 B–Q5 B×QBP!) 17 . . . Q×B 18
Q–K2 Q–B3 19 B–N2 P–N3 20 B×B
P×B 21 Q–Q3 Q–Q3 22 R–Q1
Q×QNP 23 Q×QP R–K1 24 K–N2
Q–N3 25 P–QR3 Q×Q 26 R×Q
R–K3 ½–½

30) Keres-Botvinnik, French 1 P–Q4
P–K3 2 P–K4 P–Q4 3 N–Q2 P–QB4
4 KP×P KP×P 5 KN–B3 P–QR3
6 P×P B×P 7 N–N3 B–R2 8 B–KN5
N–KB3 9 N/B3–Q4! (stops 9 . . .
B×P+!) 9 . . . 0–0 10 B–K2 Q–Q3

11 0–0 N–K5 12 B–K3 N–QB3 13
N×N B×B! 14 P×B (14 Q×P N×P!)
14 . . . P×N 15 B–Q3? (15 P–QB4!)
15 . . . N–B3 16 Q–K1 N–N5 17 Q–
R4 P–KB4 18 R–B4! N–K4 (18 . . .
N×KP 19 R–K1 N–N5 20 R×N
18 . . . R–B3 19 Q–N3!) 19 Q–N3
R–R2 20 QR–KB1 R/2–KB2 21 N–
Q4! N×B 22 P×N P–B4 23 N–B3
Q–QN3 24 R–KR4 P–R3 25 N–K5?
(25 Q–K5!) 25 . . . R–B3 26 P–Q4?
P×P 27 R×QP (27 P×P P–B5! 28
R4×P Q Q×P+!) 27 . . . Q×P 28 R×QP?
(28 P–QR4) (*30*)

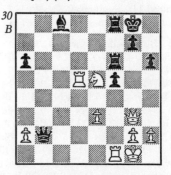

28 . . . B–K3? (28 . . . P–B5! 29 P×P
R×P!) 29 R–Q4? (29 R–Q7) 29 . . .
K–R2? (29 . . . Q×P) 30 N–Q7 (30
P–KR4!) 30 . . . B×N 31 R×B R–KN3
32 Q–B3 Q–K4 33 R–Q4 R–QN1
34 Q–B4 (34 Q×P? Q×KP+ 35 Q–B2
R–N7!) 34 . . . Q–K3 35 R–Q2 R–QN4
36 P–KR3 R–K4 37 K–R2 R–B3
38 R/B1–Q1? (38 R–B3 R–K5 39 Q–
N3) 38 . . . R–K5 39 Q–N8 R×P
40 R–Q8 Q–K4+ 41 Q×Q R×Q
42 R/1–Q2 P–N4? (42 . . . P–B5) 43 P–
N4 R–B2 44 R/8–Q7 K–N2 45 P×P
R/4×P 46 P–R3? (46 R×R+ R×R 47
K–N3 46 . . . K×R 47 R–Q6 R–B3
48 R–Q7+ K–N3 49 K–N3 R–B3
50 R–Q3 and 51 R–R3) 46 . . . R–B7+?
(46 . . . R–R4) 47 K–N3? (47 R×R R×R
48 R–B2 R–Q3 49 R–B4) 47 . . .
R7×R? (47 . . . R–B6+ 48 K–N4
R–B5+ 49 K–N3 R–QR5) 48 R×R/

Q2 R–QB2 49 R–Q4! R–B3 (49 . . .
R–B6+ 50 K–N4 R×QRP 51 R–Q7+
K–B1 52 R–KR7) 50 P–QR4? (50
R–QR4!) 50 . . . K–N3 51 P–R4 K–R4
52 P×P P×P 53 R–Q3? (53 R–Q5!) 53
. . . R–B5 54 R–R3 P–R4 55 K–R3
R–QN5 56 K–N3 R–KB5 57 R–R1
R–N5+ 58 K–R3 R–K5 59 R–R3
K–N3 60 K–N3 K–B4 61 K–B3
K–K4 62 K–N3 R–Q5 63 R–R1
K–Q4 64 R–QN1 R–QN5 (64 . . .
R×P? 65 R–N5+ K–B5 66 R×NP
R–R8 67 K–R2!=) 65 R–KB1 K–K4
66 R–K1+ K–Q5 67 K–R2 R×P
68 R–KN1 R–B5 69 R×P P–R5 70
K–N2 K–B6 71 K–B3 P–R6 72 R–QR5
K–N6 0–1
Round 16: Keres-Euwe 1–0
Reshevsky-Smyslov ½–½

31) Keres-Euwe, Ruy Lopez 1 P–K4
P–K4 2 N–KB3 N–QB3 3 B–N5
P–QR3 4 B–R4 N–B3 5 0–0 N×P
6 P–Q4 P–QN4 7 B–N3 P–Q4 8
P×P B–K3 9 Q–K2 B–K2 10 R–Q1 0–0
11 P–B4 NP×P 12 B×P B–QB4
13 B–K3 B×B 14 Q×B Q–N1 15 B–
N3 N–R4 16 QN–Q2! (16 N–Q4
P–QB4!) 16 . . . N×N (16 . . . Q–R2!)
17 R×N N×B 18 P×N R–B1 19
R–QB1 P–QB4! 20 R×BP R×R 21
Q×R Q×NP 22 N–Q4 Q–N2 23 P–R3
R–Q1 24 K–R2 P–N3 25 P–B4 P–KR4
26 R–Q3 Q–Q2 (26 . . . Q×P 27 N×B
P×N 28 Q–K7) 27 Q–N6 R–R1
28 R–R3 Q–R2 29 Q–N4? (29 Q×Q!)
29 . . . Q–Q2? (29 . . . R–QB1 and 30
. . . R–B5) 30 Q–R5 *(31)*
30 . . . B–B4? (better 30 . . . Q–R2) 31
R–QB3 R–R2 32 R–B5 B–K5 (32 . . .
B–K3 33 R–B6) 33 Q–B3 (threatens
34 P–K6) 33 . . . Q–K2? 34 N–B6 1–0

32) Reshevsky-Smyslov, Slav 1 P–Q4
P–Q4 2 P–QB4 P–QB3 3 N–KB3
N–B3 4 N–B3 P×P 5 P–QR4 B–B4
6 P–K3 P–K3 7 B×P B–QN5 8 0–0
0–0 9 Q–K2 B–N5 10 P–R3 QB×N
11 Q×B QN–Q2 12 R–Q1 P–K4 13

P–Q5 B×N! 14 P×P P–K5 15 Q–B5?
(15 Q–K2) 15 . . . B–K4 16 P×N
Q–B2 17 B–N3 P–KN3 18 Q–N5
K–N2 (threatens 19 . . . P–KR3 20
Q–R4 P–KN4) *(32)*

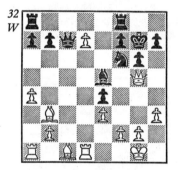

19 P–B4 P×Pep 20 P×P P–KR3 21
Q–N2 Q–N3 (21 . . . QR–Q1) 22 B–B2
KR–Q1 23 R–R3! R×P 24 R×R N×R
25 P–B4! B–B3 (25 . . . B×BP? 26 P–R5
and 27 R–B3) 26 R–N3 Q–B4 27
R–N5 Q–B5 28 R×P (28 P–N3 Q–B6
29 R×P N–B1 30 Q–Q5 Q–K8+=)
28 . . . R–QB1! (28 . . . N–B1 29 K–R2
R–B1 30 B–N3!) 29 R×N Q×B
30 Q×Q R×Q 31 B–Q2 B×P 32
K–B1 P–R3 33 K–K2 B–B8 34 K–Q1
R×B+ 35 R×R B×R 36 K×B P–N4
37 K–K2 P–B4 38 K–B3 K–B3 39 P–
K4 BP×P+ 40 K×P P×P 41 K×P
P–QR4 ½–½
Round 17: Smyslov-Keres 1–0
Euwe-Botvinnik ½–½

33) Smyslov-Keres, Queens Gambit 1
P–Q4 P–Q4 2 P–QB4 P–K3 3 N–QB3
N–KB3 4 B–N5 P–B3 5 P–K3 QN–Q2
6 P×P KP×P 7 B–Q3 B–K2 8 N–B3
0–0 9 Q–B2 R–K1 10 0–0 N–B1 11
QR–N1 N–N3 12 P–QN4 B–Q3
(better 12 . . . P–QR3 13 P–QR4
N–K5) 13 P–N5 B–Q2 (13 . . . P–KR3
14 B×N Q×B 15 P–K4 N–B5! 16
P–K5 Q–K3 17 P×B Q–N5) 14 P×P
B×P? (14 . . . P×P) 15 Q–N3 B–K2
16 B×N! (16 B–N5 N–Q2) 16 . . .
B×B 17 B–N5 Q–Q3 18 KR–B1
P–KR4 19 N–K2 P–R5 20 B×B P×B
21 Q–R4 N–K2 22 R–N7! P–R4 23
P–KR3 KR–N1 24 R/B1–N1 R×R
25 R×R P–B4 26 R–N5! (26 P×P Q×P
27 N×P P–Q5! 28 P×P Q–Q4)
26 . . . P×P 27 N/K2×P R–QB1
(27 . . . Q–B2 28 N–N3 Q–B3 29
N–B5!) 28 N–N3 B–B6 29 Q×KRP
R–B5 *(33)*

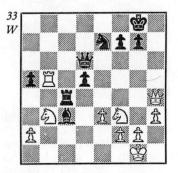

30 P–N4! P–R5 (30 . . . R–R5 or B–B3
31 N–N5) 31 N/N3–Q4 B×N 32
N×B Q–K4 (32 . . . N–B3 33 N×N
R×N 34 R–R5 Q–Q2 35 Q–N5)
33 N–B3 Q–Q3 (33 . . . R–B8+ 34
K–N2 Q–K5 35 R–N8+) 34 R–R5
R–B1 35 R×RP N–N3 36 Q–R5
Q–KB3 37 Q–B5 Q–B3 38 R–R7
R–B1 39 R–Q7 P–Q5 40 R×QP
R–R1 41 P–QR4! (41 . . . R×P 42
R–Q8+ N–B1 43 Q×P+!) 1–0

34) Euwe-Botvinnik, French 1 P–K4
P–K3 2 P–Q4 P–Q4 3 N–Q2 P–QB4
4 KP×P KP×P 5 B–N5+ B–Q2
6 Q–K2+ Q–K2 7 B×B+ N×B
8 P×P N×P 9 N–N3 Q×Q+ 10
N×Q N×N 11 RP×N B–B4 12
B–Q2 N–K2 13 B–B3 N–B3 14 0–0–0
(14 R–Q1) 14 . . . B×P *(34)*

15 B×P? (15 R×P) 15 . . . KR–N1
16 B–R6 R×P 17 R×P R–Q1 18
R×R+ N×R 19 K–Q2 N–K3 20
B–K3 K–K2 21 B×B R×B 22 K–K3
R–B4 23 R–R1 P–QR3 24 R–R4
R–KR4 25 P–R4 R–K4+ 26 K–B3
R–B4+ 27 K–K3 R–K4+ 28 K–B3
R–B4+ 29 K–K3 ½–½
Round 18: Botvinnik-Smyslov ½–½
  Keres-Reshevsky 0–1

35) Botvinnik-Smyslov, Grünfeld 1
P–Q4 N–KB3 2 P–QB4 P–KN3 3 P–
KN3 P–Q4 4 P×P N×P 5 B–N2 B–
N2 6 N–KB3 0–0 7 0–0 N–N3 8 N–
B3 P–QR4 9 B–B4 P–QB3 10 Q–B1
R–K1 11 R–Q1 N–R3 12 P–KR3
P–R5 13 P–K4 B–Q2 14 N–K5 Q–B1
15 K–R2 R–Q1 16 B–N5 P–B3 17
N×B Q×N 18 B–K3 K–R1 19 B–B1
P–KB4? (19 . . . Q–B2) 20 P–Q5!
P–B4 (20 . . . Q–B2 21 N–N5!) 21
KB–N5? (21 B×N R×B 22 B×P P×P
23 P–Q6!) 21 . . . Q–B2 22 B–KB4?
(22 P×P P×P 23 B×RP) 22 . . . B–K4
23 B×B+ Q×B 24 P–B4 Q–N2 25
Q–K3? (25 B×N R×B 26 P–K5)

25 ... P×P   26 QR–B1 (26 Q×KP
P–R6!) 26 ... P–R6! 27 P×P N–B1?
(27 ... N–B2!   28 Q×BP N/N3×P)
28 N×P N–Q3 29 B×N N×N   30
Q×N (30 B×P? Q–N7+)   30 ...
R×B 31 R×P R×RP 32 R–Q2 R/1–R1
33 Q–K6 R–QB6 34 R×R Q×R   35
Q–K5+? (35 R–K2!) 35 ... Q×Q 36
P×Q K–N2   37 K–N2 K–B2   38
R–B2+? (38 K–B3 R–R6+   39 K–K4)
38 ... K–K1 39 R–Q2 R–R6 40 R–N2
(*35*)

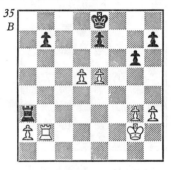

35
B

40 ... R–Q6? (40 ... R–R4! 41 R–Q2
P–K3 41 R×P R×QP) 41 R–N5 K–Q1
42 P–QR4 P–N3! (42 ... K–B2   43
P–R5 R–K6   44 P–Q6+)   43 R×P
R×QP 44 R–N8+ K–Q2 45 R–KR8
R×P 46 R×P K–K3 47 R–R4 R–K7+
48 K–B3 R–QR7!   49 R–K4+ K–B3
50 R–KB4+ K–N2 51 R–QB4 R–R6+
52 K–N4 P–K4   53 K–R4 K–R3   54
R–QN4 R–R8 55 K–N4 R–R6 56 P–R4
K–N2 57 P–R5 P×P+   58 K×P K–B3
(58 ... R×P   59 R–N4+!)   59 K–R4
K–B4   60 P–N4+ K–B3   61 R–N6+
K–B2   62 R–N7+ K–N3   63 R–N4
K–B3   64 R–N6+ K–B2 65 R–N7+
K–N3   66 R-QR7 P–K5!   67 R–R6+
K–B2 68 P–N5 P–K6 69 K–N3 P–K7+
70 K–B2 R–K6   71 K–K1 K–N2   72
R–R7+ K–N3 73 R–R8 K–N2 74 P–R5
R–K4   75 P–N6 K×P   76 P–R6 K–N2
77 R–R7+   K–N3 (77 ... K–N1   78
R–N7!) 78 R–QN7 R–QR4 79 R–N6+
K–B2   80 K×P K–K2 ½–½

F

36) **Keres–Reshevsky,** Ruy Lopez 1
P–K4 P–K4 2 N–KB3 N–QB3 3 B–N5
P–QR3   4 B–R4 N–B3   5 0–0 N×P
6 P–Q4 P–QN4   7 B–N3 P–Q4   8
P×P B–K3 9 Q–K2 N–B4 10 R–Q1
N×B   11 RP×N Q–B1   12 B-N5
(12 P–B4!)   12 ... P–R3   13 B–R4
B–QB4   14 N–B3? (14 P–B4 QP×P
15 P×P B×P 16 Q–K4!) 14 ... P–N4
15 B–N3 Q–N2! (15 ... N–K2   16
QN×NP) 16 N×QP 0–0–0! 17 N–B6
P–KN5   18 N–K1! (18 N–R4 N–Q5
19 Q-K4 Q×Q   20 N×Q B–K2   21
R–Q2 B–N4!) 18 ... N–Q5 19 Q–B1
P–KR4   20 B–B4 P–R5   21 B–K3
P–R6   22 R–Q2 P×P   23 Q×KNP
N–B6+   24 N×N B×B   25 R×R+
R×R   26 N–K1 B–Q5 (26 ... Q×Q+
27 K×Q R–Q7   28 N–K4 B–Q4   29
K–N3!)   27 N–Q3 B–KB4   28 R–K1
P–R4   29 N–K4? (29 Q×Q+)   29 ...
K–N1   30 P–N4 P–R5 (30 ... P×P
31 N×P B×NP 32 N–B5!) 31 P–QB3?
(31 N/K4–B5!)   31 ... B×N! (31 ...
B×BP   32 N×B B×N   33 R–Q1)
32 R×B (32 Q×B Q×Q   33 R×Q
B×BP 34 R–K3 R×N!) 32 ... B×BP?
(32 ... B–N3 33 N–K1 R–Q7) (*36*)

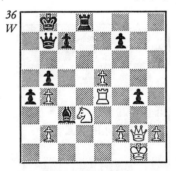

36
W

33 R–K3? (33 Q×P)   33 ... Q×Q+
34 K×Q R×N! 35 R×R B×P/N7 36
R–Q5 P–QB3   37 R–Q8+ K–B2   38
R–QR8 K–N2   39 R–KB8 B×P   40
R×P+ K–N3 41 P–B4 0–1

Round 19: Reshevsky–Botvinnik 0–1
Smyslov–Euwe 1–0

37) Reshevsky-Botvinnik, French 1
P–Q4 P–K3 2 P–K4 P–Q4 3 N–QB3
B–N5 4 P–K5 P–QB4 5 P–QR3
B×N+ 6 P×B Q–B2 7 Q–N4 P–B4
8 Q–N3 P×P 9 P×P N–K2 (9...
Q×BP 10 B–Q2) 10 B–Q2 0–0 11
B–Q3 P–QN3 12 N–K2 B–R3 13 N–
B4 Q–Q2 14 B×B N×B 15 Q–Q3
N–N1 16 P–KR4! QN–B3 17 R–R3
QR–B1 18 R–N3 K–R1 19 P–R5
R–KB2 20 P–R6 P–N3 21 R–B1
R/2–B1 22 N–K2 (22 P–B4 P×P 23
R×BP N×KP!) 22... QN–N1? (22...
N–Q1–B2) 23 K–B1 R–B5 24 K–N1
QN–B3 25 B–N5 N–KN1 (25...
K–N1) 26 R–K1 Q–KB2 27 P–QB3
N–R4 28 N–B4 R–B3! 29 B–B6+?
(29 R/3–K3 N–B5 30 R/3–K2 N5×RP?
31 B–B6+; 30... N–K2 31 B–B6+
K–N1 32 Q–N1–N4 or the plan 29
K–R2 followed by R–KR1, K–N1, B–
R4, N×P+ and P–R7) 29... N×B 30
P×N N–B5! (30... Q×P 31 R/3–K3!)
31 Q–N1? (31 N–R3 Q×P 32 P–B4)
31... Q×P 32 P–R4 P–KN4 33 N–
Q3 P–B5 34 R–R3 P–N5 35 R–R1
R–QB2 36 Q–Q1 Q–N3? (36... R–
KN1) 37 R–R4 P–B6 38 P–N3 R/2–B2
(*37*)

37
W

39 N–B4? (39 N–K5!) 39... R×N!
40 P×R R×P 41 Q–N1 (41 K–B1
R–B4) 41... R–B4! 42 Q–Q3 P–N6
43 Q–B1 P×P+ 44 K×P R–N4 45
Q–R3 R–N7+ 46 K×P N–Q7+
47 K–K3 R–N6+ 0–1

38) Smyslov-Euwe, Ruy Lopez 1 P–
K4 P–K4 2 N–KB3 N–QB3 3 B–N5
P–QR3 4 B–R4 N–B3 5 0–0 N×P
6 P–Q4 P–QN4 7 B–N3 P–Q4 8 P×P
B–K3 9 Q–K2 N–B4 10 R–Q1 N×B
11 RP×N Q–B1 12 P–B4! QP×P 13
P×P B×P 14 Q–K4! N–K2 (better
14... N–N5) 15 N–R3! P–QB3
(15... B–N6 16 R–Q3 B–K3 17 N×P
B–B4 18 N×P+) 16 N×B P×N
17 Q×P/B4 (*38*)

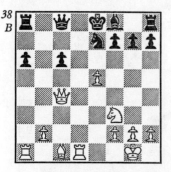

38
B

17... Q–N2 (17... Q–K3 18 R×P!)
18 P–K6! P–B3 19 R–Q7 Q–N4 20
Q×Q BP×Q 21 N–Q4 R–B1 22 B–
K3 N–N3 23 R×RP N–K4 24 R–N7
B–B4 25 N–B5 0–0 (25... B×B 26
N–Q6+) 26 P–R3! (26... P–N3 27
N–R6+ K–R1 28 B×B R×B 29 R/6–
R7) 1–0

Round 20: Euwe-Reshevsky 0–1
Botvinnik-Keres 1–0

39) Euwe-Reshevsky, Nimzo-Indian 1
P–Q4 N–KB3 2 P–QB4 P–K3 3 N–
QB3 B–N5 4 Q–B2 N–B3 5 N–B3
P–Q3 6 B–Q2 0–0 7 P–QR3 B×N
8 B×B P–QR4 9 P–K3 Q–K2 10 B–
Q3 P–K4 11 P×P P×P 12 0–0 (12
N–N5 P–R3 13 N–K4) 12... R–K1
13 B–B5? (13 B–K2) 13... B×B 14
Q×B Q–K3! 15 Q×Q R×Q 16 P–
QN4? (16 N–Q2) 16... N–K5 17
B–N2 P–B3! 18 P–N5 N–K2 19 KR–
Q1 R–Q3! 20 K–B1 (20 R×R P×R
21 R–Q1 R–QB1 22 N–Q2 N×N 23

R×N R×P 24 R×P R–B7) 20 . . .
N–B1! 21 KR–B1 P–QB4 22 B–B3
(*39*)

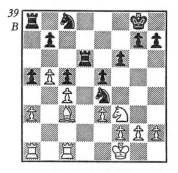

39
B

22 . . . N×B! 23 R×N P–K5 24 N–N1
N–N3 25 N–K2 P–B4 26 K–K1 QR–
Q1 27 R–B2 K–B2 28 N–N3? (28
N–B3!) 28 . . . K–K3 29 N–B1 R–Q6
30 N–N3 P–N4 31 N–K2 N–R5 32
N–N3 K–K4 33 N–B1 P–R4 34 P–B3
R–N6 35 P×P P×P 36 R–KB2 N–N7
37 R–B2 N–Q6+ 38 K–K2 R–KB1
39 N–Q2 R–B7+ 40 K–Q1 R–N7 41
R×R N×R+ 42 K–B1 R×P 0–1

40) Botvinnik-Keres, Queens Gambit
1 P–Q4 P–Q4 2 N–KB3 B–B4 3 P–B4
P–K3 4 P×P P×P 5 Q–N3 N–QB3
6 B–N5 (6 Q×NP N–N5!) 6 . . . B–K2
7 B×B KN×B 8 P–K3 (8 Q×NP
R–QN1) 8 . . . Q–Q3 9 QN–Q2 0–0
10 R–B1 P–QR4! 11 P–QR3 KR–B1
12 B–Q3 P–R5 13 Q–B2 B×B 14
Q×B N–Q1 15 0–0 N–K3 16 R–B3
P–QN4? (16 . . . P–QN3 17 KR–B1
P–QB4) 17 Q–B2 KR–N1 18 N–K1
N–QB1 (18 . . . P–N5) 19 R–B6 Q–K2
20 N–Q3 N–N3 21 N–N4 R–Q1 22
Q–KB5 R–Q3 23 KR–B1 R×R (23 . . .
QR–Q1) 24 R×R R–Q1 (*40*)
25 R×N/N6! P×R 26 N–B6 Q–B2
27 N×R Q×N 28 Q–B2 Q–B2?
(28 . . . Q–Q2) 29 Q×Q N×Q 30
N–N1 K–B1 31 K–B1 K–K2 32 K–K2
K–Q3 33 K–Q3 K–B3 34 N–B3 N–K1
35 N–R2 P–B3 36 P–B3 N–B2 37

N–N4+ K–Q3 38 P–K4 P×P+ 39
P×P N–K3 40 K–K3 N–B2 41 K–Q3
N–K3 42 N–Q5 K–B3 43 P–R4 (also
43 N×BP!) 43 . . . N–Q1 44 N–B4
K–Q3 (44 . . . P–N3 45 N–Q5 P–B4 46
N–B6) 45 N–R5 N–K3 46 K–K3 K–K2

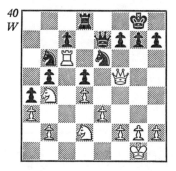

40
W

47 P–Q5 N–B4 48 N×NP K–Q3 49
N–K6! N–Q2 (49 . . . N×N 50 P×N
K×P 51 K–B4 wins; 49 . . . K–K4 50
N×N P×N 51 P–KN4 followed by
K–Q3–B3 and P–QN3) 50 K–Q4 N–
K4 51 N–N7 N–B5 52 N–B5+ K–
B2 53 K–B3 K–Q2 54 P–KN4 N–K4
55 P–N5 P×P 56 P×P N–B6 57 K–N4
N×P 58 P–K5 P–R4 59 P–K6+ K–Q1
(59 . . . N×P 60 P×N+ K×P 61
N–N7+) 60 K×P 1–0
Round 21: Euwe-Keres 0–1
Smyslov-Reshevsky ½–½

41) Euwe-Keres, Nimzo-Indian 1 P–
Q4 N–KB3 2 P–QB4 P–K3 3 N–QB3
B–N5 4 Q–B2 0–0 5 B–N5 P–KR3
6 B–R4 P–B4 7 P×P N–R3 8 P–K3
N×P 9 KN–K2? P–Q4! 10 0–0–0
(10 P–QR3 P×P!) 10 . . . B–Q2! 11
P×P R–B1 12 K–N1 (12 P×P P×P)
12 . . . N–R5? (12 . . . P–K4) 13 P×P!
P×P 14 Q–N3 B×N 15 N×B N×N+
16 P×N Q–K1 17 R–Q4! NQ4?-
(17 . . . K–R1 and 18 . . . P–K4) 18 P–
QB4 N–N3 19 B–Q3 N–R5 20 B–B2
N–B4 21 Q–B3 P–QN4 22 K–R1
P–QR4 23 P×P (23 Q×P P×P 24
R×P Q–R4!) 23 . . . B×P 24 Q–N2

(24 Q×P Q–B3!) 24 . . . Q–B3? (24 . . .
R–N1 25 R–KN4 P–K4) 25 R–KN4
R–KB2 26 B–B6 R/1–B2 27 R–Q1
(threatens 28 R–Q8+) (*41*)

35 R–B5 K–R2 36 N–Q5 R–Q5 37
N–K7 R–K5 38 N–N6 N×N 39
P×N+ K×P 40 K–N2 P–R4 41 P–
R3 P–B4 42 R–B6+ K–N4 43 R–B7

41
B

27 . . . B–Q6! (27 . . . N–Q6? 28 R×N
Q×B 27 R–Q8+ K–R2 28 B×P!)
28 B×B? (28 R×B!) 28 . . . N×B 29
R×N? (29 B×P!) 29 . . . R×B! 30
P–B3 (30 Q×R? Q–B8 mate) 30 . . .
R–B4 31 R/4–Q4 (31 R–Q8+ K–R2
32 R–QB8) 31 . . . R–B4 32 R–Q8+
K–R2 33 R–Q1 R–B7 34 Q–Q4?
(34 Q–R3) 34 . . . R–B8+ 35 K–N2
Q–B7+ 0–1

42) Smyslov–Reshevsky, Ruy Lopez 1
P–K4 P–K4 2 N–KB3 N–QB3 3 B–N5
P–QR3 4 B–R4 N–B3 5 0–0 N×P
6 P–Q4 P–QN4 7 B–N3 P–Q4 8 P×P
B–K3 9 Q–K2 N–B4 10 R–Q1 P–N5
11 B–K3 N×B 12 RP×N N Q–B1 13
P–B4 QP×P 14 P×P P–R3! (14 . . .
B–K2 15 B–N5!) 15 QN–Q2 B–K2 16
N–N3 0–0 17 B–B5 B–N5 18 Q–K4
B×N 19 P×B Q–K3 20 B×B? (better
20 P–B4) 20 . . . N×B 21 N–B5 Q–
N3+ 22 Q×Q N×Q 23 N×P N×P
24 P–N3 R–R2! (*42*)
25 N×NP R×R 26 R×R R–N1 27 N–
Q5 (27 R–R4 N×P+ 28 K–N2 N–Q7)
27 . . . R×P 28 P–B4 N×P 29 R–QB1
N–Q7 30 R×P N–B6+ 31 K–N2
N–R5+ 32 K–B1 R–N7 (32 . . . R–N8+
33 K–K2 R–KR8 34 R–B8+ K–R2 35
R–B7) 33 N–K3 R–N5 34 P–B5 P–B3

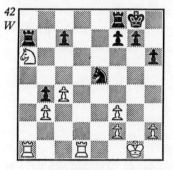

42
W

P–N3 44 R–B6 R–Q5 45 R–R6 P–R5
46 R–N6 R–Q6 47 R–R6 K–R4 48
R–R8 R–Q3 49 R–R8+ K–N4 50 K–
B3 R–Q6+ 51 K–N2 R–Q5 52 K–B3
K–B3 53 R–B8+ K–N2 54 R–QR8
R–Q6+ 55 K–N2 P–N4 56 R–R6
R–Q2 57 R–QN6 R–K2 58 R–QR6
K–B2 59 R–R6 R–K3 60 R–R8 K–N2
61 R–R5 K–N3 62 R–R8 R–QB3 63
R–N8+ K–B3 64 R–B8+ K–K4 65
R–KN8 K–B5 66 R–KR8 R–B4 67
R–R5 R–B3 68 R–R8 R–KN3 69 R–R7
K–K4 70 R–R8 K–B3 71 R–B8+
K–K3 72 R–KR8 K–B2 73 P–B4 ½–½
Round 22: Keres–Smyslov ½–½
Botvinnik–Euwe ½–½

43) Keres–Smyslov, English 1 P–QB4
N–KB3 2 N–QB3 P–Q4 3 P×P N×P
4 P–K4 N×N 5 NP×N P–KN3 6
B–R3 N–Q2 7 N–B3 B–N2 8 B–K2
P–QB4 9 0–0 0–0 10 P–Q4 P×P 11
P×P N–N3 12 Q–N3! B–N5 (12 . . .
B–K3 13 P–Q5!; 12 . . . B×P 13 QR–
Q1) 13 QR–Q1 B–Q2 14 R–B1 (14
R–N1!) 14 . . . B–R5 15 Q–N4 P–K3
16 B–N5! B×B 17 Q×B R–K1 18
KR–Q1 R–QB1 19 B–B5 Q–B2! 20
R–N1 (20 P–Q5 P×P 21 P×P N×P!
22 R×N P–N3) 20 . . . Q–B3 21 B×N
(21 P–K5 N–R5!) 21 . . . P×B 22 P–K5

(22 P–Q5 P×P 23 P×P Q×Q 24 R×Q KR–Q1!) 22... Q×Q 23 R×Q R–B3 24 P–N3? (24 R/1–N1 R/1–QB1 25 P–N4!) 24... R–R1 25 R–Q2 B–R3 26 R/2–N2 B–B8 27 R–N1 (27 R–K2 R–R4) 27... R×P 28 R×P R×R (28... R/3–B7 29 N–K1) 29 R×R R–N7! 30 R×R B×R 31 K–B1 K–B1 32 K–K2 K–K1 33 K–Q3 P–QN4 (*43*)

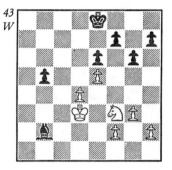

43
W

34 N–N5 P–R4 35 P–R3? (35 N–K4! K–Q2 - 35... B–R6 36 N–B3 P–N5 37 N–N5! - 36 N–Q6) 35... B–R6 36 P–B3 B–K2 37 N–K4 K–Q2 38 P–N4 K–B3 39 N–N3 P×P 40 BP×P P–N5 41 K–B4 P–N4 42 N–K4 P–N6 (42... K–N3 43 N–Q2 K–R4 44 K–N3 K–N4 45 N–B3=) 43 N–B3! (43 K×P K–Q4) 43... P–N7 44 K–N3 P–B3 45 K×P (45 P×P? B×P 46 K×P B×P wins) 45... P×P 46 P×P K–B4 47 K–B2 K–Q5 48 N–N5+ K×P 49 K–Q3 (49... K–B5 50 N–B7!) ½–½

44) Botvinnik-Euwe, Queens Gambit 1 P–Q4 P–Q4 2 N–KB3 N–KB3 3 P–B4 P–K3 4 P×P P×P 5 N–B3 P–B3 6 Q–B2 P–KN3 7 B–N5 B–N2 8 P–K3 B–B4 9 B–Q3 B×B 10 Q×B 0–0 11 0–0 QN–Q2 12 N–K5 Q–K1 13 N×N Q×N 14 P–QN4 KR–K1 (*44*) ½–½

Round 23: Symslov-Botvinnik ½–½
Reshevsky-Keres ½–½

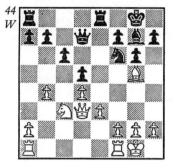

44
W

45) Smyslov-Botvinnik, Queens Gambit 1 P–Q4 P–Q4 2 P–QB4 P×P 3 N–KB3 P–QR3 4 P–K3 B–N5 5 B×P P–K3 6 QN–Q2 N–Q2 7 0–0 KN–B3 8 P–KR3 B–R4 9 P–QN3 P–B4 10 B–K2 P×P 11 N×P B×B 12 Q×B B–B4 13 B–N2 0–0 14 QR–B1 R–B1 15 KR–Q1 Q–K2 16 N/4–B3 B–N5 17 R×R R×R (*45*) ½–½

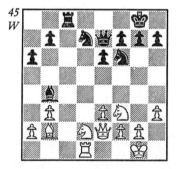

45
W

46) Reshevsky-Keres, Nimzo-Indian 1 P–Q4 N–KB3 2 P–QB4 P–K3 3 N–QB3 B–N5 4 Q–B2 0–0 5 P–QR3 B×N+ 6 Q×B P–QN3 7 B–N5 B–N2 8 N–B3 P–Q3 9 P–K3 QN–Q2 10 Q–B2 Q–K1! 11 N–Q2 P–B4 12 P×P! NP×P 13 P–QN4! (*46*) 13... P–K4? (13... N–R4! and 14... P–B4) 14 P×P P×P 15 B–K2 P–KR3 16 B×N (16 B–R4 B×P) 16... N×B 17 0–0 Q–B3 18 P–B3 KR–K1 19 B–Q3 QR–Q1 20 KR–Q1 Q–B2 21 N–K4 R–K3 22 N×N+ (22 N–B3 P–K5!)

22 ... R×N   23 B–R7+ K–R1   24 R×
R+ Q×R   25 R–Q1 R–Q3   26 R×R
Q×R ½–½

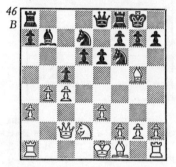

Round 24: Botvinnik-Reshevsky 1-0
Euwe-Smyslov 0–1

(47) Botvinnik - Reshevsky, Four
Knights 1 P–K4 P–K4   2 N–KB3 N–
QB3   3 N–B3 N–B3   4 B–N5 B–N5
5 0–0 0–0   6 P–Q3 B×N   7 P×B P–Q3
8 B–N5 Q–K2 9 R–K1 N–Q1 10 P–Q4
N–K3   11 B–QB1 R–Q1   12 B–B1!
N–B1? (12 ... P–B4) 13 N–R4 N–N5?
(13 ... N–K1; 13 ... N×P   14 R×N
P–KB4 15 B–B4+ K–R1 16 Q–R5!)
14 P–N3 Q–B3 15 P–B3 N–R3 16 B–
K3! (16 B×N P×B)   16 ... R–K1   17
Q–Q2 N–N3   18 N–N2! (18 B–KN5
N×N!) 18 ... B–R6 (18 ... Q×P   19
B–K2 Q–B3 – 19 ... Q×KP? 20 B×N–
20 B–QB4!) 19 B–K2 B×N   20 K×B
P–Q4! 21 P×QP P×P 22 P×P N–B4
23 B–B2 KR–Q1   24 P–QB4 P–KR4
25 P–KR4 P–N4!   26 Q–N5 Q×Q
27 P×Q P–R5? (27 ... P×P   28 B×P
N/4–K2) 28 B–Q3 RP×P 29 B×P (47)
29 ... N×P? (29 ... N×B   30 K×N
P×P) 30 QR–Q1! P–QB4 31 P×Pep
N×P/B3 32 B–K4 QR–B1 33 R×R+
N×R 34 B–B5! R–R1 35 R–K8+ K–R2
36 P×P P–B3 37 B–B7 N–K3 38 R×R
(38 R×N) 38 ... N×B   39 R×P N×P
40 R–Q7 (40 P×P!)   40 ... P×P
41 P–R4 1–0

48) Euwe-Smyslov, Grünfeld 1 P–Q4
N–KB3 2 P–QB4 P–KN3 3 N–QB3
P–Q4   4 N–B3 B–N2   5 Q–N3 P×P
6 Q×BP 0–0 7 P–K4 B–N5 8 B–K3
KN–Q2   9 Q–N3 N–N3   10 P–QR4
P–QR4 11 P–Q5 QB×N 12 P×B Q–
Q3! 13 N–N5 Q–N5+ 14 Q×Q P×Q
15 N×P (15 P–R5 B×P)   15 ... R×P
16 R–QN1 N/3–Q2   17 N–N5 R–B1
18 B–K2 (better 18 N–Q4) 18 ... P–N6!
19 N–R3 (19 0–0 R–B7)   19 ... B×P
20 R×B R×N   21 K–Q2 (21 B–Q1
N–B4!)   21 ... N–R3   22 R/1–QN1
N/3–B4 23 B–Q4 (23 B–QN5 N–K4;
23 B–Q1 R–R7) 23 ... P–K4! 24 P×Pep
(24 B–K3 or B–B3 P–B4!) 24 ... N×P3
25 B–K3 N/2–B4 26 B×N (26 B–QB4
N×P+) 26 ... N×B   27 K–B3 R–R5
28 K–Q2 K–N2! 29 K–K3 R–Q1 30
R–QB1 P–N3 31 B–B4 R/1–QR1 32
B–Q5 (32 B×NP? R–N5   33 R–B3
R–R6) 32 ... R–R7   33 R/1–QN1
R/1–R5 34 K–Q2 (48)

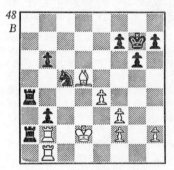

34 ... R–Q5+ 35 K–K2 N–R5! 36 R×P P×R 37 R–QR1 (37 B×NP N–B6+ 38 K–K3 R–R5 39 B–N3 R–R6 wins) 37 ... N–B6+ 38 K–K3 R–Q8 0–1
Round 25: Reshevsky-Euwe 1–0
Keres-Botvinnik 1–0

49) Reshevsky-Euwe, Queens Gambit 1 P–Q4 P–Q4 2 P–QB4 P–K3 3 N–QB3 N–KB3 4 P–K3 P–B4 5 N–B3 N–B3 6 QP×P B×P 7 P–QR3 P–QR4 8 B–K2 0–0 9 0–0 P×P 10 Q–B2 P–K4 11 B×P B–KN5 12 N–KN5 B–R4 13 B–Q3 P–R3 14 N/5–K4 N×N 15 B×N B–R2 16 B–Q2 B–N5 17 P–R3 B–K3 18 N–N5 B–N3 19 KR–Q1 Q–N4? (19 ... Q–K2) 20 N–Q6! B×RP 21 Q–N3! B–R2 22 Q×P N–K2 23 B–KB3! P–B4 (23 ... KR–N1 24 Q–B7 B–N3 25 N–K4!) 24 K–B1? (24 Q–N3+ K–R2 25 N–B7!) 24 ... P–K5 (24 ... B–N5 25 Q–N3+ K–R2 26 B×R!) 25 P×B QR–N1 (25 ... P×B 26 Q×P N–N3!; 25 ... KR–N1 26 N×KP!) *(49)*

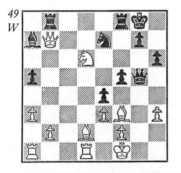

49
W

26 N×KP? (26 Q×B! P×B 27 B–B3!) 26 ... P×N 27 Q×P R–B2? (27 ... Q–B3) 28 B–KN4! Q–R5 (28 ... N–B4) 29 P–B4! K–R1 (29 ... R×P+ 30 Q×R R–KB1 31 B–K6+) 30 B–K1 Q–B3 31 B–QB3 Q–R3+ 32 B–K2 Q–B1 33 B–KN4 Q–R3+ 34 K–N2 N–B4 35 B×N R×B 36 R–Q7! 1–0

50) Keres-Botvinnik, French 1 P–K4 P–K3 2 P–Q4 P–Q4 3 N–QB3 B–N5

4 B–Q2 P×P 5 Q–N4 N–KB3 6 Q×NP R–N1 7 Q–R6 N–B3 (7 ... Q×P 8 0–0–0) 8 0–0–0 R–N3 (8 ... N×P 9 N×P) 9 Q–R4 B×N 10 B×B Q–Q4 11 P–QN3 N–K2 12 P–B3! B–Q2 (12 ... N–B4 13 Q–K1) 13 B–N2 (better 13 P×P Q×KP 14 N–B3) 13 ... B–B3 14 P–QB4 (14 P×P Q×KP 15 N–B3 N–B4!) 14 ... Q–KB4! 15 P–Q5! P×QP 16 P×KP P×KP (16 ... Q×P 17 B×N Q–K6+ 18 K–N1 N–B4 19 R–K1) 17 N–R3 N–N5 18 Q–N3 Q–B4! 19 Q×P R–B1 20 Q–B4 Q–K6+ 21 R–Q2 *(50)*

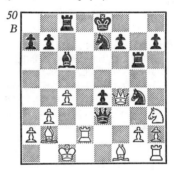

50
B

21 ... Q×Q? (21 ... Q–K8+ 22 R–Q1 Q–K6+=; 22 K–B2 N–K6+ 23 K–B3 N/2–Q4+; 22 R–Q1 Q–K6+ 23 K–N1 Q×Q 24 N×Q N–B7!) 22 N×Q P–K6 23 R–QB2! R–N4 (23 ... R–Q3 24 B–K2 N–B7 25 R–K1 and 26 R–B3; 23 ... R–R3 24 B–K2 R×P 25 R×R N×R 26 R–B3) 24 B–K2 N–B7 25 R–K1 R–Q1 (25 ... B×P 26 R–N1; 25 ... B–K5 26 R–B3 N–B4 27 P–KN4 N×P 28 K–N1) 26 P–N3? (26 B–B1! intending B–B6 and B×N) 26 ... R–KB4? (26 ... B–K5 27 R–B3 N–B4 is better but 28 B–B1! or 28 P–KN4!) 27 B–B1 R×N (28 B–QR3! was threatened) 28 P×R N–Q6+ 29 B×N R×B 30 R–B3 R×R+ 31 B×R N–B4 32 B–Q2 K–Q2 33 B×P P–N3 34 B–B2 P–B3 35 K–Q2 P–KR4 36 K–Q3 N–R3 37 B–R4 P–B4 38 R–K7+ K–Q3 39 P–KR3 1–0

2 Botvinnik–Bronstein

Moscow 16 March–11 May 1951

	1	2	3	4	5	6	7	8	9	10	11	12
Botvinnik	½	½	½	½	0	1	1	½	½	½	0	1
Bronstein	½	½	½	½	1	0	0	½	½	½	1	0

	13	14	15	16	17	18	19	20	21	22	23	24	**Total**
Botvinnik	½	½	½	½	0	½	1	½	0	0	1	½	**12**
Bronstein	½	½	½	½	1	½	0	½	1	1	0	½	**12**

1) Botvinnik–Bronstein, Dutch 1 P–Q4 P–K3 2 P–QB4 P–KB4 3 P–KN3 N–KB3 4 B–N2 B–K2 5 N–QB3 0–0 6 P–K3 P–Q3 7 KN–K2 P–B3 8 0–0 P–K4 9 P–Q5 Q–K1 10 P–K4 Q–R4 11 P×KBP B×P 12 P–B3 (12 P–B5 B–R6! gives Black good attacking chances) 12 ... Q–N3 13 B–K3 QN–Q2 14 Q–Q2 P×P 15 P×P (Better is 15 N×P N×N 16 P×N=) 15 ... B–Q1! 16 QR–B1 (Passive. Better is 16 N–N5) 16 ... B–R4! 17 P–KN4! B–Q6 18 KR–Q1 B–B5 19 Q–B2 (Better is 19 P–N3, then ... B×QP 20 P–N5±; 19. . N×QP 20 B–B2 N×N 21 N×N B–K3 22 Q×P±) 19 ... Q×Q 20 R×Q N–N3! 21 R/2–Q2 B–R3 (21 ... KN×QP 22 R×N N×R 23 R×N±; 21 ... B/B5×N∓) 22 B–B2 *(51)* 22 ... N–B5? (22 ... B/R3×N! 23 R×B B×N 24 B×N P×B 25 P×B N–Q2! and R–B5!, K–B2, K–K2, N–B4 gives Black a won ending) 23 R–B2 B–N3 24 B×B P×B 25 R–K1 N–K6 26 R–Q2 N–B5 27 R–B2 N–K6 28 R–Q2 N–B5 29 R–B2 ½–½

2) Bronstein–Botvinnik, Grünfeld 1 P–Q4 N–KB3 2 P–QB4 P–KN3 3 N–QB3 P–Q4 4 P×P N×P 5 P–K4 N×N 6 P×N P–QB4 7 B–QB4 B–N2 8 N–

51
B

K2 0–0 9 0–0 N–Q2 10 B–KN5! (weakening Black's K-side. 10 ... Q–B2 11 B×KP R–K1 12 P–Q5!) 10 ... P–KR3 11 B–K3 Q–B2 12 R–B1 P–R3 13 Q–Q2 K–R2 14 B–Q3 P–QN4 15 N–B4 (15 P–K5 N–N3 16 P–KR4 B–B4! 17 B×B P×B 18 N–B4 P–K3 19 N–R5 R–R1=) 15 ... P–K4 (this gives White's N the Q5 square. 15 ... B–N2 16 P–K5 N–N3= though White has attacking chances) 16 N–Q5 Q–Q3 17 P×BP! N×P 18 P–QB4! N×B 19 Q×N R–Q1! (19 ... P×P 20 R×P R–Q1 21 Q–B3 B–N2 22 B–B5±) 20 P–B5 Q–QB3 21 KR–Q1 B–K3 22 R–Q2 R–Q2 23 R/1–Q1 P–QR4 24 P–QR3 R/1–Q1 25 Q–N3 R–QN1 26 P–B3 R2–N2 27 Q–N2 P–N5 28 N–N6 B–KB1! 29 P×P

P×P 30 R–QB1 P–N6 31 N–Q5 B–N2 32 R–Q3 R–N4 (Better 32 ... P–B4 33 R/1–B3 P×P 34 P×P Q–R5 35 P–B6 Q×KP=?) 33 P–R4 (33 P–R3 is less weakening) 33 ... R/1–N2 34 K–R2 P–B4 35 R/1–B3 (Correct is 35 N–B3! R×P 36 B×R Q×B. Now White is in danger of losing) 35 ... P×P 36 P×P R–N5 (36 ... B×N 37 R×B R–N5∓; 37 P×B Q–B3 threat P–K5∓. The exchange sacrifice is sufficient only to draw) 37 N×R R×N 38 R–Q6 Q×KP 39 B–B2 Q–B5+ 40 B–N3 Q–B4 41 R–B3 Q–N5! 42 P–B6 (*52*)

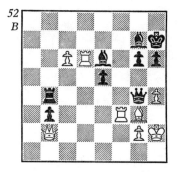

52
B

42 ... P–N4!! (43 P×P P–K5! 44 R–Q7 B×R 45 R–B7 Q–R4+ and Q×R wins) 43 P–B7! R–QB5 44 R×P P–K5 45 Q–KB2 P×P 46 B–B4 R×P 47 R×B (or 47 R/3–N6 R–B7! 48 Q×R Q×B+ 49 K–N1 P–R6!! 50 R×B B–Q5+ 51 K–R1 P×P+ 52 Q×NP Q–R5+ 53 Q–R2 Q–K8+ 54 K–N2 Q–K7+ 55 K–R3 Q–R4+ 56 K–N3 Q–B6+ 57 K–R4 B–B7+ 58 Q×B Q×Q+=) 47 ... Q×R 48 B×R Q×R 49 Q–B5+ ½–½

3) Botvinnik–Bronstein, French 1 P–Q4 P–K3 2 P–K4 P–Q4 3 N–Q2 P–QB4 4 KP×P KP×P 5 B–N5+ B–Q2 6 Q–K2+ B–K2 7 P×P N–KB3 8 KN–B3 0–0 9 0–0 R–K1 10 N–N3 B×P 11 Q–Q3 P–QR3 12 B×B QN×B 13 B–N5 B–B1 14 QR–Q1 Q–B2 15 P–B3 P–R3 16 B–R4 R–K5 17 B–N3 Q–N3 18 N/B3–Q2 R/5–K1 19 Q–B2 QR–B1

20 N–B3 P–N3 21 KR–K1 B–N2 22 R×R+ R×R 23 B–B4 B–B1 24 P–KR3 K–R2 25 N–R2 N–K4 26 B–K3 Q–B2 27 B–Q4 N–K5 28 B×N Q×B 29 N–N4 Q–B5 30 Q–B1 (30 R×P N–N6 31 Q–Q2 N–K7+ 32 K–R1 N–N6+=; 31 P×N R–K8+ 32 K–R2 Q–KB8 33 N–B6+ K–R1 34 P–N4 Q–B5+ 35 P–N3 Q–KB8 36 Q–N2 R–K7 wins) 30 ... Q–Q3 31 Q–B2 (31 P–QB4 P–KR4 32 R×P Q–B2 33 N–K3 B–R3 34 R–Q3 Q–B5 35 Q–K1 N×P 36 Q×N Q×N=) 31 ... N–B3 32 N×N+ Q×N 33 Q–Q3 (33 R×P R–K8+ 34 K–R2 Q–B5+ 35 P–N3 Q–B6 wins) 33 ... R–Q1 34 Q–K3 B–N2 35 P–N3 P–KR4 36 K–N2 R–Q3 37 N–Q4 R–Q2 38 N–B3 B–R3 39 Q–Q4 Q×Q 40 N×Q B–N2 41 N–B2 P–R4 (*53*)

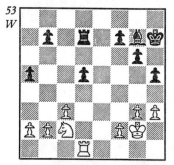

53
W

42 P–QR4 (42 N–K3 P–Q5 43 N–B2 P–Q6 44 N–Q4 wins the QP) 42 ... R–Q1 43 K–B3 B–B3 44 N–Q4 K–N2 45 N–N5 K–B1 46 N–B7 P–Q5 47 P–B4 B–K2 48 N–Q5 B–B4 49 K–K2 R–K1+ 50 K–Q3 P–N3 51 P–KN4 K–N2 52 R–KR1 P–R5 (52 ... P×P 53 P×P P–KN4 is less risky) 53 P–N5 R–K4 54 R–KN1 K–B1 55 P–B3 K–N2 56 P–B4 R–K1 57 K–Q2 R–K3 58 R–K1 (58 R–N4 B–N5+ 59 N×B P×N 60 P–KB5 P×P 61 R×P R–K6 62 R–R6 and wins; 61 ... K–N3 62 R–R6+ K×P 63 R×R P×R 64 P–B5 and wins – Benko) 58 ... R×R 59 K×R K–B1

60 K–K2 K–K1 61 K–Q3 K–Q2 62 K–K4 K–Q3 63 N–B6 K–K3 ½–½ (64 N–N4 P–Q6 65 K×P K–B4)

4) Bronstein-Botvinnik, Slav 1 P–Q4 P–Q4 2 P–QB4 P–QB3 3 N–QB3 N–B3 4 N–B3 P–KN3 5 P×P P×P 6 B–B4 B–N2 7 P–K3 0–0 8 B–K2 N–B3 9 P–KR3 N–K5 10 R–QB1 (10 N×N P×N 11 N–N5 P–K4 12 P×P N×P 13 N×KP B–B4=) 10 . . . B–K3 11 0–0 R–B1 12 N–Q2 N×N/7 13 Q×N Q–R4 14 P–R3 P–QR3 (54)

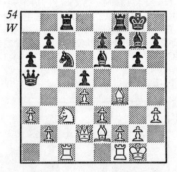

54
W

15 R–R1 (15 P–QN4 Q×RP 16 R–R1 Q–N6 17 KR–N1 N×QP 18 R×Q N×R followed by N×R and B×N∓) 15 . . . B–B4 16 KR–Q1 QR–Q1 17 P–QN4 Q–N3 18 N–R4 (18 B–B3 P–K4 19 P×P P–Q5 is unclear) 18 . . . Q–R2 19 B–B7 R–Q2 20 B–N6 Q–N1 21 P–B4 N–R2 22 P–N4 (22 N–B5 N–B1 23 N×R B×N and White's B is trapped) 22 . . . B–K3 23 B×N Q×B 24 N–B5 R–Q3 25 N×B (With B's of opposite colour the game is drawish; better P–QR4 and P–R5 to maintain the N) 25 . . . R×N 26 QR–B1 Q–N1 27 K–N2 (Black threatened P–KN4) 27 . . . R–B1 28 B–B3 R–Q3 29 R–B5 P–K3 30 R/1–B1 R×R 31 R×R (31 NP×R±) 31 . . . B–B1 32 Q–QB2 R–Q1 33 R–B3 B–Q3 34 P–KR4 K–N2 35 Q–B1 P–R3 36 R–B2 P–KN4 37 BP×P P×P 38 P–R5 (38 P×P R–R1∓) 38 . . . K–R3 39 Q–

K1 R–KB1 40 P–K4 P×P 41 Q×P R–B1 42 B–Q1 R×R+ 43 B×R Q–KR1 44 B–Q3 Q–N2 45 K–B3 P–R4 46 P×P B×P 47 K–N2 B–Q3 ½–½

5) Botvinnik-Bronstein, Nimzo - Indian 1 P–Q4 N–KB3 2 P–QB4 P–K3 3 N–QB3 B–N5 4 P–K3 0–0 5 B–Q3 P–B4 6 N–B3 P–QN3 7 0–0 B–N2 8 N–QR4 P×P 9 P–QR3 B–K2 10 P×P Q–B2 11 P–QN4 N–N5 12 P–N3 P–B4 13 N–B3 P–QR3 14 R–K1 N–QB3 15 B–B1 N–Q1 16 B–B4 B–Q3 17 B×B Q×B 18 B–N2 N–B2 19 P–B5 Q–B2 20 R–QB1 (20 N–QR4 P–QN4 21 N–N6 QR–K1 22 P–Q5 gains a tempo) 20 . . . QR–K1 21 N–QR4 P–QN4 22 N–B3 P–B5 23 P–Q5 BP×P 24 BP×P (24 RP×P P×P 25 N×QP R×R+ 26 N×R=; 25 . . . Q–B3 26 N–R4 R×R+ 27 Q×R=; 25 . . . R×R+ 26 N×R Q–K4 27 Q×N B×N 28 B×B Q×B 29 R–Q1=) 24 . . . P×P 25 Q–Q4 (25 N×QP B×N 26 Q×B N–K6 27 Q–Q2 N×B 28 Q×B R×R+ 29 R×R P–Q3=; 28 K×N Q–B3∓) 25 . . . N–B3 26 N–KR4 R–K4 27 R×R Q×R 28 Q×Q N×Q 29 N–B5 (29 R–Q1 N–B5 30 N×QP B×N 31 B×B+ N×B 32 R×N N–K6 wins) 29 . . . N–B5 (55)

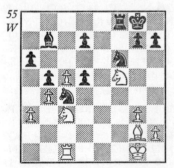

55
W

30 R–Q1? (30 N×QP N×N 31 B×N+ B×B 32 N–K7+ K–B2 33 N×B=) 30 . . . K–R1! (31 N×QP B×N

32 B×B N×B 33 R×N P–N3 wins, 34
N–Q6 N–K6) 31 R–K1 N×P 32 N–Q6
B–B3 33 R–R1 N–B7 34 R×P P–Q5
35 N/3×P B×B 36 K×B N–N5 37
N–B5 (37 N–K4 P–Q6 38 N/5–B3 N/7–
K6+ 39 K–R3 P–Q7 40 N×P N–B7+
41 K–R4 N–N7+ 42 K–N5 P–N3 43
R–KB6 K–N2 44 R×R P–R3 mate; 43
K–R6 N–N5+ 44 K–N5 R–B4+ 45
K×N N–K6+ mates) 37 . . . P–Q6 38
R–Q6 R×N 39 R×P/Q7 N5–K6+ 0–1

6) Bronstein-Botvinnik, Sicilian 1
P–K4 P–QB4 2 N–KB3 N–QB3 3 P–
Q4 P×P 4 N×P N–B3 5 N–QB3 P–
Q3 6 B–KN5 P–K3 7 Q–Q2 P–KR3 8
B×N P×B 9 0–0–0 P–R3 10 P–B4 B–
Q2 11 K–N1 B–K2 12 B–K2 N×N 13
Q×N Q–R4 14 KR–B1 P–R4 15 R–
B3 Q–QB4 (15 . . . 0–0–0 16 P–QN4
Q–B2 17 N–Q5 P×N 18 R–B3±) 16
Q–Q2 B–B3 17 R–K3 Q–R4 18 B–B3
0–0–0 19 Q–Q3 (19 N–Q5 Q×Q 20
N×B+ K–Q2 21 R×Q K×B=; now
20 N–Q5 is a serious threat) 19 . . . R–Q2
20 P–KR4 K–N1 21 P–R3 B–Q1 22 K–
R2 Q–QB4 (22 . . . B–N3? 23 P–
QN4) 23 R–K2 P–R4! 24 P–R4 B–N3
25 P–QN3 R–QB1 26 Q–B4 Q×Q 27
P×Q R–KR1 28 K–N3 R/2–Q1 29 R–
Q3 B–N8 30 R/2–Q2 K–B2 31 N–K2
B–B7 32 R–Q1 B–B4 33 N–N3 R/Q1–
KN1 34 N–K2 (34 N×P B×KP 35 N×
P B×R 36 N×R B–KN3 37 N–K7 R×
P 38 N×B P×B=; White is playing to
win) 34 . . . R–R2 35 P–B5! P–K4 36
N–B3 B–Q5 37 R×B P×R 38 R×P
(Better 38 N–K2) 38 . . . R/2–N2 39 N–
K2 R×P 40 B×R R×B 41 N–B4 R–
N6+! 42 K–N2 R–N5 43 N×P R×RP
44 N×P K–N3! 45 R×P K–B4 46 P–
K5 (46 R–Q8 B×RP 47 R–KB8 R–R7
48 R×P R×P+ 49 K–N1 R×P 50 R×
P B–B3=) 46 . . . R–Q5 (46 . . . R–B5
47 N–Q7+ B×N 48 R×B R×KBP 49
R×NP R×KP 50 K–N3 P–B3 also
draws) 47 R×R K×R 48 N–N4 B×P
49 P–K6 P×P 50 P–B6 B–K1 51 K–N3

P–K4 52 P–B3+ K–K5 53 N–R6 K–B5
54 P–B7 B×P 55 N×B P–K5 56 N–Q8
P–K6 (56)

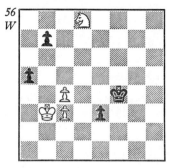

56
W

57 K–B2?? (57 N–K6+=) 57 . . . K–
N6! 0–1

7) Botvinnik-Bronstein, Dutch 1
P–Q4 P–Q4 2 P–QB4 P–K3 3 N–KB3
P–QB3 4 P–KN3 P–KB4 5 B–N2 N–
KB3 6 0–0 B–K2 7 P–N3 0–0 8 B–
QR3 P–QN3 9 B×B Q×B 10 N–K5
B–N2 11 N–Q2 QN–Q2 12 N×N N×
N 13 P–K3 (to prevent P–B5) 13 . . .
QR–B1 14 R–B1 P–B4 15 Q–K2 N–B3
16 BP×P B×P 17 B×B P×B (17 . . .
N×B 18 P–K4±) 18 N–B3 R–QB2 19–
R–B2 KR–B1 20 KR–B1 N–K5 21 N–
K5 N–B3 22 Q–Q3 P–N3 23 Q–R6 K–
N2 24 Q–K2 Q–Q3 25 P–QR4 N–K1
26 Q–Q2 N–B3 27 Q–B3 N–K5 28
Q–Q3 P×P 29 P×P (29 R×R R×R 30
R×R Q×R 31 Q×P Q–B6=) 29 . . .
P–QR4 30 K–N2 N–B3 31 Q–K2 (57)

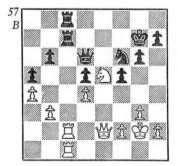

57
B

31 ... P–B5 (unnecessary - Black should hold the position) 32 P×P (better 32 R×R+ R×R 33 R×R+ Q×R 34 P×P) 32 ... N–R4 (32 ... R×R 33 R×R N–R4 34 N–Q3 R×R 35 Q×R N× P+ 36 N×N Q×N should draw) 33 R×R+ R×R 34 R×R+ Q×R 35 Q–N4 N–B3 36 Q–K6 N–R4 37 Q–Q7+! (forcing a won ending) 37 ... Q×Q 38 N×Q N×P+ 39 K–B3 N–Q6 40 N× P N–N5 41 K–B4 K–B3 42 N–Q7+ K–K2 43 N–K5 (White's winning plan is K on QB3, N on Q3 and play P–N4) 43 ... K–K3 44 K–K3 K–B4 45 P–B3 P–N4 46 K–Q2 P–R4 (46 ... K–B5 47 N–Q3+ N×N 48 K×N K×P 49 P–N4 P×P 50 P–R5 wins) 47 N–Q3 N–R3 48 N–B5 N–N5 49 N–Q3 N–R3 50 P–R3! N–B2 (50 ... P–N5 51 BP×P+ P×P 52 P×P+ K×P 53 N–K5+ and N–B6 wins) 51 K–K3 (51 K–B3 N–R3 52 P–N4 P×P+ 53 N×P K–B5 54 N×N K×P 55 N–B5 P–N5 56 P×P P×P 57 N–Q3 P–N6 58 N–K1+ K–K7 59 N–N2 is a quicker win) 51 ... N–R3 52 K–K2 K–K3 53 K–Q2 (53 N–B5+ N×N 54 P× N K–Q2 55 K–Q3 K–B3 56 K–Q4 P–R5! winning the QBP) 53 ... K–K2 54 K–B3 K–Q3 55 P–N4 P×P+ 56 N×P N–B2 57 P–R5 N–N4+ 58 K–Q3 K–K3 59 K–K3 N–R2 60 P–R6 N–N4 61 N–B6 N–B2 62 N–N4 K–B4 (62 ... N–N4 63 K–B2, K–N3 and P–B4) 63 P–R7 K–K3 64 K–B2 P–R5 65 P–B4 P×P 66 K–B3 1–0

8) Bronstein-Botvinnik, QP Meran 1 P–Q4 P–Q4 2 P–QB4 P–QB3 3 N–QB3 N–B3 4 N–B3 P–K3 5 P–K3 QN–Q2 6 B–Q3 P×P 7 B×BP P–QN4 8 B–Q3 P–QR3 9 P–K4 P–B4 10 P–K5 P×P 11 N×NP N×KP 12 N×N P×N 13 Q–B3 B–N5+ (13 ... Q–R4+ may be stronger - Botvinnik) 14 K–K2 QR–N1 15 N–B6 B–N2 16 B–KB4 (16 B×P Q–N3=) 16 ... B–Q3 17 N×Q B×Q+ 18 K×B R×N 19 B×P+ (*58*)

(19 B×B is more logical - Black might have trouble defending QB2) 19 ... K–K2 20 B–Q2 R–QN1! (weakens White's

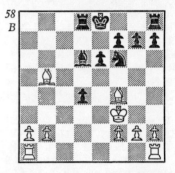

58
B

QN4) 21 P–QR4 N–Q4 22 P–QN3 (Black threatened 22 ... N–B2) 22 ... P–B4 23 KR–QB1 P–K4 24 K–K2 (White has to beware of threat 24 ... P–Q6 and P–K5 mate) 24 ... P–K5 25 R–B6 KR–QB1 26 QR–QB1 R×R 27 R×R R–N3 (27 ... P–B5 28 B–B4!±) 28 R×R N×R 29 P–R5 N–Q4 30 P–R6 B–B4 31 P–QN4 B–R2 32 B–B6 K–Q3 33 B–N7 P–R3 (33 ... P–B5 34 B×N K×B 35 B×P K–B5 36 B–Q6 K–N4 37 P–B3 P–K6 38 K–Q3 K×B 39 P–B4±) 34 P–R4 P–N4 35 P×P P×P 36 B×P N×P 37 B–B8 K–K4 38 B–Q2 N–Q4 39 B–N7 N–B6+ 40 B×N P×B 41 P–N3 ½–½

9) Botvinnik-Bronstein, Dutch 1 P–Q4 P–K3 2 P–QB4 P–KB4 3 P–KN3 N–KB3 4 B–N2 B–K2 5 N–QB3 0–0 6 P–Q5 B–N5! (6 ... P–K4 7 N–B3 P–Q3 8 0–0 and Black's B is hampered by its own pawns) 7 B–Q2 P–K4 8 P–K3 P–Q3 9 KN–K2 P–QR3 10 Q–B2 Q–K1 11 P–B3 (to prepare P–K4 but it blocks White's B on N2) 11 ... P–QN4 12 Q–N3 B–B4 13 P×P B–Q2 (13 ... P×P 14 Q×P Q×Q 15 N×Q N×P∓; 14 N×P Q–B2 15 N5–B3 P–B3∓) 14 N–R4! B–R2? (14 ... P× P=) (*59*) 15 P–N6! B×N (15 ... P×P 16 N×P

B×N 17 Q×B N×P 18 Q×QP±)
16 P–N7 B×Q 17 P×R=Q B–N3
18 P×B Q–N4 19 N–B3 Q×NP 20
R×P (better 20 0–0 Q×NP 21 R–R2
Q–N6 22 R–N1 Q–B5 23 B–KB1±)

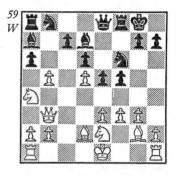

20 ... N×R 21 Q×N N×P 22 Q–R4?
(22 N×N Q×N 23 K–K2 P–B5 24
Q–Q3± ; 22 Q–K2±) 22 ... Q×Q 23
N×Q B×P 24 B–KB1? (24 N–B3 B×
B+ 25 K×B±) bringing White's R into
play) 24 ... R–R1 25 P–N3 (25 B–B4
R×N 26 B×N+ K–B1∓) 25 ...
B×B+ 26 K×B K–B1 27 B–Q3 P–N3
28 R–QB1 R–N1 29 N–B3 (29 R–B6
R–N2! there is no longer a clear win) 29
... N–N5 30 B–K2 R–R1 31 N–R4
P–B3 32 R–B4 R–N1 33 B–Q1 K–K2
34 N–N2 P–Q4 35 R–R4 P–R4 36 P–
N4 (36 N–Q3 N×N 37 K×N P–K5+
38 P×P QP×P+ 39 K–K3 K–B3∓)
36 ... RP×P 37 P×P P–B5 (better
37 ... K–B3) 38 P–N5 R–KB1 39 R–
R7+ K–Q3 40 R–KN7 P–K5 41 R×
P+ K–K4 ½–½ (42 B–N4 P–B6 43 R–B6!
R×R 44 P×R K×P 45 B×P P×B 46
K–K3 N–B7+ 47 K×P N–Q5+ 48
K–K3 N×P 49 N–Q3 P–B4 50 N×P
N×N 51 K–Q4 K–K3 52 K×N K–K4
53 P–R4 P–Q5 54 K–B4 K–K5 55 P–R5
P–Q6 56 P–R6=)

10) **Bronstein–Botvinnik,** Dutch 1 P–
Q4 P–K3 2 P–QB4 P–KB4 3 N–QB3
B–N5 4 Q–B2 N–KB3 5 P–K3 0–0 6
B–Q3 P–Q3 7 N–K2 P–B4 8 P–QR3

B×N+ 9 N×B N–B3 10 P×P P×P
11 P–QN3 B–Q2 12 B–N2 N–K4 13
B–K2 (13 0–0–0 N×B+ 14 R×B±)
13 ... B–B3 14 P–B3 N–R4 15 N–Q1
(15 0–0 Q–N4 and P–B5∓) 15 ... N–
N3 16 Q–B3 Q–N4 17 P–N3 P–K4 18
N–B2 QR–Q1 19 KR–N1 (19 P–B4
Q–R3 20 0–0 R–Q2! 21 QR–Q1
R–K2∓) 19 ... Q–K2 (19 ... P–B5!
20 N–R3 Q–R3 21 NP×P N/4×P 22
N×N P×N∓; 20 P–K4 P×NP 21 P×P
N×P 22 N–R1 N×B∓) 20 R–Q1
N–B3 21 R–Q2 P–QR3 22 K–Q1
P–N4 23 K–B1 P–N5 24 Q–B2 R×R
25 Q×R R–Q1 26 Q–B2 P–B5 27
NP×P KP×P (27 ... P–K5 28 P–B5!
is unclear) 28 P–K4 P–QR4 29 N–Q3
N–Q2 (29 ... N×P! 30 P×N B×P 31
R–Q1 P–B6 32 B–B1 N–B5∓; 31 Q–
Q2 P–B6 32 B–B1 Q–Q3 33 R–N5
P–R3 34 R–R5 Q–K2∓) 30 P×P
RP×P 31 B–R1 N/Q2–B1 32 R–Q1
N–K3 (better 32 ... Q–N4) 33 N–K5!
N×N 34 B×N Q–N4 35 R×R+
Q×R 36 Q–Q2 Q×Q+ 37 K×Q
P–N4 38 K–Q3 K–B2 39 B–B1 P–R4
40 B–K2 (40 B–R3 P–N5 41 P×P N–N4
42 B–B1 B×P+ 43 K–K2 P×P 44
B×P N–K3 45 B–Q6 B–B7 46 B–N2=)
40 ... K–K2 41 B–B1 B–Q2 42 B–R3
(White should preserve his B's – he now
gets a lost ending) 42 ... N–Q1 43
B×B K×B 44 P–R3 K–K2 45 B–N7
K–B2 46 B–K5 (60)
46 ... K–K2 (46 . . K–N3!! 47 K–K2

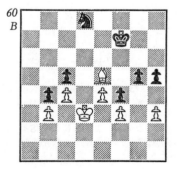

N–B3 wins; 47 B–Q6 N–K3! wins) 47
B–N7 N–N2 48 B–R6 K–B3 49 B–B8
K–B2 50 B–R6 K–N3 51 B–B8 K–B3
52 K–K2 K–B2 53 B–R6 K–N3 54
B–B8 K–B2 ½–½

11) **Botvinnik-Bronstein,** Queen's
Indian 1 P–Q4 P–K3 2 N–KB3 N–KB3
3 P–B4 P–QN3 4 P–KN3 B–N2 5 B–
N2 B–K2 6 0–0 0–0 7 P–N3 P–Q4 8
P×P P×P 9 B–N2 QN–Q2 10 N–B3
R–K1 11 N–K5 B–KB1 12 R–B1 N×N
13 P×N R×P 14 N–N5 R–K2 15
B×N P×B 16 P–K4 (16 P–QN4 with
N–Q4 and P–N5 to follow was a good
alternative) 16...P×P 17 Q–N4+
B–N2 18 KR–Q1 Q–KB1! (18...Q–
QB1 19 Q–B4±) 19 N–Q4 B–B1 20
Q–R4 P–KB4 21 N–B6 (21 B–R3!
B×N 22 R×B B–K3 23 R×BP R×R
24 Q–N5+ Q–N2 25 R–Q8+=; 23...
Q–N2 24 R×RP! is unclear) 21...
R–K1 22 B–R3 B–KR3 23 R–B2 P–K6
24 P×P B×P+ 25 K–R1 B–K3 (25...
B–N2 26 B×P Q–R3 is very strong) 26
B–N2 P–QR4 27 B–B3 K–R1 28 N–
Q4 QR–Q1 29 R×P (29 Q–B6+ Q–N2
30 Q×Q+ K×Q 31 N×B+ P×N∓)
29...B–Q4 (61)

61
W

30 R–K1? (30 R–KB1 Q–Q3 31 B×B!
Q×B+ 32 N–B3∓; 31 N×P B×B+
32 R×B Q–Q8+ 33 K–N2 R–Q7+
34 K–R3 R×P+ 35 K×R Q–N8+ 36
K–R3 Q–R8+ 37 K–N4 R–N1+ 38
K–R5 R–N4+ wins) 30...Q–Q3! 31

R–B2 (a last chance was 31 R–B3 R–K5?
32 R/3×B!∓; but 31... P–B5! wins)
31... R–K5! 32 B×R B×B+ 33
Q×B P×Q 34 N–B5 Q–N5 35 R×B
R–Q8+ 36 K–N2 R–Q7+ 37 R×R
Q×R+ 38 K–R3 Q–KB7 39 K–N4
P–B3 0–1

12) **Bronstein-Botvinnik,** Dutch 1 P–
Q4 P–K3 2 P–QB4 P–KB4 3 P–K3
N–KB3 4 N–QB3 P–Q4 5 N–R3 P–B3
6 B–Q2 B–Q3 7 Q–B2 0–0 8 0–0–0
Q–K2 9 P–B3 P×P 10 P–K4 (10 B×P
P–QN4∓) 10...P×P 11 N×P (safer
is 11 P×P P–K4) 11...P–QN4 12
N×B Q×N (62)

62
W

13 P–B4 (13 B–B4 is better) 13...N–
R3 14 B–K2 P–B4 15 B–KB3 R–N1
16 B–B3 (16 P×P is slightly better –
now Black wins a second pawn) 16...
N–QN5 17 P×P (17 B×N P×B∓)
17...N×P+ 18 K–N1 N×B+ 19
Q×N Q×QBP 20 KR–K1 P–KR3 (to
prevent N–N5, Black is preparing B–
N2) 21 R–K5 Q–B2 22 P–KN4 B–N2
23 B×B (23 R×NP B×B 24 R×R B×
R∓; 23 P–N5 P–N5 24 Q–K3 B×B
25 Q×B N–Q4, threat Q×R∓) 23...
R×B 24 P–N5 (24 R×KP N×P 25 R–
KN6 Q–B2∓) 24...N–Q4 25
R/1×N P×R 26 Q–Q4 P–B6 27 P–N3
(27 Q×QP+ Q–B2; 27 P×BP Q–B5
White's position is hopeless) 27...
Q–Q2 28 N–B2 P–B7+ 29 K–B1 P×P
30 R×NP Q–K3 31 R–K5 Q–Q3 32 K×

P R–QB2+ 33 K–Q2 Q–B4 34 Q×Q
R×Q 35 N–Q3 R–QB3 36 R×P P–R3
37 P–R4 R–R3 38 P–R5 R/R3–KB3
39 P–N4 R–B4 40 R–Q6 R/B1–B3 0–1

13) Botvinnik - Bronstein, Nimzo-
Indian 1 P–Q4 N–KB3 2 P–QB4 P–K3
3 N–QB3 B–N5 4 P–K3 P–QN3 5 N–
K2 B–N2 6 P–QR3 B×N+ 7 N×B
0–0 8 B–Q3 P–B4 9 P–Q5 P–QN4
(9 ... P×P 10 P×P N×P 11 N×N
B×N 12 Q–R5 P–B4 13 B×P±) 10
0–0 NP×P 11 B×BP P×P 12 N×P N–
B3 13 P–QN3 (13 N×N+ Q×N 14
Q×P QR–N1 and N–K4∓) 13 ...
N×N 14 B×N R–N1 15 B–N2 N–K2
16 Q–N4 N–N3 17 B×B R×B 18 P–
N4 P–QR4 19 B–B3 RP×P 20 P×P
P×P 21 B×QNP R–K1 22 B–B3 Q–R5
23 Q–B3 R–B2 24 B–Q4 N–B1 25 R–
R5 N–K3 26 B–K5 R–B3 27 B–N3
Q–QB5 (threat N–Q5, Q×R+ and
R–B8 mate) 28 R–Q5 N–B4 29 R–Q4
Q–K3 30 Q–Q5 P–R3 31 P–R3 R–R1
32 KR–Q1 Q×Q 33 R×Q N–K5 (*63*)

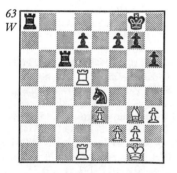

63
W

(to eliminate the dangerous White B,
34 B–K5 R–R7 35 P–B3 N–B6 36 B×N
R×B threatening R×P and R/6–B7)
34 R×P N×B 35 P×N R–R7 36 R/1–
Q2 R×R 37 R×R K–B1 38 P–N4 K–
K2 39 K–B2 R–B3+ 40 K–K2 R–R3
41 R–Q5 R–R7+ 42 K–B3 P–N4 43
R–KB5 K–B1 44 R–B6 K–N2 45 R–Q6
R–N7 46 P–N3 R–QR7 47 P–R4 R–R7
48 R–Q1 K–B3 (48 ... P×P 49 P×P

R×P 50 K–N3 wins the R) 49 P–K4
K–N3 50 P–R5+ K–B3 51 R–Q6+
K–N2 52 P–K5 R–R8 53 P–K6 P×P
54 R×P R–B8+ 55 K–K4 R–K8+ 56
K–Q5 R–Q8+ ½–½ (57 K–K5 R–K8+
58 K–Q6 R–Q8+ 59 K–K7 R–Q6)

14) Bronstein - Botvinnik, King's
Indian Reversed 1 N–KB3 P–K3 2 P–
KN3 P–Q4 3 B–N2 P–QB4 4 0–0 N–
QB3 5 P–Q3 P–KN3 6 P–K4 B–N2
7 Q–K2 KN–K2 8 P–K5 Q–B2 9 R–K1
P–KR3 10 P–B3 B–Q2 11 N–R3 P–R3
12 R–N1 N–B4 13 N–B2 QR–B1 14
P–KR4 Q–R4 15 P–R3 Q–Q1 16 B–B4
0–0 17 N–K3 N×N 18 Q×N K–R2
19 N–R2 N–K2 20 N–N4 N–N1
(better than 20 ... N–B4 which allows
N–B6+) 21 Q–Q2 B–QB3 22 P–Q4
P×P 23 Q×P B–N4 24 P–N3 P–QR4
25 P–R4 B–R3 26 Q–Q2 Q–K2 27 P–
N4 B–B5 28 P×P (28 B–K3 P×P 29
P×P Q–Q2 30 B–B5 R×B=; 28 N–K3
P–KN4 29 N×B P×B 30 N–Q6 BP×P
31 N×R NP×P+∓) 28 ... B–R3 29
B–B1 Q–B4 30 B–QN5 Q×QBP 31
Q×Q R×Q 32 B×B (better 32 B–Q2)
32 ... P×B 33 R–N6 (33 R/K1–QB1
better) 33 ... R–B5 34 N–R2 N–K2
35 R×RP N–B3 36 N–B3 N–N5 37
R–N6 N–Q6 38 R–R1 N×B 39 P×N
R×BP 40 K–N2 (better 40 R–R3) 40
... P–N4 41 P×P P×P 42 N×P+
K–N3 43 N–B3 R–KN1 (*64*)
44 R–R3 (Bronstein first wrote 44 R–N7
on his score-sheet, 44 ... K–R2!! 45 N–

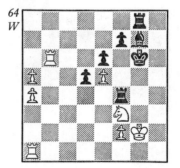

64
W

N5+ K–R3! 46 N×BP+ R×N 47
R×R B×P+ ∓) 44 ... B–B1 45 R–Q3
R×P 46 K–B1 R–R8+ 47 K–K2 R–
R7+ 48 R–Q2 R×P 49 R–N8 R–KR1
(49 ... K–R2 50 R–N7 R–N2 51 R–N8
with counterplay) 50 N–Q4 B–N2 51
R×R B×R 52 P–B4 R–R6 53 R–Q1
R–R7+ 54 K–B3 R–R6+ 55 K–N4
B–N2 56 K–R4 B–B1 (56 ... R–R5
with some winning chances) 57 P–B5+
P×P 58 R–KN1+ K–R2 59 N×P R–
R3 60 R–N5 B–R3 61 R–N3 R–K3 62
R–KB3 R×P 63 N×B K×N 64 R×P
K–N3 65 R–B4 R–B4 66 K–N4 ½–½

15) **Botvinnik-Bronstein,** French 1 P–
Q4 P–K3 2 P–K4 P–Q4 3 N–Q2 P–
QB4 4 KP×P KP×P 5 KN–B3 N–KB3
6 B–N5+ B–Q2 7 B×B+ QN×B
8 0–0 B–K2 9 P×P N×P 10 N–Q4!
Q–Q2 (to prevent N–B5) 11 N2–B3
0–0 12 N–K5 Q–B1 13 B–N5 R–K1
14 N–Q3 N×N 15 Q×N Q–N5 16 B–
K3 B–B4 17 P–KR3 Q–N3 (after this
exchange the QP is weaker, but the KB4
square is controlled) 18 Q×Q RP×Q
19 QR–Q1 R–K5 20 P–QB3 P–N3
(better is 20 ... B×N 21 R×B R×R
22 B×R R–K1 23 B–K3 – White has
only a minute advantage) 21 N–B2 R–
Q1 22 R–Q3 K–B1 23 KR–Q1 K–K2
24 K–B1 (P–KN4 is more aggressive)
24 ... K–Q2 25 B–N5 K–B3 26 P–
QN4 B–B1 27 N–K3 R–K4 (65)
28 P–KB4? (28 B×N P×B 29 P–KB4
R–R4 30 P–B4 B×P 31 N×P B–Q3

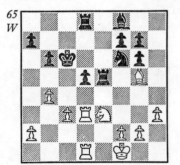

65
W

32 N×BP R4–R1 33 N–K4 B–K2 34
R×R R×R 35 R×R B×R 36 K–K2
P–B4 37 N–N5 with a won ending)
28 ... R–K5 29 P–B5 R–K4 30 B–B4
R–K5 31 B–N5 R–K4 32 B–B4 R–K5
33 B–N5 ½–½

16) **Bronstein-Botvinnik,** Dutch 1 P–
Q4 P–K3 2 P–QB4 P–KB4 3 P–KN3
N–KB3 4 B–N2 B–K2 5 N–QB3 0–0
6 P–K3 P–Q4 7 KN–K2 P–B3 8 P–N3
B–Q3 9 0–0 Q–K2 10 Q–B2 N–K5 11
N–Q1 N–R3 (11 ... P–B4 12 BP×P
KP×P 13 N/1–B3±) 12 N–N2 B–Q2
13 P–B5 B–B2 14 N–Q3 B–K1 15 P–
QN4 N–N1 16 B–N2 P–QR4 17 P–
QR3 N–Q2 18 N–K5 N/K5–B3 19
N–B1 P–KN4! (to gain control of K5)
20 P–B3 P–N5 21 N1–Q3 NP×P 22
B×P N–K5 23 QR–K1 (better 23 B–N2
or 23 K–R1) 23 ... N/Q2–B3 24 N–
KB4 K–R1 25 R–K2 N–N4 26 B–N2
R–KN1 27 B–QB3 N/N4–K5 28 B–K1
P×P 29 P×P N–R4 30 N/B4–Q3
N/R4–B3 31 Q–N1 B–R4 32 R–N2
B–K1 33 R–R2 R×R 34 Q×R B–N1
35 Q–N2 P–R3 36 N–KB4 K–R2 37
K–R1 N–N5 38 N×N R×N 39 B–R3
R–N4 40 Q–R1 B–KB2 41 B–N2
R–N1 42 B–B3 N–B3 43 Q–N2 N–N5
44 Q–K2 N–B3 45 R–N1 N–K5 46
R–B1 (46 P–R3 and P–N4 – Boleslavsky)
46 ... Q–K1 47 Q–Q3? (better 47 Q–
Q1 to maintain control of KR5) 47 ...
B×N 48 KP×B R–R4 49 Q–R3 (49 B–
N2 Q–R1∓; 49 B×N QP×B 50 Q–R3
B–B6+ and 51 ... Q–R5∓) 49 ...
B×B+ 50 R×B R–N2 51 K–N2 Q–Q1
52 K–B1 Q–B3 53 R–Q3 P–R4 54 P–R4
R–N1 55 R–Q1 (55 Q–R7 gives some
counterplay) 55 ... Q–N2 56 Q–KB3
K–R3 57 K–N2 (57 R–Q3 R–QR1 58
R–R3 R×R 59 Q×R Q×QP 60 Q–R8
Q–B5+ 61 K–N1 N–B3 wins) 57 ...
R–QR1 58 R–Q3 R–R7+ 59 K–B1
R–R8 60 Q–N2 Q–N5 61 Q–KR2
Q–N1 62 P–N5 Q–QR1 63 Q–QN2
Q–R4 64 R–K3 P×P 65 R–K2 Q–R5

66 K–N2 R–Q8 (66 . . . Q–Q8 67 Q×P
R–N8 is quicker) 67 B–B2 Q–B5 68 P–
B6 Q×BP? (68 . . . P×P 69 Q–R3 P–N5
70 Q–R8 N–B3 wins) 69 Q–N4 Q–K1
70 R–B2 R–Q6 71 B–K1 Q–KN1
72 Q–K7 (*66*)

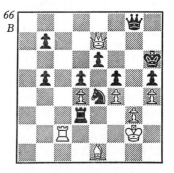

66
B

72 . . . R×P+? (72 . . . R×QP∓; 72 . . .
P–N5∓) 73 B×R Q×B+ 74 K–R1
Q–K8+ 75 K–R2 ½–½

17) Botvinnik-Bronstein, Nimzo -
Indian 1 P–Q4 N–KB3 2 P–QB4 P–K3
3 N–QB3 B–N5 4 P–K3 P–QN3 5 N–
K2 B–R3 6 P–QR3 B–K2 7 N–N3
P–Q4 8 P×P B×B 9 N×B P×P 10 N–
N3 Q–Q2 11 Q–B3 N–B3 12 0–0
P–N3 13 B–Q2 0–0 14 QN–K2 (better
14 P–QN4) 14 . . . P–KR4! (15 N–B4
P–R5 16 N/3–K2 N–K5∓) 15 KR–B1
P–R5 16 N–B1 N–K5 17 N–B4 P–R4
18 R–B2 (18 Q–R3 P–B4 19 N×NP
N–N4 20 N×B+ Q×N wins) 18 . . .
B–Q1 (18 . . . N–Q1 19 R×P Q×R 20
N×P N×B 21 N×N Q–N2 22 N×B+
Q×N 23 Q×R wins; 20 . . . Q–Q3
21 Q×N N–K3 22 N×B+ Q×N 23
P–Q5 wins) 19 B–K1 N–K2 20 Q–K2
N–Q3 21 P–B3 P–KN4 22 N–Q3
Q–K3 (fixing the KP) 23 P–R4 N–N3
24 P–R3 P–B4 25 B–B3 B–B3 26 R–K1
QR–K1 27 Q–Q1 R–B2 28 P–QN3
KR–K2 29 B–N2 P–B5 (30 P×P Q×R
31 N×Q R×N 32 Q–Q2 N×P with a
winning attack. White has no answer to
the threat of N–B4 and N–N6) (*67*)

30 N–K5 B×N 31 P×B N–B2 (31 . . .
N×P 32 P×P N×P+ 33 Q×N Q×R
34 Q×P+∓) 32 P×P N×BP 33 N–R2
P–B4 34 N–N4 P–Q5 35 N–B6+?
(35 R–K4 N–Q4 and N–R3 wins; 35 B–
B1 P–Q6 36 R–Q2 N–K7+ 37 K–B2
N×P 38 N×N Q×N 39 R×P Q–N6+
40 K–B1 N–B5 wins) 35 . . . Q×N 0–1

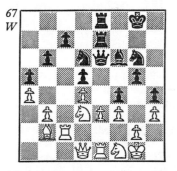

67
W

18) Bronstein-Botvinnik, Slav 1 P–Q4
P–Q4 2 P–QB4 P–QB3 3 N–QB3 N–
B3 4 N–B3 P–K3 5 P–K3 P–QR3 6 B–
Q3 P–QN4 7 P–QN3 QN–Q2 8 0–0
B–N2 9 P–B5! B–K2 (9 . . . P–K4 10
P×P N–N5 11 P–K6 P×P 12 N–Q4
N×QBP 13 Q×N N×B 14 Q×KP+
Q–K2 15 Q–B5+) 10 P–QR3 P–QR4
11 B–N2 0–0 12 Q–B2 P–N3 13 P–
QN4 P×P 14 P×P Q–B2 15 QR–K1
KR–K1 16 N–K2 (16 N–K5 and P–
B4±; 16 . . . N×N 17 P×N Q×P
18 N–K4 wins) 16 . . . B–KB1 17 P–R3
B–N2 18 N–K5 N–B1 19 P–B3 N/3–
Q2 20 P–B4 P–B3 21 N–KB3 R–K2
(21 . . . P–K4 22 BP×P BP×P 23 P–
K4+) 22 N–B3 P–B4 23 R–R1 R/2–K1
24 N–K5 R×R 25 R×R R–R1 26 Q–N1
Q–B1 (*68*)
27 B×NP!! N×N 28 BP×N B–KR3
29 B–QB1 P×B 30 N×NP N–Q2 31
N–Q6 R×R 32 Q×R Q–R1 33 Q–B3
(33 Q–N2±) 33 . . . B–KB1 34 P–N5
B×N 35 KP×B Q–R5 36 Q–N2 (33
Q–N2 now 36 K–R2 K–B2 37 B–Q2
N–B3 38 Q–N4 Q–B7 39 Q–R5 wins)
36 . . . K–B2 37 K–R2 P–R3 38 P–K4

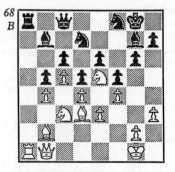

68
B

(38 B–Q2±) 38 ... P–B5 (38 ...
BP×P 39 B×P±; 38 ... QP×P 39
P–Q5!±) 39 P–K5 P–N4 40 Q–K2
K–N2 (69)
41 Q–Q3 (Sealed. 41 P–B6 B×P 42
P×B Q×BP 43 B×P! P×B 44 Q–N4+
K–B2 45 Q×BP+ K–N2 46 Q–N4+
K–B2 47 Q–R4! N–B1 48 Q×P wins)
41 ... N–N1!! 42 P–R4 Q–B5 43 Q–
KR3 Q×NP! (43 ... Q×B 44 P×P

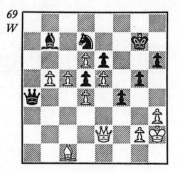

69
W

P×P 45 Q×P Q–K6 46 Q–B6+ K–R2
47 Q×NP Q–KN6+ 48 Q×Q P×Q+
49 K×P±) 44 P×P P P×P 45 Q×P Q–
Q6! 46 Q–B6+ K–R2 47 Q–B7+ K–
R1 48 Q–B6+ K–R2 49 B×P P×B 50
Q–B7+ K–R1 51 Q–K8+ K–N2 52
Q–K7+ K–R1 53 Q–K8+ K–N2 54
Q–K7+ K–R1 55 Q–B8+ K–R2 56
Q–B7+ K–R1 57 Q×B Q–N6+
58 K–R1 ½–½

19) Botvinnik–Bronstein, Grünfeld
1 P–Q4 N–KB3 2 P–QB4 P–KN3 3 P–
KN3 B–N2 4 B–N2 P–Q4 5 P×P
N×P 6 N–KB3 0–0 7 0–0 P–QB4 8 P–
K4 KN–B3 9 P–K5 N–Q4 10 P×P
N–N5 11 N–B3 QN–B3 12 P–QR3
N–Q6 (12 ... N–R3 13 P–QN4 N×KP
14 N×N B×N 15 B–N2±; 12 ...
Q×Q 13 R×Q N–B7 14 R–N1 B–B4
15 N–KR4±) 13 B–K3 B–N5 (13 ...
N×NP 14 Q–K2±) 14 P–KR3 B×N
15 Q×B N/Q6×KP 16 Q–K4 Q–Q6
17 Q–QR4 Q–B5 (17 ... N–B5 18
QR–Q1 N×NP 19 R×Q N×Q 20
N×N±) 18 QR–Q1 QR–Q1 19 B–Q5
Q×Q 20 N×Q P–K3 21 B–R2 (21
B–N2 N–B5 22 B–B1 N–Q5 23 B×P
N–K7+ 24 K–N2 N×B 25 R×N
N×NP∓) 21 ... N–B6+ 22 K–N2
N/B6–Q5 23 P–KN4 P–KR3 24 R–Q2
K–R2 25 P–B4 (25 N–B3 P–B4 26 P–
B3! and KR–Q1±) 25 ... P–B4 26
N–B3 P–K4 27 P×KP B×P 28 N–Q5
P×P 29 P×P R×R 30 K×R R–B1+
31 R–B2 R×R+ 32 B×R P–R3 33 K–
N2 K–N2 34 B–B4 N–K3 35 P–N4
B–N7 (35 ... P–KR4=) 36 P–R4 N–K4
37 B–K2 B–Q5 38 B–N3 P–QR4 39
P×P N×BP 40 N–B7 N–B3 41 P–R6
P×P 42 N×P (70)

70
B

42 ... N–K5 (42 ... N×P 43 B–N5
N–B4 44 N×N B×N 45 B×N B–K6
46 K–B3 B–N4 47 B–B4 B×B 48 K×B
P–N4+ and P–R4=; 46 B–KR4 P–R4
47 P–N5 B–B8=) 43 B–B7 N–B6 44

B–B3 N–K4 45 P–R5 P–R4 (45 . . .
N×B 46 K×B K–B3 and P–R4=) 46
P–N5 N–B5? (46 . . . N×B) 47 N–N4
N–N4 48 B–Q8 K–B1 49 N–B6 B–B4
50 B–K2 N–K6+ 51 K–B3 N–Q5+
52 N×N B×N 53 B–Q3 N–N5 (53 . . .
K–N2 54 B–N6 wins) 54 B×P N–K4+
55 K–K4 N–B3 56 B–N6 B×B 57
P×B P–R5 58 B–B5 K–K2 59 K–B4
K–Q3 60 B–K4 1–0

20) Bronstein-Botvinnik, Reti 1 P–
QB4 P–K3 2 N–KB3 N–KB3 3 P–
KN3 P–QN3 4 B–N2 B–N2 5 0–0
B–K2 6 P–N3 0–0 7 B–N2 P–Q4
8 P×P P×P 9 Q–B2 R–K1 10 P–K3
QN–Q2 11 P–Q3 B–KB1 12 N–B3
P–QR3 13 QR–Q1 P–QN4 14 P–QR4
P–N5 15 N–K2 P–B4 16 N–Q2 (16 P–
Q4 R–B1 17 Q–N1 P–B5∓) 16 . . .
N–K4 17 N–KB4 R–B1 18 Q–N1
P–QR4 19 KR–K1 R–B2 20 P–Q4
N–N3 21 N×N RP×N 22 P×P B×P
23 Q–R1 Q–K2 24 R–QB1 N–N5 25
B–Q4 (25 B×NP P–B3 26 P–R3 N–
K4∓) 25 . . . KR–QB1 26 N–B3
N–B3 27 B–R3 B×B 28 N×B R×R
29 R×R R×R+ 30 Q×R N–K5 31 B–
B8 N–B6 32 B×B Q×B 33 P–B3
K–B1 34 Q–B1 Q–B1 35 K–N2 P–N4
36 P–N4 P–N3 37 Q–K1 Q–K1 38 Q–
Q2 Q–K4 (38 . . . N×P 39 P×N Q×RP
40 Q–B1±) 39 Q–Q3 Q–B3 40 N–B2
K–K2 41 Q–Q4 Q×Q 42 N×Q N–
Q8! 43 N–B2 (43 N–B6+ K–Q3 44
N×RP K–B2∓) 43 . . . N–N7 44 N–
Q4 N–Q8 45 N–B2 N–N7 46 N–Q4
½–½

21) Botvinnik-Bronstein, King's
Indian 1 P–Q4 N–KB3 2 P–QB4 P–Q3
3 N–QB3 P–K4 4 N–B3 QN–Q2 5 P–
KN3 P–KN3 6 B–N2 B–N2 7 0–0 0–0
8 P–K4 P–B3 9 P–KR3 N–R4 10 B–K3
Q–K2 11 N–R2 K–R1 12 R–K1 P–QR3
13 P–R3 (if this is not followed up by
P–QN4 the QN3 square will remain
weak) 13 . . . QR–N1 14 B–KB1 N4–

B3 15 Q–Q2 P–QN4 16 BP×P RP×P
17 QR–Q1 N–N3 18 B–R6 (more
natural is 18 P×P P×P 19 P–QN4
Q–N2 20 N–B3=) 18 . . . B×B 19
Q×B B–K3 20 N–B3 B–N6 21 R–Q2
KN–Q2 22 Q–K3 B–B5 (71)

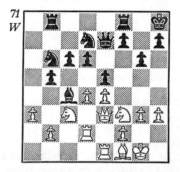

71
W

(Black dominates QB5, QN6∓) 23 B–
N2 P–B3 24 R–B2 B–N6 25 R2–K2
N–B5 26 Q–Q3 N–R4 (26 . . . N/Q2–
N3 27 N–Q5=) 27 R–Q2 N–N3 28
Q–N1 (28 P×P QP×P 29 Q–Q6 Q×Q
30 R×Q N/N3–B5 wins a P) 28 . . .
N/N3–B5 29 R/Q2–K2 P–N5 30
RP×P R×P 31 P–R4 N–N3 32 N–QR2
B×N 33 Q×B N/N3–B5 34 P–R5
KR–QN1 35 RP×P RP×P 36 Q–N1
(36 R–N1 Q–N2 threatening R–R1 and
N–N6) 36 . . . K–N2 37 P×P BP×P
38 Q–B1 N×P 39 Q–B3 N–R5 40 Q–
B1 R–B5 41 Q–N5 Q×Q 42 N×Q
N–N6 43 P–B4 N–Q5 44 R–R2 R–N7
45 R×R N×R 46 K–R2 (46 R–R1 R–
B8+ 47 R×R N–K7+ and wins easily
with the passed QBP) 46 . . . N–Q6 47
R–K3 R–B6 48 B–B1 R–B7+ 49 K–R3
(49 K–N1 N–B8 wins) 49 . . . N–B7+
50 K–R4 R–B8 51 B–N2 R–KN8 52
B–R3 R–KR8 53 P×P P×P 54 R–R3
K–B3 55 N–R7+ (55 R–R7 R×B+ 56
N×R N–B6 mate) 55 . . . K–K2 56 N–
N5 K–Q3 (56 . . . N–K3 wins a piece)
57 N–B7+ K–K2 58 K–N5 K×N 59
R–R7+ K–K1 60 B–Q7+ K–Q1 61
K×P N×P 62 P–N4 R–KB8 (62 . . .
N–QN4 63 R–N7 N–B4 64 B×P N×R

65 B×R with drawing chances) 63 B–
B5 N×B 64 P×N K–K1 0–1

22) Bronstein-Botvinnik, Dutch 1 P–
Q4 P–K3 2 P–QB4 P–KB4 3 P–KN3
N–KB3 4 B–N2 B–K2 5 N–QB3 0–0
6 P–K3 P–Q4 7 KN–K2 P–B3 8 P–
N3 N–K5 9 0–0 N–Q2 10 B–N2
QN–B3 11 Q–Q3 P–KN4 12 P×P
KP×P 13 P–B3 N×N 14 B×N P–N5
15 P×P N×P (15 . . . P×P 16 P–K4±)
16 B–R3! (prevents the N going to B3 or
K5, and threatening B×N and P–K4)
16 . . . N–R3 17 N–B4 B–Q3 18 P–
QN4 P–R3 19 P–R4 Q–K2 20 QR–N1
P–N4 (20 . . . N–B2 21 P–N5 N–N4
22 B–KN2 N–K5 23 P×RP P×P 24
B–R5±) 21 B–KN2 N–N5 22 B–Q2
N–B3 23 R–N2 B–Q2 24 R–R1 N–K5
25 B–K1 KR–K1 26 Q–N3 (threatening
27 P×P RP×P 28 R×R R×R 29
N×P±) 26 . . . K–R1 27 R/N2–R2
Q–B1 28 N–Q3 QR–N1? (better 28 . . .
Q–R3 with a counter-attack on the KP)
29 P×P RP×P 30 R–R7 R–K2 31 N–
K5 B–K1 (31 . . . B×N 32 P×B B–K3
gives a defensible position) (72)

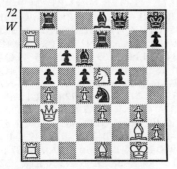

72
W

32 P–N4! P×P 33 B×N P×B 34 B–R4
R×N (34 . . . R×R 35 R×R wins;
34 . . . R–KN2 35 R×R Q×R 36 R–
KB1 B–K2 37 N–B7+ wins; 34 . . .
R/K2–QN2 35 Q–K6 B×N 36 Q×B+
K–N1 37 R×R R×R 38 R–R8 K–B2
39 Q–R5+ wins) 35 P×R B×P 36 R–

KB1 Q–N1 37 B–N3 B–N2 38 Q×Q+
1–0

23) Botvinnik-Bronstein, Grünfeld 1
P–Q4 N–KB3 2 P–QB4 P–KN3 3 P–
KN3 P–B3 4 B–N2 P–Q4 5 P×P P×P
6 N–QB3 B–N2 7 N–R3 B×N 8 B×B
N–B3 9 B–N2 (better 9 0–0) 9 . . . P–K3
10 P–K3 0–0 11 B–Q2 R–B1 12 0–0
N–Q2 13 N–K2 Q–N3 14 B–QB3
(14 Q–N3±) 14 . . . KR–Q1 15 N–B4
N–B3 16 Q–N3 (16 N–Q3 N–K5 17
B–K1 P–K4!∓) 16 . . . N–K5 17 Q×Q
P×Q 18 B–K1 N–R4 19 N–Q3 B–B1
(19 . . . N–B5 20 B–N4 B–B1 21 B×B
K×B 22 KR–B1=; 20 R–Q1 B–
B1∓) 20 P–B3 N–Q3 21 B–B2? (21
R–B2 N/4–B5 22 R–K2 N–B4 23 B–B2
B–R3±) 21 . . . B–R3? (21 . . . R–
B7!∓) 22 QR–B1 N/4–B5 23 KR–K1
N–R4 (23 . . . N–B4 24 P–B4=; 24 P–
KN4 N/4×KP 25 B–R3 N×KNP 26
P×N B×R 27 R×B N–Q7!∓) 24 K–
B1 B–N2 25 P–KN4 N–B3 26 P–N3
N–N4! 27 K–K2 B–B1 28 P–QR4 N–
B2 29 B–N3 N–R3 30 B–B1 P–B3 31
KR–Q1 (31 K–Q2 N–R4! 32 R–B3
R×R 33 K×R R–B1+ 34 K–N2 N–N5
35 N×N B×N∓) 31 . . . N–R4 32
R×R R×R 33 R–B1 R×R 34 N×R
B–R6 35 K–Q1 B×N (better 35 . . . K–
B2) 36 K×B N×P+ 37 K–B2 N–R4
38 K–B3 K–B2 39 P–K4 P–B4 40
NP×P NP×P 41 B–Q3 K–N3 (73)
42 B–Q6? (sealed. It should not win. The
right way is 42 B–N1 BP×P 43 P×P

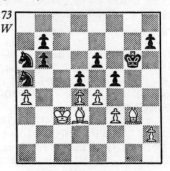

73
W

P×P 44 B×P+ K–N2 45 B×P N×B
46 K–B4±; 42 B–N1 N–B3 43 P×QP
P×P 44 B–R2 N–K2 45 B–R4±)
42... N–B3 43 B–N1 K–B3 (43...
N–R2! 44 P×QP P×P 45 B–R2 P–
N4=) 44 B–N3!! BP×P (44... N/R3–
N5 45 B–K5+!! K–N3 46 B–Q6 N–R3
47 P×QP P×P 48 B–R2±; 45...
N×B 46 P×N+ K×P 47 K×N wins)
45 P×P P–R3 46 B–B4 P–R4 47 P×P
P×P 48 P–R4 N/R3–N1 49 B–N5+
K–B2 50 B–B5 N–R2 (50... N–K2
51 B×N K×B 52 B–N6 N–B3 53
B×P N–R2 is unclear) 51 B–B4 N/1–B3
52 B–Q3 N–B1 53 B–K2 K–N3 54 B–
Q3+ K–B3 55 B–K2 K–N3 56 B–B3
N/3–K2 (56... N/1–K2 57 B–B7 N–B4
58 B×QP N/4×QP 59 B×P wins)
57 B–N5! 1–0 (74)

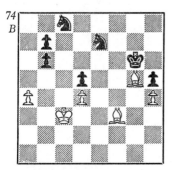

74
B

(Bronstein did not consider 57... N–B3
58 B×QP N–Q3; Smyslov gives 59 B–

B3 K–B4 60 B–B1! P–N4 61 B×N
P×B 62 P–R5 and White should win
anyway.

24) Bronstein-Botvinnik, Slav 1 P–Q4
P–Q4 2 P–QB4 P–QB3 3 N–QB3 N–
B3 4 N–B3 P–K3 5 B–N5 P×P 6 P–
QR4 B–N5 7 P–K4 P–B4 8 B×P P×P
9 N×P P–KR3! 10 B–K3 N×P 11
0–0 N–KB3 (11... N×N 12 P×N
B×P 13 B–N5+ B–Q2 14 N×P -
Black has difficulties) 12 Q–B3 0–0
13 QR–Q1 Q–K2 14 KR–K1 N–B3
15 Q–N3 (15 N×N P×N 16 Q×P
B–N2∓) 15... K–R1 16 N×N P×N
17 B–Q4 R–Q1 18 R–Q3 B–N2 19
KR–K3 (better 19 KR–Q1) 19...
R×B 20 R×R B–B4 21 R–Q1 B×R
22 Q×B ½–½ (75)

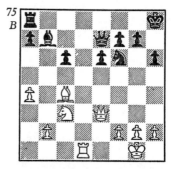

75
B

(Black could force a draw by 22...
N–Q4 23 N×N BP×N 24 B×P B×B
25 R×B R–Q1 or play to win.)

3 Botvinnik–Smyslov

Moscow 16 March–13 May 1954

	1	2	3	4	5	6	7	8	9	10	11	12
Botvinnik	1	1	½	1	½	½	0	½	0	0	0	1
Smyslov	0	0	½	0	½	½	1	½	1	1	1	0

	13	14	15	16	17	18	19	20	21	22	23	24	Total
Botvinnik	1	0	1	1	½	½	½	0	½	½	0	½	12
Smyslov	0	1	0	0	½	½	½	1	½	½	1	½	12

1) Smyslov-Botvinnik, French 1 P–K4
P–K3 2 P–Q4 P–Q4 3 N–QB3 B–N5
4 P–K5 P–QB4 5 P–QR3 B–R4 6 P–
QN4 P×QP 7 N–N5 B–B2 8 P–KB4
N–K2 9 N–KB3 QN–B3 10 B–Q3
B–N1 11 QN×QP P–QR3 12 B–K3
B–R2 13 0–0?! (13 Q–K2 N×N 14
B×N B×B 15 N×B Q–N3 16 Q–
B2±) 13 ... N×N 14 B×N B×B+
15 N×B Q–N3 16 K–R1 B–Q2 17
P–B3 R–QB1 18 Q–K1 P–R3 (76)

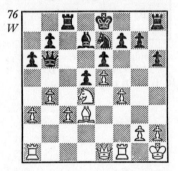

76
W

(18 ... 0–0? 19 Q–R4 N–N3 20 B×N
BP×B 21 R–B3) 19 P–QR4 P–QR4
20 N–N3 Q–B2! 21 N–B5 (21 N×P?
P–QN3! 22 N–N3 Q×BP 23 Q×Q
R×Q 24 N–B1 0–0∓) 21 ... B–B3
22 Q–B2 (22 P–B5 N×P 23 B×N P×B
24 R×P 0–0=) 22 ... 0–0 23 N–N3

B–Q2 24 Q–B5? (24 KR–B1 P–B3
25 Q–N3 unclear) 24 ... Q×Q 25
N×Q R–B2 26 N×B R×N 27 P×P
R–R1 28 P–R6 P×P 29 P–B4 P×P
30 B×P R–Q5! (∓) 31 B–K2 N–Q4
32 P–N3 N–B6 33 B–B3 R–N1 34 R–
R3 N–N8! (34 ... N×P 35 KR–R1
R/1–N5 36 B–Q1 N–B4 37 R–B3=?)
35 R–R2 N–Q7 36 R–KB2 N–B5
37 P–R4 P–N4! 38 RP×P P×P 39 P×P
N×P 40 B–K2 R–N8+?! 41 K–N2
(sealed) 41 ... P–R4 42 R–B2 R–N6
(42 ... R×P 43 R–B5 R–K5! 44 R×RP
R–N6∓) 43 R–KB4? (43 R–QB5!
N–Q6 44 B×N R/5×B 45 R×RP
R×P+ 46 K–R2∓/=) 43 ... R–Q4!
44 R–K4 K–N2 45 B–R5 N–N3 46 R–
KN4 R–K6! 47 B×N K×B 48 R–B2
R–KB4 49 R×R P×R 50 R–QB4
R–K5 51 R–B7 R×P 52 R–R7 R–R6
53 K–R3(?) (53 K–B2 P–R5 54 K–N2
K×P 55 R×BP R–N6 wins) 53 ...
P–B5 54 K–R4 P×P 55 R–R6+ K–B4
56 R–B6+ K–K5 57 K–R3 R–KB6
58 R–QR6 R–B4 0–1

2) Botvinnik-Smyslov, Nimzo-Indian
1 P–Q4 N–KB3 2 P–QB4 P–K3 3 N–
QB3 B–N5 4 P–K3 P–QN3 5 N–K2
B–R3 P–QR3 B–K2 (6 ... B×N+!)
7 N–B4 P–Q4 8 P×P B×B 9 K×B (9

P×P B–R3 10 P×P+ K×P 11 P–K4
P–B4∓) 9 . . . P×P 10 P–KN4! P–B3?
(10 . . . P–KN4 11 N–R5 N×N 12 P×N
P–QB3 13 Q–B3 N–R3 14 P–K4±)
11 P–N5 KN–Q2 12 P–KR4 B–Q3?
(12 . . . 0–0 13 P–K4 P×P 14 N×P
N–B4 15 N×N P×N 16 B–K3±)
13 P–K4! P×P 14 N×P B×N 15 B×B
0–0 16 P–R5 R–K1 (16 . . . N–R3 17
P–R6 P–N3 18 Q–R4!) 17 N–Q6 R–K3
18 P–Q5! R×N (18 . . . P×P 19 Q×P
N–R3 20 N×P! K×N 21 P–N6+
P×P 22 P×P+ K–K2 23 B–Q6+
K–B3 24 Q–B3+ wins) 19 B×R
Q×P (77)

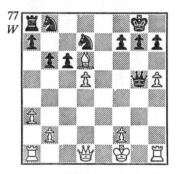

20 Q–B3! Q×QP (20 . . . P×P 21 R–
KN1 Q–R5 22 R–N4 Q–Q1 23 R–B1
wins) 21 Q×Q P×Q 22 R–B1 N–R3
23 P–N4 P–R3 24 R–R3 K–R2 25 R–Q3
N–B3 26 P–N5 N–B4 27 B×N P×B
20 R×BP R–QN1 29 P–R4 R–N2
38 R/Q3-QB3 1–0

3) Smyslov-Botvinnik, French 1 P–K4
P–K3 2 P–Q4 P–Q4 3 N–QB3 B–N5
4 P–K5 P–QB4 5 P–QR3 B–R4 6 P–
QN4 P×QP 7 N–N5 B–B2 8 P–KB4
N–K2 9 N–KB3 B–Q2 10 N/5×QP
QN–B3 11 P–B3! N×N 12 P×N
N–B4 13 B–K2 R–QB1 14 P–QR4!±
P–B3? (14 . . . P–KR4!?; 14 . . . P–OR3
15 0–0 B–N3 16 K–R1 Q–B2) 15 0–0
0–0 16 P–N4! N–K2 17 B–Q3 Q–K1
18 P–QN5 N–N3 19 P–B5! (winning)
19 . . . N–K2 (19 . . . KP×P 20 NP×P

P×P 21 P×N P–K5 22 P×P+ K–R1
23 N–R4 wins) 20 Q–K2 KP×P (78)

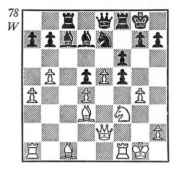

(20 . . . Q–B2 21 KP×P Q×P 22 B–N5
Q–B2 23 QR–K1 wins) 21 P–K6 P×P
22 N–R4! B–N3 23 B–N2 N–N3 24
N×N P×N 25 QR–K1? (25 P×B Q×Q
26 B×Q R–B7 27 P–R5 wins; or 25 P–
R5 B–Q1 26 P×B Q×Q 27 B×Q
R–B7 28 B–R3 R×B 29 B×R K×B
30 KR–K1 wins) 25 . . . P–B4 26 P×B
Q×P 27 Q–K6+? (27 Q–N2! KR–K1
28 P–R3 B–R4 29 R–K5 wins) 27 . . .
Q×Q 28 R×Q K–B2 29 KR–K1 (29
R–K5 KR–K1! 30 R×QP R–K6! 31 B–
N1 R–K7=/±) 29 . . . KR–K1 30
R×R R×R 31 R×R K×R= 32 B–B3
K–Q2 33 P–R5 B–Q1 34 B–N4 P–N3
35 P–R6 B–B3 36 B–B3 K–K3 37 K–
N2 P–N4 38 B–K2 P–N3 39 B–Q1
B–K2 40 B–Q2 B–Q1 41 B–K3 (sealed)
½–½

4) Botvinnik - Smyslov, Queen's
Gambit Accepted 1 P–Q4 P–Q4 2 P–
QB4 P×P 3 N–KB3 P–QR3 4 P–K3
B–N5 5 B×P P–K3 6 Q–N3 B×N 7
P×B P–QN4 8 B–K2 N–Q2 9 P–QR4
P–N5 10 N–Q2 KN–B3 11 N–K4 P–
B4= 12 N×N+ Q×N 13 P–Q5 P–K4
14 P–R5 B–Q3 15 P–K4 0–0 16 B–K3
P–B5!? (16 . . . Q–R5 intending P–KN3,
P–KB4 or 16 . . . KR–B1 intending
N–B1–N3–B5=) 17 Q×BP KR–B1 18
Q–N3 Q–N3 19 K–B1 P–B4 20 R–KN1
Q–R4 21 R–N2! N–B4 22 Q–Q1 (22

Q×P? QR–N1 - 22 . . . N×P?   23 Q–
N7 - 23 Q–R3 P×P 24 P×P Q–R5∓)
22 . . . Q–R5(?) (22 . . . P–B5!) 23 K–
N1 P–B5 (23 . . . P×P? 24 B–N5 Q–R6
25 P×P±) 24 B–Q2 QR–N1 25 K–R1
R–B1 (25 . . . R–B2!?) 26 B–B4 R–B3
(26 . . . Q–R6) 27 Q–KN1 B–B1 28 R–
N4 Q–R4 29 Q–N2 Q–B2 30 P–N3
K–R1 31 R–KN1± R–Q3 32 B–QB1
N–Q2 33 B–N2 R–K1 34 Q–B1 (34 R–
N5 P–N3 35 Q–B1 Q–B3) 34 . . . Q–
R4! 35 Q–N2 (35 B×RP N–B3!) 35 . . .
Q–R3 36 R–N5 P–N3 37 Q–B1 B–N2
38 B–B1 (38 B×RP B–B3 39 R–N4
R–R1 40 B–N5 R×P 41 B×N R×B 42
Q–B4±) 38 . . . B–B3 39 R/5–N4 B–
K2 (39 . . . B–Q1!) 40 B–Q2 N–B3 41
R/4–N2 (sealed) 41 . . . R–Q2 42 B×RP
R–R2 43 B–N5 R–KN1 44 P–R6 P–N4!
45 Q–Q3? (45 P–Q6 B×P 46 B–B4 R/1–
N2 47 Q–Q3 wins; 45 Q–R1 B–Q3 46
B×NP B×B 47 Q×P wins) 45 . . . B–
Q3 46 Q–K2 R/2–KN2 47 Q–Q1 Q–R5
48 B–K2 P–N5   49 B–K1! (49 P×P?
N×KP 50 B–K1 N–N4 51 P–B3 Q–R6
52 Q–Q3 P–K5 wins) 49 . . . P–R4 50
P×P P×P (79)

79
W

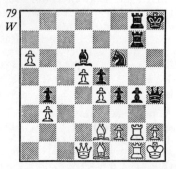

51 B×KNP R×B?! (51 . . . N×B 52
P–B3 Q–R2 53 R×N R×R 54 R×R
R×R 55 P×R Q×KP+ 56 K–N1
B–B4+= or 53 Q–B2 N–K6 54 R×R
R×R 55 Q–B8+ R–N1 56 R×R
wins; 53 P×N Q×KP 54 B–B2! wins)
52 P–B3 R×R (52 . . . R–N6 53 B×R
P×B 54 R×P R–R1 55 Q–B2 wins)

53 B×Q R×R+ 54 Q×R R×Q+
55 K×R N–K1 56 P–R7 N–B2 57 K–
B1 K–N2 58 K–K2 K–B2 59 B–B2
K–K1 60 K–Q3 K–Q2 K–B4 1–0

5) Smyslov-Botvinnik, Slav 1 P–QB4
P–QB3 2 P–Q4 P–Q4 3 N–KB3 N–B3
4 N–B3 P–K3 5 B–N5 P×P 6 P–K4
P–N4 7 P–K5 P–KR3 8 B–R4 P–N4
9 KN×P P×N 10 B×NP QN–Q2
11 P×N B–QN2 12 P–KN3! Q–N3
(12 . . . P–B4? 13 P–Q5 P×P 14
Q–K2+) 13 B–N2 0–0–0 14 0–0
N–K4 (80)

80
W

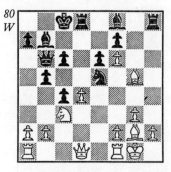

(14 . . . P–B4 15 P×P B×P=) 15
Q–K2!? (15 P×N R×Q 16 R/B1×
R±; 15 B–K3 P–B4 16 P×P B×P
17 QB×B Q×B 18 B×B+±) 15 . . .
Q×P 16 B–K3! Q–Q6 (16 . . . Q–N5
17 P–B3 Q–R4 18 P–KR3±) 17 KR–
Q1! Q×Q 18 R×R+ K×R 19 N×Q
N–Q6! (19 . . . N–N5 20 B×RP N×RP
- 20 . . . N×P/B3 21 P–QR4± - 21
B–N6+ K–B1 22 R–Q1±; 19 . . .
K–B2? 20 B–B4 B–Q3 21 R–Q1 R–Q1
22 R×B!) 20 P–N3 K–B2 21 P×P P×P
22 B×RP= (22 R–N1 B–B4   23
B×B±; 22 N–B3 P–B4 23 R–N1 B×B
24 K×B P–R3 25 N–K4±; 22 N–B3
B–R6!±) 22 . . . P–B4 23 R–N1 B×B
24 B–N8+! (24 K×B? B–Q3) 24 . . .
K–B3 25 K×B B–R3! 26 P–B4 P–K4!
27 P–QR4 (27 K–B3 P×P 28 P×P
B–B1!; 27 P×P? B–Q7 27 B×P N×B
28 P×N R–K1) 27 . . . P×P 28 P×P

(28 P–R5 N–N5!) 28 ... P–B6= 29
N×P B×P 30 B×B N×B+ 31 K–N3
N–R4+ 32 K–N4 N×P+ 33 K–N5
N–Q4 34 N×N K×N 35 P–R4
P–B3+ 36 K–N4 P–B5 37 P–QR5
P–B6 38 P–R6 R–R1 39 K–B5 R×P
40 P–R5 R–R7 41 K×P (sealed) ½–½

6) **Botvinnik-Smyslov,** Grünfeld 1
P–Q4 N–KB3 2 P–QB4 P–KN3 3
N–QB3 P–Q4 4 P×P N×P 5 P–K4
N×N 6 P×N B–N2 7 B–QB4 0–0
8 N–K2 P–N3 9 0–0 (9 P–KR4!±)
9 ... B–N2 10 P–B3 P–B4 11 B–KN5?
(11 B–K3 Q–B2 12 R–B1 N–Q2=)
11 ... P×P 12 P×P N–B3 13 B–Q5!?
(13 P–Q5 N–R4 14 R–B1 N×B∓;
13 B–K3 N–R4∓) 13 ... Q–Q2! 14
Q–Q2 P–K3 15 B×N B×B 16 KR–K1
(16 B–R6? B×B 17 Q×B B–N4∓)
16 ... B–N4 17 QR–Q1 (*81*)

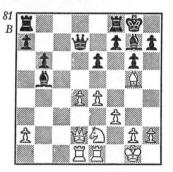

81
B

17 ... QR–B1? (17 ... KR–B1! 18
B–R6 B–R1∓) 18 B–R6! B×B 19
Q×B B×N (19 ... R–B7 20 N–B4
R×P 21 P–K5 B–B3 22 N–R5=)
20 R×B Q–R5 21 R/Q1–Q2 Q–R6
22 K–B2 KR–Q1 23 R–K3= Q–B8
24 R–K1 Q–B6 25 Q–K3 Q–N5 26
R/K1–Q1 R–B6 27 Q–N5 R–Q2 28
P–KR4 Q–K2 29 Q×Q (29 Q–N3
P–KR4=) 29 ... R×Q 30 P–Q5 P×P
31 R×P R–R6 32 R/Q1–Q2 P–KR4
33 R–B2 K–N2 34 R–Q6 ½–½

7) **Smyslov-Botvinnik,** French 1 P–
K4 P–K3 2 P–Q4 P–Q4 3 N–QB3

B–N5 4 P–QR3 B×N+ 5 P×B P×P
6 Q–N4 N–KB3 7 Q×NP R–N1 8
Q–R6 P–B4 9 N–K2 R–N3 10 Q–K3
N–B3 11 P×P (*82*)

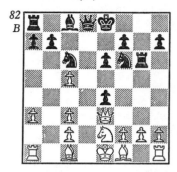

82
B

11 ... N–KN5? (11 ... Q–R4! 12
B–Q2 B–Q2 13 P–QB4 N–KN5!∓)
12 Q×P! Q–Q8+ 13 K×Q N×P+
14 K–K1 N×Q 15 N–B4! R–KN1
(15 ... R–N2 16 N–R5±) 16 B–Q3
(±) N×P/B4 17 B×P R–R1 (17 ...
R–N2?? 18 N–R5 R×P 19 K–B1 wins)
18 B–Q3 N×B+ 19 P×N B–Q2 20
B–K3 0–0–0 21 K–B2 P–K4 22 N–K2!
B–N5 23 P–R3 B–R4 24 P–Q4!
(24 P–N4 B–N3 25 P–Q4 P–B4=;
24 QR–Q1 P–B4=) 24 ... B×N
(24 ... P–B4 25 P×P N×P 26 B–
Q4±) 25 K×B P×P 26 P×P N×P+
27 K–B2 (±) 27 ... P–N3 28 KR–Q1
N–K3 (28 ... N–N6 29 QR–N1 R×R
30 R×R R–Q1 31 R–QN1 N–R4±)
29 QR–B1+ K–N2 20 R×R R×R
31 P–KR4 R–KR1 32 P–N3 P–N4
33 K–B3 P–R4 34 K–K4 (34 B–B2!)
34 ... R–K1! 35 K–B3 R–KR1 36
R–B3 (36 B–B2 P–B4 37 R–K1 R–K1
38 K–N2!±) 36 ... P–B4 37 R–Q3
(37 R–B1! intending B–B2 R–K1–K5)
37 ... K–B3 38 B–Q2 R–R1 39 B–B3
K–B4 40 B–B6 P–N5 41 P–R5!
(sealed) 41 ... R–R2 42 R–K3 K–Q3
43 B–K5+! K–Q4 44 B–N2 K–Q3
45 R–Q3+ K–B4 46 R–Q2 R–R2
(46 ... P×P!) 47 R–R2 K–Q3? (47 ...
K–B5! – unclear) 48 P–R4! (48 P–N4

P×P+   49 K×P K–Q4 50 B–B6! R–
KB2! 51 K–B5 N–B1) 48 . . . K–K2?
(48 . . . K–Q4!) 49 P–N4! P–B5 (49 . . .
P×P+   50 K×P K–Q3 51 K–B5 N–
N2+   52 B×N R×B 53 P–R6 wins)
50 R–Q2 (51 R–Q5 wins) 1–0

8) Botvinnik-Smyslov, Queen's
Gambit Declined 1 P–Q4 P–Q4 2 N–
KB3 B–B4 3 P–B4 P–K3 4 Q–N3
(4 P×P P×P 5 Q–N3 N–QB3 6 B–Q2
R–N1 7 N–B3 N–B3 8 B–N5±) 4 . . .
N–QB3 5 B–Q2 P×P? (5 . . . R–N1 6
P–K3 N–B3 7 N–B3 B–K2=) 6
Q×NP KN–K2 (6 . . . B–K5 7 N–B3
R–N1 8 Q–R6 N–N5 9 Q–R4+ B–B3
10 Q–Q1±) 7 Q–N5! R–QN1 8 Q–R4
R×P 9 N–R3 Q–Q2 10 N×P R–QN1
11 P–K3 N–N5 (11 . . . N–Q4 12 P–
QR3±) 12 Q×Q+ K×Q 13 B×N
R×B 14 N4–K5+ K–K1 15 B–Q3 P–
KB3 16 B×B N×B (16 . . . P×B! 17
N–Q3 R–N3 18 K–K2 N–Q4) 17
N–Q3 R–N3 18 K–K2 B–R6 19 N–
Q2 N–Q3 20 KR–QN1! N–B1 (20
. . . K–Q2? 21 R–N3 R×R 22 P×R
N–N4 23 P–QN4 wins) 21 N–QB4
R×R 22 R×R B–K2 23 R–N8 K–
Q1 (23 . . . K–Q2? 24 N–K5! P×N
25 N×P K–Q1 26 N–B7 wins) 24
P–QR4! R–K1 25 P–R5 K–Q2 26 P–
R6 B–B1 (26 . . . N–N3 or 26 . . . N–Q3
27 N–K5+!) 27 R–N7 B–K2 (27 . . . N–
N3? 28 N×N+ P×N 29 P–R7 R–R1
30 R–N8 wins) 28 N–R5! B–Q3 29 P–
K4 B–B1 30 P–B3 N–N3 31 R×RP
R–N1 32 N–N3 N–R5 33 R–N7 R–
R1 34 P–R7 B–K2 (*83*)
35 K–K3? (35 P–B4 K–B1 36 N–R5 K–
Q2 37 P–K5 N–N3 38 N–B5 B×N 39
P×B N–Q4 40 P–B6+ K–B1 41 N–B4
N×P+   42 K–Q2 P×P 43 N–Q6+
wins) 35 . . . K–B1 36 N–R5 K–Q2 37
P–N3 N–N3 38 N–N3? (38 N–B5+
B×N 39 P×B N–B1 40 P–B6+ K–Q3
41 R–N8 R×P 42 N–B4+ K–B4 43
R×N K×N 44 R–KR8 wins) 38 . . .
K–B1 39 R–N8+ (39 N–R5?? N–B5+

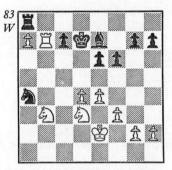

wins; 39 N/3–B5 B×N 40 N×B N–
Q2!=) 39 . . . R×R 40 P×R=Q+
K×Q 41 N/N3–B5 (sealed) (41 N/Q3–
B5 P–K4 42 P–Q5±) 41 . . . P–K4 42
P×P P×P 43 P–B4 N–B5+= 44 K–
B3 P×P 45 P×P P–N3 46 P–K5 P–B3
47 N–N3 K–B2 48 K–K4 K–N3 49
P–B5 P×P+ 50 K×P N–K6+ ½–½
9) Smyslov-Botvinnik, French 1 P–
K4 P–K3 2 P–Q4 P–Q4 3 N–QB3 B–
N5 4 P–K5 P–QB4 5 P–QR3 B–R4 6
P–QN4 P×QP 7 Q–N4 N–K2 8 P×B
P×N 9 Q×NP R–N1 10 Q×RP N–
Q2 (10 . . . QN–B3! 11 P–B4 Q×P 12
N–B3 B–Q2 unclear) 11 N–B3 N–B1 12
Q–Q3 Q×P 13 P–KR4! B–Q2 14 B–
N5 R–B1 (14 . . . N–B3!?) 15 N–Q4!±
N–B4 (15 . . . R–B5 16 Q–K3 N–B4??
17 N×N R–K5 18 N–Q6+) 16 R–
QN1! R–B5 (16 . . . N×N 17 Q×N
P–N3 18 B–Q3; 16 . . . P–N3 17 P–
N4 N×N 18 Q×N Q×P 19 B–Q3±)
17 N×N P×N 18 R×P (*84*)

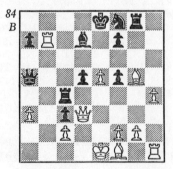

18 ... R–K5+ (18 ... R×B 19 P×R
R–K5+ 20 B–K2 N–N3 21 K–B1 wins)
19 Q×R! QP×Q 20 R–N8+ B–B1 21
B–N5+ Q×B 22 R×Q N–K3 23 B–
B6 R×P 24 P–R5 B–R3 25 P–R6 1–0

10) Botvinnik-Smyslov, Queen's
Gambit Accepted 1 P–Q4 P–Q4 2 P–
QB4 P×P 3 N–KB3 P–QR3 4 P–K3
B–N5 5 B×P P–K3 6 Q–N3 B×N 7
P×B P–QN4 8 B–K2 N–Q2 9 P–QR4
P–N5 (*85*)

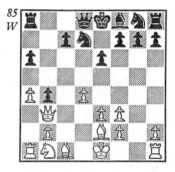

85
W

10 P–B4! KN–B3 (10 ... P–QB4 11
P–Q5!±) 11 B–B3 R–R2 12 B–B6
B–K2 13 N–Q2 0–0 14 N–B4 P–QR4
(14 ... N–N1 15 N–R5 Q–Q3 16
Q–B4±) 15 N–K5 (15 0–0 N–N1 16
B–N2 P–B4 17 P×P B×P 18 Q–B2±)
15 ... N–N1 16 B–Q2 N–Q4! 17
P–K4 (17 P–B5? Q–Q3 18 R–QB1
P–B3 19 P×P P×N 20 B×N P×P 21
P×P P–B3 22 B–QB4 Q×QP∓) 17 ...
N–N3 18 B–K3 B–Q3 19 B–N5 Q–R5!
20 R–QB1 (20 0–0–0 P–QB4 21 P×P
B×P 22 B×B R–B2 23 K–N1 R×B
24 Q–K3±) 20 ... K–R1 21 B–K2?!
(21 B–Q2 22 Q–N3! 21 N–B3 Q–N5
22 K–K2) 21 ... B×N 22 QP×B
N/N1–Q2 23 B–N5 (23 0–0 P–N4!
23 B–B3! and 24 K–K2) 23 ... R–Q1
24 B–Q2? (24 R–Q1; 24 B×N/Q7
R×B 25 B×N P×B 26 Q–N3 Q–Q1∓)
24 ... N×KP! 25 Q–K3 N–N5 (winning) 26 Q–KN3 Q×Q 27 BP×Q N–B7
28 K×N R×B 29 K–K3 R×NP 30

R–QN1 R×R 31 R×R P–QB4 32
R–Q1 R–R1 33 R–Q6 R–QN1 34 K–
Q2 P–B5 35 K–B2 P–N3 36 R–B6
P–B6 37 K–N3 R–QB1 0–1

11) Smyslov-Botvinnik, Ruy Lopez 1
P–K4 P–K4 2 N–KB3 N–QB3 3 B–N5
P–QR3 4 B–R4 N–B3 5 0–0 P–Q3
6 B×N+ P×B 7 P–Q4 P×P?! (7 ...
N–Q2!?; 7 ... N×P!?) 8 N×P P–B4
9 N–KB3 B–K2 10 N–B3 (10 P–K5
N–Q2 11 B–B4 N–N3=) 10 ... 0–0
11 R–K1 B–N2 12 B–N5 P–R3 13
B–R4 (*86*)

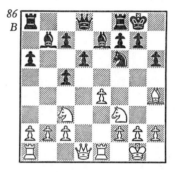

86
B

13 ... R–K1 (13 ... N–Q2!? 14 B×B
Q×B 15 N–Q5±) 14 P–K5! P×P
(14 ... N–Q2 15 B×B R×B 16 N–Q5
B×N 17 Q×B N–N3 18 Q–Q3±)
15 R×P! (15 N×P Q–Q5!) 15 ...
Q×Q+ 16 R×Q B–Q3 17 R×R+
N×R 18 N–Q2± (18 B–N3 B×N 19
RP×B P–B4!; 18 N–Q5 R–N1 19 P–
QN3 P–B5!) 18 ... B–K4 19 N–N3
B×N 20 P×B P–B5 21 N–B5 (21 N–
R5 B–K5 22 R–Q2 R–N1 23 P–B3
B–B4=) 21 ... B–B3 22 R–Q8 P–N4
23 R×R B×R 24 B–N3 P–QR4 25 P–
B3 P–B4 26 B–K5 K–B2? (26 ... P–B5
27 K–B2 K–B2 28 P–N3 P×P 29 P×P
P–R4=) 27 P–B4! N–Q3 28 N–R6
N–K1 (28 ... N–K5! 29 N×P B–B3=
/?) 29 K–B2 B–K5 (29 ... P–N5!?) 30
P–N3 K–N3 31 K–K3 K–R4 32 K–Q4
K–N5 33 K×P K–R6 34 P×P! P×P
35 N×P (35 K–N5? N–Q3+!) 35 ...

N×N 36 B×N K×P 37 K–N5 K–R6?
(37 . . . B×P!? 38 K×P K–R6 39 P–B4
K–N5! 40 K–N5 - 40 P–B5 P–B5 41
P×P P×P 42 P–B6 B–K5 43 K–N5
B–Q6+!!= - 40 . . . P–B5 41 P×P
P×P 42 P–R4 P–B6 43 B–N6 K–N6
44 P–R5 wins) 38 P–B4 K–N5 39 P–
B5 P–B5 40 P×P P×P 41 B×RP
K–B4 (sealed) 1–0

12) Botvinnik-Smyslov, Slav 1 P–Q4
P–Q4 2 P–QB4 P–QB3 3 N–KB3
N–B3 4 N–B3 P×P 5 P–QR4 B–B4
6 P–K3 P–K3 7 B×P B–QN5 8 0–0
QN–Q2 9 N–R4 (9 Q–K2±) 9 . . .
0–0 (9 . . . B–N5!? 10 P–B3 B–KR4
unclear) 10 P–B3! B–N3 11 P–K4 P–K4
12 N×B (12 B–K3? N–N5!; 12 P×P!
N×P/K4 13 B–K2±) 12 . . . RP×N
13 B–K3 Q–K2 (13 . . . Q–N3! 14
R–K1 P×P 15 Q×P B–B4 16 Q–Q2
QR–Q1=) 14 Q–K2 P×P 15 B×P
B–B4 16 B×B Q×B 17 K–R1 P–KN4!?
(87)

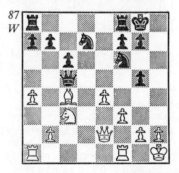

87
W

(17 . . . QR–Q1)　18 P–KN3! QR–Q1
(18 . . . N–K4 19 B–R2 P–N5 20 P–B4
N–B6 21 P–K5 N–Q4 22 N×N P×N
23 P–R3±) 19 B–R2 KR–K1 20 QR–
Q1 N–B1　21 R×R R×R　22 P–K5
N–Q4　23 N×N (23 N–K4 Q–K6!)
23 . . . P×N 24 Q–Q2 N–K3 25 P–B4
P×P　26 P×P Q–B3?! (26 . . . Q–Q5
27 Q×Q N×Q　28 R–Q1 N–K3±)
27 P–B5 N–B4　28 Q–N5 R–Q2?
(28 . . . P–B3! 29 Q–N2±) 29 R–KN1!

P–B3 30 P×P N–K5 30 P×P N–K5
31 P–B7+! R×P　32 Q–Q8+ K–R2
(32 . . . R–B1　33 B×P+ K–R2　34
R×P+ K×R　35 Q–K7+ wins) 33
B×P N–B7+ 34 K–N2 Q–B3 35 Q×Q
R×Q 36 K×N R×P+ 37 B–B3 R–B5
38 R–N4 1–0

13) Smyslov-Botvinnik, Sicilian 1
P–K4 P–QB4　2 N–QB3 N–QB3　3
P–KN3 P–KN3 4 B–N2 B–N2 5 P–Q3
P–N3 (5 . . . P–K3 6 . . . KN–K2=)　6
KN–K2 P–Q3　7 0–0 B–N2　8 P–B4
(8 B–K3!? N–Q5　9 B×N P×B　10
N–N5 P–K4 11 P–QR4) 8 . . . P–B4!
9 P–KN4?! (9 P×P P×P　10 B–K3
N–B3 11 P–KR3 0–0 12 P–Q4 Q–Q2=)
9 . . . P×NP 10 P–B5 Q–Q2 11 N–B4
(11 N–Q5! N–Q5 unclear) 11 . . . P×P
12 P×P (12 N/B3–Q5 N–Q5 13 P–B3
P–K4　14 N–R5 N–B6+　15 B×N
P×B　16 Q×P P–KB5±) 12 . . . B–
Q5+! 13 K–R1 B×N! (88)

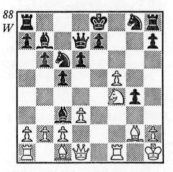

88
W

14 P×B N–K4　15 Q–K2 N–KB3　16
B×B Q×B+　17 Q–N2 Q×Q+　18
K×Q P–B5! 19 B–K3 N–B6 20 B–Q4
N×B　21 P×N R–QB1 22 R–B2 P×P
23 P×P (23 N×P R–B5! wins) 23 . . .
K–B2　24 R–K1 KR–Q1　25 N–K6
R–Q2　26 R/K1–K2 R–N2　27 K–N3
R–KN1 28 K–R4 P–KR3 29 R–KN2?!
R/N2–N1　30 R–QB2 R/QN1–QB1
31 P–R4 R×R　32 R×R N–Q4! 33
R–B2 K–B3 34 K–N3 P–KR4 (winning)
35 K–R4 N–K6! 36 P–Q5 N×P+ 37

K×P P–R3 38 R–QN2 N–K6 39 R–B2
N–B4 40 R–QN2 P–N4 41 P×P P×P
(sealed) (42 R×P P–N6! 43 P×P N–K6
and 44... R–R1; 42 P–Q4 P–N5 43
R–KB2 P–QN6 44 R–QN2 P–N6 45
P×P N×P+ 46 K–R4 N–B4+ 47
K–R5 R–R1+ wins) 0–1

14) Botvinnik-Smyslov, King's Indian
1 P–Q4 N–KB3 2 P–QB4 P–KN3 3 P–
KN3 B–N2 4 B–N2 0–0 5 N–QB3
P–Q3 6 N–B3 QN–Q2 7 0–0 P–K4
8 P–K4 P–B3 9 B–K3(?) (9 P–KR3!)
9... N–N5 10 B–N5 Q–N3! (10...
P–B3 11 B–B1 P–KB4 12 B–N5±)
11 P–KR3 P×P! (11... KN–B3 12
Q–Q2 P×P 13 N×P N–B4 14 QR–Q1
R–K1 15 KR–K1 KN–Q2 16 B–K3±)
12 N–QR4 Q–R3 13 P×N P–N4 14
N×P (14 B–K7 R–K1 15 B×P P×N
16 N×P N–K4∓; 14 P×P P×P 15
N×P P×N 16 P–K5 B–N2 17 B×B
Q×B 18 P×P Q×P∓ 14 P–B5 P×N
15 B–K7 P×P∓) 14... P×N 15 N×P
(15 P–N3 N–K4 16 P–B3 P–Q4!∓)
15... Q×N 16 P–K5 Q×P 17 B×R
N×P 18 R–B1 (18 B–N2 B–K3 19
Q×QP Q×NP 20 B–B4 N–B6+ 21
B×N Q×KB 22 Q–Q1 Q–N2∓)
18... Q–N5! (18... Q–N4 19 B–K7
B×P 20 Q–Q5!) 19 P–R3! (19 B–N2
B–QR3 20 R–K1 N–Q6∓) 19...
Q×QNP 20 Q×RP B–N2! (*89*)

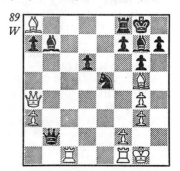

89
W

21 R–N1? (21 B×B Q× B 22 R–B3
N–B6+ 23 R×N Q×R 24 B–K7=)

21... N–B6+ 22 K–R1 B×B (22...
N–Q7+? 23 B×B N×R/N8 24 B–
QB6=; Q×R?? 23 R×Q B×B 24
B–K7 N–Q7+ 25 K–N1 N×R 26
B×R B×B 27 Q–N4 wins) 23 R×Q
N×B+ 24 K–R2 N–B6+ 25 K–R3
B×R (winning) 26 Q×P B–K5! 27
P–R4 K–N2 28 R–Q1 B–K4 29 Q–K7
R–B1! 30 P–R5 (30 R×P? R–B8)
30... R–B7 31 K–N2 N–Q5 32 K–B1
B–B6 33 R–N1 N–B3 0–1

15) Smyslov-Botvinnik, Sicilian 1
P–K4 P–QB4 2 N–QB3 N–QB3 3 P–
KN3 P–KN3 4 B–N2 B–N2 5 P–Q3
P–Q3 6 KN–K2 P–K4! 7 N–Q5 (7 0–0
KN–K2 8 P–B4 0–0 9... P–B4=)
7... KN–K2 8 P–QB3?! (8 B–N5!?;
8 N/K2–B3!?) 8... N×N 9 P×N
N–K2 10 0–0 (10 P–Q4 BP×P 11 P×P
P×P 12 N×P 0–0!∓) 10... 0–0 11
P–KB4 (11 P–Q4 KP×P 12 P×P P–
B5∓) 11... B–Q2 12 P–KR3? (12
P×P P×P 13 B–N5!?) 12... Q–B2
13 B–K3 (13 P×P P×P 14 B–N5 P–B3
15 B–K3 N–B4 16 B–B2 N–Q3∓)
13... QR–K1 14 Q–Q2? (14 B–B2!?)
14... N–B4 15 B–B2 P–KR4∓ 16
QR–K1 (16 P–KN4) 16... Q–Q1!
(16... B–R3? 17 P–KN4 RP×P 18
RP×P N–K2 19 P–N5 B–N2 20 N–
N3=) 17 K–R2 B–R3 18 P–KR4 (*90*)

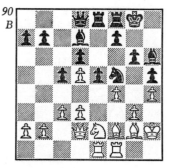

90
B

(18 P–KN4 RP×P 19 RP×P N–R5
20 P–N5 N×B 21 K×N P×P 22 P×B
Q–N4+ 23 K–R2 Q–R4 + 24 K–N1

Q–N5+ 25 K–R2 R×N 26 R×R P–B6
wins) 18 . . . Q–B3! 19 B–K4 P×P
20 N×P N×RP 21 B–K3 N–B4 22
B×N (22 N×RP P×N 23 B×N – 23
B×B Q×B! – 23 . . . B×QB 24 R×B
Q–N4!! – not 24 . . . B×B 25 R/K3–
B3 R–K4 26 P–Q4 P×P 27 P×P R×P
28 Q–KB2) 22 . . . Q×B 23 Q–N2
(23 N–K6 B×B! 24 Q×B Q×P/Q4
wins) 23 . . . Q–N5 (winning) 24 Q–
K2 Q×Q+ 25 R×Q R–K4 26 R/K2–
K1 KR–K1 27 B–B2 (27 B–Q2 B×N
28 P×B R–K7+ wins) 27 . . . P–R5 28
R×R R R×R 29 P–Q4 P×P+ 30 K×P
R–N4+ 31 K–R2 R–B4 32 B–K3 P×P
33 P×P K–R2 34 R–B2 P–KN4 35
N–K2 R×R+ 36 B×R P–B4 0–1

16) Botvinnik–Smyslov, King's Indian
1 P–Q4 N–KB3 2 P–QB4 P–KN3 3 P–
KN3 B–N2 4 B–N2 0–0 5 N–QB3 P–
Q3 6 P–K3 QN–Q2 7 KN–K2 P–K4
8 P–N3 R–K1 9 B–QR3 R–N1!?
(9 . . . P–KR4!? 9 . . . P–K5 10 Q–B2
Q–K2 11 P–KN4±) 10 0–0 P–QR3
11 P×P N×P (11 . . . P×P!) 12 P–B5!±
P×P 13 B×BP P–N3? (13 . . . Q×Q
14 QR×Q P–N3 15 B–Q4 P–B4 16
B×N R R×B 17 P–K4±; 13 . . . N/K4–
Q2 14 B–R7 R–R1 15 B–Q4 P–B4 16
B×N N×B 17 R–B1±) 14 Q×Q
R×Q 15 B–Q4 R–K1 (91)

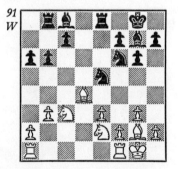

91
W

16 P–K4! B–N2 (16 . . . N–B3 17
B–K3 B–N2 18 B–B4±) 17 P–B4
N/K4–N5 (17 . . . N–B3 18 B×N B×B

19 P–K5 and 20 N–Q5±) 18 P–KR3!
P–B4 19 B×N N×B 20 P–K5 B×B
21 K×B N–Q2 22 QR–Q1 N–B1
23 R–Q6 N–K3 (23 . . . R–K3 24 KR–
Q1 P–B3 25 R×R N×R 26 R–Q6
K–B2 27 P×P B×P 28 R–Q7+ K–N1
29 N–Q5 wins) 24 N–K4! KR–Q1 25
KR–Q1 B–B1 26 R×R R×R 27 R×R
N×R 28 N–B6+ K–N2 29 N–Q5
(29 K–B3–K4!?; 29 N–K8+ K–N1 30
N–B7) 29 . . . P–QN4 30 N–B7 P–N4
31 K–B3 P×P 32 P×P P–B5 33 P×P
P×P 34 N×P P–B3 35 N–B7 P×P
36 P×P K–N3 37 K–K4 K–N4 38
P–QR4 K–R5 39 P–R5 N–B3 40 P–
R6 K×P 41 N–N5 (sealed) 41 . . .
P–B6 42 N/N5×P K–N5 43 N–Q4
N–R2 44 N–Q5 P–R4 45 N–B6+ 1–0

17) Smyslov–Botvinnik, King's Indian
1 N–KB3 N–KB3 2 P–KN3 P–KN3
3 B–N2 B–N2 4 0–0 0–0 5 P–Q3
P–B4 6 P–K4 N–B3 7 P–B3 P–Q4 8
P–K5?! (8 QN–Q2) 8 . . . N–K1 9
P–Q4 B–N5! 10 P–KR3 B×N 11
B×B P–K3 12 B–K3 (12 B–N2 P×P
13 P×P Q–N3∓) 12 . . . P×P 13 P×P
P–B3 14 B–N4! (14 P×P B×P 15
N–B3 N–Q3∓) 14 . . . P×P 15 P×P!
(15 B×P+ K–R1 16 P×P N–B2 17
B–N4 P–Q5 18 B–Q2 N×P) 15 . . .
P–Q5 16 B–Q2! (16 B×P+ K–R1
17 B–KB4 N–B2 18 B–N3 N–Q4∓)
16 . . . N×P 17 B×P+ K–R1 18 B–
KB4! N–QB2 19 B–N3 N–B3 20
Q–N4! N–Q4 (20 . . . N–R4 21 N–Q2
N×B 22 N×N; 20 . . . R–B4!?) 21
B–N5 Q–R4 22 N–Q2! (92)
22 . . . N–K6! 23 P×N Q×N 24 R×R+
R×R 25 R–KB1 R×R+ (25 . . . R–
QN1 26 Q–Q7 P×P – 26 . . . N–K4
27 Q–K7 P×P 28 B–B6 N–B6+ – 27
Q×B K×Q 28 R–B7+=) 26 K×R
Q–B8 27 K–N2 (27 K–K2? N–K4 28
Q–K6 P–Q6+ wins) 27 . . . Q–Q7+
28 K–B1 Q–B8+ 29 K–N2 Q×P+
30 K–B1 Q–B8+ 31 K–N2 (31 . . .
Q–N7+ 32 K–B1 Q–R6 33 Q–B8+

Q–B1+ 34 Q×Q B×Q 35 P×P N×P
36 B–B6+ B–N2 37 B×N B×B=)
½–½

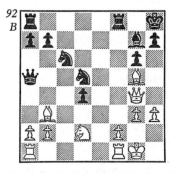

92
B

18) Botvinnik–Smyslov, King's Indian
1 P–Q4 N–KB3 2 P–QB4 P–KN3 3
P–KN3 B–N2 4 B–N2 0–0 5 N–QB3
P–Q3 6 P–K3 QN–Q2 7 KN–K2 P–
QR3?; 8 P–N3 R–N1 9 P–QR4 P–K4
10 B–QR3 (10 P–R5!±) 10 . . . P–N3!
11 0–0 B–N2 12 P–Q5 (12 P×P N×P
13 P–K4 P- QR4=?) 12 . . . P–QR4 13
P–K4 N–B4 (13 . . . N–R4   14 P–
QN4±) 14 Q–B2 (14 P–QN4 P×P
15 B×P B–QR3!=)   14 . . . P–R4!?
15 QR–K1 P–R5 (15 . . . N–R2 16 P–B4
P×P 17 P×P P–B4 18 P×P P×P 19
N–N5±) 16 B–B1 B–B1 17 N–N5
(17 P–B4? RP×P 18 RP×P P×P 19
P×P N–N5 intending 20 . . . Q–R5∓)
17 . . . B–Q2 18 B–N5! P–R6 19 B–R1
B×N   20 BP×B Q–Q2   21 B×N!
B×B   22 N–B1 B–N2   23 N–Q3
P–B4 24 N×N QP×N   25 B–B3!
Q–Q3 26 P–KN4 P–B5 (26 . . . P×NP!?
B×P B–R3 intending B–B5, K–N2,
R–KR1) 27 P–N5! (*93*)
K–B2 (27 . . . Q–K2   28 K–R1 Q×P
29 R–KN1±) 28 K–R1 K–K2 29 R–
KN1 R–KR1 30 R–Q1! R–R5 31 R–
Q3 Q–Q2 32 Q–K2 (32 P–Q6+!?)
32 . . . R/N1–KR1 (32 . . . K–Q3!) 33
B–N4 Q–Q3 (33 . . . Q–Q1? 34 P–
Q6+ P×P 35 R/1–Q1±) 34 Q–B1
B–B1 35 R–KB3 (35 R×P R×R 36
B×R P–B5! 37 P×P Q–R6=) 35 . . .

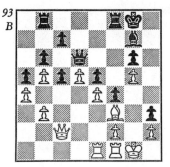

93
B

K–Q1 36 Q–Q3 B–K2 37 B–K6 R/R1–
R4 38 R×RP R×R (38 . . . R×P? 39
B–N4!! R/N4×B 40 R×RN4 R×R/N5
41 R–R8+ B–B1 42 Q–R3 R–N4 43
Q–R6 or 43 Q–R4 wins) 39 B×R P–B5!
(39 . . . R×P? 40 B–N4 41 P–R4 wins
39 . . . B×P? 40 Q–KB3 B–R3 41 Q–
N4 wins) 40 P×P Q–R6 (40 . . . Q–
N5!?) 41 Q×Q (sealed) B×Q 42 B–
B5! (42 B–N4 R–R1 43 K–N2 B–K2
44 R–Q1 R–R5=) 42 . . . P×B 43 P–
N6 (43 P×P K–K2 44 P–B3! K–B2
45 R–N4 B–K2! 46 P–R4 B×P!=!?)
43 . . . B–B1 (43 . . . R–R1? 44 P–N7
R–N1 45 P–R4 B–K2 46 P–R5 B–B3
47 P–R6 K–K2 48 R–N6 wins) 44
P×P B–N2! 45 P–B6 B×P 46 P–N7
B×P 47 R×B P–B6! 48 R–N4 R–R6!
49 R–N3 (49 R–K4 K–Q2 50 R×P
R–R5!) 49 . . . R–R5 50 R×P R×P
51 R–QR3 K–Q2 52 K–N2 K–Q3 53
K–N3 K×P 54 P–R3! K–K3 55 K–B3
K–B4 56 K–N3 K–N4 57 K–B3 R–B5
58 K–N3 ½–½

19) Smyslov–Botvinnik, French 1
P–K4 P–K3 2 P–Q4 P–Q4 3 N–QB3
B–N5 4 P–QR3 B×N 5 P×B P×P
6 Q–N4 N–KB3 7 Q×NP R–N1 8
Q–R6 P–B4 9 N–K2 N–B3 10 P×P
R–N3 11 Q–Q2! B–Q2 12 R–QN1!
Q–B2 (12 . . . Q–R4 13 N–B4! R–KN1
14 R×P 0–0–0 15 R–N5±) 13 Q–Q6
(13 N–Q4 P–QR3   14 P–N3 P–K4!)
13 . . . 0–0–0 (14 . . . Q–R4   15 . . . B–
K1) 14 Q×Q+ K×Q (*94*)

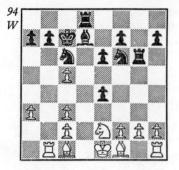

94
W

15 N–Q4 (15 N–N3! 16 B–K2 17
0–0) 15 . . . P–QR3 16 B–B4+ K–B1 17
P–N3 (17 N×N B×N 18 P–B4± 17
B×P? P×B 18 R–N6 N–Q4! 19 N×N
N×B 20 N×R N×P 21 K–Q2 K×N∓)
17 . . . N–Q4 18 B–Q2 P–K4 19 N–N3
(19 N×N B×N 20 B–R3 K–N1 21
B–B5 P–K6! 22 P×P N×KP 23 B×N
B×R 24 B×R RP×B∓) 19 . . . B–
N5∓ 20 B–N2 P–B4 (20 . . . B–B6
21 B–R3+! and 22 0–0) 21 0–0 B–B6
22 B–R3 R–B1 23 KR–K1 K–B2?
(23 . . . P–KR4! 24 P–B4 N–B5 25
B×N P×B 26 N–Q2 P–R5∓) 24
B–N2 P–KR4 (24 . . . B×B! 25 K×B
P–KR4∓) 25 P–B4! N–B5 (25 . . .
N/Q4–K2 26 N–R5 N×N 27 B×N+
K–B1 28 B×B±) 26 B×B (26 N–R5?
N×B 27 R×P+ K–B1 28 KR–N1
P–K6! wins) 26 . . . P×B 27 B×N P×B
28 N–Q2 (28 P–B3 R–Q1! 29 N–Q4
N×N 30 P×N R×QP 31 R–K7+
K–B3!) 28 . . . P×P 29 N×P! (29
RP×P? P–R5) 29 . . . P×RP+ 30 K×P
R/B1–KN1 (30 . . . R–N5 31 K–R3
R×P 32 N–N5!) 31 K–R3 (31 R–N1
R–N5 32 K–R3? N–K4!) 31 . . . R–
N5 (31 . . . R–N7 32 R–K2 R/N1–
N6+ 33 P×R R×R 34 N–R4!)
32 R–K6! R×P 33 R–B6 R–N2 34
R×BP R×P/B7 (34 . . . N–Q5=) 35
N–N5 R–K2 36 K–R4 N–Q5 37 R–
B4 N–N4 38 P–R4 N–B6 39 R–B4
R/K2–K7 40 R–N6 N–Q4 41 R×R
(sealed) (41 . . . R×R 42 N–K6+ K–Q2!

43 R–Q6 K–K2   44 R×N K×N   45
R–Q6+=) ½–½

20) Botvinnik–Smyslov, King's Indian
1 P–Q4 N–KB3 2 P–QB4 P–KN3 3
P–KN3 B–N2 4 B–N2 0–0 5 N–QB3
P–Q3 6 P–K3 QN–Q2 7 KN–K2 P–K4
8 P–N3 R–K1 9 B–QR3 P–KR4!?
10 P–R3 P–R3 11 P×P P×P 12 P–K4?
(12 N–K4!?; 12 Q–B2 intending 13
R–Q1) 12 . . . N–R2 13 0–0 P–R5 14
B–QB1 (14 P–KN4 KN–B1–K3∓)
14 . . . P–QB3 15 B–K3 P×P 16 P×P
Q–K2 17 Q–Q2 P–QN4 18 QR–Q1?
(18 P×P RP×P 19 P–QR4! P–N5 20
N–Q1 B–QR3 21 N–N2) 18 . . .
P×P 19 P×P Q–N5! 20 R–B1? (20
R–N1! Q×P 21 KR–B1 Q–K3 22
N–R4 unclear) 20 . . . B–B1 21 K–R2
N–B4 22 N–QN1 P–R4! 23 Q–B2
B–K3 24 KR–Q1 KR–N1 25 B–B1
P–R5 26 B–Q2 Q–N3 27 B–K3 P–R6!
28 N/K2–B3 Q–R4 29 Q–B2 B–K2
30 R–B2 N–B3 31 N–Q2 R–N7 32
R/Q1–B1 R–Q1 (intending 33 . . .
N–Q6; 32 . . . K–N2! and 33 . . . R–
KR1∓) 33 B×N (95)

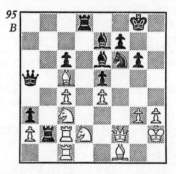

95
B

33 . . . Q×B? (33 . . . B×B! 34 Q×N–
34 Q–K2 Q×N! 35 R×Q R/Q1×N –
34 . . . R×N+ 35 R×R R×R+ 36
B–N2 B–Q5 wins) 34 Q–K2 (34 Q×Q?
R×N+) 34 . . . Q–N5 35 N–N3 R×R
36 R×R N–K1 (36 . . . N–Q2!? 36 . . .
K–N2 and 37 . . . R–KR1) 37 N–N1
N–Q3 38 N/N1–Q2 N–N2 39 P–R4

N–B4 40 N×N (40 B–R3! B×B 41 K×B N–Q6 42 N–B3 unclear) 40... Q×N 41 N–N3 (sealed) Q–Q3 (41... Q–R2 42 B–R3 B×B 43 K×B B–N5! 44 R–B1! Q–Q2+ 45 K–N2 Q–Q6 46 Q–N4!) 42 R–Q2 (42 B–R3 B×B 43 K×B Q–Q2+ 44 K–N2 B–N5∓) 42...Q–N5 43 R–B2 P–B3 44 B–R3 B–B2 45 B–N4 K–N2 46 K–N2 Q–Q3! 47 R–Q2 Q–N1 48 R–B2 B–N5 49 P–R5 Q–Q3 50 P×P B×NP 51 B–R5 Q–Q6? (51...B×B 52 Q×B Q–Q8! 53 R–K2 R–KR1 54 Q–N4+ K–B2 wins) 52 B×B Q×Q+ 53 R×Q K×B 54 R–KB2! K–B2 55 R–B1 K–K3 56 R–B3 B–K2 57 R–B1 B–N5 58 R–B3 K-K2 59 R–B1 K–B2 60 R–B3 K–N3 61 R–B2 R–Q3 62 R–B5 B–Q7 (62...B–B6–Q5 and P–QB4, R–N3–N5×N wins) 63 R–B3 B–N4 64 P–B5 R–Q2 65 R–B3? (65 N–R5 R–Q7+ 66 R–B2 R–N7 67 K–B3 B–Q7 68 N–B4 B–B8 69 R–K2 unclear) 65...P–B4 66 K–B3 K–B3! 67 P×P (67 N–R5 P×P+ 68 K×P R–Q5+ 69 K–B3 P–K5+ 70 K–B2 R–Q7+ wins) 67...K×P 68 P–N4 K–K3 69 K–K2 (69 N–R5 R–Q7 70 R×P - 70 N×P R×P 71 N–N4 R–R7 72 K–K4 P–R7 73 R–QR3 R–K7 and 74...R–K6+ wins - 70... K–Q4 71 N–N3 P–K5+ 72 K–N3 R–QB7 73 R–R8 P–K6 wins) 69... P–K5 70 R–B4 K–K4 71 R–R4 R–KR2 72 R×P R–R7+ (73 K–Q1 P–K6 74 N–B1 R–R8+ 75 K–B2 R×N+! wins) 0–1

21) Smyslov-Botvinnik, French 1 P–K4 P–K3 2 P–Q4 P–Q4 3 N–QB3 B–N5 4 P–QR3 B×N+ 5 P×B P×P 6 Q–N4 N–KB3 7 Q×NP R–N1 8 Q–R6 P–B4 9 N–K2 R–N3 10 Q–Q2 QN–Q2! 11 B–N2 P–N3 (11... Q–B2!) 12 P–R3 (12 N–B4 R–KN1 13 B–N5 B–N2 - 13...Q–B2! - 14 P×P P×P 15 P–QB4±) 12...B–N2 13 R–KN1 Q–B2 14 0–0–0 0–0–0 (14...

P×P!? 15 P×P N–Q4 16 P–N4 R–B1=) 15 Q–B4 Q–B3 (15...P–K4 16 P×KP N×P 17 Q–B5+±) 16 P–N4 (16 P–B4! Q–B2 17 Q×Q K×Q 18 P–QB3±/=) 16...N–Q4! 17 Q×KP (17 Q×BP N/Q2–B3 18 P–QB4 R–Q2 19 P×N Q×P 20 N–B4? Q–N4!) 17...Q–R5 *(96)*

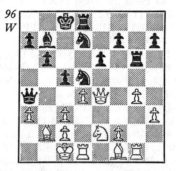

96
W

18 B–N2 (18 P–QB4? N–N5 19 P–Q5 B×P 20 R×B N×R 21 B–N2 N/Q2–B3 22 B×N R×B 23 P×N Q×RP+ 24 K–N1 P×P wins) 18...P–B4 19 Q–Q3 (19 NP×P? R×B!) 19... P–QB5 20 Q–N3 (20 Q–Q2! N/Q2–B3 – 20...P×P 21 P×P R×P? 22 B×N wins - 21 P×P P×P 22 N–B4±) 20...N/Q2–B3 21 N–B4 N×N 22 B×B+ K×B 23 Q×N N–Q4 24 Q–B3 R–KB1 25 QR–K1 Q–K1! 26 P–N5 (26 P×P R×R 27 R×R R×P 28 R–N7+ K–R3 29 Q–K2 Q–B3 30 R×KRP N–B3 31 R–K7 R×P!! wins) 26...P–KR3 27 P–KR4 P×P 28 R×NP! R×R 29 P×R R–N1 30 Q–K2 (30 K–Q1 Q–B3 31 Q–R5 K–R3! – intending 32 ... N–B5 – 32 Q–B7? R×P 33 R×P R–N8+ 34 K–Q2 Q–N4 wins; 31 B–B1 – unclear: 30...R×P?? 31 Q×N) 30...Q–B3 31 Q×KP Q×Q 32 R×Q R×P 33 R–K5 K–B3 34 K–Q2 P–R4 (34...P–N4=) 35 P–R4 R–R4 36 R–K6+ (36 K–K2 R–R8 37 R×P R–QN8 38 B–R3 R–QR8 39 B–B8 N×P 40 K–Q2 N–Q4∓; 36 B–R3 R–R6∓) 36...

K–B2 37 R–K5 K–B3 38 R–K6 K–B2
39 R–K5 K–B3 40 R–K6+ ½–½

22) **Botvinnik-Smyslov,** Grünfeld 1
P–QB4 N–KB3 2 P–Q4 P–KN3 3
N–QB3 P–Q4 4 B–B4 B–N2 5 P–
K3 0–0 6 B–K5?! P–K3! (6 . . . P×P!?
7 KB×P N–B3) 7 N–B3 QN–Q2 8
B–N3 P–B3 9 B–Q3 P–N3 10 0–0
B–N2 11 Q–K2 Q–K2 12 KR–Q1
(12 P–KR3 P–B4!=; 12 P–K4 P×KP
13 N×P N×N 14 B×N N–B3 15
B–B2 N–R4 16 B–R4 Q–B2 and 17 . . .
P–B4∓) 12 . . . N–R4! 13 B–R4
Q–Q3 14 P–KN4!? KN–B3 15 B–N3
Q–K2 16 P–KR3 (16 N–K5!?) 16 . . .
P–B4 17 BP×P N×P 18 N×N P×N!
(18 . . . B×N 19 P–K4 B–QB3 20
B–N5) 19 B–R6 B×B 20 Q×B P×P!
(20 . . . P–B5 21 Q–N7! Q–K3 22 N–
N5) 21 P×P (21 N×P N–B4 22 Q–
N5 N–K5∓) 21 . . . N–B3 22 QR–B1
P–R4 (22 . . . N–K5!? 23 R–B7 Q–B3)
23 R–B7 Q–N5 (23 . . . Q–K5? 24 N–
N5 Q–K1 25 Q–N7!) 24 P–N5 N–K5
25 Q–R3 Q–N4 (25 . . . P–R4 26
B–K5±) 26 Q–N3 Q–K1 27 Q–K3?
(27 Q×QP!? N×B 28 P×N Q–K6+
29 K–B1! QR–K1 30 R–B2±/?) 27 . . .
R–B1? (97)

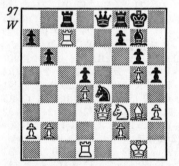

(27 . . . N×B 28 Q×Q KR×Q 29 P×N
R–K7 30 R–KB1 R×P 31 N–K5
B×N∓) 28 R/Q1–QB1 R×R 29 R×R
N×B 30 Q×Q R×Q 31 P×N R–K7
32 R×RP R×P 33 R–R8+ K–R2 34

R–R7 K–N1 (34 . . . P–N4 35 R×P
R×P 36 R–N7 R–QN7 37 N–K5±)
35 R–R8+ K–R2 36 R–Q8 R×P 37
R×P R–R2 (37 . . . R–QN7 38 R–Q7
K–N1=) 38 K–B2 P–B3?! (38 . . .
K–N1, 38 . . . R–R7+=) 39 P×P (39
R–Q6 P×P 40 N×P+ K–R3 41 N–K6
R–QN2 42 N–B4 P–QN4=) 39 . . .
B×P 40 R–Q6 K–N2! (40 . . . R–KB2
41 K–K2±) 41 R×P (sealed) 41 . . .
P–N4 (41 . . . R–R7+ 42 K–K3 R–KN7
43 K–B4 P–N4+!=) 42 P–N4 R–R7+
43 K–B1 (43 K–K3 P×P 44 P×P R–
KN7=) 43 . . . R–R8+ 44 K–B2
R–R7+ 45 K–B1 R–R8+ ½–½

23) **Smyslov-Botvinnik,** King's Indian
Attack 1 P–K4 P–K3 2 P–Q3 P–QB4
3 N–Q2 N–QB3 4 P–KN3 P–KN3
5 B–N2 B–N2 6 KN–B3 KN–K2 7 0–0
0–0 8 P–B3 P–Q3 (8 . . . P–Q4!?) 9 P–
QR4 P–B4?! (9 . . . P–K4!) 10 Q–N3
P–Q4 11 P×QP P×P (11 . . . Q×P 12
N–B4 Q×P? 13 R–Q1 Q–K7 14 B–K3)
12 R–K1 (13 N–B1 14 B–B4) 12 . . .
P–KB5! 13 N–B1 B–N5! (13 . . . P×P
14 BP×P±) 14 P×P (14 B×P? B×N
15 B×B P–KN4 wins; 14 Q×NP? R–
N1 15 Q–R6 R–N3 wins; 14 N–N5
Q–Q2! 15 B×BP? P–KR3!) 14 . . .
B×N (14 . . . Q–Q3!?) 15 B×B K–R1
16 B–Q2 B–R3 (98)

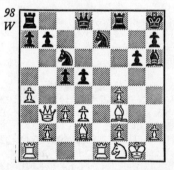

(16 . . . Q–Q3 17 R–K2 and 18 QR–
K1±; 16 . . . Q–Q2 17 Q–N5! P–N3?
18 R×N!) 17 R–K6! B×P 18 QR–K1

B×B (18 . . . N–K4? 19 R/1×N B×R
20 R×B R×B 21 B–N5 R–B2 22 Q×
NP wins; 18 . . . P–B5!) 19 N×B N–B4
(19 . . . P–N3!?; 19 . . . R–B4!?) 20 B–
N2! (20 Q×QP or 20 Q×NP 20 . . .
Q–N4+!) 20 . . . N–R5 21 Q×QP
N×B 22 Q×N/N2 (22 Q×Q? N×Q
23 R–K8 N×R wins) 22 . . . Q×P 23
N–K4 R–B4? (23 . . . R–B5 24 Q–N3! –
24 N×P? Q–B4; 23 . . . Q–Q4 24 N–
Q6 – 24 R–Q6 Q–B4!) 24 N–Q6 R–B6
(24 . . . R–R4 25 P–KB4!± – 25 N×P?
N–K4! 26 R/6×N R×R 27 R×R Q–
Q8+ 28 Q–B1 Q–N5+= –) 25 N×P
QR–KB1 26 N×P (26 R×N? R×P 27
Q×R R×Q 28 K×R Q–Q7+=)
26 . . . Q–B4 27 R–K8! K–N1 (27 . . .
Q×N 28 Q×R!) 28 R×R+ (28 . . .
K×R 29 N–K6 K–N1 30 N–N5 R–
Q6 31 Q×N Q×N+ 32 Q–N2 Q–Q7
33 Q–K4 wins; 28 . . . Q×R 29 N–K6
Q–B3 30 N–N5 R–B4 31 R–K8+
K–N2 32 N–K6+ K–R3 33 Q×N
wins) 1–0

24) Botvinnik-Smyslov, King's Indian
1 N–KB3 N–KB3 2 P–B4 P–KN3 3 N–
B3 B–N2 4 P–Q4 P–Q3 5 P–KN3 0–0
6 B–N2 QN–Q2 7 0–0 P–B3 8 P–K4
P–K4 9 P–KR3 P–QR4 10 B–K3 P×P?!

(10 . . . P–R5!?) 11 N×P R–K1 (11 . . .
N–B4? 12 P–K5 P×P 13 N×P) 12 Q–
B2 N–B4 13 QR–Q1! KN–Q2 (13 . . .
P–R5? 14 N×BP P×N 15 B×N) 14
N–N3! Q–K2 15 N×N P×N (15 . . .
N×N 16 B–Q4!) 16 P–B4 (16 N–
R4!±) 16 . . . N–N3! 17 P–N3 (17 Q–
B2 B–B1) 17 . . . P–R5 18 Q–B2!
B–B1 19 P–K5 (19 KR–K1!?) 19 . . .
P–B4 20 R–Q3 (20 R–Q6! Q–B2 21
R–Q3± – 21 QB×P? N–Q2! –) 20 . . .
P×P 21 P×P B–K3 22 KR–Q1 (*99*) ±

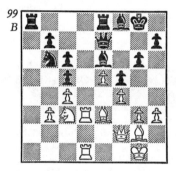

99
B

22 . . . P–R6 23 Q–B2 KR–R1 24 R–
Q6± – 24 . . . N–Q2? 25 N–Q5 P×N
26 R×B! –) 22 . . . R–R3!? ½–½

4 Botvinnik–Smyslov

Moscow 5 March–27 April 1957

	1	2	3	4	5	6	7	8	9	10	11
Botvinnik	0	½	½	1	1	0	½	0	½	½	½
Smyslov	1	½	½	0	0	1	½	1	½	½	½

	12	13	14	15	16	17	18	19	20	21	22	Total
Botvinnik	0	1	½	½	½	0	½	½	0	½	½	9½
Smyslov	1	0	½	½	½	1	½	½	1	½	½	12½

1) Botvinnik-Smyslov, English 1 P–QB4 N–KB3 2 N–QB3 P–KN3 3 P–KN3 B–N2 4 B–N2 0–0 5 P–K4 (Slightly weakening on the dark squares; more logical was 5 P–Q3 followed by N–B3 and 0–0) 5...P–B4! 6 KN–K2 N–B3 7 0–0 P–Q3 8 P–QR3 B–Q2 9 P–R3 N–K1 10 P–Q3 N–B2 11 R–N1 R–N1 12 B–K3 P–QN4 13 P×P N×P 14 N×N R×N 15 P–Q4 Q–B1 16 P×P (Black gets freedom for his pieces after this; best seems 16 K–R2 and if 16...P×P 17 N×P N×N 18 B×N B×B 19 Q×B when 19...B×P 20 B×B R–KR4 fails against 21 P–KN4 Q×P 22 Q–K3) 16...P×P 17 K–R2 R–Q1 18 Q–B1 N–Q5 19 N–B3 R–N2 20 P–B4 B–QB3 21 R–B2 P–QR4 22 Q–B1 N–N4 23 P–K5 (*100*) (Or 23 N×N B×N 24 Q–B1 B–Q6 25 R–R1 P–B5; 23 B×P B×N 24 P×B N×BP 25 R×R Q×R 26 P–K5 B×B 27 Q×B Q–B2 28 B–K3 R–Q6 and White has no good square for the bishop) 23...N×N 24 P×N B×B 25 R×B R×R 26 Q×R Q–B3 27 R–Q2 R×R 28 B×R P–B5! 29 B–K3 P–B3 30 B–Q4 K–B2 31 Q–Q1 P–R5 32 Q–K2 Q–Q4 33 K–N1 B–B1 34 P–B5 BP×P 35 P×P+ P×P 36 B×P P–K3 37 Q–B2+ K–K1 38 Q–B6 B×P 39

Q×NP+ K–Q2 40 Q–R7 (This give Black much less trouble than 40 Q–N7 though Black should still win) 40...B–

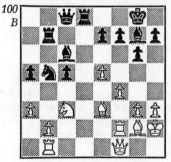

100 B

K2 41 B–B6 (Sealed) 0–1. (The winning process is 41...Q–B4 42 K–N2 P–R6 43 B×B Q×B 44 Q–B2 Q–B4 and if Q–R4+ Q–B3, so...Q–QR4 and...Q–R5 and Q–N6...cannot be prevented)

2) Smyslov-Botvinnik, Sicilian 1 P–K4 P–QB4 2 N–KB3 N–QB3 3 P–Q4 P×P 4 N×P N–B3 5 N–QB3 P–Q3 6 B–KN5 P–K3 7 Q–Q2 P–QR3 8 0–0–0 P–R3 (To relieve the pin, for if 9 B–R4 B–Q2 10 P–B4 N×P etc, but slightly weakening; better is 8...B–Q2) 9 B–K3 N–KN5 10 N×N P×N 11 B–B5 (*101*)

11 ... B–N2 12 P–KR3 P×B 13 Q×
Q+ R×Q 14 R×R+ K×R 15 P×N
B–Q3 16 N–R4 K–B2 17 B–B4 R–Q1
18 P–QN3 B–QB1 19 R–K1! (A strong
centralising move threatening P–K5
shutting off Black's pieces) 19 ... P–B3

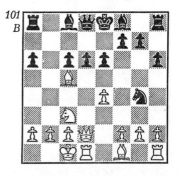

101
B

20 N–N2 B–B5+ 21 K–N1 B–Q7 22
R–KB1 B–B5 23 N–Q3 B–Q3 24 K–B1
P–QR4 25 P–R4 B–K2 26 R–K1 B–Q3
27 P–K5 B×P 28 N×B P×N 29 R×P
K–Q3 30 R–K3 R–B1 31 P–KB3
P–K4 32 K–Q2 R–B5 33 P–N3 R–B1
34 R–Q3+ K–B2 35 R–K3 K–Q3 36
B–K2 B–K3 37 R–Q3+ K–B2 38 R–
B3 K–Q3 39 K–K3 B–Q4 40 R–Q3
K–B2 41 R–Q1 R–B3 42 R–KR1 K–
Q3 43 P–QB4 B–B2 44 B–Q3 K–K2
45 B–K4 R–Q3 ½–½

3) **Botvinnik-Smyslov,** King's Indian
1 P–QB4 N–KB3 2 N–QB3 P–KN3
3 P–KN3 B–N2 4 B–N2 0–0 5 P–Q4
P–Q3 6 N–B3 N–B3 7 0–0 P–QR3
8 P–Q5 N–QR4 9 N–Q2 P–B4 10 Q–
B2 P–K4 11 P–QR3 P–N3 12 P–QN4
N–N2 13 R–N1 B–Q2 14 N2–K4
N×N 15 N×N Q–B2 16 P×P N×P
17 N×N NP×N 18 B–Q2 KR–N1
19 P–K4 (*102*)
19 ... R×R 20 R×R R–N1 21 R–N3
R×R 22 Q×R B–KB3 (To bring the
bishop to Q1 giving it greater scope)
23 P–KR4 B–Q1 24 K–R2 Q–N3 25
Q–B2 P–KR4 26 B–R3 B–K1 (Black
avoids exchange of QB in view of the

pawn structure since also White would
be threatening to penetrate by Q–R4)
27 B–B3 Q–N2 28 K–N2 K–R2 29 K–
B1 P–R4 30 P–R4 Q–R3 31 Q–N3
Q–N3 32 Q–R2 Q–N2 33 K–N1 K–N1
34 K–R1 K–R2 35 K–N2 K–N1 36 Q–
B2 K–R2 37 B–Q2 B–KB3 38 K–R2
Q–N3 39 B–B3 B–N2 40 B–B8 B–R3
41 K–N2 ½–½

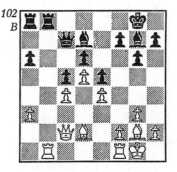

102
B

4) **Smyslov-Botvinnik,** Sicilian 1 P–
K4 P–QB4 2 N–KB3 N–QB3 3 P–Q4
P×P 4 N×P N–B3 5 N–QB3 P–Q3
6 B–KN5 P–K3 7 Q–Q2 P–QR3
8 0–0–0 P–R3 9 B–K3 B–Q2 10
P–B3 (Passive; more aggressive is 10
P–B4) 10 ... P–QN4 11 N×N B×N
12 Q–B2 Q–B2 13 B–Q3 B–K2 14
Q–N3 P–N3 15 K–N1 0–0–0 16 Q–
B2 K–N2 17 N–K2 P–K4 18 N–B1
(A timid move, a fine attack could be
obtained by 18 P–QB4 P×P 19 B×BP
B×P+ 20 B–Q3 B×B+ (20 ... B–B3
21 R–QB1) 21 R×B threatening both
B–N6 and R–N3) 18 ... P–Q4 19 P×P
N×P 20 KR–K1 P–B4 21 N–N3 N×B
22 Q×N B–Q3 23 P–QB4! P×P 24
B×QBP Q–N3 25 Q–K2 (There was
no need to avoid exchange of queens,
and White's advantage would persist
after 25 R–QB1 Q×Q 26 R×Q
threatening both B×P+ and N–R5+)
25 ... K–R2 26 R–QB1 B–N2 27 KR–
Q1 P–K5? (Better 27 ... B–N1) 28 B–
Q5 B–B5 29 B×B? (An unsound
sacrifice that overlooks, amongst other

things the force of Black's 30th move. Correct was 29 R–B5) 29 . . . B×R 30 B–Q5 B–K6 31 P×P P×P 32 Q–B4 (A stronger fight was 32 N–R5 Q×N 33 Q×B+) 32 . . . R–R2 33 Q×P R2–Q2 34 R–Q3 B–N4 35 Q–B3 (*103*)

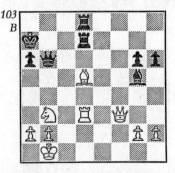

(Black now has a decisive combination based on the fact that the White king has no safe outlet on the second rank. If 35 P–QR4 R×B 36 R×R Q×N wins a piece) 35 . . . R×B! 36 R×R Q–N8+ 37 K–B2 R–B1+ 38 K–Q3 Q–N8+ 39 K–Q4 Q×P+ 40 K–K4 R–K1+ 41 K–Q3 0–1

5) Botvinnik-Smyslov, King's Indian 1 P–QB4 N–KB3 2 N–QB3 P–KN3 3 P–KN3 B–N2 4 B–N2 0–0 5 P–Q4 P–Q3 6 N–B3 B–N5 (This early development of the QB is premature and yields White the advantage of two bishops. Better is the normal 6 . . . QN–Q2 or 6 . . . N–B3) 7 P–KR3 B×N 8 B×B N–B3 9 B–N2! (Hitherto White has castled, e.g. 9 0–0 N–Q2 10 B–N2 N×P 11 B×P R–N1 12 B–N2. This move keeps options open on both flanks) 9 . . . N–Q2 10 P–K3 P–K4 11 P–Q5 N–K2 12 P–K4 P–KB4 (It would be preferable to disentangle the knights first by 12 . . . P–QR4 and 13 . . . N–QB4) 13 P–KR4! P–B5 (This together with next move leaves Black no counter-resources; 13 . . . P–QR4! and 14 . . . N–QB4) 14 B–R3 R–B3 15 Q–K2 B–R3 16 B–Q2 N–QB4 17

P–QN4 P–B6 18 Q–B1 B×B+ 19 K×B N–R3 20 P–R3 P–B3 (Preferable was 20 . . . P–B4 closing some attacking lines for White) 21 Q–Q3 N–B2 22 QR–QN1 R–N1 23 KR–QB1 (*104*)

P–QR4 24 P–N5 P–B4 (Failing to see the force of White's reply; 24 . . . P×QP!) 25 P–N6 N–K1 26 R–K1 N–N2 27 R–K3 Q–KB1 28 R–N5 R–R1 29 N–R4 Q–B2 30 Q–B3 P–R4 31 R×RP R–N1 32 N–N2 K–R2 33 Q–N3 N–N1 34 N–Q3 N–R3 35 R–K1 N–N5 36 Q–R4 Q–K2 37 K–B2 R3–B1 38 R–R7 N–K1 39 B×N P×B 40 Q–N5 N–B3 41 P–R4 K–N1 42 Q–R5 Q–Q1 43 N–N2 N–Q2 44 N–Q1 N–B3 45 Q–N5 Q–K2 46 P–QR5 Q–R2 47 N–Q3 R–B2 48 Q–N2 N–R4 (Desperately seeking counterchances with . . . N–B5 50 P×N P×P with eventual . . . P–N6 but Botvinnik blocks this) 49 R–N1 P–N4 50 P×P QR–KB1 51 Q–Q2 R–B5 52 N–B3 N×P 53 R×N Q–R7 54 Q–K1 1–0

6) Smyslov-Botvinnik, Grünfeld 1 P–Q4 N–KB3 2 P–QB4 P–KN3 3 N–QB3 P–Q4 4 N–B3 B–N2 5 Q–N3 P×P 6 Q×BP 0–0 7 P–K4 B–N5 8 B–K3 KN–Q2 9 0–0–0! (at the time this move was an innovation that Smyslov had been keeping up his sleeve; usual 9 Q–N3) 9 . . . N–QB3 10 P–KR3 B×N 11 P×B N–N3 12 Q–B5 P–B4 13 N–K2 (This turns out well for White because of Black's weak 14th move; 13 P–Q5! and if . . . N–K4 then 14 B–K2) 13 . . . Q–Q3 14 P–K5 (*105*)

14 . . . Q×Q? (This compromises Black's game beyond repair; 14 . . . Q–Q4!) 15 P×Q N–B5 16 P–B4! Black's bishop is now buried alive. 16 . . . KR–Q1 17 B–N2 (Threats B×N and B–Q5) 17 . . . N×B 18 P×N N–N5 (Giving up a Pawn; if 18 . . . P–K3 19 B×N P×B 20 N–Q4 wins easily) 19 B×P QR–N1 20 P–B6 K–B2 21 N–Q4 P–K3 22 N–N5 N–Q4 23 R×N! P×R (23 . . . R×R 24 N×BP R–B4+ 25 K–N1 when N–R6 is decisive) 24 N×BP KR–QB1 25 B×R R×B 26 N×P R×P+ 27 K–Q2 K–K3 28 N–B3 1–0

7) Botvinnik-Smyslov, Nimzo-Indian 1 P–QB4 N–KB3 2 N–QB3 P–K3 3 P–Q4 B–N5 4 P–K3 P–QN3 5 N–K2 B–R3 6 P–QR3 B×N+ (gets a difficult game; preferable 6 . . . B–K2) 7 N×B P–Q4 8 P–QN3 0–0 9 B–K2 P×P 10 P×P N–B3 11 N–N5 N–QR4 (To drive the knight away by P–B3. Striking at the centre by 11 . . . P–K4 12 P–Q5 N–QR4 13 B–N2 allows White's bishops play) 12 B–Q2 P–B3 13 B×N P×B (Doubled pawns cannot be avoided; if 13 . . . P×N 14 B–QN4 R–K1 15 P×P White wins a pawn) 14 N–B3 P–B4 15 N–R4 (15 P–Q5! P×P 16 N×P N×N 17 Q×N Q×Q 18 P×Q B×B 19 K×B and White has a won ending; 17 . . .

Q–N3! 18 0–0 QR–Q1 21 Q–R5 R–Q7± though with counter-play for Black) 15 . . . P×P 16 P×P Q–Q3 17 0–0 QR–Q1 18 Q–Q2 Q×QP 19 Q×P Q–K5 20 N–B3 Q–B3 21 N–N5 Q–N3 22 Q×Q P×Q 23 KR–Q1 N–K5 ½–½

8) Smyslov-Botvinnik, Sicilian 1 P–K4 P–QB4 2 N–KB3 N–QB3 3 P–Q4 P×P 4 N×P N–B3 5 N–QB3 P–Q3 6 B–KN5 P–K3 7 Q–Q2 P–QR3 8 0–0–0 P–R3 9 B–K3 B–Q2 10 P–B4 R–B1 (After this Black has no safe place for the King, 10 . . . Q–B2! followed by 11 . . . 0–0–0) 11 K–N1 P–QN4 12 B–Q3 N–KN5 (Tempting but inferior; Black should continue development with 12 . . . B–K2 and if 13 KR–K1 then N–QR4 with threat of . . . N–B5 13 B–N1 N×N (13 . . . B–K2!) 14 B×N P–K4 15 B–N1 P×P 16 N–Q5! N–K6 17 B×N P×B 18 Q×P B–K3 19 Q–R7 B×N 20 P×B B–K2 21 KR–K1 Q–B2 22 Q×P 0–0 (*106*)

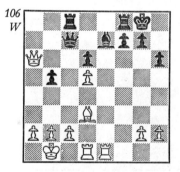

23 P–B3! (Not 23 Q×NP B–B3 threat 24 . . . R–N1 24 Q–B6 Q–R2 25 Q× QP R–N1 26 P–QN3 R–N3 winning) 23 . . . B–B3 24 B×P R–R1 25 Q–B6 Q–N1 26 Q–B4 R–B1 27 B–B6 R–R2 28 Q–N3 Q–B2 29 R–K4 P–N3 30 R–KB1 B–K4 31 P–KR3 K–N2 32 R–QN4 R–B1 33 P–R3 P–R4 34 K–R2 Q–Q1 35 Q–B2 P–B4 36 Q–B2 R/2–KB2 37 P–QR4 P–N4 38 R–N5 P–N5

39 P–R5 P–B5   40 P×P P×P   41 P–R6
1–0

9) Botvinnik-Smyslov, King's Indian
1 P–QB4 N–KB3   2 N–QB3 P–KN3
3 P–KN3 B–N2   4 B–N2 0–0   5 P–Q4
P–Q3   6 N–B3 P–B3   7 0–0 B–B4
(Point of move 6, to protect QN2
against N–KR4; but better are more
usual 6 ... QN–Q2, 6 ... P–B4, 6 ...
N–B3) 8 N–KR4 B–K3   9 P–Q5 P×P
10 P×P B–Q2 11 B–K3 N–R3 12 B–Q4
Q–R4 13 R–K1 N–B4 14 P–K4 N–R5
15 N×N Q×N   16 P–N3 Q–R6 (preferable 16 ... Q–R4 followed by ...
KR–B1) 17 P–B4 B–N4 (Better 17 ...
KR–B1   18 P–K5 N–K1)   18 P–K5
N–Q2 19 P–K6 B×B+ 20 Q×B Q–B4
21 N–B3! P×P   22 P×P (Elegant
winning method was 22 QR–B1 Q×P
23 Q×Q P×Q   24 N–Q4 B–B3   25
N×B P×N   26 R×KP N–N3   27 R×
BP) 22 ... N–B3   23 QR–B1 Q–R4
24 N–N5 B–B3 25 B×B P×B 26 R×P
N–N5   27 P–KR4 P–KR3   28 N–B7
K–R2 29 P–N4 (107)

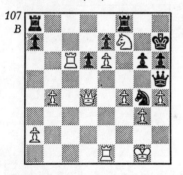

107
B

29 ... QR–B1   30 R×R R×R   31 N×
QP P×N   32 Q×P K–R1   33 Q–Q7
(2.25) R–B6 (Forcing a perpetual check)
34 Q–Q8+ K–R2   35 Q–Q7+ K–R1
36 Q–Q8+ K–R2   37 Q–K7+ K–R1
38 Q–K8+ K–R2   39 Q–K7+ K–R1
40 Q–K8+ K–R2 ½–½

10) Smyslov-Botvinnik, Ruy Lopez,
Morphy 1 P–K4 P–K4   2 N–KB3

N–QB3 3 B–N5 P–QR3 4 B–R4 N–B3
5 0–0 B–K2 6 R–K1 P–QN4 7 B–N3
0–0 8 P–B3 P–Q3 9 P–KR3 N–QR4
10 B–B2 P–B4 11 P–Q4 Q–B2 12 QN–
Q2 N–B3   13 P×BP P×P   14 N–B1
B–K3   15 N–K3 QR–Q1   16 Q–K2
P–N3   17 N–N5 B–B1   18 P–QR4
Q–N2 19 P×P P×P   20 P–R4 B–Q3
21 N–Q5 N–KR4 22 N–B3 (Or 22 P–
KN4 N–B5 23 B×N P×B 24 N–B6+
K–N2 25 N/5×RP R–R1 – White loses
two pieces for a rook) 22 ... P–B3 23
B–R6 R–B2 24 KR–Q1 B–N5 25 Q–K3
N–N2 26 R–Q2 N–K1 27 N–R2 B–K3
28 Q–N3 K–R1   29 QR–Q1 R/1–Q2
30 N–B1 B–N1   31 B–K3 N–R4   32
B×P N–B5 33 R–K2 N×P (108)

108
W

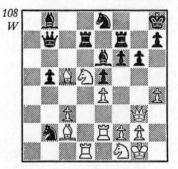

34 R–N1 Q–B3 35 B–N4 N–B5 36 P–
R5 P–N4 37 N/1–K3 N/1–Q3 38 B×N
N×B 39 B–Q3 R–QN2 40 R/2–N2
P–R3 41 Q–B3 B–R2 42 P–B4 P×P
43 R×R N×R 44 N×QBP K–N2 45
B–K2 B–Q5   46 N/5–K3 KB×N
47 N×B N–Q3 ½–½

11) Botvinnik-Smyslov, King's Indian
1 N–KB3 N–KB3   2 P–KN3 P–KN3
3 B–N2 B–N2 4 P–B4 P–B3 5 P–Q4
P–Q4 6 P×P P×P 7 N–B3 0–0 8 N–K5
N–B3   9 0–0 B–B4   10 N×N P×N
11 N–R4 N–Q2 12 P–N3 P–K4 13 P×P
B×P 14 B–R6 R–K1 (Best; After 14 ...
B×R 15 Q×B Q–B3 16 Q×Q N×Q
17 B×R K×B   18 R–B1 White has
favourable endgame) 15 R–B1 R–QB1

16 Q–Q2 (16 B–K3!? B–N1 17 B–Q4; 16 ... Q–B2 17 B×QP; 16 ... Q–R4 17 R–K1 and 18 B–Q4) 16 ... Q–K2 17 KR–K1 B–Q3 18 Q–Q4 Q–B3 19 Q×Q N×Q 20 N–B5 N–Q2 21 N×N (More promising line is 21 P–K4) 21 ... B×N 22 P–K4 B–QR6 23 QR–Q1 B–KN5 ½–½

12) Smyslov–Botvinnik, Sicilian 1 P–K4 P–QB4 2 N–KB3 P–KN3 3 P–B4 B–N2 4 P–Q4 P–Q3 5 N–B3 N–QB3 6 B–K3 B–N5? (Failing to take into account White's 11th move. 6 ... P×P 7 N×P N–B3; 6 ... N–B3 7 P×P Q–R4 are better) 7 P×P P P×P 8 Q×Q+ R×Q 9 B×P B×N+ 10 P×B N–B3 11 N–Q4! N×P 12 N×N P×N 13 B×RP B–B4 (13 ... N×QBP!? 14 B–N6 R–Q2 15 P–B3 B–K3) 14 P–B3 N–Q3 15 P–QR4 R–R1 16 B–N6 0–0 17 P–B5 N–B1 18 P–N4 B–K3 19 P–R5 N×B 20 BP×N KR–N1 (*109*)

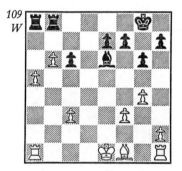

21 B–Q3 R×NP 22 P×R R×R+ 23 K–Q2 R–R7+ 24 K–K3 B–B1 (24 ... R–QN7 25 R–QN1 R×R 26 B×R B–B1 27 K–Q4 B–N2 28 K–B5 and 29 B–K4) 25 R–Q1 (Threat 26 B×B P RP×B 27 R–Q8+ K–N2 28 R×B followed by R×BP) 25 ... R–QN7 26 B–B4 K–N2 27 R–Q8 B–K3 28 B×B P×B 29 R–N8 P–K4 30 P–QB4 K–B2 31 P–B5 K–K3 32 R–Q8 P–N4 33 P–R3 (Unnecessary; 33 K–Q3!) 33 ... R–N8 34 K–Q2 R–N4 35 K–Q3 R–N8 36 K–B4 R–QB8+

37 K–N4 R–N8 38 K–R4 R–R8 39 K–N4 R–N8+ 40 K–R3 R–QR8+ 41 K–N2 R–R4 42 R–Q3 R–R1 43 K–N3 R–R4 Sealed 1–0. (White wins by 44 K–N4 R–R1 45 R–R3 and now 45 ... R×R 46 K×R K–Q2 47 K–N4 K–B1 48 K–B3 P–K5 49 P–B4! P×P 50 P–R4; 45 ... R–Q1 46 R–R7 R–Q5+ 47 K–R5 R–QB5 48 P–N7 R×P+ 49 K–N6 R–N4+ 50 K×P etc.)

13) Botvinnik–Smyslov, Nimzo-Indian 1 P–QB4 N–KB3 2 N–QB3 P–K3 3 P–Q4 B–N5 4 P–K3 P–QN3 5 N–K2 B–R3 6 P–QR3 B×N+ 7 N× B P–Q4 8 P–QN3 0–0 9 P–QR4 P–B4 10 B–R3 QP×P 11 NP×P (11 QP×P! with initiative e.g. 11 ... Q×Q+ 12 R×Q BP×P 13 P–B6 R–B1 14 P–B7! or 11 ... NP×P 12 QB×P Q×Q+ 13 N×Q R–B1 14 P–QN4) 11 ... N–B3 12 N–N5 B–N2 13 B–K2 N–K5 14 B–B3 (*110*)

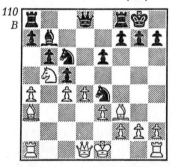

14 ... N–N4? (Anti-positional; 14 ... N–R4!) 15 B×N! B×B 16 P–B3 P–QR3 17 N–B3 P–B4 18 0–0 Q–B3 19 Q–Q3 KR–Q1 20 P–Q5 N–B2 21 P–K4 KP×P 22 BP×P B–Q2 23 B–N2 N–K4 24 Q–K2 P–KB5 25 N–Q1 P–QN4 26 N–B2 P–B5 27 P×P P×P 28 Q–Q2 QR–B1 29 KR–B1 R–K1 30 B–B3 (Stronger 30 R–R7 and if Q–QN3 31 B–Q4) 30 ... R–B2 31 K–R1 R–N2 32 R–R2 P–R4 33 R/1–R1 P–N5 34 B×P Q–QN3 35 B–B3 Q–K6 36 N–Q1 Q×Q 37 R×Q(2.29) N–Q6(2.29) 38

B–Q4 R/1–N1 39 N–B3 R–N6 40 P–R4
R/1–N2(2.29.50) 41 R–R8+(2.40) 1–0

14) Smyslov-Botvinnik, French 1 P–
Q4 P–K3 2 P–K4 P–Q4 3 N–QB3
B–N5 4 P–K5 P–QB4 5 P–QR3 B×
N+ 6 P×B Q–B2 7 Q–N4 P–B4
8 Q–N3 N–K2 9 B–Q2 0–0 10 B–Q3
P–QN3 11 N–R3 B–R3 12 N–B4 Q–
Q2 13 P–KR4 (Best seems 13 B×B
N×B and then 14 P–KR4) 13 . . . B×B
14 P×B QN–B3 15 B–K3 P×P 16
P×P QR–B1 17 P–R5 N–R4 (17 . . .
N–Q1!?) 18 P–R6 P–N3 19 0–0 K–R1
20 QR–N1 N–N1 21 B–Q2 N–QB3
22 N–K2 N–Q1 23 KR–B1 N–B2
24 Q–R4 R×R+ 25 R×R R–B1 26 P–
B3 R×R+ 27 B×R (*111*)

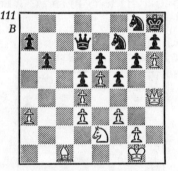

111
B

27 . . . Q–K2 (As it turns out, better is
27 . . . Q–N4 28 B–N5 N×B 29 Q×N
Q×P 30 K–B2 Q×P 31 Q–Q8 Q–
K2) 28 Q×Q N×Q 29 N–B4 N–
Q1 30 P–N4 P×P 31 P×P N/2–B3
32 N–K2 K–N1 33 K–B2 K–B1 34 K–
K1 N–B2 35 P–N5 K–K2 36 K–Q1
K–Q2 37 K–B2 P–N4 38 K–N3 P–R3
39 P–R4? (A mistake that could have
proved fatal; 39 B–Q2!) 39 . . . K–B2
(Better chance was 39 . . . P×P+ e.g.
40 K×P N×QP 41 N×N N×KP 42
K–R5 N×P 43 B–Q2 P–K4 44 N–B3
K–K3 45 N–R4) 40 P×P P P×P 41 B–Q2
K–N3 42 K–R3 K–N2 43 K–N2 K–R3
44 K–R3 N/2–Q1 45 B–K1 N–K2
46 N–B1 ½–½

15) Botvinnik-Smyslov, Nimzo-
Indian 1 P–QB4 N–KB3 2 N–QB3
P–K3 3 P–Q4 B–N5 4 P–K3 P–QN3
5 N–K2 B–R3 6 P–QR3 B×N+
7 N×B P–Q4 8 P–QN3 0–0 9 B–K2
P×P 10 P×P N–B3 11 P–QR4 Q–Q2
12 N–N5 KR–Q1 13 B–N2 N–QR4
14 Q–B2 P–B3 15 N–R3 Q–K2 16 0–0
P–B4 17 N–N5 B–N2 18 B–R3 N–B3
19 KR–Q1 P–QR3 20 N–B3 N–QN5
21 Q–N3 P–QR4 22 N–N5 P–R3 (This,
and the next few moves, are rather
desultory. 22 . . . R–Q2! followed by
QR–Q1; 22 . . . N–K1! followed by
. . . N–B2) 23 B–N2 QR–B1 24 P–B3
P×P 25 P×P N–R4 26 B–KB1 Q–N4
27 B–R3 N–B5 (Threat 28 . . . N–R6+
29 K–R1 N–B7+) 28 K–R1 P–R4 (28
. . . R×BP!) 29 B×N P×B 30 Q×P
P–R5 31 R–R3 R–B4 32 R–K1 R–B4
33 N–Q6 (Better seems 33 P–Q5) 33
. . . N×P 34 B×N P–R6 35 B×P
B×P+ 36 R×B R×R (*112*)

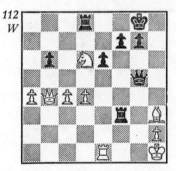

112
W

37 N×P! R×N (Not 37 . . . K×N 38
B×P+ K–B3 39 B–Q5 R×B 40 Q–
K7+ K–B4 41 Q–K6+ K–B5 42 R–
K4 mate) 38 B×P R×P 39 Q×P R–B5
40 B×R+ R×B 41 Q–K6 Q–B5 42 Q–
QB6 (More definite is 42 Q–Q5 etc.)
42 . . . R–B4 43 Q–R8+ K–R2 44 Q–
K4 Q×Q+ 45 R×Q R–QR4 46 K–N2
K–N3 47 K–B3? (Best is 47 R–B4 R×P
48 K–B3 with Black king is cut off from
passed pawn) 47 . . . K–B4 48 R–B4+
K–K4 49 R–K4+ K–B4 50 R–B4+

K–K4 51 K–N4 R×P 52 K–N5 R–R3
53 P–R4 R–QB3 54 P–R5 K–K3 55
K–N6 K–K4 56 K–N5 K–K3 ½–½

16) Smyslov–Botvinnik, Ruy Lopez,
Morphy 1 P–K4 P–K4 2 N–KB3 N–
QB3 3 B–N5 P–QR3 4 B–R4 N–B3
5 0–0 B–K2 6 R–K1 P–QN4 7 B–N3
0–0 8 P–B3 P–Q3 9 P–KR3 N–QR4
10 B–B2 P–B4 11 P–Q4 Q–B2 12 QN–
Q2 N–B3 13 P×BP P×P 14 N–B1
B–Q3 15 N–R4 P–N3 16 B–R6 R–Q1
17 Q–B3 N–K1 18 N–K3 P–B3 19 N–
Q5 Q–B2 20 N–N6 R–N1 21 N×B
QR×N 22 P–KN3 B–B1 23 B–K3
K–R1 24 N–N2 N–B2 25 QR–Q1
R×R 26 R×R R–Q1 27 R×R N×R
28 P–QR4 Q–K3 29 P×P P×P (*113*)

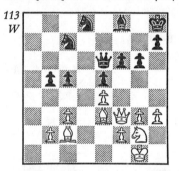

113
W

30 P–R4 K–N2 31 P–R5 P–N4 32 B–B1
N–N2 33 N–K3 N–Q3 34 N–B5
(34 N–N4!?) 34 ... N×N 35 P×N
Q–Q4 36 B–K4 Q–Q3 37 B–K3 P–R3
38 K–N2 (Imprecise; 38 K–R2!) 38 ...
B–K2 39 P–N3 K–B1 40 B–B6 Q–Q6
41 K–R2 K–B2 42 B–N7 P–K5 43
B×KP? (43 Q×P Q×P 44 Q–B6 etc.)
43 ... Q×P   4 B–Q5+ N×B 45
Q×N+ K–B1 46 K–N2 Q–B7 47 P–
KN4 Q–K7 48 K–N3 Q–B7 49 K–B3
Q–B6 50 K–N2 Q–B7 51 Q–R8+
K–B2 52 Q–Q5+ K–B1 53 K–B3
Q–B6 54 Q–R8+ K–B2 B5 Q–Q5+
K–B1 ½–½

17) Botvinnik–Smyslov, King's Indian
1–N–KB3 N–KB3 2 P–KN3 P–KN3

3 P–B4 P–B3 4 B–N2 B–N2 5 P–Q4
0–0 6 N–B3 P–Q4 7 P×P P P×P 8 N–K5
P–N3 9 B–N5 B–N2 10 B×N B×B
11 0–0 P–K3 12 P–B4 B–N2 13 R–B1
P–B3 14 N–B3 N–B3 15 P–K3 Q–Q2
16 Q–K2 (16 R–KB2! followed by B–B1
to control QB4) 16 ... N–R4 17 P–
KR4 N–B5 18 B–R3 (More vigorous
was 18 P–KN4) 18 ... N–Q3 19 K–R2
P–QR4 20 KR–K1? (Ineffective; 20 R–
KN1!)   20 ... P–QN4   21 N–Q1
P–N5 22 N–B2 B–QR3 23 Q–Q1
KR–B1 (*114*)

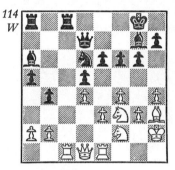

114
W

24 R×R+ (Better to try for a K-side
attack by 24 P–N4) 24 ... R×R 25
B–B1 B×B 26 R×B Q–B3 27 N–Q3
Q–B7+? (27 ... N–K5!)   28 Q×Q
R×Q+ 29 R–B2 R×R+ 30 N×R
N–B5 31 N–Q1 K–B2 32 P–N3? N–Q3
33 K–N2 (33 P–N4!)   33 ... P–R4!
34 K–R3 (Better 34 N–K1 followed by
N–Q3) 34 ... N–K5 35 P–N4? (35 N–
K1) 35 ... P×P+ 36 K×P P–B4+
37 K–R3 B–B3 38 N–K1 K–N2 39 N–
Q3 N–B6 40 N×N P×N 41 N–K1
K–R3 42 N–B2 B–K2 43 K–N3?
(43 P–R3 K–R4 44 P–N4) 43 ... K–R4
44 K–B3? (44 P–R3 was still best chance)
44 ... K×P 45 N–K1 P–N4 46 P×P
K×P 47 N–B2 B–Q3 48 N–K1?
K–R5 49 N–B2 K–R6 50 N–R1 K–R7
51 K–B2 B–N6+ 52 K–B3 B–R5!
53 N–B2 K–N8 54 K–K2 K–N7 55 N–
R1 B–K2 56 N–B2 K–N6 57 N–K1
B–Q1 58 N–B2 B–B3 59 P–R3 B–K2

60 P–N4 P–R5 61 N–K1 B–N4 62 N–
B2 B–B3 63 K–Q3 K–B7 64 N–R1
B–Q1 65 N–B2 B–N4 66 P–N5 B–Q1
67 N–N4 B–N3 68 N–B2 B–R4 69 N–
N4 K–K8 0–1 (60 P–R4 would have
drawn)

18) Smyslov-Botvinnik, French 1 P–
K4 P–K3 2 P–Q4 P–Q4 3 N–QB3
B–N5 4 P–QR3 B×N+ 5 P×B P×P
6 Q–N4 N–KB3 7 Q×NP R–N1
8 Q–R6 P–B4 9 N–K2 R–N3 10 Q–K3
N–B3 11 B–Q2 N–K2 12 N–N3 B–Q2
13 P×P Q–B2 14 P–QB4 B–B3 15 B–
K2 N–N5 16 B×N R×B 17 P–R3
R–N3 18 N×P N–B4 19 N–Q6+ (115)

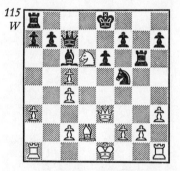

115
W

19 . . . Q×N 20 P×Q N×Q 21 B×N
B×P 22 R–KN1 K–Q2 23 P–KR4
P–KR4 24 P–B5 (This and the next
move form a faulty plan. Best is 24 B–
N5 B–K5 25 0–0–0 QR–KN1 26 R–N3
P–B3 27 B–B4 P–K4 28 R×R R×R
29 B–N3) 24 . . . QR–KN1 25 R–N1
B–B6 26 R×R R×R 27 K–Q2 P–K4
28 K–Q3 (Better 28 R–N3 R–N7 29 B–
Q4 B–Q4 30 P–QB4 B–B3 31 B×P
R×P+ 32 K–K1 R–B4 33 R–K3)
28 . . . P–B3 29 B–Q2 R–N7 30 K–K3
B–B3 31 B–B3 K–K3 32 P–B4 R×P
33 K–Q3 R–KN7 34 P×P P–B4 35 R–
N4 B–K5+ 36 K–Q4 R–N5 37 B–K1
P–R4 38 R–N2 B–Q4+ 39 K–Q3
R–R5 40 K–K2 R×QRP 41 R–Q2
B–B5+ 42 K–B2 K–Q2 43 R–Q4
B–N4 44 B–Q2 P–R5 45 B–N5 R–Q6

46 R×R B×R 47 B–B1 B–N4 48 K–K3
K–K3 49 K–B4 B–Q2 50 B–N2 K–Q4
51 B–R3 B–B1 52 B–B1 B–K3 (116)

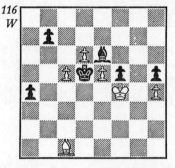

116
W

53 B–R3 B–Q2 54 B–B1 K–Q5 55 B–
R3 B–K3 56 B–N4 B–B1 57 B–R3
B–K3 58 B–N4 B–Q2 59 B–R3 B–B1
60 B–B1 K–Q4   61 B–R3 B–Q2
62 B–B1 ½–½

19) Botvinnik-Smyslov, English 1 P–
QB4 P–KN3 2 N–QB3 P–QB4 3 P–
KN3 B–N2 4 B–N2 N–QB3 5 P–K3
P–K3 6 KN–K2 KN–K2 7 P–Q4
P×P 8 N×P P–Q4 (Also 8 . . . N×N
9 P×N P–Q4=) 9 P×P N×N 10
P×N N×P 11 0–0 0–0 12 Q–N3 (117)

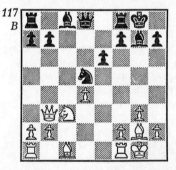

117
B

12 . . . Q–N3 (If 12 . . . B×P 13 B–R6
R–K1 14 QR–Q1 Q–N3 15 N×N
P×N 16 B×P etc.) 13 N×N P×N
14 B×P Q×Q 15 B×Q B×P ½–½

20) Smyslov-Botvinnik, French 1 P–
K4 P–K3 2 P–Q4 P–Q4 3 N–QB3
B–N5 4 P–K5 P–QB4 5 P–QR3 B×N+

6 P×B Q–B2 7 Q–N4 P–B3 8 N–B3
N–B3 9 Q–N3 Q–B2? (9 ... P×QP!
10 BP×P Q–B2 11 B–Q3 KN–K2)
10 QP×P KN–K2 11 B–Q3 P×P
(11 ... N–N3!) 12 N×P N×N 13
Q×N 0–0 13 0–0 N–B3 15 Q–N3
P–K4 16 B–K3 B–B4 17 QR–N1 B×B
(Probably 17 ... QR–N1 is better)
18 P×B QR–K1 19 P–KB4 Q–B2? (*118*)

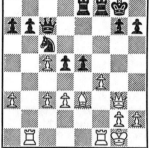

118
W

(19 ... P–K5! and if 20 P–Q4 N–R4
followed by ... N–B5) 20 P×P R×R+
21 R×R Q×P 22 Q×Q N×Q 23 R–
Q1 K–B2 24 P–R3 N–B3 25 B–B4

R–K2 26 B–Q6 R–Q2 27 R–B1+
K–K3 28 R–K1+ K–B2 29 K–B2
P–QN3 30 R–QN1 K–K3 31 R–N5
P–Q5 32 P–B4 P×P 33 B–R2 R–B2+
34 K–K2 R–K2 35 R×P K–Q2+
36 K–Q2 R–K3 37 R–KN5 P–N3 38
R–Q5+ K–B1 39 B–N1 R–B3 40 B×P
N×B 41 R×N R–B7+ 42 K–B3
Sealed. 1–0 (The two united passed
pawns win easily for White, e.g.
42 ... R×P 43 R–B4 P–KR4 44 R–B7
K–N1 45 P–B5 R–N6 46 R–N7)

21) Botvinnik-Smyslov, King's Indian
1 P–Q4 N–KB3 2 P–QB4 P–KN3
3 P–KN3 P–B3 4 B–N2 P–Q4 5 P×P
P×P 6 N–QB3 B–N2 7 N–B3 0–0
8 N–K5 B–B4 9 0–0 N–K5 10 N×N
QB×N 11 P–B3 B–B4 12 B–K3 N–Q2
13 N×N Q×N $\frac{1}{2}$–$\frac{1}{2}$

22) Smyslov-Botvinnik, French 1 P–
K4 P–K3 2 P–Q4 P–Q4 3 N–QB3
N–KB3 4 B–N5 P×P 5 N×P QN–Q2
6 N–KB3 B–K2 7 N×N+ B×N 8 B×
B Q×B 9 Q–Q2 0–0 10 Q–N5 Q×Q
11 N×Q $\frac{1}{2}$–$\frac{1}{2}$

5 Smyslov–Botvinnik

Moscow 4 March–8 May 1958

	1	2	3	4	5	6	7	8	9	10	11	12
Smyslov	0	0	0	½	1	0	½	½	½	½	1	0
Botvinnik	1	1	1	½	0	1	½	½	½	½	0	1

	13	14	15	16	17	18	19	20	21	22	23	Total
Smyslov	½	0	1	½	½	0	1	½	½	1	½	10½
Botvinnik	½	1	0	½	½	1	0	½	½	0	½	12½

1) Smyslov-Botvinnik, Caro-Kann
1 P–K4 P–QB3 2 N–QB3 P–Q4 3 N–B3 B–N5 4 P–KR3 B×N 5 Q×B N–B3 6 P–Q3 P–K3 7 B–K2 QN–Q2 8 Q–N3 P–KN3 9 0–0 B–N2 10 B–B4 Q–N3 (10 . . . 0–0? 11 B–Q6 R–K1 12 P–K5±) 11 QR–N1 0–0 12 B–B7 Q–Q5 13 B–B3 P–K4 14 B–Q6 KR–K1 15 B–R3 P×P (*119*)

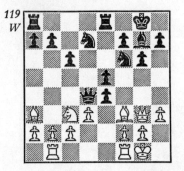

119
W

16 P×P?! (16 N×P N×N 17 B×N=) 16 . . . P–QN4 17 KR–Q1 Q–N3 18 P–N3 N–B4 19 B–B1 Q–B2 (19 . . . P–N5 20 N–R4 N×N 21 P×N Q–B4 22 B–K3 Q–B5∓) 20 B–K3 N–K3 21 P–QR4 P–QR3 22 P–N4 QR–Q1∓ 23 B–K2 Q–K2 24 P×P RP×P 25 R×R R×R 26 B–N6? R–R1 27 P–B3 R–R6 28 Q–K1 B–R3∓ 29 B–B1 N–

Q5 30 B–B5 Q–K3 31 B–Q3 N–Q2 32 B×N P×B 33 N–K2 B–K6+ 34 K–R1 N–K4 (Threat: . . . N×P) 35 Q–KB1 Q–Q3 36 P–KB4 (36 Q–Q1 N–B5∓) 36 . . . N×B 37 P×N R×P 38 Q–B3 R–Q7 39 R–KB1 Q×NP 40 P–K5 Q–B5 41 N–N3 R–QB7 42 P–B5 R–B8 43 P–K6 BP×P 44 P×NP R×R+ 45 N×R P×P 46 Q–B6 P–N5 47 K–R2 P–N4! 48 N×B P×N 49 Q×NP+ K–B2 50 Q×P P–N6 51 Q–K5 P–B4 52 Q–B7+ K–N3 53 Q–N8 K–B4 54 Q–B8+ K–K5 55 Q–B6 Q–Q4 56 Q–B3+ K–Q5 57 Q–Q1+ K–K4 58 Q–K2+ K–Q3 59 Q–R6+ K–K2 60 Q–R7+ K–B3 61 Q–R7 Q–K4+ 62 K–R1 P–N7 0–1

2) Botvinnik-Smyslov, King's Indian
1 P–Q4 N–KB3 2 P–QB4 P–KN3 3 N–QB3 B–N2 4 P–K4 P–Q3 5 P–B3 0–0 6 B–K3 P–QR3 7 B–Q3 N–B3 8 KN–K2 R–N1 9 P–QR3 N–Q2 10 B–QN1 N–R4 11 B–R2 P–QN4 12 P×P P×P 13 P–QN4 N–B5 14 B×N P×B 15 0–0 (15 P–N5!±) 15 . . . P–QB3 16 Q–Q2 N–N3?! (16 . . . R–K1) 17 B–R6 B×B 18 Q×B P–B3 19 P–QR4 N–R1 20 KR–N1± P–KB4 21 Q–K3 P×P 22 P×P N–B2 23 P–Q5 P×P 24 P×P B–N2 (24 . . . R–B4!?

114

25 R–KB1 Q–Q2 26 Q–Q4 (26 Q–R7±) 26 ... P–K3 27 P×P N×P! (27 ... Q×KP 28 N–B4 Q–K4 29 QR–Q1) 28 Q–N4 (28 Q×BP P–Q4 unclear) 28 ... KR–K1 29 N–Q4 Q–N2 30 QR–Q1 (30 N×N Q×N 31 Q–B4 K–R1 32 QR–B1 Q–K4 unclear) 30 ... N–B2 31 Q–B4 R–K4 (*120*)

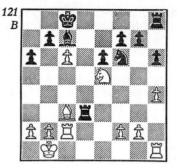

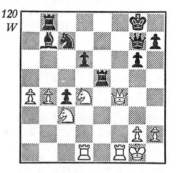

32 N–B6! B×N 33 Q×P+ P–Q4 34 Q×B R–Q1 35 Q–N6 Q–K2 35 Q–Q4 Q–Q3 37 R/B1–K1 R/Q1–K1 38 R×R R×R 39 P–N5 N–K3 40 Q–R7 P–Q5 41 N–K4 1–0 (41 ... Q–B1 42 P–N6 N–B5 43 P–N7 R–K1 44 P–N8=Q R×Q 45 N–N5 wins)

3) Smyslov-Botvinnik, Caro-Kann 1 P–K4 P–QB3 2 N–QB3 P–Q4 3 P–Q4 P×P 4 N×P B–B4 5 N–N3 B–N3 6 P–KR4 P–KR3 7 N–B3 N–Q2 8 B–Q3 B×B 9 Q×B Q–B2 10 B–Q2 KN–B3 11 0–0–0 P–K3 12 K–N1 0–0–0 13 P–B4 P–B4 14 B–B3 P×P 15 N×P P–R3 16 Q–K2 B–Q3 17 N–K4 N×N 18 Q×N N–B3 (18 ... N–B4 19 Q–B2 B–K4 20 KR–K1 B–B3 21 P–KN3 R–Q2!=) 19 Q–K2 R–Q2 20 R–QB1 Q–B4 21 N–N3 Q–B4+ 22 R–B2 B–B2 23 P–B5 R–Q4 24 P–B6 B–N3 25 N–Q2 Q–Q6 (25 ... Q×P?? 26 N–B4 KR–Q1 27 P–R4 wins) 26 N–B4 B–B2 27 Q×Q R×Q 28 N–K5?? (*121*) (28 P×P+ K×P 29 B–K5 B×B 30 N×B R–Q4 31 P–B4 N–Q2 32 KR–

QB1 N×N 33 R–B7+ K–N3 34 P×N R–KB1 35 P–QN4 K–N4! 36 R–N7+ K–R5 37 R–B5 R×R 38 P×R R–B1=) 28 ... R×B 29 P×P+ K×P 30 R×R B×N∓ 31 R–N3+ K–R2 32 R–QB1 R–QN1 33 R×R K×R 34 R–B4 N–Q4 35 K–B2 P–KR4 36 P–QN4 K–N2 37 K–N3 B–Q3 38 P–R3 B–B2 39 R–B2 B–N3 40 K–B4 N–B5 41 P–N3 N–R6 42 P–B3 N–N8 43 P–B4 N–B6 44 P–R4 N–Q5 45 R–Q2 N–B4 46 P–R5 B–K6 47 R–Q8 (47 R–Q7+ K–B3 48 R×P N–Q3+) 47 ... B–B7 48 P–N5 K–B2 49 R–KN8 P×P+ 50 K×P B×P 51 P–R6 B–B7 52 K–R5 P–N3 53 R–QR8 B–K8+ 54 K–N5 N–Q3+ 55 K–R4 N–B1 (Also 55 ... B×P 56 P–R7 B–B7 57 K–N3 B×P wins) 56 K–N5 B–B7 57 K–R5 B–R2 58 K–N5 P–B3 59 K–N4 P–K4 60 P×P P×P 61 K–B3 B–N1 62 K–Q3 N–N3 63 P–R7 N×R 64 P×B=Q+ K×Q 65 K–K4 N–N3 66 K×P N–Q2+ 0–1

4) Botvinnik-Smyslov, Grünfeld 1 P–Q4 N–KB3 2 P–QB4 P–KN3 3 N–QB3 P–Q4 4 N–B3 B–N2 5 Q–N3 P×P 6 Q×BP 0–0 7 P–K4 B–N5 8 B–K3 KN–Q2 9 B–K2 N–N3 10 Q–B5 P–QB3 11 R–Q1 QN–Q2 12 Q–R5 P–K4! 13 P–Q5 (13 N×P B×B 14 K×B N×N 15 P×N Q–R5 16 P–B4 P–N4∓) 13 ... P×P 14 N×QP N×N 15 Q×N B–K3 16 Q–Q2 (16 Q×NP Q–

R4+ 17 P–QN4 Q×P 18 Q–R6=)
16 . . . N–B3 17 Q–N4 P–QR4 18 Q–
N5 (18 Q–R3!? Q–N1 19 N–N5 B–Q2
20 B–B5 P–R3 21 B×R B×B 22 Q–
KB3 B–N5+ 23 K–B1 unclear) 18 . . .
Q–K1! 19 N–Q2 Q×Q 20 B×Q B×P
21 K–K2 (21 P–QN3 KR–B1 22 R–R1
R–B6 23 B–QB4 P–QN4) 21 . . . B–K3
22 P–B3 KR–B1 23 R–QB1 N–K1 24
B–Q3 N–Q3 25 R×R+ R×R 26 R–R1
R–R1 27 B–N6 P–R5 28 N–N1? (28 P–
QN3 B–Q2 29 P×P R×P 30 R×R
B×R 31 N–B4 N×N 32 B×N B–
QB3∓) 28 . . . N–B5 29 B×N B×B+
30 K–K1 B–B1 (30 . . . P–B4) 31 N–R3
B–N6 (31 . . . B–K3!) 32 R–B1 R–R3
33 B–K3 R–B3?! 34 R×R P×R 35 K–
Q2 P–KB4 36 K–B3 P×P 37 P×P K–
B2 38 N–B4 K–K3 39 B–R7? (39 N–R5
B–R7 40 K–B2! K–Q2 41 N–N7 and
N–B5) 39 . . . B–R7 40 B–N8 B–R3!
41 B–B7 (41 P–KN3!?) 41 . . . B–N8
42 N–Q2 B×N+ 43 K×B (*122*)

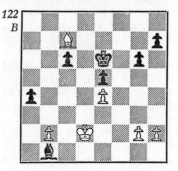

122
B

43 . . . B×P 44 P–KN3 K–Q4 45 K–B3
B–N7?! (45 . . . P–N4! 46 B–N8 B–B6
47 B–B7 P–K5 48 K–Q2 K–B5∓) 46
P–R4 B–B6 47 B–N8 P–B4 48 B–B7
B–K5 49 B–N8 B–N8 50 B–B7 P–K5
51 B–B4 B–Q6 52 B–K3 P–B5 53 B–B4
(53 B–Q4 B–B8! 54 B–N6 K–K4 55
K–Q2 K–B4 56 B–Q4 K–N5 57 K–K1
K×P! 58 K×B K×P wins; 53 B–Q4
B–B8! 54 B–B2 K–K4 55 K–Q2 K–B4
56 B–K1 P–B6+! 57 K×P – 57 P×P
K–K4 and –Q4–B5 – 57 . . . K–N5 58

K–Q4 K–B6 wins) 53 . . . K–K3 54 K–
Q2 K–B4 55 B–Q6 K–N5 (55 . . . P–R4!
Zugzwang: 56 K–K3 P–B6 57 P×P
K–K3 and . . . K–Q4) 56 K–K3 B–N8
57 B–K5!= P–B6 58 B×P K×P 59 B–
B6 K–N5 60 B–K7 K–B4 61 B–N5
K–K4 62 B–R6 B–B7 63 B–N5 B–N6
64 B–R6 B–Q4 65 B–N5 K–B4 66 B–
R6 K–N5 67 B–N5 K–N6 68 B–Q8
K–N7 69 B–K7 K–B8 70 B–N4 P–R3
71 B–B8 P–N4 72 P–R5 P–N5 73
B×P P–N6 74 B–B4 P–N7 75 B–R2
B–B2 76 K×P B×P 77 K–Q3 P–
N8=Q 78 B×Q K×B 69 K–B2 B–
N3+ 80 K–B3 B–B2 81 K–B2 B–R7
P–N4 ½–½

5) Smyslov–Botvinnik, Sicilian 1 P–
K4 P–QB4 2 N–KB3 N–QB3 3 P–Q4
P×P 4 N×P N–B3 5 N–QB3 P–Q3
6 B–K2 P–KN3 7 B–K3 B–N2 8 P–
KR4!? 0–0 9 P–R5 P–Q4 10 RP×P
RP×P 11 P×P (11 N×N P×N 12 P–
K5 N–K5 13 N×N Q×N 14 B–
Q4±) 11 . . . N×P 12 N/Q4×N P×N
13 N×N Q×N 14 Q×Q P×Q 15
0–0–0 B–N2 16 P–KB4 P–Q5 17 B×P
B×P 18 KR–N1 B–K5 19 B×B K×B
20 R–Q7 K–B3 21 R–Q4 B–B4 22
KR–Q1 QR–B1 23 R/Q1–Q2 R–B2
24 P–N3 R–KR1 (24 . . . P–K4∓) 25
B–B4! R–R6 26 K–N2 R–K6 27 P–R4
P–K4 28 P×P+ K×P 29 P–R5 B–K3
30 B×B K×B 31 R–Q8 K–K2 32 R–
QN8 R–K3 33 P–B4± P–R3 34 K–B3
P–B4 35 R/Q2–Q8 (35 P–N4!? followed
by P–B5, R–N6) 35 . . . P–B5 36 R–
K8+ (36 R–KB8 P–N4 37 R–B5 R–
KB3 38 R×NP P–B6 unclear) 36 . . .
K–B3 37 R×R+ K×R 38 K–Q4
(38 R–KB8 P–N4 39 P–N4!?) 38 . . .
R–B2 39 K–K4 K–Q3? (39 . . . R–B4
40 R–N6+ K–B2 41 K–B3 R×P= or
41 . . . P–N4) 40 R–N6+ K–B4?? (*123*)
(40 . . . K–B2 41 R×RP R–B1 42
R×P P–B6 43 R–N1 R–QN1 44 R–
KB1 R×P 45 R×P R–N8 may draw)
41 K–Q3 1–0 (42 P–N4 mate)

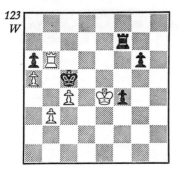

123
W

Q3!) 34 N–N7! R–Q4 35 N–B5 P–K4 36 N–K4 R×P 37 R×R P×R 38 N×P K–K2 (38 . . . B–B5? 39 N–Q7+) 39 N×P B–N8 40 B–R6! (40 K–B2 P–Q6 41 N–N5 P–Q7 42 K–K2 B–Q6+) 40 . . . N–Q4 41 K–B2 N–K6 42 B–K2 K–K3 43 N–N5+ K–Q4 44 N–K4 B×N 45 P×B+ K×P 46 P–KN4 K–B5 47 P–R5 P×P 48 P×P K–N4 49 K–B3 1–0

6) Botvinnik–Smyslov, King's Indian 1 P–QB4 P–KN3 2 P–K4 B–N2 3 P–Q4 P–Q3 4 N–QB3 P–QR3 5 B–K3 N–KB3 6 P–B3 P–B3 7 B–Q3 P–QN4 8 Q–Q2 P×P 9 B×P P–Q4 10 B–N3 P×P 11 N×P (11 P×P! P–K4 12 N–B3±) 11 . . . 0–0 12 N–K2 P–QR4! 13 0–0 P–R5 14 B–QB4 QN–Q2 15 QR–B1 R–N1 16 N×N+ B×N 17 N–B3 N–N3 18 B–K2 B–K3 19 KR–Q1 B–N2? (19 . . . Q–Q2 20 B–B1 KR–Q1∓) 20 B–KR6 B×B 21 Q×B P–B3 22 R–Q2 B–B2 23 P–R4 Q–Q2 24 P–R3 KR–Q1 25 N–K4 Q–K1 26 B–B1 B–Q4 27 N–B5 (*124*)

7) Smyslov–Botvinnik, Sicilian 1 P–K4 P–QB4 2 N–KB3 N–QB3 3 P–Q4 P×P 4 N×P N–B3 5 N–QB3 P–Q3 6 B–K2 P–KN3 7 B–K3 B–N2 8 P–KR4 0–0 9 P–R5 P–Q4 10 RP×P BP×P?! 11 P×P N×P 12 N×N/Q5 (12 B–QB4! P–K3 13 N×N/Q5 P×N 14 B–N3 N×N 15 B×N Q–K2+ 16 K–B1±) 12 . . . Q×N 13 B–B3 Q–B5 14 P–B3 N×N 15 P×N B–K3 16 Q–N3 ½–½ (*125*)

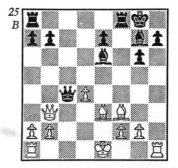

25
B

(16 . . . R×B! 17 P×R Q–B3 18 Q–Q1 B–Q4 19 R–R3 Q–K3∓)

8) Botvinnik–Smyslov, King's Indian 1 P–QB4 N–KB3 2 N–QB3 P–K4 3 P–KN3 P–B3 4 N–B3 P–Q3 5 B–N2 P–KN3 6 0–0 B–N2 7 P–Q4 QN–Q2 8 P–K4 0–0 9 P–KR3 N–K1 10 B–N5 P–B3 11 B–K3 P–KB4 12 Q–Q2 Q–B3 13 KP×P NP×P 14 B–N5 Q–B2 15 P–N3 P–B5! 16 QP×P N×P (16 . . . P×P 17 N–K4!) 17 B×P N×N+ 18 B×N B×P (*126*) 19 B–N2 (19 KR–K1! B–K4 20 B×B

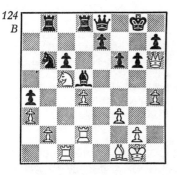

124
B

27 . . . Q–B1 28 Q×Q+ K×Q 29 N–R6± R/N1–B1 30 N–N4 B–N6!? (30 . . . R–Q3 31 R/Q2–B2 K–K1 32 B–N5 K–Q2! 33 N×B N×N 34 B× RP N–N3 35 B–N3 R×P±) 31 R×P R×R 32 N×R R–Q3 33 N–R5 B–R7 (33 . . . P–K4 34 N×B P×N 35 R–

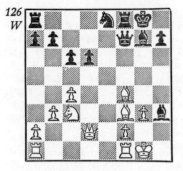

126
W

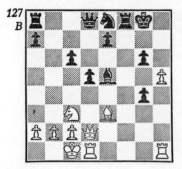

127
B

Q×B 21 Q–N5+ K–B2 22 Q–B4+±;
19 KR–K1! B–R3 20 R×N) 19 ... B×B
20 K×B N–B3 21 Q–Q3 P–Q4 22
QR–Q1 N–R4?! (22 ... QR–Q1=) 23
B–Q2 P×P 24 Q×P Q×Q 25 P×Q
QR–Q1 26 N–K2 N–B3 27 N–B4
KR–K1 28 B–B1 K–B2 29 B–K3
P–N3 30 R–KR1 P–KR3? (30 ...
N–N5 31 B–B1 P–KR3) 31 R×R?
(31 B–Q4!±) 31 ... R×R 32 K–B3
P–B4 33 P–R4 R–Q3 34 R–QB1 (34
N–R5 N×N 35 R×N R–Q6 36 R–Q5
R×R 37 P×R B–B1 38 K–K4 K–B3=)
34 ... N–Q2 35 K–K2 N–K4 36 B–
Q2? N–B3? (36 ... R–Q5) 37 N–Q5
R–K3+ 38 B–K3 B–Q5 39 R–KR1
B–N2 40 R–QB1 N–Q5+ 41 K–Q3
½–½ (41 ... N–B3∓ - but then 42 K–
K2 draws by threefold repetition!)

9) Smyslov–Botvinnik, Sicilian 1 P–
K4 P–QB4 2 N–KB3 N–QB3 3 P–Q4
P×P 4 N×P N–B3 5 N–QB3 P–Q3
6 B–K2 P–KN3 7 B–K3 B–N2 8 P–
KR4 P–KR4 9 P–B3 0–0 10 Q–Q2
P–Q4 11 N×N! P×N 12 P–K5 N–K1
(12 ... N–Q2 13 P–K6!?) 13 P–B4
P–B3 14 0–0–0 (14 P–KN4! RP×P
15 0–0–0) 14 ... P×P 15 P×P B×P
16 P–KN4 B×P 17 B×B P×B 18
P–R5 (127)
18 ... P–N4 19 B×NP Q–Q3 20 R–
R4 N–B3 21 B×N Q×B 22 R×P+
K–R1 23 K–N1 R–KN1 (23 ... QR–
N1? 24 R–N6! R×P+ 25 K–R1)

24 R–N4! (24 R–N6 R×R 25 P×R
K–N2 26 R–R1 R–R1 27 R×R K×
R∓) 24 ... P–R4 25 R–N6 B×N
26 P×B QR–N1 27 R×R R×R+
28 K–R1 R–N1= 29 Q–K3 R–N5 30
P–R3 R–K5 31 Q–Q3 Q–K4 32 K–N2
R–K6 33 Q–Q4 Q×Q 34 P×Q K–N2
(34 ... P–K4 is better) 35 R–N1+
K–B2 36 P–R6 R–R6 37 R–N7+
K–B3 38 R–R7 R–R5 39 K–B3 R–R6+
40 K–N2 R–R5 ½–½

10) Botvinnik–Smyslov, English 1 P–
QB4 N–KB3 2 N–QB3 P–Q4 3 P×P
N×P 4 P–KN3 P–KN3 5 B–N2 N×N
6 NP×N B–N2 7 B–QR3 (7 P–KR4 P–
KR3 8 N–R3±) 7 ... N–Q2 8 N–B3
P–QB4 9 Q–R4 0–0 10 R–QN1 P–QR3
11 P–B4 R–N1 (11 ... Q–B2 12 0–0
R–R2!, e.g. 13 B–N2 P–QN4 14 Q–B2
P–K4) 12 0–0 Q–B2 13 P–Q3 R–Q1 14
B–N2 N–B1 15 B×B K×B 16 R–N2
N–K3 17 KR–N1 P–QN4 18 P×P P×P
19 Q–K4 B–Q2 (128)
20 N–K5 (20 Q–K5+ P–B3 21 Q–
K3±) 20 ... B–K1 21 N–B6 B×N
22 Q×B Q×Q 23 B×Q P–N5 24 R–
QB1 N–Q5 25 B–R4QR–R1 26 B–N3
R–R4 27 K–B1 P–K3 28 K–K1 K–B3
29 B–B4 K–K2 30 P–KR4 R/Q1–QR1
31 P–K3 N–N4 32 P–Q4 (32 B×N R×B
33 P–Q4=) 32 ... N–Q3 33 B–N3
P×P 34 P×P R–Q1 35 R–B7+ K–B3
36 R–Q2 N–K5 (36 ... N–B4 37 P–Q5
P×P 38 R–N7=) 37 R–Q3 R–KB4

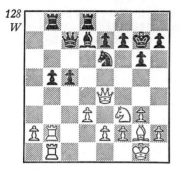

128
W

38 P–B4 N–B4 39 R–Q1? (39 R–Q2)
39 . . . N×B 40 P×N R/B4–Q4 (40 . . .
R–QR4!∓) 41 R–B4 R–QN1 42 R–R1
K–B4 43 K–B2 K–N5 44 R–R7 ½–½
11) **Smyslov-Botvinnik**, Grünfeld 1
P–Q4 N–KB3 2 P–QB4 P–KN3 3 N–
QB3 P–Q4 4 N–B3 B–N2 5 Q–N3
P×P 6 Q×BP 0–0 7 P–K4 B–N5 8 B–
K3 KN–Q2 9 R–Q1 N–N3 10 Q–N3
N–B3 11 P–Q5 N–K4 12 B–K2 N×N+
13 P×N B–R4 14 P–KR4 Q–Q2 15 P–
R4!? (15 P–B4 B×B 16 N×B P–QB3=)
15 . . . P–R4 (15 . . . B×N+ 16 P×B!
Q×RP 17 Q×Q N×Q 18 K–Q2±)
16 N–N5 N–B1 17 B–Q4 N–Q3?!
(17 . . . B×B 18 N×B N–N3±) 18
B×B K×B 19 N–Q4! K–N1 20 R–KN1
Q–R6 (20 . . . P–QB3 21 P×P P×P 22
N–B5!) 21 Q–K3 (*129*)

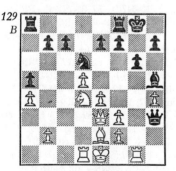

129
B

21 . . . P–QB4? (Best chance is 21 . . .
Q×RP: a) 22 P–K5 N–K1 23 Q–R6
Q–R7! 24 R–N3 N–N2 unclear; b)

22 Q–R6 P–K4! 23 P×Pe.p. P×P 24
N×P - if 24 R–N4 Q–R8+ 25 K–Q2
Q–R7 26 N×P Q–K4! - 24 . . . R–B2
25 N–N5 R–K2 26 R×N P×R 27 B–
B4+ K–R1 28 B–B7! wins) 22 P×Pe.p.
P×P 23 Q–N5! P–QB4 (23 . . . K–R1
24 Q×KP QR–Q1 25 Q–B6+ and
N–B6) 24 N–B6 1–0

12) **Botvinnik-Smyslov**, Reti 1 P–
QB4 N–KB3 2 P–KN3 P–B3 3 N–
KB3 P–Q4 4 P–N3 B–B4 5 B–KN2
P–K3 6 B–N2 QN–Q2 7 0–0 P–KR3
8 P–Q3 B–K2 9 QN–Q2 0–0 10 P–
QR3 P–QR4 11 Q–B2 B–R2 12 B–B3
P–QN4! 13 P×NP P×P 14 P–QN4?!
(Better 14 B–Q4 N–K1 15 B–R3)
14 . . . Q–B2 15 Q–N2 N–N3 16 B–K5
Q–Q2 17 N–N3 P×P 18 P×P R×R
19 R×R N–R5 (19 . . . B×NP?? 20 Q–
Q4) 20 Q–Q2 R–B1 21 R–QB1 R×R+
22 N×R N–K1 (Stronger 22 . . . Q–B1
followed by . . . N–Q2–N1–R3) 23 N–
Q4 K–B1 24 B–R3 B–N1 25 N/Q4–N3
P–B3 26 B–R1 Q–R2 27 P–Q4 N–Q3
28 Q–R2 N–B5 29 N–B5 (Or 29 N–Q3
Q–R3 30 B–B3) 29 . . . B×N 30
QP×B (*130*)

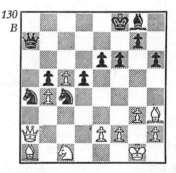

130
B

(30 NP×B? Q–R4! 31 K–B1 N–Q7+
32 K–N2 N–K5 33 N–Q3 Q–Q7∓)
30 . . . P–K4?! (30 . . . Q–KB2) 31 Q–
N1 P–Q5 32 Q–B5 Q–QB2 33 N–Q3
B–B2 34 Q–R7 B–N1 35 Q–K4!
B–B2 36 Q–R8+ B–K1 37 B–KN2
K–K2 38 P–B4! N–K6? (38 . . . N–B6

39 P×P P×P   40 P–B6!± threatens
Q–N7) 39 P×P P×P   40 Q–K4 N×B
41 N×P! 1–0

13) Smyslov-Botvinnik, Queen's
Gambit, Slav 1 P–Q4 P–Q4 2 P–QB4
P–QB3 3 N–KB3 N–B3 4 N–B3 P–K3
5 P–K3 QN–Q2 6 B–Q3 P×P 7 B×BP
P–QN4 8 B–Q3 P–N5 9 N–K4 N×N
10 B×N B–N2 11 0–0 B–Q3 12 B–Q2
0–0 13 R–B1 R–B1   14 Q–K2 Q–N3
15 KR–Q1 B–K2 16 B–K1 N–B3 17
B–N1 P–B4 18 P×P R×P 19 R×R
Q×R 20 N–Q4 R–Q1 21 N–N3 Q–N3
22 R×R+ B×R   23 P–B3 B–Q4=
24 B–KB2 B×N 25 P×B B–K2 26 B–
Q3 B–B4 27 B–B4 N–K1 28 K–B1
N–Q3 29 B–Q3 P–N3 30 Q–Q2 P–B4
31 B–B4 K–B2 32 B–N3 (*131*)

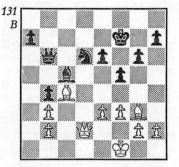

131
B

32 ... Q–B3 (32 ... N×B? 33 Q–Q7+
K–B3 34 B–R4+ P–N4 35 B×P+!
K×B 36 Q–N7+ etc.) 33 Q–Q3
P–QR4 34 K–K2 K–K2 35 B–R4+
K–B2 36 B–N3 K–K2 37 B–B4 B–N3
(Threat: 38 ... N×B 39 P×N P–R5!)
38 B×N+ Q×B   39 Q×Q+ K×Q
40 B–N5 B–Q1 41 P–B4 ½–½

14) Botvinnik-Smyslov, English 1 P–
QB4 N–KB3 2 N–QB3 P–Q4 3 P×P
N×P 4 P–KN3 P–KN3 5 B–N2 N×N
6 NP×N B–N2 7 R–N1 N–Q2 8 P–
QB4 0–0 9 N–B3 R–N1 (9 ... P–K4!)
10 0–0 P–N3 11 P–Q4 P–K4 12 B–
QR3 R–K1 13 P×P (13 P–Q5!?; 13
N×P N×N 14 P×N Q×Q 15 KR×Q

B–B4 16 P–K4 B–N5 17 P–B3 B–K3=)
13 ... B–N2! (13 ... N×P   14 N×N
B×N 15 B–B6 B–R6 16 B×R Q×B
17 R–K1 B–B6 18 Q–Q3 B×R 19
R×B±) 14 Q–B2 N×P 15 KR–Q1
Q–B1 16 N×N B×B 17 K×B R×N
18 R–Q5 Q–K3 19 R×R B×R 20
R–Q1 R–K1 21 Q–K4 B–B3 22 Q×Q
R×Q   23 K–B3 R–B3±   24 R–QB1
B–Q5 25 P–K3 B–B4 26 B–N2 P–B4
27 K–K2 K–B2 28 P–KR3 B–K2 29 P–
QR4 P–KR4 30 K–Q3 P–R5?! 31 P–
N4! R–B4 32 B–B3 R–B3 33 R–KN1
R–Q3+ 34 K–B2 B–B3 35 P×P P×P
36 B×B K×B 37 R–N8± R–B3 38 K–
B3 P–R3 39 R–KR8 K–N4 40 R–N8+
K–B3 41 R–KR8 K–N4 42 K–Q4 R–
B4 (42 ... R–Q3+? 43 K–K5+) 43
R–R7 K–N3 (43 ... R–B3! 44 R–Q7
K–B3 45 R–Q5 K–K3 46 K–B3 R–
Q3=; 43 ... R–B3! 44 R–R8 R–B4
45 P–B4+ K–N3 46 R×P R–R4 47 R–
R8 R×P 48 R–QB8 P–B4+ 49 K–Q5
R–R6=) 44 R–Q7 K–B3 45 R–Q5
R–B3 46 K–B3 R–K3 47 R–Q4 K–N4
48 R–Q7 R–QB3   49 K–N4 K–B3
50 R–Q4 K–N4 51 R–Q8 R–K3 52
R–QB8 P–B5 (52 ... R–QB3 53 R–R8
P–B5 54 P–K4. Botvinnik's plan is to
force ... P–QR4 when P–B4+ wins the
KRP) 53 P×P+ K×P 54 R×P K–B6
55 R–KR7 R–K5   56 R–R6 P–N4
(56 ... K–N7(!) 57 R×NP K×RP 58
R×P K–N7 59 P–R5 P–R6 60 R–N6+
K×P 61 R–KR6 K–N7 62 P–R6 R–K8
63 P–B5 R–QR8 64 K–N5 R–N8+
65 K–B6 P–R7 66 P–R7 R–QR8 67
K–N7 R–N8+ 68 K–R8 R–QB8 69
P–B6! R×P 70 R×P+ K×R 71 K–N7
wins) 57 RP×P? (57 R×QRP P×BP
58 R–B6 P–B6+ 59 K–N3 K×P 60
R×P± - R–QR3 comes) 57 ... P×P
58 R–B6+ K–N7 59 K×P (*132*)
59 ... R–K7? (59 ... K×P 60 P–B5 R–
K8 61 P–B6 R–N8+ 62 K–R6 R–R8+
63 K–N7 R–N8+ 64 K–B8 K–N7 65
P–B7 P–R6 draws. Also 59 ... R–K8
60 P–B5 K×P 61 R–B4 R–N8+ 62

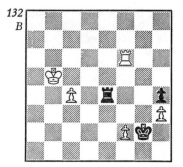

132
B

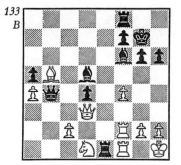

133
B

K–R6 R–R8+ 63 K–N7 R–N8+ 64 K–B7 R–KR8! draws) 60 P–B5 R–N7+ 61 K–R6 R–R7+ (61 ... R–B7 62 K–N6 R–N7+ 63 K–B7 K×P 64 R–B4! R–N8 65 P–B6 R–KR8 66 K–Q7 R–Q8+ 67 K–K6 R–QB8 68 K–Q5 R–Q8+ 69 R–Q4 wins) 62 K–N7 R–N7+ 63 R–QN6 R–B7 (63 ... R×P 64 R–N3±) 64 P–B6 K×RP 65 P–B7 K–N7 66 R–QB6 R–N7+ 67 R–QN6 R–B7 68 P–B4 1–0

15) Smyslov-Botvinnik, Caro-Kann 1 P–K4 P–QB3 2 P–Q4 P–Q4 3 P–KB3 P–K3 4 N–B3 N–B3 5 B–KN5 P–KR3 6 B–R4 Q–N3 7 P–QR3 P–B4! 8 KN–K2 N–B3 9 QP×P B×P 10 N–R4 Q–R4+ 11 N2–B3 (11 P–QN4 Q×N 12 N–B3 B×P!∓) 11 ... B–K2 12 B×N B×B 13 P×P N–Q5! 14 B–Q3 (14 P×P B×P∓) 14 ... P×P 15 0–0 0–0 16 P–B4 P–KN3 17 Q–K1 B–N2 18 K–R1 B–Q2 19 P–QN4 Q–Q1 20 R–Q1 P–N3 21 Q–B2 B–K3 22 B–R6 Q–B3 23 R–Q2 QR–Q1 24 N–Q1 N–B4 25 N/R4–B3 P–Q5 26 N–K4 Q–K2 27 B–Q3 P–QR4! 28 P×P P×P 29 P–QR4 Q–N5 30 R–K2 B–Q4 31 N–N3 N×N+ 32 Q×N R/Q1–K1 33 R/K2–B2 (33 R×R R×R 34 P–B5 P×P 35 R×P R–K8+ 36 R–B1 R×R+ 37 B×R B–B3∓) 33 ... B–KB3 34 Q–R3 K–N2 35 B–N5 R–K8 36 Q–Q3 *(133)*

36 ... B–K5 37 Q–QN3 R×R+ 38 R×R Q–Q7 39 N–B2 B–R1 40 Q–Q3

Q×KBP∓ 41 P–R3 P–R4 42 Q–K2 Q–K6 43 Q×Q P×Q 44 N–Q1 R–B1?! (44 ... B–Q5 45 R–K1 P–B4 46 N×P P–B5 47 N–Q1 P–B6∓) 45 N×P R–B6 46 B–Q3 R–B4 47 N–B4 R–KN4 48 R–B2 B–B3 49 N–Q6 R–K4 50 N–B4 R–KN4 (50 ... R–K8+ 51 R–B1 R×R+ 52 B×R B×P 53 N×P B×P∓, but not so easy!) 51 N–Q6 R–Q4 52 N–N5 R–K4 53 R–K2 R×R 54 B×R B–K2 55 K–N1 1–0 (On time. The position is still ∓)

16) Botvinnik-Smyslov, English 1 P–QB4 N–KB3 2 N–QB3 P–Q4 3 P×P N×P 4 P–KN3 P–KN3 5 B–N2 N×N 6 NP×N B–N2 7 R–N1 N–Q2 8 N–B3 0–0 9 0–0 P–K4 10 P–Q4 P–QB3 11 P–K4 Q–R4 12 Q–B2 P×P 13 P×P N–N3 14 B–Q2 (14 B–K3!) 14 ... Q–R5 15 Q×Q N×Q 16 KR–B1 N–N3 17 B–K3 P–KB4 18 N–K5 P×P 19 B×P B–B4 20 B×B R×B 21 P–N4 R/B4–KB1 22 P–QR4 QR–K1 23 P–R5 N–Q4 24 R×NP N×B 25 P×N B×N 26 P×B R×P *(134)*
27 R×BP (27 R×RP R–K5! 27 P–R3 R×KP 29 R×BP P–N4=) 27 ... R–B2! 28 P–R6 R×P 29 R/B6–B7 R–K8+ 30 K–N2 R–K7+ 31 K–N3 R–K6+ 32 K–N2 R–K7+ 33 K–N3 R–K6+ 34 K–R4 R×R 35 R×R P–R3 36 P–N5 P–R4 ½–½

17) Smyslov-Botvinnik, Caro-Kann 1 P–K4 P–QB3 2 N–QB3 P–Q4 3 N–B3

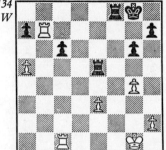

134
W

P×P 4 N×P N–B3 5 N×N+ NP×N
6 B–B4 B–N2 7 P–KR3 B–B4 8 0–0
P–K3 9 R–K1 0–0 10 P–Q4 N–Q2
11 B–B4 R–K1 12 Q–Q2 B–N3 (12 . . .
Q–K2!? 13 P–B3 Q–B1) 13 P–B3
N–N3 14 B–QN3 P–QR4 15 P–R3
N–Q4 16 B–R6 Q–N3 (16 . . . B×B
17 Q×B Q–N3 18 B×N BP×B 19
P–KR4 Q×NP 20 P–R5 Q×BP 21
P×B RP×P unclear) 17 B×B K×B
18 B–R2 QR–Q1 19 P–B4 N–K2 20
QR–Q1 Q–B2 21 Q–B3 B–R4 22 R–
Q3 B–N3 23 R–Q2 R–Q2 24 N–R2
P–R4 25 N–B3 R/K1–Q1 26 R/K1–Q1
P–N3 27 N–R4 N–B4 28 N×B P×N
29 B–N1 P–B4 30 B×N (135)

135
B

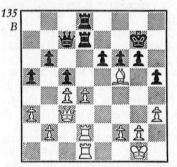

30 . . . P×P 31 R×P (31 B×KP P×Q
32 R×R+ R×R 33 R×R+ Q×R 34
B×Q P×P) 31 . . . R×R 32 R×R R×R
33 Q×R NP×B 34 P–QN4 P×P
35 P×P K–B2 36 K–B1 K–K2 37 K–
K2 Q–N2 38 P–B5 Q–R3+ 39 Q–Q3
Q–R7+ 40 K–B3 Q–R1+ 41 K–N3

P×P 42 P×P P–R5+! 43 K–R2 (43
K×P Q×P 44 Q–N3 Q–K5+ 45 K–
R5 P–K4=) 43 . . . Q–N1+ 44 K–N1
Q–B2 45 Q–R3 (45 Q–N5!) K–B2
46 Q–N4 Q–B3 47 Q–N6 Q–K5 48
Q–R5 Q–N8+ 49 K–R2 Q–N1+ ½–½

18) **Botvinnik–Smyslov,** English 1 P–
QB4 N–KB3 2 N–QB3 P–Q4 3 P×P
N×P 4 P–KN3 P–KN3 5 B–N2 N×N
6 NP×N B–N2 7 Q–N3 N–B3 8 N–
B3 0–0 9 0–0 N–R4 10 Q–B2 P–QB4
11 P–Q3 B–B4 12 P–K4 B–Q2 13 B–
N5 R–B1 14 Q–Q2 B–N4 15 KR–Q1
B–R5 16 R–K1 P–B3 17 B–R6 (17 B–
K3 P–K4∓) 17 . . . B×B 18 Q×B
Q×P!? (18 . . . P–K4) 19 P–K5! N–B3
20 R–K3 Q–B7 21 P×P P×P 22 QR–
K1 QR–Q1 (136)

136
W

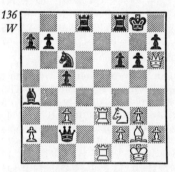

23 B–R3 (23 N–Q4!! P×N 24 B–Q5+!
R×B – 24 . . . K–R1 25 R–K7 – 25
R–K8 wins; 23 N–Q4!! N×N 24 B–
Q5+ R×B 25 R–K7 wins) 23 . . . N–
K4 24 N×N P×N 25 P–KB4 B–B3
26 Q–N5?? (26 R×P Q×BP 27 R–K7
R–B2!) 26 . . . R/Q1–K1?? (26 . . . R–
Q7 27 B–K6+ R–B2 28 B×R+ K×B
wins) 27 R×P Q×BP 28 R×R B×R?
(28 . . . R×R) 29 Q–K5 Q×Q 30 R×Q
P–N3 31 R–K7 P–QR4 32 R–QN7
R–B3 33 R–N8 K–B2 34 K–B2 R–Q3
35 K–K3 B–R5 (35 . . . P–R4!) 36 R–
N7+ K–N1 37 R–N8+ K–N2 38 R–
N7+ K–N1 39 R–N8+ K–B2 40 R–
N7+ K–B1 41 R×RP P–B5 42 R–QB7

P–QN4 43 K–K4 P–N5 44 R×P R–Q7 45 K–K5 R×QRP 46 R–B8+ B–K1?? (46 ... K–N2 47 R–B7+ K–B1 48 R–B8+ draws) 47 B–Q7 R–K7+ 48 K–B6 P–N4 (48 ... P–N6 49 R–N8 P–N7 50 B×B R×B 51 R×P and K×P) 49 P×P R–B7+ 50 K–K5 (50 B–B5 P–N6 51 P–N6 wins) 50 ... R–K7+ 51 K–B4 P–N6 52 R–N8 P–N7 53 B×B R×B 54 R×P P–R5 55 R–R2 R–R1 56 R–R3 K–B2 57 P–R4 K–N3 58 K–K4 K–R4 59 K–Q4 R–Q1+ 60 K–B4 R–K1 61 K–Q5 R–Q1+ 62 K–K5 R–QR1 63 K–Q5 R–Q1+ 64 K–B5 R–QN1 55 R×P R–N6 66 K–Q6 R×P 67 K–K7 R–N6 68 R–R6 R–N2+ (68 ... K×P 69 P–N6 wins) 69 K–B6 R–N5 70 R–Q6 R–R5 (70 ... R×P 71 K–B5!) 71 R–K6 R–QN5 72 K–B7 R–N2+ 73 R–K7 R–N5 74 K–N7 1–0

19) Smyslov-Botvinnik, Caro-Kann 1 P–K4 P–QB3 2 N–QB3 P–Q4 3 N–B3 B–N5 4 P–KR3 B×N 5 Q×B N–B3 6 P–Q3 P–K3 7 P–R3! B–K2 8 P–KN4 KN–Q2 (Best is 8 ... P×P 9 P×P KN–Q2 and ... B–N4) 9 P–Q4 N–B1? 10 B–K3 N–N3 11 Q–N3 B–R5 12 Q–R2 N–Q2 13 0–0–0± Q–N1 14 P–B4 P×P 15 N×P N–B3 16 N×N+ B×N 17 Q–B2 B–R5 18 Q–B3 N–K2 19 B–Q3 P–KN3 20 P–B5! (*137*) 20 ... KP×P (20 ... Q–N6 21 Q×Q B×Q 22 P×KP P×P 23 B–KR6!±) 21

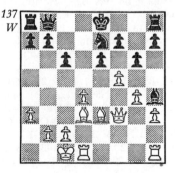

137
W

B–KB4 Q–Q1 22 P×P Q–Q4 23 Q–N4 B–B3 24 KR–K1 P–KR4 25 Q–N3 P–R5 (25 ... 0–0–0 26 B–N8 Q–R4 27 P×P P×P 28 R–K6+) 26 Q–N4 P×P 27 B×P K–B1 28 B–K4 Q–R7 29 P–B3 R–Q1 30 R–B1 N–Q4 31 B–Q2 R–Q3 (31 ... B–N2 32 R×P+! wins) 32 Q–B8+ K–K2 34 Q×P+ (34 R/Q1–K1!) 34 ... R–Q2 35 R/Q1–K1 Q–R8+ 36 B–N1+ 1–0 (36 ... K–Q3 37 R×B+ N×R 38 B–B4+ K–Q4 39 Q–N3 mate)

20) Botvinnik-Smyslov, English 1 P–QB4 P–QB4 2 N–KB3 P–B4 3 P–Q4 P×P 4 N×P P–KN3 5 P–KN3 B–N2 6 B–N2 N–QB3 7 N–N5 N–B3 8 KN–B3 0–0 9 0–0 P–N3 10 P–N3 B–N2 11 B–N2 R–B2 12 Q–Q2 Q–KB1 13 N–R3 R–Q1 14 QR–Q1 N–QR4 15 B×B N×B 16 N/R3–N5 P–QR3 17 N–Q4 (17 N–B7!±) 17 ... B–R3 18 Q–B2 P–B5 19 N–B3 P–Q3 20 N–Q4 R–R1 21 N–Q5 (21 N–K6 Q–B1 22 N×P B×N 23 P×B Q–N5+ unclear) 21 ... N×N 22 P×N R–B1 23 Q–N1 Q–K1 24 B–R3 N–Q1 25 Q–K4 Q–Q2 (*138*)

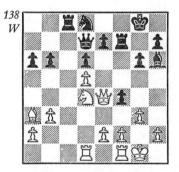

138
W

26 K–N2 (26 N–K6±) 26 ... Q–N5 27 P–B3 (27 P–R3 Q–R4 28 P–KN4 Q–K4 29 Q×Q P×Q 30 N–B3±) 27 ... Q–R4 28 N–K6 Q–B4! 29 N–Q4?! (29 Q×Q R×Q 30 N×N R×N 31 P–KN4 R/B4–KB1=) 29 ... Q×Q 30 P×Q P×P 31 R×R K×R 32 P×P

B–N2 ∓ 33 B–N2 P–QN4 34 R–Q2
K–K1 35 K–B2 K–Q2 36 N–B3 B×B
37 R×B N–B2 38 K–K3 R–B6+
(38 . . . R–B8!? 39 K–Q2 R–KR8 40
R–B2 R–R6 41 R–B6 unclear) 39 K–Q2
P–N5 40 R–N1 P–KR4 41 P–R3 P–R4
42 P×P P×P 43 R–QR1 N–R3 (43 . . .
R×P 44 R–R7+ K–K1 45 R–R8+
N–Q1 46 P–K5! R–R6 47 R–N8)
44 R–R7+ K–K1 45 R–R8+ K–B2
46 P–K5 P×P 47 N–N5+ K–N2
48 N–K6+ ½–½

21) Smyslov-Botvinnik, Sicilian 1 P–
K4 P–QB4 2 N–KB3 N–QB3 3 P–Q4
P×P 4 N×P N–B3 5 N–QB3 P–KN3
6 N×N QP×N 7 Q×Q+ K×Q 8 B–
QB4 K–K1 9 P–QR4?! (9 B–B4; 9 P–
K5) 9 . . . P–K4 10 P–B4 B–K3 11
B×B P×B 12 R–B1 B–R3 (139)

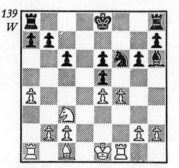

13 P–B5 (13 P×P B×B 14 R×B N–
N5=) 13 . . . B×B 14 R×B K–K2
15 R–Q1 NP×P 16 P×P QR–Q1 17
R×R R×R 18 P–QN3 R–KN1 19 P–
N3 P–KR4 20 P×P K×P 21 R–B2
P–R5 P×P R–KR1 23 N–Q1 ½–½

22) Botvinnik-Smyslov, Dutch 1 P–
Q4 P–KB4 2 P–KN3 N–KB3 3 B–N2
P–K3 4 N–KB3 B–K2 5 0–0 0–0 6 P–
B4 P–B3 7 N–B3 P–Q4 8 B–N5
QN–Q2 9 P×P Q–K3 Q–K1 (9 . . . N–K5
10 B×B Q×B=; 9 . . . P×P? 10 N–
Q2) 10 Q–B2 K–R1 11 N–K2 P–KR3
12 B×N B×B 13 P×P KP×P 14 N–
B4 P–KN4 15 N–Q3 R–KN1 16 Q–B3

B–K2 17 N/B3–K5 N–B3 18 P–B3
B–K3 19 N–B5? (19 P–QN4 R–Q1
20 P–QR4±) 19 . . . B×N 20 Q×B?
(20 P×B) 20 . . . N–Q2! 21 N×N
Q×N 22 QR–K1 R–N2 23 R–B2
P–N3 24 Q–B3 Q–Q3 25 R–B2 B–Q2
26 P–QN4 (26 P–K4! P–B5 27 P–K5
Q–K3 28 P–KN4±) 26 . . . P–KR4!
27 K–R1 P–R5 28 P×P P×P 29 P–B4
QR–KN1 30 B–B3 B–K1 31 Q–Q2
Q–R3 32 Q–K2 P–R6 33 R/B2–B1
(140)

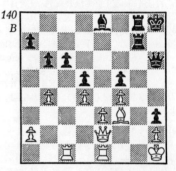

33 . . . R–N7! 34 B×R R×B 35 Q–B3?
(35 Q–B1 B–R4 36 P–K4! BP×P 37
R–B3 B–B6 38 R×B P×R 39 Q×P
unclear) 35 . . . Q–R5 36 P–N5 B–R4
37 Q×R P×Q+ 38 K–N1 P–B4 0–1

23) Smyslov-Botvinnik, Reti 1 N–
KB3 N–KB3 2 P–KN3 P–KN3 3 P–
QN4 P–N3 4 B–QN2 B–QN2 5 N–R3
B–N2 6 B–N2 0–0 7 0–0 P–Q3
8 P–B4 P–B4 9 N–B2 Q–B2 10 P–Q3
QN–Q2 11 P–K4 P–K3 12 N–K3
N–N5 13 B×B N×N 14 P×N K×B
15 N–N5 QR–K1 16 P–QR3 P–Q4!∓
17 NP×P NP×P 18 Q–N3 P–Q5 19
P×P P×P (141)
20 P–B5! (Idea: 20 . . . N×P 21 QR–B1
Q–K4 22 Q–N5 unclear) 20 . . . P–
KR3 21 N–B3 P–K4 22 QR–B1 B–B3
23 N–R4 R–QN1 24 Q–Q1 Q–Q1
25 B–R3 N–B3 26 N–B3 Q–K2 27
Q–B2 R–N2 28 N–Q2 R–B2 (28 . . .
KR–QN1? 29 N–B4! Q×P 30 N×P)

141
W

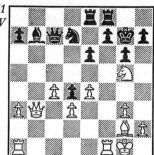

29 Q–B4 N–R2 30 N–B3 R–QN1 31
R–KB2 N–N4 32 N×N P×N 33 P–R4
B–K1 34 B–N4 P–R4 35 B–Q1 R/N1–
B1 36 R/B2–B2 B–Q2 37 B–K2 K–N1
38 K–N2 K–N2 39 K–N1 K–B1 40
B–Q1 K–N1 (40 . . . Q–K3!) 41 Q–N3
(41 P–R3?! B×KRP 42 P–N4 R×P!
43 Q×R R×Q 44 R×R Q–B3∓) ½–½
(41 . . . K–B1 42 Q–B4 Q–K3! 43
Q×Q B×Q 44 P–B6 K–K2 45 R–B5
K–Q3 46 R×RP R×P 47 R×R+
R×R∓)

6 Botvinnik-Tal

Moscow 15 March–7 May 1960

	1	2	3	4	5	6	7	8	9	10	11
Botvinnik	0	½	½	½	½	0	0	1	1	½	0
Tal	1	½	½	½	½	1	1	0	0	½	1

	12	13	14	15	16	17	18	19	20	21	**Total**
Botvinnik	½	½	½	½	½	0	½	0	½	½	8½
Tal	½	½	½	½	½	1	½	1	½	½	12½

1) Tal-Botvinnik, French 1 P–K4
P–K3 2 P–Q4 P–Q4 3 N–QB3 B–N5
4 P–K5 P–QB4 5 P–QR3 B×N+
6 P×B Q–B2 7 Q–N4 P–B4 8 Q–N3
N–K2 9 Q×P R–N1 10 Q×P P×P
11 K–Q1 (An eccentric line; Gligoric-
Petrosian, Candidates 1959, continued
11 . . . QN–B3 12 N–B3 N×P 13 B–
KN5! - 13 . . . N×N 14 B–N5+! -)
11 . . . B–Q2 12 Q–R5+ N–N3 13 N–
K2 (Threat 14 N–B4 exploiting the pin;
Black must now take care, e.g. 13 . . .
Q×KP 14 P×P or 13 . . . P×P 14
N–B4 K–B2 15 B–Q3 with a number
of threats, viz. 15 . . . QN–B3 16 B×P
P×B 17 P–K6+ B×P 18 Q–R7+ R–
N2 19 Q×R+!; 13 . . . B–R5 14 N–B4
Q×BP 15 B–Q3 Q×R 16 N×N
N–B3 17 N–B4+!; 13 . . . N–B3 14
P×P R–QB1 15 R–R2) 13 . . . P–
Q6!(1.01) 14 P×P(0.31) B–R5+ (This
move is not quite correct; 14 . . . N–
B3! and . . . 0–0–0–) 15 K–K1 Q×KP
16 B–N5! N–B3 17 P–Q4 Q–B2 18
P–R4! P–K4 19 R–R3 Q–B2 20 P×P
QN×P 21 R–K3 K–Q2 (21 . . . R–R1
22 R×N+ K–Q2 23 R–K7+ Q×R 24
Q×N) 22 R–N1 P–N3 23 N–B4 QR–
K1 24 R–N4! B–B3 25 Q–Q1! (142)
25 . . . N×N (After 25 . . . N–N5 26 R–
K2 or 26 R×R R×R+ 27 B–K2

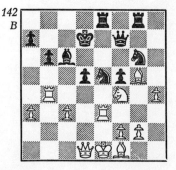

142
B

Black is lost) 26 QR×N N–N3 27
R–Q4 R×R+ 28 P×R K–B2 29
P–B4 P×P 30 B×P Q–N2 31 B×R
Q×B(2.22) 32 P–R5(1.31) 1–0

2) Botvinnik-Tal, Modern Benoni 1
P–Q4 N–KB3 2 P–QB4 P–QB4 3 P–
Q5 P–K3 4 N–QB3 P×P 5 P×P P–Q3
6 N–B3 P–KN3 7 B–N5 B–N2 8 N–
Q2 (More flexible than 8 P–K4, e.g.
8 . . . 0–0 9 B–K2 P–KR3 10 B–R4
P–KN4 11 B–N3 P–N4! 12 B×NP
N×KP 13 N×N Q–R4+ 14 Q–Q2
Q×B) 8 . . . P–KR3 9 B–R4 P–KN4
10 B–N3 N–R4 (To be rid of White's
active QB) Usual continuation has been
10 . . . P–R3 11 P–QR4 and then
remove the bishop.) 11 N–B4 N×B
12 RP×N 0–0 13 P–K3 (Stronger than

P–K4, which might encourage . . . P–KB4. Attempting to win the pawn on Q3 via 13 N–K4 P–N4 14 N/B×P P–B4 15 N×B P×N 16 P–Q6 Q–R4+ 17 Q–Q2 Q×Q+ 18 K×Q R×B fails) 13 . . . Q–K2 14 B–K2 R–Q1 15 0–0 N–Q2 16 P–QR4 N–K4 17 N×N Q×N 18 P–R5 R–N1 19 R–R2! (Now Black's queen and bishop are ineffective. White's knight will be free to go to QB4 via N–N5–R3) 19 . . . B–Q2 20 N–N5 B×N(0.55) 21 B×B *(143)*

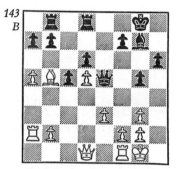

143
B

21 . . . P–N3? (21 . . . P–R3! 22 B–B4 P–N4 23 P×Pe.p. R×P 24 P–N3 R–R1) 22 P–R6! R/N–B1 23 Q–Q3 R–B2 24 P–N3 Q–B6 25 Q×Q B×Q 26 R–B2 B–B3 27 P–KN4 R–K2 28 R–B4 R–QB1 (Primarily to prevent 29 P–N4 on which is possible 29 . . . R/2–B2 30 R/1–B1 B–N7! 31 R1–B2 B–R6 32 P×P B×P) 29 P–N3 B–N2 30 R–Q1 R–B1 31 R–Q3 Gets in the way of his own bishop. The black king starts a diversion. 31 . . . K–R2 32 K–N2 K–N3 33 R–Q1 P–R4 34 P×P+ K×P 35 P–N4+ K–N3 36 R–B2 R–KR1 37 B–Q3+ K–B3 38 K–N3 R2–K1 39 B–N5 R–K5 40 R–B4 R×R 41 P×R K–K2 42 B–R4 B–K4+ 43 K–B3 R–R5 44 R–KN1 (Probably not taking into accouht Black's next move. On 44 B–B2 R–R6+ 45 K–K4 R–R7 46 R–KB1 B–N6; 47 K–B3 B–R5!) 44 . . . P–B4(2.07) ½–½

3) Tal–Botvinnik, Caro-Kann 1 P–K4 P–QB3 2 N–QB3 P–Q4 3 N–B3 B–N5 4 P–KR3 B×N 5 P×B!? (Roundly condemned. Popularly similar pawn doublings are regarded as weakening, etc. In this case White strengthens his centre and opens the KN-file) 5 . . . P–K3 6 P–Q4 N–Q2 7 B–KB4 (Dubious; better 7 B–K3 controlling important KB4 square; on 7 . . . B–N5 8 P–R3 is a good reply) 7 . . . B–N5 8 P–KR4 (A miscalculation. 8 P–QR3! B–R4 9 P–N4 B–B2 10 B–K3) 8 . . . KN–B3 9 P–K5 (After this move, White is positionally lost) 9 . . . N–R4 10 B–KN5 Q–R4 11 B–Q2 Q–N3 12 P–R3 B–K2 13 B–K3 P–N3! (Fixing White's weaknesses) 14 N–R4 Q–Q1 15 Q–Q2 N–N2 *(144)*

144

(avoiding any kind of complication; after 15 . . . B×RP 16 B–R6 threatening B–R3–N4 White's position would be more satisfactory than in game) 16 B–KN5 P–KR3! 17 B×P N–KB4 18 B–KB4 R×P 19 R×R N×R 20 0–0–0 P–QN4! 21 N–B5 N×N 22 P×N B×P 23 B–K2 B–K2 23 K–N1! Q–B2 25 R–R1 0–0–0 26 B–N3 N–B4 27 R–R7 R–B1 (The rook is not so solidly placed on this square; White's bishop quickly plays an active role in the game; 27 . . . B–B4! followed by R–Q2 should lead to Black victory) 28 B–KB4 Q–Q1 29 B–Q3 R–R1 30 R×R Q×R 31 Q–R5 (White now obtains an attack seemingly strong enough to hold a draw) 31 ... Q–R8+ 32 K–R2 Q×P 33 Q–R6+ K–N1 34 Q×BP! Q×B/5 35 B×P Q×KP 36 Q–K8+ K–N2 (More prudent was 36 ... K–B2) 37 Q–B6 K–N1 ½–½

4) Botvinnik-Tal, Nimzo-Indian 1 P–Q4 N–KB3 2 P–QB4 P–K3 3 N–QB3 B–N5 4 P–QR3 B×N+ 5 P×B 0–0 6 P–B3 P–Q4 7 P×P P×P 8 P–K3 B–B4 (Probably the most logical. White intends an eventual P–K4 and this helps to hinder White's intention) 9 N–K2 QN–Q2 (On 9 ... P–B4, unpleasant is 10 P–KN4 B–K3 – the piece sacrifice 10 ... N×P 11 P×N Q–R5+ 12 K–Q2 B–K5 13 R–KN1 Q×RP 14 Q–K1 as in Averbakh–Khasin, Moscow Championship 1957 was not correct – 11 N–N3 with prospects for an attack on the king) 10 N–N3 B–N3 11 B–Q3 P–B4 12 0–0 R–K1 13 R–K1 Q–B2 14 B×B (This exchange strengthens Black's king defences. 14 P–K4 14 ... BP×P 15 BP×P P×P 16 P×P Q–B6 17 B–K3 N–Q4!) 14 ... RP×B 15 P–K4 BP×P 16 BP×P QR–B1 (*145*)

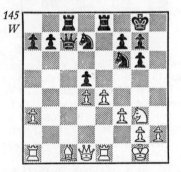

145
W

17 B–N5 Q–B7 18 B×N Q×Q (Bl. R. on B7 gives White the possibility to activate his pieces with a tempo, e.g. 18 ... N×B 19 P–K5 N–Q2 20 Q×Q! R×Q 21 KR–N1! N–N3 22 P–QR4 R–K2 23 R–N5 with the possible N–B1–K3) 19 KR×Q N×B 20 P–K5

N–R4?! (On 20 ... N–Q2 White would get the better endgame, e.g. 21 QR–N1 N–N3 22 P–QR4 R–B2 23 P–R5 N–B5 24 R–N5 R–Q1 25 KR–N1 KR–Q2 26 R–R1) 21 N–K2 R–B7 22 K–B1 P–KN4 23 KR–B1 KR–QB1 24 P–N3 P–B3 25 R×R R×R 26 R–N1 P–QN3 27 R–N5 P×P 28 P×P R–B4 29 N–Q4 K–B2 30 K–K2 (Now Black brings the knight, which has "lost its way" into the game. 30 P–B4! when Black can hope for a draw with 30 ... P–N3 31 P×P N–N2 32 R–N3 K–K2) 30 ... P–N3 31 K–Q3 N–N2 32 R–N1 R–R4 33 N–B2! N–K3 34 R–N4 R–B4 35 P–KR4 P×P 36 R×RP P–Q5 37 N×P R×P 38 N×N K×N 39 P–R4 R–KN4 40 R–K4+ K–B3 (1.53) ½–½

5) Tal-Botvinnik, Caro-Kann 1 P–K4 P–QB3 2 P–Q4 P–Q4 3 N–QB3 P×P 4 N×P B–B4 5 N–N3 B–N3 6 KN–K2 P–K3 7 P–KR4 P–KR3 8 N–B4 B–R2 9 B–B4 N–B3 10 Q–K2 (10 0–0!; White is trying to provoke 10 ... Q×P after which 11 0–0 N–K5 12 B–K3 gives a large positional plus for the pawn) 10 ... B–Q3 11 B–K3 QN–Q2 (If 11 ... B×N 12 B×B Q×P 13 B–K5) 12 N3–R5 N×N 13 N×N R–KN1 14 P–KN4 Q–B2 15 P–N5 B–N3! 16 0–0–0 0–0–0 17 N–N3 (17 B–Q3! though after 17 ... B×B 18 R×B P–KN3 19 N–N3 P×P! 20 B×P P–B3; 20 P×P P–KB4! 21 P× Pep N×P 22 B–KN5 B–B5+ Black need not fear anything) 17 ... P×P 18 B×NP B–B5+ 19 B×B Q×B+ 20 Q–K3 (*146*)
20 ... Q–R3! 21 B–Q3 B×B 22 R×B N–N3 23 Q×Q P×Q 24 R–KB3 P–KB4 25 R–K1 R–Q3 26 P–B3 R–N5 27 N–K2 N–Q4! (∓) (Sharpening the game with 27 ... R×RP 28 N–B4 K–Q2 29 N–N6 R–R7 30 N–B8+ K–K2 31 R×BP only assists White) 28 R–R1 R–Q1 29 R–N3 R×R 30

P×R R–N1 31 K–Q2 R–N5 32 K–K1 K–Q2 33 K–B2 R–K5 34 R–K1! K–Q3 35 N–B1 R×R 36 K×R P–B4 37 K–K2 P×P 38 P×P N–B3 39 K–Q3 N–R4 40 N–K2 P–K4 41 P–R4!? (After 41 P×P+ K×P 42 K–K3? N×P! 43 N×N P–B5+ 44 K–B3 P×N 45 K×P P–KR4 Black wins ensuing pawn endgame) 41 ... N–B3 42 P×P+ K×P 43 P–QN4 ½–½

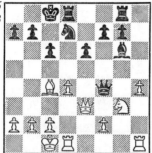

146
B

6) **Botvinnik-Tal,** King's Indian 1 P–QB4 N–KB3 2 N–KB3 P–KN3 3 P–KN3 B–N2 4 B–N2 0–0 5 P–Q4 P–Q3 6 N–B3 QN–Q2 7 0–0 P–K4 8 P–K4 P–B3 9 P–KR3 Q–N3 10 P–Q5 P×P 11 BP×P N–B4 12 N–K1 (12 R–K1 or 12 N–Q2 are usual here) 12 ... B–Q2 13 N–Q3 N×N 14 Q×N KR–B1 (A critical position, the essence of which is the breakthrough ... P–KB4. The direct 14 ... N–R4 does not achieve this goal in view of 15 B–K3 Q–Q1 16 Q–K2! P–B4 17 P×P Black is forced to a positionally difficult game after 17 ... P×P) 15 R–N1 N–R4 16 B–K3 Q–N5 17 Q–K2 R–B5 18 KR–B1 R1–QB1 19 K–R2 P–B4! 20 P×P B×P 21 R–QR1 (On 21 P–R3 Q–N6 22 N–K4 R–B7 23 R×R R×R 24 Q–Q1 Black can try the interesting piece sacrifice 24 ... N–B5!?) 21 ... N–B5 22 P×N P×P 23 B–Q2 (23 P–QR3 – 23 B×RP Q–R4 – Q–N6 24 B×RP leads to interesting complications as White's

extra piece can be locked out with ... P–N3) 23 ... Q×P 24 QR–N1 (24 N–Q1 loses to 24 ... Q–K4, e.g. 25 Q×Q B×Q 26 R×R R×R 27 R–B1 P–B6; 25 Q×Q B×Q 26 B–B3 R–B7) 24 ... P–B6 (Black had placed his hopes on this move but White has a surprising continuation for the initiative viz: 25 B×BP B×R 26 R×B Q–B7 27 B–K4!! – 27 R–QB1 Q–N7 28 R–QN1 etc. – 27 ... R×B 28 N×R!! Q×R 29 N×P R–B1 30 Q–K6+ K–R1 31 N–B7+ R×N 32 Q×R Q–B4 33 Q×Q P×Q 34 K–N3 B–K4+ 35 B–B4; 28 ... B–K4+ 29 K–N2 Q×R 30 N×P! B×N 31 Q–K6+ K–N2 32 Q–Q7+ with better endgame) 25 R×Q? P×Q 26 R–N3 R–Q5 27 B–K1 (27 B–K3 R×N 28 R3×R R×Q8) 27 ... B–K4+ 28 K–N1 (147)

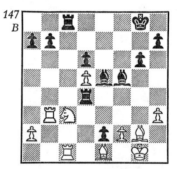

147
B

28 ... B–B5 (Black missed 28 ... R×N! 29 R3×R R–Q8 30 R–B4 B–N7) 29 N×P R×R 30 N×R/4 R×B+ 31 B–B1 B–K5 32 N–K2 B–K4 33 P–B4 B–B3 34 R×P B×P 35 R–QB7 B×P 36 R×QRP B–B5 37 R–R8+ K–B2 38 R–R7+ K–K3 39 R–R3 P–Q4 40 K–B2 B–R5+ 41 K–N2 K–Q3 42 N–N3 B×N 43 B×B P×B 44 K×B K–Q4 45 R–R7 P–B6 46 R–QB7 K–Q5 0–1

7) **Tal-Botvinnik,** Caro-Kann 1 P–K4 P–QB3 2 P–Q4 P–Q4 3 N–QB3 P×P

4 N×P B–B4 5 N–N3 B–N3 6 KN–K2
N–Q2 7 P–KR4 P–KR3 8 N–B4
B–R2 9 B–B4 P–K4 10 Q–K2 Q–K2
11 P×P Q×KP 12 B–K3 B–QB4
13 B×B Q×Q+ 14 K×Q (14 N3×Q!
N×B 15 0–0–0 N–B3 16 N–Q4; now
the knight on KN3 is poorly placed)
14 ... N×B 15 KR–K1 N–B3 16 P–N4
QN–Q2 17 K–B1+ K–B1 18 B–N3
P–KN4! (Black forces the White knight
back and vacates KN2 for king) 19
P×P P×P 20 N–R3 R–KN1 21 KR–
Q1!? (Objectively stronger was 21
QR–Q1 but a drawish position arise
after 21 ... R–K1 22 R×R K×R
23 R–K1+ K–B1 24 R–Q1 K–K2 etc.)
21 ... P–R4 22 P×P R×P 23 R–Q6
K–K2 24 QR–Q1 R–K4 25 N–R5
B–N3? (148)

148
W

(25 ... R–KR1!)   26 R×N+ N×R
27 R×N+ K×R 28 N–B6+ K–Q3
29 N×R R–QB4   30 N–R6 P–B3
31 N–N4 B×P? 32 N×BP B×B 33
P×B R–QN4 34 N×P R×P 35 P–B4
R–N8+ 36 K–K2 R–N7+ 37 K–B3
R–N6+ 38 K–N4 R–N7 39 P–N3
P–N4 40 N6–K4+ K–Q4 41 P–B5
P–N5 42 P–B6 R–QR7 43 P–B7
R–R1 44 N–R7! P–N6 (44 ... K×N
45 N–B6+ 46 N–K8) 45 N–Q2 P–N7
46 K–B3 K–Q5 47 K–K2 P–B4 48
P–B8/Q R×Q 49 N×R P–B5 50
N–K6+ K–Q4 51 N–B4+ K–Q5
52 N–N1(1.24) (3.17) 1–0

8) **Botvinnik-Tal,** King's Indian 1 P–
Q4 N–KB3 2 P–QB4 P–K3 3 N–KB3
P–B4 4 P–Q5 P×P 5 P×P P–KN3
6 N–B3 B–N2 7 B–N5 0–0 8 P–K3
R–K1 (More elastic is 8 ... P–Q3)
9 N–Q2 P–Q3 10 B–K2 P–QR3 11
P–QR4 QN–Q2 12 0–0 Q–B2 13 Q–
B2 N–N3 14 B–B3 (149)

149
B

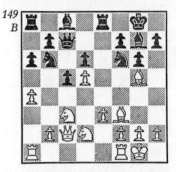

14 ... P–B5? (This pawn sacrifice is
inadequate; better was 14 ... B–B4 15
P–K4 B–Q2 followed by ... N–B1)
15 B×N B×B 16 P–R5 N–Q2 17 QN–
K4 B–K4 18 Q×P Q–Q1 19 Q–R2
P–B4? (19 ... N–B3! with piece play
on K-side) 20 N–B3 P–KN4 21 N–B4
P–N5 22 B–K2 Q–B3 23 N–R4 K–R1
24 P–KN3 P–R4 25 P–B4! B–Q5
26 Q–R3! QR–N1 27 N/R–N6 P–R5
28 QR–Q1 B×N 29 P×B N–B4 30
P×P B–Q2 31 Q–B3 Q×Q 32 P×Q
B–N4 33 KR–K1 N–K5 34 R–QB1
(A blunder which could have led to
undeserved defeat) 34 ... QR–B1??
(As is seen later 34 ... KR–QB1 is
correct) 35 N–R5 B×B 36 R×B
N×P 37 R×N! R×R 38 N×P R1×P?
(Necessary was 38 ... R–QN1 39
N×P R–Q6 40 N×P R×QP 41 P–K4
R×N 42 P×R R×P with a drawn end-
game) 39 R×R R×R 40 N×P R–Q6
41 N–B7+ 1–0

9) **Tal-Botvinnik,** Caro-Kann 1 P–K4
P–QB3 2 P–Q4 P–Q4 3 N–QB3 P×P
4 N×P B–B4 5 N–N3 B–N3 6 KN–

K2 N–B3 7 P–KR4 P–KR3 8 N–B4
B–R2 9 B–B4 P–K3 10 0–0 B–Q3
11 N×P! (*150*)

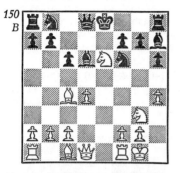

11 . . . P×N 12 B×KP (With a piece for
two pawns, open K-file and bishop on
K6 preventing Black castling. If Black
seeks relief by the exchange 12 . . .
B×N 13 P×B B–N1 then 14 Q–K1!!;
if 14 . . . Q–K2 then 15 B–B8) 12 . . .
Q–B2 13 R–K1 QN–Q2 14 B–N8+
K–B1! 15 B×B R×B 16 N–B5 P–
KN3! 17 B×P+ K–N1 18 N×B
Q×N 19 B–N5 R–K2 20 Q–Q3
K–N2 21 Q–KN3?? (A very weak move
probably resulting in a lost ending. 21
P–KB4! and after 21 . . . QR–K1 22 R–
K5! with very good practical chances)
21 . . . R×R+ 22 R×R Q×Q 23
P×Q R–KB1! 24 P–B4 N–N5 25 P–
Q5 P×P 26 P×P N2–B3 27 P–Q6
R–B2 28 R–QB1 R–Q2 29 R–B7
K–B2 30 B×N N×B 31 K–B2 K–K3
32 R×R K×R 33 K–B3 K×P 34 K–
B4 K–K3 35 P–KN4 N–Q4+ 36 K–K4
N–B3+ 37 K–B4 N–Q4+ 38 K–K4
N–N5 39 P–R3? (With 39 P–R4 Black
has increased difficulty in realising his
extra piece) 39 . . . N–B3 40 P–R5 P–
KN4 41 P–R6 K–B3 42 K–Q5 K–N3
43 K–K6 N–R4 44 P–R4 N–N6 45
K–Q6 P–R4 46 K–Q5 K×P 47 K–B4
N–B8 48 K–N5 N–Q6 49 P–QN3
N–B8 50 K×P N×P+ 51 K–N4 N–B8
52 K–B3 K–N3 53 K–B2 N–K7 54
K–Q3 N–B8+ 55 K–B2 N–K7 56 K–
Q3 N–B5+ 57 K–B4 K–B3 58 P–N3
N–K7 0–1

10) Botvinnik-Tal, King's Indian 1 P–
Q4 N–KB3 2 P–QB4 P–KN3 3 N–
QB3 B–N2 4 P–K4 P–Q3 5 P–B3 0–0
6 B–K3 P–K4 7 P–Q5 P–B3 8 Q–Q2
P×P 9 BP×P P–QR3 10 P–KN4
QN–Q2 11 KN–K2 P–KR4 12 B–N5
P×P 13 P×P N–B4 14 N–N3 B×P
15 P–N4 QN–Q2 16 P–KR3 B–B6
17 R–R2 P–R4 (*151*)

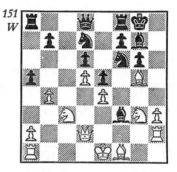

18 P–N5 Q–N3 19 Q–KB2 Q×Q+
20 R×Q B–R4 21 P–N6 KR–B1 22
N–N5 N–K1 23 N×B (Loses the
advantage. Better possibilities from 23
R–N1! when Black would have a
difficult struggle, e.g. 23 . . . N×P 24
N×P N×N 25 R×N) 23 . . . P×N
24 B–K3 N–B4 25 B×N R×B 26 B–
Q3 QR–B1 27 K–K2 R–B8 28 R×R
R×R 29 R–B1 R–B4 30 R–QN1 B–B3
31 N–R3 B–Q1 32 N–B4 (In trying
rightly to transfer the knight to KB5
White misses a small tactical subtlety.
32 N–B2!) 32 . . . P–B4! 33 N–K3
P×P 34 B×P K–R1! 35 K–Q3 N–B3
36 B–N2 K–N1 37 P–QR4 B–K2 38
B–B3 B–B1 39 R–N1+ K–R2 40 B–
K4+!! N×B 41 K×N B–R3 (Missing
41 . . . R–B6! after which Black, pos-
sessing an extra Pawn has good winning
chances) 42 N–B5 R–B5+ 43 K–Q3
R×P 44 N×P R–Q5+ 45 K–K2 R×P
46 N–K4 K–R1 47 N–B6 R–Q7+ 48

K–B3 R–Q1   49 R–N6 P–QR5?
(49 ... B–N2! 50 N×P B–B1 51 N–
B6 B–K2 followed by push of the
QRP) 50 R×B+ K–N2 51 R–R7+
K×N 52 R×NP R–Q6+ 53 K–N2
R–QN6 54 R–QR7 P–R6 55 P–N7
K–B4 56 R×P R×NP 57 R–R4! R–
N7+ 58 K–B3 R–N6+ 59 K–N2
R–K6 60 R–R4(3.55) ½–½

11) Tal–Botvinnik, Réti's Opening
1 N–KB3 N–KB3 2 P–KN3 P–KN3
3 B–N2 B–N2 4 0–0 0–0 5 P–B4 P–B3
6 P–N3 N–K5 7 P–Q4 P–Q4 8 B–
N2 B–K3 (This leads to difficulties for
Black. White finds an interesting tactic
involving a pawn sacrifice as the bishop
is not favourably posted on K3. Probably stronger was 8 ... P–QR4) 9
QN–Q2 N×N 10 Q×N! N–R3 11
QR–B1 Q–Q3 12 N–K5 KR–Q1 13
KR–Q1 QR–B1 14 Q–R5! (*152*)

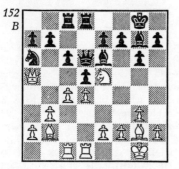

152
B

(This active posting gives rise to tactical
possibilities: 14 ... Q–B2 15 N×QBP;
14 ... Q–N5 15 N×QBP! P×N 16
Q×N P×P 17 B–QR3 Q–N3 18
Q×Q P×Q 19 P×P; 14 ... B×N
15 P×B Q–N5 16 B–QB3!) 14 ...
P×P 15 N×P/4 Q–B2 16 Q–K1 Q–N1
17 P–K4 B×N 18 R×B N–B2 19 B–
KR3 P–K3 20 B–QB1 Q–R1! 21
B–N5 R–K1 22 Q–Q2 P–KB4 23
B–R6 B×B 24 Q×B R–K2 25 R–K1
QR–KB1 26 R–B5 Q–Q1 27 R–K5
R–B1 26 R–B5 Q–Q1 27 R–K5

R2–B2! 28 Q–Q2(2.02) Q–Q3(2.15)
29 B–B1 R–Q2 30 P×P R×P 31 R5–
K4 R–B3? (Black can force a draw by
31 ... R–Q4! 32 B–B4 R×P 33 R×R
Q×R 34 Q×Q R×Q 35 B×P+) 32 P–
KR4! K–N2 33 P–R5 P×P 34 R–R4
K–N1 35 B–Q3 R–N2 36 R–K5! R3–
B2 37 Q–R6 Q–K2 38 R5×RP N–Q4!
39 Q–Q2! N–B3 40 R–R6 Q–Q3 41
R–B4 Q–B1 42 Q–K3 N–Q4 43 R×R
Q×R 44 Q–K5! N–B2 45 Q–QB5!
(*153*)

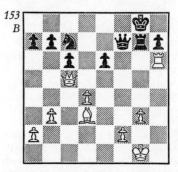

153
B

45 ... Q–B6 46 B×P+ R×B 47 Q–
N5+ K–R1 48 Q–Q8+ K–N2 49
R×R+ K×R 50 Q×N+ K–N3 51
Q×NP Q–K5 52 Q–R6! Q–K8+
53 K–N2 Q–K5+ 54 K–B1 Q–N8+
55 K–K2 Q–B7+ 56 K–B3 Q–B4+
57 K–K3 Q–N4+ 58 K–K2 Q–R4+
59 K–Q2 K–B3 60 Q×BP Q–R4+
61 Q–B3 Q×P+ 62 K–K3 K–B2 63
P–Q5! (Creating two connected passed
pawns for White) 63 ... P×P 64 Q–
B7+ K–B3 65 Q–B6+ K–K2 66
Q×P Q–R8 67 Q–K4+ K–B2 68 K–
B4 Q–B8+ 69 K–N4 Q–QR8 70 Q–
Q5+ K–B1 71 K–B5 Q–N8+ 72
K–B6 1–0

12) Botvinnik–Tal, Queen's Gambit
1 P–QB4 N–KB3 2 P–Q4 P–K3 3 N–
KB3 P–Q4 4 N–B3 P–B4 5 P–K3
N–B3 6 P–QR3 B–Q3 7 QP×P B×BP
8 P–QN4 B–Q3 9 B–N2 0–0 10 P×P
P×P 11 N–QN5 B–N1 12 B–K2

P–QR4 13 P×P N×P 14 0–0 R–R3 15 B–K5! Reducing Black's attacking chances. 15 . . . B×B 16 N×B R–K1 17 N–Q3 N–K5 18 N–B4 R–K4 19 R–B1 R–R3 (*154*)

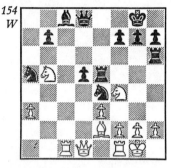

154
W

20 N–Q4 (If 20 N×P? N–QB3 it seems the White pieces are hanging in the air, e.g. 21 N–B4 Q–R5 22 P–R3 P–KN4 23 N–R5 P–N5 24 P×P B×P 25 B×B R/K×N) 20 . . . N–QB3 21 P–N3 (White can win the exchange by 21 N–B3 R–B4 22 P–N4 but after 22 . . . R×N 23 P×R B×P Black has a position promising the initiative) 21 . . . P–KN4 22 N–Q3 R–K1 23 B–N4! B×B 24 Q×B N×N 25 P×N Q–B3 26 N–K5 N–Q7 27 KR–Q1 R×N (Black must give up the exchange but has 28 P×R N–B6+ 29 K–B1 Q–R3 30 K–N2 R×P+ 31 K×N Q×P+ 32 K–K2 Q–R7+! 33 K–Q3 Q–R3; 29 . . . N×QP 30 Q–B8+ K–N2 31 P–R3 with a pawn and attack for the exchange) 28 R×N R–K5 29 Q–B8+ K–N2 30 Q×P Q–K3 31 R–B1? R–K8 32 Q–N5 Q–R6 33 P–B3 Q–K3 34 R2–KB2 R–B3 35 R×R Q×R+ 36 K–N2 P–N5 37 Q–Q3 P–R4 38 R–B1 Q–K3 39 P×P R×R 40 K×R P×P 41 P–QR4 Q–QN3 42 K–B2 Q–N5? (42 . . . Q–N7+ 43 K–K3 Q–B8+ 44 Q–Q2 Q–KN8+ 45 K–B4 K–B3 and draws) 43 K–K3 Q×RP 44 K–B4 Q–R7 45 Q–K3! Q×P 46 Q–K5+ K–B1 47 Q–Q6+ K–N2 48 Q×P

Q–B7+ 49 K×P P–B4+ 50 K–N5 Q×P+ 51 K×P Q–N3+ 52 K–B4 Q–B3+ 53 K–K3 K–B1 54 K–Q3 Q–B8+ 55 K–K4 Q–N7+ 56 K–K5 Q–N4+ 57 K–K6 Q–K2+ 58 K–B5 Q–QB2! (Securing a draw) 59 Q–R8+ K–K2 60 Q–K4+ K–Q1 61 Q–R4+ K–B1 62 Q–R8+ K–N2 63 Q–K5 Q–B2+ 64 K–K4 Q–N3+ 65 Q–B5 Q–Q3 66 Q–B7+ K–B1 67 Q–B5+ K–Q1 68 Q–R5+ K–K1 69 P–Q5 K–K2 70 Q–R7+ K–Q1 71 Q–R8+ K–Q2 72 K–B5 K–K2 ½–½

13) Tal–Botvinnik, Queen's Indian 1 P–QB4 P–QB4 2 N–KB3 N–KB3 3 P–KN3 P–QN3 4 B–N2 B–N2 5 0–0 P–KN3 6 P–Q4 P×P 7 Q×P B–N2 8 N–B3 N–B3! 9 Q–R4 P–KR3! (Preventing 10 B–R6 and threatening 10 . . . P–KN4) 10 N–Q5 P–K3 (*155*)

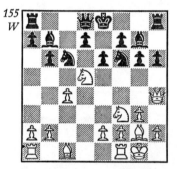

155
W

(White would have more difficulties after 10 . . . N–QR4, as 11 N–Q2 R–QB1 12 R–N1 is necessary) 11 N×N+ Q×N 12 Q×Q B×Q 13 R–N1 N–QR4 (On 13 . . . N–N5 then 14 B–Q2! 14 . . . N×P?? 15 R–R1) 14 P–N3 B–K5 15 B–N2! B×B 16 R×B ½–½

14) Botvinnik – Tal, Nimzo–Indian 1 P–Q4 N–KB3 2 P–QB4 P–K3 3 N–QB3 B–N5 4 P–QR3 B×N+ 5 P×B N–K5 6 N–R3 (Not best. White should put direct pressure on the centre, e.g. 6 Q–B2 P–KB4 7 P–K3 P–QN3 8 B–

Q3 B–N2 9 N–K2 Q–R5! 10 0–0 0–0
11 P–B3 N–N4) 6 . . . P–QB4 7 P–K3
Q–R4 8 B–Q2 P×P 9 BP×P N×B
10 Q×N Q×Q+ 11 K×Q P–QN3
12 B–Q3 B–R3 13 KR–QB1 N–B3
14 QR–N1 K–K2 (156)

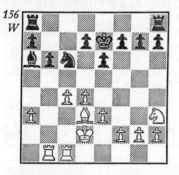

156
W

15 P–B5 B×B 16 K×B QR–QN1 17
R–N5 P×P 18 R1×P P–QR3! (More
precise than 18 . . . R×R) 19 R×R
R×R 20 K–B2 R–QB1 21 N–B4
P–Q3 22 R–B3 P–N4 ½–½

15) Tal-Botvinnik, Caro-Kann 1 P–K4
P–QB3 2 P–Q4 P–Q4 3 N–QB3 P×P
4 N×P B–B4 5 N–N3 B–N3 6 B–QB4
P–K3 7 KN–K2 B–Q3 8 P–KR4 P–
KR3 9 N–B4 B×N (If 9 . . . B–R2
10 N3–R5 Black has to play 10 . . .
K–B1) 10 B×B N–B3 11 Q–Q2 QN–
Q2 12 0–0–0 N–Q4 13 QR–K1
(Probably stronger was 13 B–Q3)
13 . . . N2–N3 14 B–N3 N×B 15
Q×N N–Q4 16 Q–K5! 0–0 17 N–K4!
Q–N1 (157)
18 N–Q6! R–Q1 19 N–B4 N–N3 20
Q×Q QR×Q 21 N–K5 B–R2 22 R–
R3 N–Q2 (On acceptance of the pawn
22 . . . R×P then 23 N×KBP! and if
K×N 24 B×P+ K–B1 25 R–B3+;
24 . . . K–N3 25 R–N3+ K–R4 26
R×P.) 23 P–QB3 N×N 24 R×N P–
QN3 25 KR–K3 QR–B1 26 B–B4
R–B2 27 P–QN4 K–B1 28 P–N4!
B–N1! 29 B–N3 B–R2 30 P–KB4 B–
N1 31 K–N2 B–R2 32 P–R5 R1–

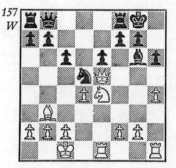

157
W

QB1 33 B–B2 B–N1!! (Correct evaluation of the position; after 33 . . . B×B
34 K×B P–QB4 35 NP×P P×P
36 P–Q5 and White has the advantage)
34 P–KN5 P–B3 35 R5–K4 P–QB4
36 B–N3? (Better was 36 QP×P NP×P
37 P–N5 with advantage on the Q–side)
36 . . . P×QNP 37 BP×P RP×P 38
P×P P×P 39 R–N3 R–B2 40 R×NP
R–KB7+ 41 K–R3 R–QB2 ½–½

16) Botvinnik-Tal, Nimzo-Indian 1 P–
Q4 N–KB3 2 P–QB4 P–K3 3 N–QB3
B–N5 4 P–QR3 B×N+ 5 P×B N–K5
6 Q–B2 P–KB4 7 N–R3 P–Q3 8 P–B3
N–KB3 9 P–K4 P×P 10 P×P P–K4
(On 10 . . . 0–0 White has the possibility
of provoking sharp play with 11 P–K5
P×P 12 P×P N–N5 13 B–Q3; 13 B–
N5) 11 N–B2 0–0 12 B–K2 P–B4
13 P×KP P×P 14 0–0 N–B3 15 B–N5
Q–K1 16 N–Q1 Q–N3 17 B×N
R×B 18 N–K3 R×R+ 19 R×R B–K3
20 Q–Q3 R–Q1 21 N–Q5 (158)
21 . . . R–KB1? (A better defence to the
threat 22 N–K7+ is 21 . . . R–Q2 and
then offer exchange of rooks by . . . R–
KB2) 22 N–B7! R×R+ 23 B×R Q–
B2 (Retreating the bishop is worse; 23
. . . B–B2 24 Q–Q7; 23 . . . B–B1 24
Q–Q5+ Q–B2 25 N–N5 and Black is
hard pressed to avoid a loss) 24 Q–Q6
B–B1 25 N–R6! Q–B5 26 Q–Q5+
K–R1 27 Q×BP B–K3 28 N–B7 B–N1
29 Q–B2 Q×KP 30 N–K8 Q–N3 31

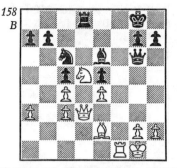

K–R1) 40 R×RP+(2.29) K–N1 41 Q–
R4 1–0

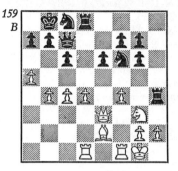

Q–B8 P–K5 32 N–Q6 N–K4 33 P–B5
(Strengthening the position of the knight
and freeing B4 for bishop) 33 . . .
N–Q6? (33 . . . Q–N4!) 34 N–B5 N–
K4 35 N–K7 Q–B2 36 Q×Q B×Q
37 K–B2 B–B5! 38 B×B (After 38 P–
B6 P×P 39 N×P P–K6!! Black can
hold a draw) 38 . . . N×B 39 P–B6
P×P 40 N×P P–QR4 41 P–QR4 ½–½
17) Tal–Botvinnik, Caro–Kann 1 P–K4
P–QB3 2 P–Q4 P–Q4 3 N–QB3
P×P 4 N×P B–B4 5 N–N3 B–N3
6 B–QB4 P–K3 7 KN–K2 N–B3 8 N–
B4 B–Q3 9 N×B RP×N 10 B–KN5
QN–Q2 11 0–0 Q–R4 12 P–B4?!
(Somewhat weakening the black squares;
12 Q–Q2!) 12 . . . 0–0–0 13 P–QR3 Q–
B2 14 P–N4 N–N3 15 B–K2 B–K2 16
Q–Q3 KN–Q4 (Probably better is 16 . . .
P–B4 e.g. 17 P–B3 P–B5; 17 QP×P
R×P 18 P×N R×Q 19 P×Q B–B4
20 K–R1 R×N etc.) 17 B×B Q×B
18 P–B4 N–B3 19 QR–N1 Q–Q2!
20 QR–Q1 K–N1 21 Q–N3 Q–B2 22
P–QR4 R–R5 23 P–R5 N–B1 24 Q–K3
(*159*)
24 . . . N–K2 25 Q–K5 R5–R1 26 P–N5
P×P 27 Q×NP P–R3 28 Q–N2 R–Q2
29 P–QB5 K–R1 30 B–B3 N–B3 31
B×N Q×B 32 R–B3 Q–R5! 33 KR–
Q3! KR–QB1 34 R–N1 Q×P?!
35 R–N3! Q–B2 36 Q–R3 K–R2
(36 . . . Q–Q1! for . . . R–B3) 37 R–N6
Q×KBP 38 N–K2 Q–K5 39 Q–QN3
Q–Q4 (In the time scramble Botvinnik
fails to find correct defence 39 . . .

18) Botvinnik–Tal, Nimzo–Indian 1 P–
Q4 N–KB3 2 P–QB3 P–K3 3 N–QB3
B–N5 4 P–QR3 B×N+ 5 P×B
N–K5 6 Q–B2 P–KB4 7 N–R3 0–0!
8 P–B3 N–KB3 9 P–B5 P–QN3 10
P×P BP×P (The hackneyed capture
towards the centre is less favourable
as the open QR-file is of little value
whereas White now has weakness at
QB4) 11 P–K3 Q–B2 12 B–Q2 N–K1!
13 P–QB4 B–R3 14 R–B1 N–Q3
15 Q–R4 Q–B3! (*160*)

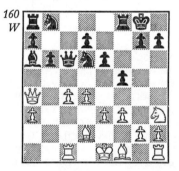

16 Q×Q N×Q 17 B–N4 N×B 18
P×N B×P! 19 B×B KR–B1 20
B×P+ P×B 21 K–Q2 K–B2 22 N–B4
P–QR4 23 P×P P×P 24 K–Q3 P–R5
25 R×R R×R 26 R–R1 N–B5? (After
this Black has to fight for a draw;
26 . . . R–QR1!) 27 R–QN1 P–R6
28 R–N7+ K–B3 29 R–R7 P–N4??

(Suicidal. Black could force a draw with 29 ... N–N7+ 30 K–Q2 N–B5 31 K–K2 N–N7! 32 R×QRP R–B7 33 K–K1 N–B5) 30 N–R5+ K–N3 31 P–N4 N–N7+ 32 K–Q2 N–B5+ 33 K–Q3 N–N7+ 34 K–Q2 N–B5+ 35 K–K2! R–B3! 36 P–KR3! P–K4 37 QP×P? (In time pressure Botvinnik misses the stronger 37 P–Q5; now Black has chances of a draw) 37 ... P×P 38 RP×P N×P/4 39 R×QRP R–B7+ 40 K–B1 K–B2 41 P–K4 R–Q7 42 K–K1 R–KN7! 43 R–N3 K–K2 44 N–N7 N×P+ 45 R×N R×P 46 N–B5+ K–K3 47 N–N3 P–R4 48 N×P R×P+ 49 K–B2 K–K4 50 K–N3 R–KR5 51 N–N7 R–KB5 52 R–R3 (If 52 R–K3+, then possible is 52 ... K–B3 53 N–R5 K–B4) 52 ... R–Q5 53 R–R6 R–Q3 54 R–R7 R–Q5 55 R–KB7 R–KB5 56 R–K7+ K–B3 57 R–R7 R–K5 58 N–R5+ K–N3 59 K–B3 R–QN5 60 N–N3 R–B5+ 61 K–K3 R–B2 62 R–R5 R–B3 63 N–K4 R–B4 64 R–R6+ K–N2 65 N–N3 R–K4+ 66 K–Q4 R–N4 67 K–K4 K–B2 68 N–B5 R–N5+ 69 N–Q4 R–N8 70 N–B3 R–N5+ 71 N–Q4 R–N8 72 N–B6 K–N3 73 N–K5+ K–R4 74 R–R5 R–K8+ 75 K–B3 R–B8+ 76 K–N3(4.11) R–B5(3.04) $\frac{1}{2}$–$\frac{1}{2}$

19) Tal–Botvinnik, Dutch Defence 1 P–QB4 P–KB4 2 N–KB3 N–KB3 3 P–KN3 P–KN3 4 B–N2 B–N2 5 P–Q4 P–Q3 6 N–B3 P–K3 7 0-0 0-0 8 Q–B2 N–B3 9 R–Q1 Q–K2 10 R–N1 P–QR4 11 P–QR3 N–Q1 12 P–K4 P×P 13 N×P N×N 14 Q×N N–B2 15 B–R3! Q–B3 16 B–Q2 P–Q4 (16 ... P–B3! and on 17 B–B3 either 17 ... P–K4 18 B×B QR×B 19 P×P P×P threat ... N–Q3; 17 ... P–Q4) 17 Q–K2 P×P 18 B–B4 N–Q3 19 N–N5 R–K1 90 B–N2 R–R3 21 N–K4 N×N 22 B×N P–QN4 23 P–N3 P×P 24 Q×P R–B1 25 Q×NP (25 QR–B1) 25 ... R–N3 26 Q–K3 R×R

27 B×R B–N2 28 B–R2 B–Q4 29 B×B P×B 30 B×P P–R5 31 R–Q3 Q–B4 32 B–K5 B–R3 33 Q–K2 R–B1 34 R–KB3 Q–R6 *(161)*

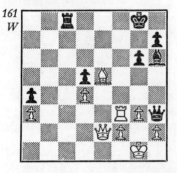

161
W

35 B–B7! B–B1 (The best defence was 35 ... Q–Q2 despite White winning a tempo with 36 B–B4) 36 Q–N5! Q–K3 37 B–K5 Q–QB3 38 Q–R5 R–R1(2.29½) (Avoiding 38 ... B×P? 39 R×B Q–B8+ 40 K–N2 Q×R 41 Q×P+ K–B1 42 B–Q6+) 39 Q–Q2 (2.21) R–B1(2.29½) 40 K–N2 Q–Q2 (2.29½) 41 P–R4(2.27) Q–N5 1-0

20) Botvinnik–Tal, Nimzo–Indian 1 P–Q4 N–KB3 2 P–QB4 P–K3 3 N–QB3 B–N5 4 P–QR3 B×N+ 5 P×B N–K5 6 P–K3! P–KB4 7 Q–R5+!! P–KN3 8 Q–R6 (White's opening experiment has resulted in the weakening of the dark squares on Black's K–side. After 8 ... Q–N4 9 Q×Q N×Q 10 P–KR4±; 8 ... Q–B3 9 N–KB3! P–Q3 10 P–KR4 P–K4 11 P–R5 with sharp play favouring White) 8 ... P–Q3 9 P–B3 N–B3 10 P–K4! P–K4 11 B–N5 Q–K2 12 B–Q3 R–B1 (12 ... N–B3 13 P×BP P×KP+ 14 K–B1!; 12 ... P–B5 13 P–KN3!) 13 N–K2 (Missing the stronger 13 Q–R4! Q–B2 14 B–R6 R–R1 15 N–R3) 13 ... Q–B2 14 Q–R4 BP×P 15 BP×P N–N5 *(162)* 16 P–R3 Q–B7+ 17 K–Q2 Q×Q 18 B×Q N–B7 19 KR–KB1 N×B 20 R×R+! K×R 21 K×N B–K3 22

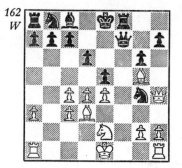

162
W

N–N3 (The continuation 22 B–Q8!? would have been interesting, viz. 22 . . . P–B3 23 B–B7 K–K2 24 P×P P×P 25 B×P N–Q2 would be worth a draw) 22 . . . N–Q2 23 N–B1 P–QR3! 24 B–B2 K–N2 25 N–Q2 R–KB1 26 B–K3 P–N3 27 R–QN1(1.51) N–B3(1.55) ½–½

21) Tal-Botvinnik, Queen's Indian 1 P–Q4 N–KB3 2 P–QB4 P–K3 3 N– KB3 P–QN3 4 P–KN3 B–N2 5 B–N2 B–K2 6 0–0 0–0 7 N–B3 N–K5 8 Q– B2 N×N 9 Q×N P–KB4 10 P–N3 B–KB3 11 B–N2 P–Q3 12 QR–Q1 Q–K2 13 N–K1 B×B 14 N×B N–B3 15 Q–B3 Q–Q2 16 N–B4 QR–K1 17 P–Q5 (Evaluating the endgame after 17 . . . B×B 18 P×P N–K4 19 P×Q N×Q+ 20 P×N R–K2 in White's favour in view of 21 P–QN4! R×P 22 P–N5) 17 . . . N–Q1 (*163*) ½–½

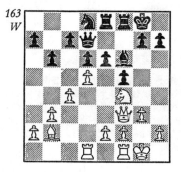

163
W

7 Tal–Botvinnik

Moscow 16 March–12 May 1961

	1	2	3	4	5	6	7	8	9	10	11
Tal	0	1	0	½	½	½	0	1	0	0	0
Botvinnik	1	0	1	½	½	½	1	0	1	1	1

	12	13	14	15	16	17	18	19	20	21	**Total**
Tal	1	0	½	0	½	1	0	1	½	0	**8**
Botvinnik	0	1	½	1	½	0	1	0	½	1	**13**

1) Botvinnik-Tal, Nimzo-Indian 1 P–QB4 N–KB3 2 N–QB3 P–K3 P–Q4 B–N5 4 P–K3 0-0 5 B–Q3 P–Q4 6 P–QR3 P×P 7 B×P B–Q3 8 N–B3 N–B3 9 N–QN5?! (9 P–QN4!) 9 ... P–K4 10 N×B Q×N (10 ... P×N) 11 P×P Q×Q+ 12 K×Q N–KN5 13 K–K2 QN×P 14 B–Q5 P–B3 (14 ... R–Q1 15 B–K4 P–QN3! 16 B×R B–R3+ 14 ... R–Q1 15 R–Q1) 15 B–K4 B–K3 (15 ... P–QN3!) 16 N–Q2!? (16 N×N N×N 17 P–B4 B–B5+ 18 K–B2 N–Q6+ 19 B×N B×B 20 B–Q2 and 21 B–B3=) 16 ... QR–Q1 (16 ... P–KB4!) 17 P–R3 N–B3 18 B–B2 R–Q2 (18 ... P–QN3!? and 19 ... B–B1) 19 P–QN3 KR–Q1 20 R–Q1 N–Q6 21 B×N R×B 22 B–N2 (*164*) 22 ... R/6–Q2? (22 ... P–B4!) 23 B×N! P×B 24 P–QN4! B–B4?! (24 ... B–Q4) 25 N–N3 B–Q6+?! (25 ... R×R 26 R×R R×R 27 K×R P–N3) 26 K–K1 P–N3 27 QR–B1 B–K5 28 P–B3?! (28 R×R R×R 29 K–K2!) 28 ... R×R+ 29 R×R R×R+ 30 K×R B–Q4? (30 ... B–B4! 31 N–Q4 B–Q2) 31 N–Q4 P–QB4 32 P×P P×P 33 N–N5 P–QR3 34 N–B7 B–B5 35 N–K8! P–B4 36 P–KR4 K–B1 37 N–Q6 B–B8 38 P–

N3 K–K2 39 N×P+ K–K3 40 P–K4 K–K4 41 K–Q2 (sealed) 1–0

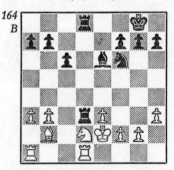

164
B

2) Tal-Botvinnik, Caro-Kann 1 P–K4 P–QB3 2 P–Q4 P–Q4 3 N QB3 P×P 4 N×P B–B4 5 N–N3 B–N3 6 B–QB4 P–K3 7 KN–K2 N–B3 8 N–B4 B–Q3 9 0-0 N–Q4! (9 ... Q–B2 10 Q–B3!?) 10 N/N3–R5 (10 N×N BP×N 11 B–N5+ N–B3; 10 N–Q3 Q–R5) 10 ... 0-0 11 B–N3 N–Q2 12 N×B (12 P–B4 N×N 13 N×N B–KB4=) 12 ... RP×N 13 N–N3 Q–R5! 14 Q–Q3 QR–Q1?! (14 ... QN–B3 threat 15 ... N–KN5; 14 ... KN–B3 intending 15 ... P–B4) 15 R–K1 QN–B3 16 P–KR3 B–B5 17 P–QB3 (17 N–K4) 17 ... P–N3 18 Q–B3 B×B 19 QR×B Q–B5 20 Q–K2

138

P–B4 21 QR–Q1 Q–B2 22 P×P P×P
23 N–K4 N×N 24 Q×N N–B3 25
Q–K2 R×R 26 R×R R–Q1 27
R×R+ Q×R= (*165*)

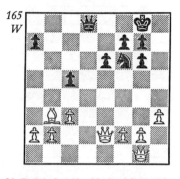

165
W

28 B–B4 Q–N1 29 Q–Q2 Q–B2 30
B–B1 K–B1 31 P–QN4 P×P 32 P×P
N–Q4 33 P–R3 Q–B6 34 Q–N5 Q–
KB3? (34 . . . P–B3! 35 Q×P Q×RP=)
35 Q–N3 Q–B5 36 Q–Q3 Q–B8?
(Botvinnik was short of time; 36 . . .
Q–B2!=) 37 P–QR4! K–N1?! (37 . . .
Q–B6 or 37 . . . Q–B2) 38 P–R5 Q–K8
39 Q–Q4 P–R3 40 P–N5 P×P 41 P–
R6 Q–R4 42 P–R7 P–N5 43 B–B4!
P–B3 44 B–N5! P–N6 45 Q–QR4! 1–0
(45 . . . Q×Q 46 B×Q N–N3 47 B×P
K–B2 48 B–R4 followed by B–B6)

3) Botvinnik-Tal, Nimzo-Indian 1 P–
P–QB4 N–KB3 2 N–QB3 P–K3
3 P–Q4 B–N5 4 P–K3 0-0 5 B–Q3
P–Q4 6 P–QR3 P×P 7 B×P B–Q3
8 N–B3 N–B3 9 P–QN4! P–K4 10 B–
N2 B–N5 11 P–Q5!? (11 P×P) 11 . . .
N–K2 12 P–R3 B–Q2 13 N–KN5!
N–N3? (13 . . . P–KR3 14 N/5–K4
N×N 15 N×N B–KB4=) 14 N–K6!
P×N 15 P×P K–R1 16 P×B Q×P
17 0-0 Q–B4 18 N–Q5! (*166*)
18 . . . N–N1? (18 . . . Q–K5? 19 N×N
Q×B 20 N×P!; 18 . . . P–K5 19 N×N
P×N 20 Q–B2 threat P–B4; 18 . . .
QR–Q1 19 N×N P×N is best) 19 Q–
N4 Q–B7 20 Q–K2 Q–B4 21 Q–N4
Q–B7 22 Q–K2 Q–B4 23 P–K4 Q–Q2

166
B

24 QR–Q1 QR–Q1 25 Q–N4 Q–K1
26 P–N3 N–R3 27 Q–R5 N–N1 28
Q–K2 N/3–K2 29 N–K3 N–R3 30
N–N4! N×N (30 . . . Q–R4 31 K–N2
threat 32 N×P) 31 P×N N–B3 32
K–N2 B–K2 33 B–Q5 N–Q5 34
B×N P×B 35 B–B4 (35 B×P! P–Q6
36 Q–K3!) 35 . . . P–B4? (35 . . . P–
KN3 followed by . . . K–N2) 36 P–QN5
B–B3 37 P–B4 P–Q6 38 R×P R×R
39 B×R B–Q5 40 P–K5 P–KN3 41
R–KR1 K–N2 42 Q–K4 P–N3 43 B–
B4 (sealed) 1-0 (43 . . . Q–Q2 44 Q–B6
Q×Q 45 P×Q R–B1 46 P–K6!;
43 . . . Q–K2 44 P–N5 threat Q–B6
and Q–B6+; 43 . . . Q–K2 44 P–N5
R–B1 45 P–B5 P×P 46 R×P+ K×R
47 Q–R4+ K–N2 48 Q–R6 mate)

4) Tal-Botvinnik, Caro-Kann 1 P–K4
P–QB3 2 P–Q4 P–Q4 3 P–K5 P–
QB4?! 4 P×P P–K3 5 N–QB3 (5 N–
KB3! B×P 6 B–Q3 with advantage)
5 . . . N–QB3 6 B–KB4 KN–K2 7 N–
B3 N–N3 8 B–K3!? (8 B–N3 B×P
9 B–Q3) 8 . . . KN×P 9 N×N N×N
10 Q×R5 (10 Q–Q4!? N–B3 11 B–
QN5) 10 . . . N–B3 11 0-0-0 B–K2
(11 . . . P–KN3 12 Q–K2 B–N2 13
N×P!) 12 P–B4 P–KN3 13 Q–R6
B–B1 14 Q–N5 Q×Q?! 15 P×Q P–
QR3 16 N–R4 B–Q2 17 B–KB4
P–R3! 18 N–N6 R–Q1 19 B–B7 P×P
20 P–B4 P–Q5 21 P–QN4 B–N2 (*167*)
22 B×R? (22 P–N5! N–N1 23 P–
QR4 P–K4 24 R–K1 P–B3 25 P–N3

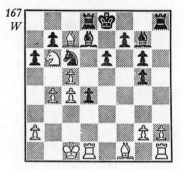

167
W

B3 29 P–QR4 N–K4 30 P–N5 R–B6
31 N–Q4 R–R1   32 R/Q–R1 P–QR4
33 R–Q1 (*168*)

168
B

followed by B–N2 should win. 22 . . .
K×B 23 P–N5 N–N1 24 B–K2 P–B4!
25 B–B3 P×P 26 P×P B×P 27 B×P K–
B2 28 P–QR4 (28 B–B3? P–N5, 28
B–R8? N–R3) 28 . . . B×P 29 N×B
K×B 30 K–Q2 N–Q2 31 R–N1+ K–
B3 32 KR–QB1 B–K4 33 K–Q3 R–R1?
(33 . . . B–B2!) 34 R–N6+! N×R 35
P×N+ K–Q2 (35 . . . K–N4 36 R–B5+
followed by R×B; 35 . . . K–Q3 36
P–N7 R–QN1 37 N–B5) 36 N–B5+
K–K2 37 R–K1 R–R6+ 38 K–B4
R–B6+ 39 K–N5 R–K6 40 R–QR1
B×P 41 R–R7+ K–K1 (adjourned;
41 . . . K–B3 42 R–R7!++) ½–½ (42
R–R7 B–B5 43 N–Q7 P–Q6 44 N–
B6+ with perpetual check)

5) Botvinnik–Tal, Nimzo-Indian 1 P–
QB4 N–KB3 2 N–QB3 P–K3 3 P–Q4
B–N5 4 P–K3 0–0 5 B–Q3 P–Q4 6 P–
QR3 P×P 7 B×P B–Q3 8 N–B3 N–
B3 9 P–QN4 P–K4 10 B–N2 N–N5 11
P×P N×KP (11 . . . B×KP 12 Q×Q
QR×Q 13 P–N5 B×KN 14 P×B N–
QR4=) 12 B–K2 Q–K2 13 N–QN5
KR–Q1 14 Q–B2 P–QR3?! (14 . . . B–
R4) 15 N×B P×N 16 Q–Q1 QR–
B1= 17 0–0 N–K5 18 N–Q4 B×B 19
Q×B N–B5 20 QR–B1 P–Q4 21 Q–
N4 Q–Q2 22 Q×Q (22 N–B5?! P–KN3
23 N–R6+ K–B1) 22 . . . R×Q 23 R–
B2 N/K–Q3 24 R–Q1 R/2–Q1?! (24
. . . R/2–B2) 25 N–N3 N×B 26 R×N
N–B5 27 R–R2 P–QN3 28 K–B1 P–

33 . . . R/R–QB1? (33 . . . N–Q6! 34
N–B6 K–B2 35 R/2–Q2 N–N5 36
N×N P×N 37 R×P R×RP=) 34 N–
B5 R/1–B2 35 R×P K–B2 36 R–Q1?!
(36 P–K4) 36 . . . K–K3 37 N–Q4+ K–
B2 38 K–K2 R/2–B5 39 P–R3 R–N5
40 N–B2 R/N–QB5   41 R–Q2 (ad-
journed) 41 . . . K–K2 42 N–Q4 P–N3
43 R–Q1 N–Q2 44 N–B6+ K–K1 45
R–Q6 R–B7+   46 R×R R×R+   47
K–B3 R–R7 48 R–K6+ K–B1 49 R–
Q6 K–K1 50 R–K6+ K–B1 51 K–N3
R×RP?! (51 . . . P–R4) 52 R–K7 N–B4
53 R×P N–K5+   54 K–R2 N–Q3 55
R–R8+?! (55 R–Q7)   55 . . . K–B2=
56 R–QN8 N–B5 57 R–B8 N–Q7 58
P–N4 R–R7 59 R–QN8 N–K5   60
R×P R×P+   61 K–N1 R–N7 62 N×P
N–Q7   63 N–B6 N–B5   64 R–N7+
K–K3   65 P–R4 K–Q4   66 R–Q7+
K–B4   67 R–Q3 K×P   68 N–Q4+
K–B4   59 N–B3 R–K7 70 P–R5 P×P
71 P×P N×P   72 P–R6 R–N7+   73
K–R1 R–N3 ½–½

6) Tal–Botvinnik, Caro-Kann 1 P–K4
P–QB3 2 P–Q4 P–Q4 3 P–K5
P–QB4?! 4 P×P P–K3 5 Q–N4!?
N–Q2 6 N–KB3 (6 B–QN5 Q–B2
7 N–KB3 Q×P 8 N–B3; 7 . . . N–K2
8 N–B3 N–N3   9 Q–N3 B×P=)

6 . . . N–K2 7 B–KN5 P–KR3 8 B×N (8 B–R4? P–KN4 9 B–N3 P–KR4 10 Q×NP B–R3 11 Q–R4 B–B8!) 8 . . . Q×B 9 N–B3 Q×P 10 0–0–0– P–R3 (10 . . . Q×P?) 11 K–N1 N–N3 12 N–Q4 B–Q2 13 P–KR4 0–0–0= 14 R–R3 K–N1 15 P–B4 (15 R–B3) 15 . . . R–B1 (*169*)

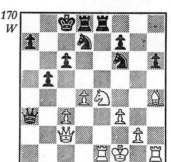

170
W

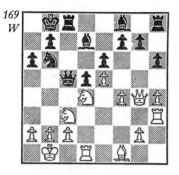

169
W

Q–R8+ 23 Q–Q1 Q×P+ 24 K–B2 N–K4) 21 . . . N×N+ 22 P×N P–B3 23 R–R1 Q–K2 24 R×P Q×P 25 Q×Q R×Q 26 R–R8+ N–N1 27 B– N3 K–N2 28 KR–R1 R–QB1 29 R/8–R7+ K–N3 30 B×N P–N5 31 B–Q6 P×P 32 B–B5+ K–N4 33 R/1– R4 1–0

8) Tal-Botvinnik, Caro-Kann 1 P–K4 P–QB3 2 P–Q4 P–Q4 3 P–K5 P– QB4?! 4 P×P P–K3 (4 . . . N–QB3 5 B–QN5!) 5 Q–N4!? N–QB3?! (5 . . . N–Q2) 6 N–KB3 Q–B2 7 B–QN5 B–Q2 8 B×N Q×B 9 B–K3 N–R3?! (9 . . . N–K2 10 QN–Q2 N–B4 11 N– N3 N×B 12 P×N; 9 . . . P–KR4 10 Q–N3 N–R3 11 N–Q4!) 10 B×N P×B 11 QN–Q2 Q×P 12 P–B4! 0–0–0 (12 . . . P×P 13 0–0 B–B3 14 QR–B1) 13 0–0 K–N1 14 KR–Q1 Q–N3?! (14 . . . B–K2) 15 Q–R4! P– QR4? 16 QR–B1 R–N1 17 N–N3! P–R5? 18 P–B5 Q–B2 19 N/N–Q4 . . . R–B1 20 P–QN4 P×Pep 21 P×P Q–Q1 22 Q×Q R×Q 23 P–QN4 R–N5 24 P–N5 R–B1 25 P–B6 B–K1 26 R–B2 B–N2 27 R–R1 B×KP 28 N×B R×N 29 N–Q7+! 1–0 (*171*) (29 . . . K–B2 30 P–N6+ K–Q1 31 P×P; 29 . . . B×N 30 P×B R–Q1 31 R–B8+ R×R 32 R–R8+)

9) Botvinnik-Tal, Keres System 1 P– QB4 N–KB3 2 N–QB3 P–K4 3 P–KN3 P–B3 4 N–B3 P–K5 5 N–Q4 P–Q4 6 P×P Q–N3?! (6 . . . B–QB4?! 7 N–

16 P–R5 R–N1 17 N–N3 Q–B2 18 B– Q3 N–B5 19 B×N Q×B 20 N–Q4 B–K2 21 R/R–Q3 Q–B2 22 Q–K2 Q–N3 23 Q–N4 Q–B2 24 Q–K2 Q–N3 25 Q–N4 Q–B2 ½–½

7) Botvinnik-Tal, Nimzo-Indian 1 P– QB4 N–KB3 2 N–QB3 P–K3 3 P–Q4 B–N5 4 P–QR3 B×N+ 5 P×B P– QN3?! 6 P–B3 B–R3 7 P–K4 P–Q4 8 BP×P B×B 9 K×B P×P 10 B–N5! P–KR3 11 Q–R4+! (11 B×N Q×B! 12 P×P 0–0) 11 . . . P–B3 (11 . . . QN– Q2 12 B×N Q×B 13 P×P; 11 . . . K–B1 12 B×N; 11 . . . Q–Q2 12 Q×Q+ QN×Q 13 B×N N×B 14 P–K5 N–Q2 15 N–K2 with advan- tage); 12 B–R4 P×P 13 R–K1 P– KN4?! (13 . . . 0–0 14 P×P Q–B2!) 14 B–B2 Q–K2 15 N–K2 P–N4 16 Q–B2 Q×P? (16 . . . P–K6 17 B×P . . . 0–0 18 N–N3 N–Q4 19 B–B1 Q–B3) 17 P–R4 NP×P? (17 . . . P–N5) 18 B×P QN–Q2 19 N–N3 . . . 0–0–0 20 N×P KR–K1 (*170*) 21 K–B2! (21 N×N? R×R+ 22 K×R

171
B

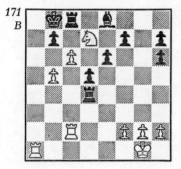

N3 B–N3   8 P×P N×P;   6 . . . P×P)
7 N–N3 P×P (7 . . . N–N5!?)   8 B–N2
P–QR4?! (8 . . . N–B3)   9 P–Q3 P–R5
10 B–K3 Q–N5 11 N–Q4 P–R6 (11 . . .
Q×P   12 N/B3–N5)   12 N–B2! Q×P
13 B–Q4 B–QN5   14 N×B Q×N   15
B×N P×B   16 0–0 B–K3   17 R–B1
(17 Q–B1! is even stronger)   17 . . .
N–B3   18 P×P P×P   19 N×P B×P
20 N–Q6+ K–B1   21 N×NP N–K4
22 N–B5 R–QN1   23 N–R6?! (172)

172
B

(23 P–B4) 23 . . . B–N6 24 N×Q B×Q
25 KR×B R×N   26 R–R1 R–N7   27
K–B1 K–N2 28 R×P R–QB1 29 B–K4
R–K1   30 R–R4 R–K2   31 B–B5 R–B2
32 R–R4 P–R3   33 R–R4 R–B4   34 P–
R3 N–B5   35 B–Q3 N–K4   36 B–K4
N–B5   37 B–Q3 N–K4   38 B–K4 N–B5
39 K–K1 N–K4   40 R/R4–Q4 R–B6
41 R/Q1–Q2 (sealed)   41 . . . R–B8+
42 R–Q1 R–B6 43 P–B4 P–B4 44 B×P
N–B5 45 R/Q4–Q3 R/B6–B7 46 B–N4

R–R7 47 R–N3 K–N3 48 K–B2 N–Q7
49 R–K3 N–B5   50 R–N3 N–Q7   51
R–K3 N–B5 52 R–K8 N–Q7 53 R–K5
K–B3   54 R–B5+ K–N3   55 R–K5
K–B3   56 B–R5 R–B6   57 P–R4 R–B5
58 B–B3 R/B5–B7   59 B–Q5 R–R5
60 B–B3 R/R5–R7 61 R–K1 R–R5   62
P–R5 R–B6   63 B–N2 R–B7   64 R–Q1
R–R6   65 B–Q5 R–R5   66 K–K1 R–Q5
67 B–N2 N–N6 68 R×R N×R   69 K–
B2 N–K3 70 B–K4 R–N7 71 R–B5+
K–N2   72 R–Q5 K–B3   73 K–B3 1–0

10) **Tal-Botvinnik,** Caro-Kann 1 P–K4
P–QB3   2 P–Q4 P–Q4   3 P–K5 B–B4!
4 P–KR4 P–KR3   5 P–KN4 B–Q2
(5 . . . B–R2?   6 P–K6 P×P   7 B–Q3)   6
P–R5 P–QB4   7 P–QB3 N–QB3   8 B–
R3 P–K3 9 B–K3? (9 N–K2; 9 P–KB4
Q–N3 10 N–B3)   9 . . . Q–N3 10 Q–
N3? (10 N–Q2 Q×P 11 N–K2)   10 . . .
P×P!   11 Q×Q (11 P×P B–N5+   12
12 N–B3 N–R4 13 Q–B2 R–B1)   11 . . .
P×Q   12 P×P? N–R4!   13 N–QB3 P–
QN4 14 B–KB1 P–N5 15 N–N5 K–Q1
16 N–KB3 N–B5 (16 . . . N–N6   17
R–QN1 R×P 18 N–Q6 B×N 19 P×B
N–B3   20 N–K5)   17 B×N P×B   18
N–Q6 B×N 19 P×B B–B3 20 N–K5
B×R   21 N×P+ K–K1   22 N×R
B–K5 (173)

173
W

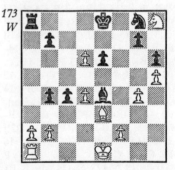

23 P–Q5 P×P   24 B–Q4 N–B3   25
K–Q2 K–Q2 26 N–B7 K–K3 27 N–
K5 K×P   28 P–B3 B–R2   29 P–N5
P×P 30 P–R6 P×P 31 N–B7+ K–K3

32 N×RP N–N1 33 N–N4 B–B4 34
N–K3 B–N3 35 N–N4 B–B4 36 N–K3
B–N3 37 N–N4 K–Q3 38 N–K5 B–
B4! 39 N–B7+ K–Q2 40 N×P N–K2
41 P–B4 N–B3 42 N–B3 K–Q3
(sealed) 0–1

11) Botvinnik-Tal, Queen's Gambit
Declined, Slav 1 P–Q4 N–KB3 2 P–QB4
P–B3 3 N–QB3 P–Q4 4 P×P P×P
5 N–B3 N–B3 6 B–B4 B–B4 7 P–K3
P–K3 8 B–QN5! B–QN5?! (8...
N–Q2) 9 N–K5 Q–R4 10 B×N+
P×B 11 0–0 B×N 12 P×B Q×BP?
(12... P–B4) 13 Q–B1! (*174*)

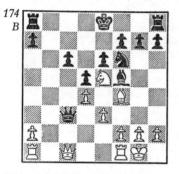

174
B

13... Q×Q 14 KR×Q 0–0?! (14...
N–R4) 15 P–B3 P–KR3 16 N×QBP
KR–K1 17 P–QR4 N–Q2 18 B–Q6
N–N3 19 B–B5 B–Q6 (19... N–B5
20 P–K4 B–R2 21 P×P P×P 22 N–
K7+) 20 N×P R×N 21 B×N R–R3
22 P–R5 B–B5 23 R–R3 P–B3 24 P–
K4 K–B2 25 K–B2 R/R3–R1 26 K–K3
KR–QN1 27 R/R3–B3 R–QB1 28
P–N4 QR–N1 29 P–R4 R–B3 30 P–
R5! R/N1–QB1 31 P–K5 P–N3? 32
P×P+ K×P 33 R/B3–B2 P×P 34
P×P R–KR1 35 R–KR2 R/B3–B1
36 K–Q2 B–N6 37 P–R6 B–B5 38 P–
R7 R–R2 39 R–QR1 R–QR1 40 B–K3
R–QN2 41 R×P+ K–N2 42 R/R1–R1
R–N7+ 1–0

12 Tal-Botvinnik, French 1 P–K4
P–K3 2 P–Q4 P–Q4 3 N–QB3 B–N5
4 P–K5 P–QB4 5 P–QR3 B×N+

6 P×B Q–B2 7 Q–N4 P–B4 (7...
N–K2; 7... P–B3! 8 N–B3 P–B5!;
7... P–B3! 8 B–N5±) 8 Q–N3 N–
K2!? (8... P×P 9 P×P N–K2 10 B–Q2
0–0 11 B–Q3 P–QN3 12 N–K2 B–R3
13 N–B4 Q–Q2=) 9 Q×P R–N1 10
Q×P P×P 11 K–Q1!? B–Q2 12 Q–
R5+ K–Q1! 13 N–B3!? (13 N–K2;
13 P–KB4!?) 13... Q×BP 14 R–R2
QN–B3 15 R–N2 K–B2 16 R–N5
R–R1 17 Q×R (17 Q–N5 QR–KN1
18 Q–Q2 N–N3) 17... R×Q 18 B–
N2 Q×N+! (18... Q–R4? 19 R×Q
N×R 20 B×P) 19 P×Q (*175*)

175
B

19... N–N3? (19... R–R5! 20 P–
KB4! with an obscure position) 20 P–
KR4! N/N3×KP (20... R×P 21 R×R
N×R 22 P–KB4) 21 P–R5 N–B2?! 22
P–KB4! N–Q3 23 R–N3 N–K5 24 K–
K1 R–R3 25 B–K2 B–K1 26 R–Q3
N–B3 27 B×P N×B 28 R×N B×P?
29 R–Q3 R–R2 (29... B×B 30 R–
B3+!) 30 R/Q–R3 B–N3 31 R×R+
N×R 32 R–R6 N–B1 33 R–R8 N–Q2
34 R–KN8 B–B2 35 R–N7 B–K1 36
R–K7 K–Q1 37 R×P B–B2 38 R–
KR6 K–K2 39 B–Q3 B–K3 40 R–R5
N–B3 41 R–N5 (sealed) 1–0

13) Botvinnik-Tal, King's Indian 1 P–
Q4 N–KB3 2 P–QB4 P–KN3 3 N–
QB3 B–N2 4 P–K4 P–Q3 5 P–B3 0–0
6 B–K3 P–K4 7 P×P P×P 8 Q×Q
R×Q 9 N–Q5 N×N 10 BP×N P–
QB3 11 B–QB4 P–QN4?! (11...

P×P 12 B×QP N–B3) 12 B–N3 B–N2
13 0-0-0– (13 R–B1! P×P? 14 R–B7
R–Q2 15 R×B!++) P–QB4?! (13 . . .
P×P) 14 B–QB2 N–Q2 15 N–K2
B–KB1 16 N–B3 P–QR3 17 P–QN3
QR–B1 18 B–Q3 N–N3 19 B–K2
R–Q3 20 K–N2 P–B4 (20 . . . P–B5)
21 R–QB1 R–KB3? (21 . . . P–KB5)
22 P–QR4! (176)

177
B

176
B

22 . . . P×RP 23 P×RP P–QR4 24
K–B2 P–QB5 25 R–QN1 B–N5 26
N–R2 B–B4 27 B×B R×B 28 N–B3
B–B1 29 R–N2 B–Q2 30 R/R1–QN1!
B×P+ 31 N×B N×N 32 R–N8+
K–N2 33 R/N1–N7+ R–KB2 34 P–
Q6 R×R 35 R×R+ K–B3 36 R×P
R–B1 37 P–Q7 R–Q1 38 B×P N–B4
39 R–B7± K–N4 40 B–N5 P×P
41 P×P 1–0

14) **Tal-Botvinnik,** Caro-Kann 1 P–
K4 P–QB3 2 P–Q4 P–Q4 3 P–K5
B–B4 4 P–KR4 P–KR4!? 5 N–K2
P–K3 6 N–N3 P–KN3 (6 . . . B–N3
7 B–K2 P–QB4! 8 P–QB3 N–QB3
9 B–K3=) 7 N×B NP×N 8 P–QB4!
P–B4 9 BP×P (9 B–N5!) 9 . . . Q×QP
10 N–B3 Q×QP 11 Q–B3 (11 B–
N5+! N–B3 12 Q–K2) 11 . . . N–
QB3 12 B–QN5 N–K2 13 B–N5
Q×KP+ 14 K–B1 B–R3 15 R–K1
Q–Q5 16 B×N K×B 17 Q×BP
QR–Q1 18 R–R3 (177)
18 . . . Q–Q7! 19 Q×QBP+ Q–Q3

20 Q–B4 (20 Q×Q+ R×Q 21 N–K4)
20 . . . Q–N5 21 Q–K2 Q–N5 22
B×N Q×Q+ 23 N×Q (23 R×Q
P×B 24 R–B3) 23 . . . P×B 24 R–R3
R–Q2 25 R–R6 R–QN1 26 N–N3?!
R×P! 27 N–B5+ K–B3 28 N×B
R/Q2–Q7 29 K–N1! R×BP 30 R–
KB1 R×R+ 31 K×R K–N2 32
R×RP K×N 33 R×P ½–½

15) **Botvinnik-Tal,** King's Indian 1 P–
Q4 N–KB3 2 P–QB4 P–KN3 3 N–
QB3 B–N2 4 P–K4 P–Q3 5 P–B3 0-0
6 B–K3 P–B3 7 B–Q3 P–K4 8 KN–K2
P×P (8 . . . QN–Q2) 9 B×P P–B4?!
10 B–KB2 N–B3 11 0-0 P–QR3
12 Q–Q2 B–K3 13 QR–Q1 Q–R4
14 P–QN3 QR–N1 15 B–N1 KR–Q1
16 P–B4 B–N5 17 P–KR3 B×N 18
N×B Q×Q 19 R×Q R–K1 20 N–N3
(20 P–K5 P×P 21 B×BP P–K5)
20 . . . B–B1 21 R–K1 R–K3 22 N–B1
QR–K1 23 R/Q2–K2 B–N2 24 P–
KN4 N–Q2 25 K–N2 R/K3–K2 26
N–R2 N–B1 27 B–R4 N–K3 28 R–
KB1 R–Q2?! (28 . . . P–B3) 29 P–N5
(178)
29 . . . P–KR4?! (19 . . . P–N4) 30 P×
Pep B×P 31 N–N4 B–N2 32 N–B6+
B×N 33 B×B N–N2 34 R–Q2 N–
KR4 35 B–B3 R/K1–Q1 36 B–B2
K–B1 37 B–Q1 K–K2 38 B–KN4
R–B2 39 P–B5 K–K1 40 P–B6 P–
QN4 41 R–Q5 P×P 42 P×P (sealed)
R–N2 43 K–B3 R–N5 44 B×R N×B

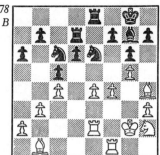

178
B

R–B2   39 P–B4 K–Q2   40 Q–K3?!
K–Q1 (*179*)

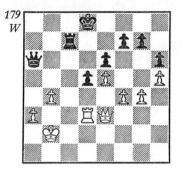

179
W

45 B×N N×R 46 KP×N P×B 47 R–
QN1 K–B1 48 R–N6 K–N1 49 K–B4
K–R2   50 K–N5 R–N1+   51 K×P
R–N6   52 P–KR4 R–K6   53 R×QP
R–K4+   54 K–N4 K–N3   55 K–B4
R–B4+   56 K–B3 R–R4   57 R×P
R×RP 58 K–Q3 K–B4 59 R–B6 R–R7
60 R×P R×P 61 R–B7 K×P 62 R–Q7
K–K4 63 R–K7+ 1–0

16) **Tal–Botvinnik,** Caro-Kann 1 P–
K4 P–QB3   2 P–Q4 P–Q4   3 P–K5
B–B4 4 P–KR4 P–B4?! 5 P×P Q–B2
6 N–QB3 N–QB3   7 N–B3 R–Q1
8 N–QN5 Q–B1 9 KN–Q4 (9 P–B3!)
9 ... B–N5 10 P–KB3 B–Q2 11 N×N
P×N 12 N–Q4 Q–N1 13 Q–K2 P–K3
(13 ... Q–N5+? 14 P–B3 Q×BP 15
B–K3) 14 N–N3 B×P 15 N×B Q–
N5+   16 PB3 Q×N   17 B–K3 Q–R4
18 P–QN4!? (18 Q–KB2! R–R1 19 Q–
N3)   18 ... Q–B2   19 B–B5 N–K2
20 P–R5 P–KR3   21 B–Q6 Q–N2
22 O–O–O!? (22 P–N4 followed by K–
B2) 22 ... R–R1 (22 ... N–B4 23 B–
B5! N–N6 24 Q–KB2 N×R 25 Q–R4
B–B1 26 B–Q3) 23 P–N4 P–R4 24
Q–KB2 P×P 25 P×P P–QB4 26 B×N
K×B   27 Q×P+ K–K1   28 K–N2 R–
QB1   29 Q–Q4 B–R5   30 R–B1 R×R
31 K×R K–Q2 (31 ... Q–B3+?   32
K–Q2 Q–B7+ 33 K–K3 Q×P 34 B–
K2) 32 K–N2 R–QB1 33 B–Q3 B–N4
34 R–Q1 Q–R3   35 P–R3 B×B   36
R×B K–K2 37 Q–K3 K–K1 38 Q–Q2

R–B2   39 P–B4 K–Q2   40 Q–K3?!
K–Q1 (*179*)

41 R–Q1?! (sealed) K–B1   42 Q–Q3
Q–N3   43 Q–Q4 Q–N4   44 Q–K3
K–N2   45 R–Q4?! (45 R–Q3)   45 ...
Q–B8   46 P–R4 Q–N7+   47 R–Q2
Q–B8   48 R–QB2 R×R+   49 K×R
Q–N7+   50 K–N3 Q×P   51 P–R5
Q–Q8+! 52 K–N2 Q–B8 53 Q–N6+
K–R1   54 Q–B6+ K–R2   55 Q–B7+
K–R1   56 Q–B8+ K–R2   57 Q–B7+
K–R1   58 P–B5 Q–K8   59 Q–B8+
K–R2   60 Q–B7+ K–R1   61 Q–B8+
K–R2   62 Q–B5+ K–N2   63 Q–N6+
K–R1   64 Q–B6+ K–R2   65 Q–B5+
K–N2   66 Q–Q4 Q–K7+   67 K–R3
Q–N4 68 P×P P×P 69 Q–B3 Q–B8
70 K–R2 Q–K7+   71 K–N3 Q–Q8+
72 Q–B2 Q–KB8 73 K–R2 Q–N4 74
K–R3 Q–B8 75 Q–B3 Q–QN8 76 P–
R6+ K×P   77 Q–B6+ K–R2   78 Q–
Q7+ K–N1   79 Q×KP Q–R8+   80
K–N3 Q–Q8+   81 K–N2 Q–Q5+
82 K–R2 Q×NP   83 Q–N8+ K–B2
84 Q×P+ K–Q1   85 Q–B6+ K–Q2
86 Q–B4 Q–K3 87 K–N2 K–K1 88
Q–R4+ K–B2 89 Q–B4+ K–K1 90
K–B2 Q–R3 ½–½

17) **Botvinnik–Tal,** King's Indian 1P–
Q4 P–KN3 2 P–K4 B–N2 3 P–QB4
P–Q3 4 N–QB3 N–KB3 5 P–B3
QN–Q2 6 B–K3 O–O 7 B–Q3 P–K4
8 KN–K2 N–R4 9 P×P P×P 10 O–O
P–QB3 11 Q–Q2 Q–K2 12 QR–Q1

N–B4 13 B–N1 N–K3 14 Q–K1 B–
B3?! 15 K–R1 N/R4–B5 16 P–KN3
N×N 17 N×N P–KR4?! 18 Q–B2
P–N3 19 P–B4 P×P 20 P×P B–QN2
(20 . . . B×P? 21 P–KB5) 21 P–K5
P–B4+ 22 R–Q5! B–N2 23 K–N1
N–B2 24 N–B3 (24 R–Q6! QR–Q1 25
KR–Q1) 24 . . . N×R 25 P×N QR–
Q1 26 B–K4 B–QR1 27 Q–N3 P–QN4
28 Q–B2 Q–Q2 29 B×BP KR–K1
30 Q–N3 (30 P–N4) R–QB1 31 P–N4
K–R1 32 Q–B3 (32 P–K6! P×P 33
Q×P B×N 34 Q×P+ K–N1 35 K–
R1 B×QP 36 R–N1+) 32 . . . P–R3
33 K–R1 P–B4! (180)

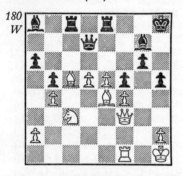

180
W

34 P×Pep. (34 B–QB2 B–B1! 35 B×B
R×N) 34 . . . B×BP 35 B×P Q–N5
36 Q–Q3? R–KN1 37 B–K4 QR–K1
38 B–B3? Q×P 39 N–K2 Q–R5 40
B–B2 Q–N4 (adjourned) 41 N–N3
R–Q1 42 B–K3 Q–K4 43 R–Q1 R–N5
44 P–QR3 B–QN2 45 B–N6 R–Q2
46 B–K3 R–R5 47 N–B1 R–QB5 48
B–N2 R–N2 49 Q–Q2 P–R5 50 P–R3
Q–N7 51 Q×Q B×Q 52 B–B5 R–Q2
53 N–K3 R–B8 54 R×R B×R 55 B–
Q4+ K–N1 56 N–N4 B–N4 57 K–N1
B×P 58 N–K5 B×B 59 N×R B×P
60 N–B5 B–B1 61 K–B2 K–R2? 62
P–R4 P×P 63 N×P/R4 B–B5 64 K–B3
P–R6 65 B–N1 P–R7 66 B×P B×B
67 K–K4 B–Q2 68 N–B5 B–N4 69
K–Q5 K–N3 70 N–K4 K–B4 71 N–B3
B–B8 72 K–B5 B–K4 73 N–N1 K–
K3?! 74 N–Q2 B–Q3+ 75 K–N6

B–N7 76 N–N3 B×P 77 K×P B–B8+
78 K–N6 K–Q3 79 N–R5 B–B4+
80 K–N7 B–K7 81 N–N3 B–K6 82
N–R5 K–B4 83 K–B7 B–B5+ 0–1

18) **Tal-Botvinnik,** Caro-Kann 1 P–
K4 P–QB3 2 P–Q4 P–Q4 3 P–K5 B–B4
4 P–KR4 P–KR3 5 P–KN4 B–Q2 6 P–
QB3?! P–QB4 7 B–N2 P–K3 8 N–K2
B–N4! 9 N–R3? (9 N–Q2 or 9 B–K3)
9 . . . B×N 10 Q×B P×P 11 P×P
B×N 12 P×B N–QB3 13 B–K3 (13
B–N2 Q–R4+ 14 Q–Q2 Q×Q+
15 K×Q N–R4) 13 . . . Q–R4+ 14
K–B1 KN–K2 15 R–QN1 R–QN1
16 B–R3 Q–R5 17 R–Q1 Q×RP 18
K–N2 Q–R3 19 Q×Q P×Q 20 P–R5
K–Q2 21 R–QN1 R–N3 22 K–N3
N–R4 23 R×R?! P×R 24 P–B4 N–B5
25 B–QB1 N–B3 26 R–Q1 N–N5 27
P–R3 N–R7 28 P–B5 N×B 29 R×N
P–QN4 30 R–QR1 K–K2 31 K–B4
R–QB1 32 P–N5 P×P+ 33 K×P
P×P 34 B×P R–B3 35 K–B4 R–R3?!
36 B–N4 R–QB3 37 R–QB1? (37 P–
R4! and if 37 . . . P–N5 38 B–B3)
37 . . . P–B3 38 B–B5 P×P+ 39 P×P
N×KP 40 R–Q1 K–Q3 41 B–K4
R–B4 (sealed) 0–1

19) **Botvinnik-Tal,** King's Indian 1 P–
Q4 N–KB3 2 P–QB4 P–Q3 3 N–QB3
P–KN3 4 P–K4 B–N2 5 P–B3 0–0
6 B–K3 P–QR3 7 Q–Q2 P–B3 8 B–Q3
P–K4 9 P×P P×P 10 N–R4? P–QN4
11 N–N6 R–R2 12 B–QB2 (12 N×B
R–Q2 13 N–N6 R×B 14 Q–K2 Q–
Q3) 12 . . . B–K3 13 Q×Q R×Q 14
N–K2 (14 P–QR4!) 14 . . . R–N2 15
P–B5 P–QR4 16 K–B2 B–KB1 17
KR–Q1 R×R 18 R×R KN–Q2
19 N×N N×N 20 B–N1 B×BP 21
B×B N×B 22 R–QB1 N–R3 23 P–
B4 P×P 24 N×P P–QB4 (24 . . . B–
Q2) 25 K–K3 K–B1 26 P–K5 K–K2
27 B–K4 R–B2 28 P–QR4 P×P 29 R–
QR1 B–N6 30 N–Q5+ B×N 31
B×B R–Q2 32 B–B4 N–N5 33 R×P

R–Q5 34 B–N5 K–K3 35 R×P N–
Q4+ 36 K–B2 K×P 37 B–K2 K–Q3
38 R–R6+ K–Q2 39 R–R7+ N–B2
40 P–QN3 R–Q7 41 K–B3 (*181*)

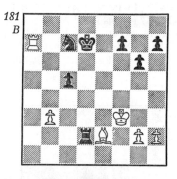

41 ... P–B4 (sealed) 42 P–R4 K–B3
43 B–B4 P–R3 44 P–N3 R–Q5 45 K–
B2 P–N4 46 P×P P×P 47 R–R2 P–N5
48 R–R1 K–N3 49 R–K1 N–N4 50
R–K6+ N–Q3 51 K–K3 K–B2 52 B–
Q3 K–B3 53 B–B2 R–N5 54 R–B6
K–Q4 55 R–B8 K–K4 56 R–QR8
N–K5 57 R–K8+ K–Q4 58 R–Q8+
K–K3 59 K–B4 N–Q7+ 60 K–K3
N×P 61 R–K8+ K–Q2 62 R–K5 K–
Q3 63 R×KBP N–Q5 64 R–B2
N×B+ 65 R×N K–Q4 66 R–KR2
R–K5+ 67 K–Q2 P–B5 68 R–R8 R–
Q5+ 69 K–K3 R–Q6+ 70 K–B4
P–B6 71 R–Q8+ K–B5 72 R–B8+
K–N6 73 R–N8+ K–R7 74 R–QB8
K–N7 75 R–N8+ K–B8 0–1 (76 K×P
P–B7 77 R–QB8 K–N7 78 R×P+
K×R 79 K–B4 R–Q8 80 P–N4 K–Q6
81 P–N5 K–Q5 82 P–N6 R–B8+ 83
K–N5 K–K4 84 P–N7 R–N8+ 85 K–
R6 K–B3++)

20) Tal-Botvinnik, Caro-Kann 1 P–K4
P–QB3 2 P–Q4 P–Q4 3 P–K5 B–B4
4 P–KR4 P–KR3 5 N–K2!? P–K3 6 N–
N3 N–K2 (6 ... B–R2!) 7 N–B3 N–Q2
(7 ... B–R2 8 B–Q3 B×B 9 P×B
N–R3) 8 B–K3 B–R2 9 B–Q3 B×B
10 P×B! P–KR4! 11 QN–K2 (11 N×
RP?!) N–KB4 12 P–KN3 P–B4) 11 ...

P–KN3?! (11 ... N–KN3!= or 11 ...
Q–R4+ 12 B–Q2 Q–R3) 12 Q–Q2
N–KN1! 13 0–0–0 B–R3 14 K–N1
B×B? 15 P×B N–R3 16 P–K4 Q–K2
17 P×P? (17 N–B4!) 17 ... KP×P
18 Q–R5 N–B1 19 QR–KB1 N–K3
20 R–B3 Q–Q1 21 Q–R4 Q–N3 22
R–QB1 N–N5 23 N–B1 0–0 24 N–K3
P–KB4 25 P–KN3 N–R7 26 R–KB4
N–N5 27 N–N2 QR–K1 28 Q–R3
R–B2 29 R–QB3 P–R3 30 R–N3 Q–
R2 31 Q–Q6 Q–N1 32 Q×Q R×Q
33 R–B1 N–R7 34 R–B1 R–K1 35
N/N2–B4 N×N?! 36 P×N N–N5 37
R–N6 K–N2 38 R–R1 N–R3 39 N–B3
R–B2 40 N–R4 N–B2 41 K–B2 N–Q1
42 K–Q2 (adjourned) N–K3 43 K–K3
R–Q2 (*182*)

44 P–N4 K–B2 45 N–B5 N×N 46
NP×N R–QR1 47 K–Q2 K–K3?
(47 ... R–K2=) 48 R–KN1 R–N2 49
K–B3 R–QR2 50 K–N4 P–R4+ 51 K–
R4 R–R1? 52 R/N1–N1 R–QR2 53
R/N1–N5 R–N1 54 P–R3 R–K1 55
R×RP R/K1–QR1 56 R×R R×R+
57 K–N4 P–N4 58 RP×P P–R5 59 R–
R4 P–R6 60 K–R3 P–R7 61 R–N1
R–R1 62 P–N6? R–KN1 63 R–KR1
R×P 64 R×P R–N6 65 R–R6+ K–Q2
66 R–R7+ K–B1 67 P–K6 R×P+
68 K–N2 R–K6 69 P–K7 K–Q2 70 P–
K8=Q+ K×Q 71 R×P K–Q1 72
P–R5 R–K7+ 73 K–N3 R–K8 74 K–
N2 R–K7+ 75 K–B3 R–QR7 76 R–N6
K–B2! 77 P–R6 R–R8 78 K–N2 R–R5

79 K–N3 R–R8   80 R–N7+ K–B1
81 R–N6 K–B2 82 R–N7+ K–B1 83
R–QR7 R–N8+   84 K–B3 R–QR8
85 R–R8+ K–B2   86 K–N3 R–N8+
87 K–B3 R–QR8   88 K–N3 R–N8+
(adjourned)   89 K–R2 R–N4   90 P–R7
R–R4+   91 K–N3 K–N2   92 R–KB8
R–N4+   93 K–R4 K×P   94 R×P R–N8
95 R–B6 (95 R–B7+ K–R3   96 R–B7
R–N5+!=) K–N2   96 P–B5 R–R8+
97 K–N4 R–N8+   98 K–B3 R–B8+
99 K–Q2 R–B8 100 K–K3 K–B2 101
R–B7+ K–Q1 102 K–K2 R–B5 103
K–Q3 R–B6+   104 K–Q2 K–B1 105
K–K2 R–B5 106 K–K3 R–B8   107 R–
B8+ K–Q2   108 R–B6 K–B2 109 R–
B7+ K–Q1   110 K–K2 R–B5 111 K–
Q3 R–B6+   112 K–B2 K–B1 113 P–B6
K–Q1 114 R–B8+ K–B2 115 K–Q2
K–N2   116 K–K2 R–B5   117 K–K3
R–B8 118 R–B7+ K–B1 119 K–Q2
R–B6 120 K–B2 K–Q1 121 R–B8+
K–B2 ½–½

21) **Botvinnik–Tal,** King's Indian 1 P–
Q4 N–KB3   2 P–QB4 P–KN3   3 N–
QB3 B–N2   4 P–K4   P–Q3   5 P–B3

QN–Q2   6 B–K3 P–K4   7 KN–K2 0–0
8 P–Q5 N–R4   9 Q–Q2 P–KB4   10
0–0–0 P–QR3   11 K–N1 QN–B3   12
P×P P×P   13 N–N3 Q–K1   14 B–Q3
N×N?!   15 P×N P–B4?!   16 B–R6
Q–N3   17 P–KN4 P–N4   18 B×B K×B
19 R–R4 P×BP   20 B–B2 P–R3   21
QR–R1 Q–N4   22 Q×Q+ P×Q   23
R–R6 P×P   24 P×P B×P   25 R–N6+
K–B2   26 R–KB1 K–K2   27 R–N7+
K–K1 (*183*)

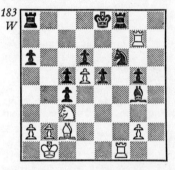

183
W

28 N–K4 N–Q2   29 N×P+ K–Q1
30 R×R+ N×R   31 N×P B–Q2   32
R–B7 K–B2   33 P–Q6+ 1–0

8 Botvinnik–Petrosian

Moscow March 22–May 20 1963

	1	2	3	4	5	6	7	8	9	10	11
Botvinnik	1	½	½	½	0	½	0	½	½	½	½
Petrosian	0	½	½	½	1	½	1	½	½	½	½

	12	13	14	15	16	17	18	19	20	21	22	**Total**
Botvinnik	½	½	1	0	½	½	0	0	½	½	½	9½
Petrosian	½	½	0	1	½	½	1	1	½	½	½	12½

1) Petrosian-Botvinnik, Nimzo-Indian 1 P–Q4 N–KB3 2 P–QB4 P–K3 3 N–QB3 B–N5 4 Q–B2 P–Q4 5 P×P P×P 6 B–N5 P–KR3! 7 B×N Q×B 8 P–QR3 B×N+ 9 Q×B P–B3 10 P–K3 0–0 11 N–K2 R–K1! 12 N–N3?! (12 N–B4?? Q×N!; 12 N–B1!? & 13 N–Q3) 12 ... P–KN3 13 P–B3? (13 B–Q3!? P–KR4 14 0–0) 13 ... P–KR4 14 B–K2 N–Q2 15 K–B2 P–R5 16 N–B1 N–B1 17 N–Q2 R–K2 18 KR–K1 B–B4 19 P–R3?! (19 N–B1!?/ 19 P–QN4!?) 19 ... QR–K1 20 N–B1 N–K3 21 Q–Q2? (*184*)

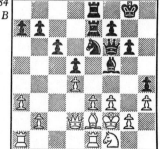

184
B

21 ... N–N2? (Better 21 ... N–N4! threatening B×RP forcing the position open with mating threats, e.g. 22 K–N1 B×P 23 P×B N×RP+ 24 K–N2 R×P!! 25 N×R Q–N4+ 26 N–N4 Q×Q 27 N–B6+ K–R1 28 N×R 28 ... Q–N4+ and mates, or 23 ... N–K5+ 24 K–N2 Q–N4+ 25 K–R2 N–B7 26 P–B4 Q–B3 27 Q–Q2 R×P 28 N×R Q×BP+ 29 K–N2 N–K5! threatening mate and queen) 22 QR–Q1 N–R4 23 R–B1 Q–Q3 24 R–B3 N–N6 25 K–N1 (25 N×N P×N+) 25 ... N–R4 26 B–Q1 R–K3 27 Q–KB2 Q–K2 28 B–N3 P–KN4 29 B–Q1? (29 P–K4!? N–B5 30 Q–Q2 31 R/3–K3!?) 29 ... B–N3 30 P–KN4? (30 B–B2!?) 30 ... P×Pep. 31 N×P N–B5! 32 Q–R2 P–QB4! 33 Q–Q2 P–B5 34 B–R4 P–N4! 35 B–B2 (35 B×P!? R–N1 36 B–R4 N–Q6 and Black rooks penetrate) 35 ... N×P+ 36 K–B1 Q–B3 37 K–N2 N–B5+ 38 P×N R×R 39 P×P Q–K3 40 P–B4 R–K7+! 0–1

2) Botvinnik-Petrosian, Queen's Gambit accepted 1 P–Q4 P–Q4 2 P–QB4 P×P 3 N–KB3 N–KB3 4 P–K3 P–B4 5 B×P P–K3 6 0–0 P–QR3 7 P–QR4 N–B3 8 Q–K2 P×P 9 R–Q1 B–K2 10 P×P 0–0 11 B–KN5 N–Q4 12 B×B N/3×B 13 N–K5 (13 R–R3!?) 13 ... B–Q2 14 N–Q2 B–B3 15 N–K4 N–B5 16 Q–B3 B×N 17

149

L

Q×B (17 Q×N B–Q4 18 B–Q3 N–N3=) 17...N/5–Q4 18 R–R3 R–B1 19 R–R3 N–KN3! (185)

185
W

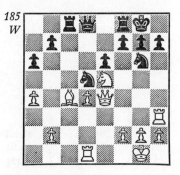

20 B×N P×B (20...Q×B? 21 Q×Q P×Q 22 R–QN3 R–B2 23 N–Q3 intending 24 N–B5∓) 21 Q–B5 Q–Q3! 22 R–QN3 (23 N×P?! Q–B5 23 Q–R5 R–B8!) 22...R–B2 23 P–N3 P–N3 (23...N×N!? 24 P×N Q–K3 25 Q×Q P×Q=) 24 R–K1 N–K2 (24...N×N? 25 Q×N and exchange of queens would leave Black's BP's vulnerable) 25 Q–B4! R–B7! 26 N–Q3 Q–Q1! (26...Q×Q 27 N×Q N–B3 28 R×P N×P 29 K–N2±) 27 Q–N5 N–B1! 28 Q×Q R×Q 29 P–R5 (29 N–N4 R–B5 30 N×QP R×RP=) 29...P×P 30 R–N8 R–B1 31 R–R1 N–K2 32 R×R+ K×R 33 R×P R–Q7 34 R×P R×N 35 R–R8+ N–B1 ½–½

3) Petrosian-Botvinnik, Queen's Indian
1 P–Q4 N–KB3 2 N–KB3 P–K3 3 P–KN3 P–QN3 4 B–N2 B–N2 5 P–B4 B–K2 6 0–0 0–0 7 N–B3 N–K5 8 N×N B×N 9 N–K1 B×B 10 N×B P–Q4 11 Q–R4 P–QB4 12 B–K3 Q–Q2 13 Q×Q N×Q 14 BP×P KP×P 15 N–B4 N–B3 16 P×P (to prevent Black playing P–B5) 16...P×P 17 QR–B1 (186)
17...P–Q5 (17...QR–B1?! 18 R–B2 R–B2 19 KR–B1 KR–B1 20 P–QN4!) 18 B–Q2 P–QR4 (Anticipating White playing P–QN3; intending P–R5 attack-

186
B

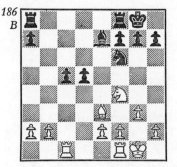

ing it) 19 N–Q3 N–Q2 20 P–K3! (Isolating the Black pawns) 20 ... P×P 21 B×KP KR–N1 22 KR–Q1 P–R5 23 K–N2 P–R3?! (23...P–N3!) 24 R–Q2 R–N4 25 N–B4 N–B3 26 K–B3 QR–N1 27 N–Q3 N–Q2 28 B–B4 R/N1–N2 29 B–K3 P–B3? (Too weakening; 29...B–B3 or 29...R–N1 was better) 30 P–R4! P–R4 31 R–B4? N–N3 32 R/B4–B2 P–B5 33 B×N P×N 34 R–B8+ K–B2 35 B–Q4 P–N4! 36 R–B4 R–N5 37 R×R R×R 38 B–B3 R–B5 39 P×P P×P 40 R×P B–B3 41 P–R3 P–R5! 42 P×P B×B 43 R×B R×P 44 R–B5 (44 R–B6 R–R6+ 45 K–N4 R–QN6 46 K×P R×NP 47 P–B4 R–N6 draws) 44...K–B3 45 R–N5 R–B5+ 46 K–K3 R–R5 47 R–N4 K–K4! 48 K–Q3 K–K3 49 R–N5 K–B3 50 K–K2 R–K5+ 51 K–B1 R–R5 52 K–N1 R–N5+ 53 K–R2 R–R5+ 54 K–N2 R–N5+ 55 K–R3 R–R5+ 56 K–N3 R–Q5! 57 K–B3 R–B5+ 58 K–K3 R–R5 59 R–N8 K–K3 60 R–K8+ K–B3 61 K–Q2 K–B2 62 R–K3 R–KB5 63 P–B3 R–R5 64 K–B3 R–R6 65 K–Q4 R–R7 66 P–N4 P×Pep 67 R×P K–K3 68 K–B5 K–Q2 69 K–Q5 R–K7 70 P–R4 K–B2 71 P–R5 R–QR7 72 R–N5 R–R5! 73 K–K5 P–N5 74 P–B4 P–N6 75 R–N3 R×P+ 76 K–K6 R–R3+ 77 K–K7 R–KN3 78 R–B3+ K–N3 79 R–B1= P–N7 80 R–KN1 K–B2 81 P–B5 R–N6 82 P–B6 R–K6+ 83

K–B7 R–KN6 84 K–K6 R–K6+ 85 K–
B5 R–KN6 86 P–B7 R–B6+ ½–½

4) Botvinnik-Petrosian, English 1 P–
QB4 P–QB4 2 N–QB3 N–QB3 3 N–
B3 P–KN3 4 P–K3! N–B3 5 P–Q4
P×P 6 P×P P–Q4 7 P×P KN×P
8 Q–N3 N×N 9 B–QB4! (187)

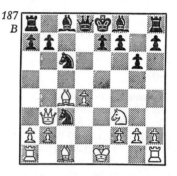

187
B

9 . . . P–K3 (9 . . . B–N2 10 B×P+
K–B1 11 P×N N–R4 12 Q–Q5± - or
9 . . . N–Q4 10 B×N P–K3 11 B×N+
P×B 12 0–0 B–KN2±) 10 P×N B–
N2 (10 . . . N–R4 11 B–N5+ B–Q2
12 Q–R4 N–B3 13 P–Q5 P×P 14 0–0
with a strong attack) 11 B–R3 B–B1
12 B–QB1 B–N2 13 B–QN5 B–Q2
14 B–R3 B–KB1 15 B×B (0–0!) 15 . . .
K×B 16 0–0 K–N2 17 B–K2 P–N3
18 P–B4 Q–B3 19 Q–K3 KR–K1 20
N–K5 QR–Q1 21 QR–Q1 Q–K2 22
P–B5?! (22 P–B4 P–B3 23 N–B3 Q–
Q3) 22 . . . N×N 23 Q×N+ Q–B3
24 P×P P×P ½–½

5) Petrosian-Botvinnik, Grünfeld 1 P–
QB4 P–KN3 2 P–Q4 N–KB3 3 N–
QB3 P–Q4 4 N–B3 B–N2 5 P–K3
0–0 6 B–K2 P×P 7 B×P P–B4 8 P–Q5
P–K3 9 P×P (9 P–K4 P×P 10 P×P
R–K1+) 9 . . . Q×Q+ 10 K×Q
B×P 11 B×B P×B 12 K–K2 N–B3
(12 . . . N–Q4!?) 13 R–Q1 QR–Q1
(13 . . . K–B2!) 14 R×R R×R 15 N–
KN5 R–K1 16 N/5–K4 N×N 17
N×N P–N3 18 R–N1 N–N5 (188)

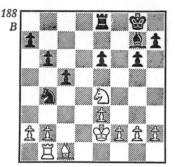

188
B

19 B–Q2! N–Q4 (19 . . . N×P?! 20 R–
QR1 N–N5 21 B×N P×B 22 R×P
B×P 23 R–QN7±) 20 P–QR4 R–
QB1 21 P–QN3 B–B1 22 R–QB1
B–K2! (22 . . . P–QR3 23 P–QN4 P–B5
24 P–N5 P×P 25 P×P B–K2±) 23 P–
QN4! P–B5 (23 . . . K–B2) 24 P–N5
K–B2 25 B–B3 B–R6 26 R–B2 N×B+
27 R×N B–N5 28 R–B2 K–K2 29 N–
Q2 P–B6 (29 . . . B×N 30 K×B K–Q3
31 K–B3 K–B4 32 R–Q2 and wins)
30 N–K4 B–R4 31 K–Q3 R–Q1+
32 K–B4 R–Q8 33 N×P R–KR8
(Better is 33 . . . B×N 34 K×B R–KR8
35 P–R3 K–Q2 with some chance of
holding the position) 34 N–K4 R×P
35 K–Q4 K–Q2 36 P–N3 (36 P–N4
P–R4!) 36 . . . B–N5 37 K–K5 R–R4+
38 K–B6 B–K2+ 39 K–N7 P–K4 40
R–B6 R–R8 41 K–B7! R–R8 42 R–K6
B–Q1 43 R–Q6+ K–B1 44 K–K8 B–
B2 45 R–QB6 R–Q8 (45 . . . R×P 46
N–B3 winning) 46 N–N5 R–Q1+ 47
K–B7 R–Q2+ 48 K–N8 1–0

6) Botvinnik - Petrosian, Queen's
Gambit accepted 1 P–Q4 P–Q4 2 P–
QB4 P×P 3 N–KB3 N–KB3 4 P–K3
P–K3 5 B×P P–B4 6 0–0 P–QR3
7 P–QR4 N–B3 8 Q–K2 B–K2 9 P×P
B×P 10 P–K4 N–KN5 (10 . . . P–K4
11 B×P+) 11 B–B4 Q–B3 12 B–KN3
N/5–K4 13 N×N N×N 14 N–Q2 0–0
15 QR–Q1 P–QN3 16 Q–R5 N×B
17 N×N P–R4 (189)

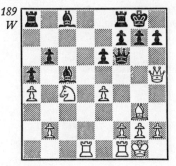

189
W

18 N–K5 (18 B–K5!?) 18 ... Q–K2
19 R–Q2 P–B3 20 N–Q3 P–K4 21
N×B Q×N 22 Q–Q1 B–K3 23 R–K1
QR–B1 24 P–R3 Q–N5 ∓ 25 R–K3
R–B5 26 P–N3! R–B3 27 K–R2
P–QN4 ½–½

7) Petrosian–Botvinnik, English 1 P–
QB4 P–KN3 2 N–KB3 B–N2 3 N–
B3 P–K4 4 P–KN3 N–K2 5 B–N2 0–0
6 P–Q4! P×P 7 N×P QN–B3 8 N×N
N×N 9 0–0 P–Q3 10 B–Q2! B–N5!
11 P–KR3 B–K3 12 P–N3 Q–Q2 13
K–R2 QR–K1? (better 13 ... N–K2
14 B×P B×P) 14 R–B1 P–B4 15 N–
Q5! K–R1 16 B–K3 B–N1 17 Q–Q2
N–Q1 18 KR–Q1 N–K3 19 N–B4
N×N 20 B×N Q–B1 21 P–KR4 R–K2
22 B–B3 B–B2 23 Q–R5! B–K1 24 P–
B5! P–Q4 25 B–Q6! (*190*)

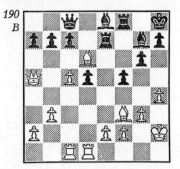

190
B

25 ... Q–Q2 26 B×R Q×B 27 R×P
(27 P–K3! P–Q5 28 R–K1!) 27 ...
P–B5 28 Q–Q2 B–QB3 29 R–Q3 B–

N4 30 R–Q4 P×P+ 31 P×P B×R
32 Q×B+ Q–N2 33 Q×Q+ K×Q
34 R–B2 R–K1 (34 ... R–QN1 35
P–B6! P–N3 36 R–Q2 R–KB1 37 P–
R4 B–R3 38 R–Q7+ R–B2 39 B–
Q5 wins) 35 K–N2 K–B3 36 K–B2
B–B3 37 B×B P×B 38 R–B4 K–K4
39 R–R4 R–QR1 40 R–R6 K–Q4 41
P–QN4 K–B5 42 P–R3 K–N4 43 R–
R5+ K–B5 44 K–K3 P–QR3 45 K–B4
K–Q4 46 K–N5 R–K1 47 R×P R×P+
48 R–R7 R–K4+ 49 K–B4 R–K2 50
R–N7 K–K3 51 P–R4 K–Q2 52 R–
N8 1–0

8) Botvinnik – Petrosian, Queen's
Gambit Accepted 1 P–Q4 P–Q4 2 P–
QB4 P×P 3 N–KB3 N–KB3 4 P–K3
P–K3 5 B×P P–B4 6 0–0 P–QR3 7 P–
QR4 N–B3 8 Q–K2 B–K2 9 P×P B×P
10 P–K4 N–KN5 11 P–K5! N–Q5 12
N×N Q×N 13 N–R3!! (Plan 14 N–
B2) 13 ... B×N (13 ... N×KP 14 P–
QN4!? N×B 15 N×N Q×R 16
P×B±) 14 R×B N×KP (*191*)

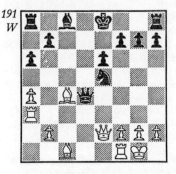

191
W

15 P–QN3! Q–B4! (15 ... N×B 16
P×N 0–0 17 R–KN3 P–B3 18 B–R6 R–
B2 19 R–Q1 Q–N3 20 Q–N2! Q–B2
21 R×P+ R×R 22 Q×BP±) 16 ...
R–R2 N×B 17 P×N B–Q2 18 B–R3
Q–B4! 19 R–Q2 B–B3 20 R–K1 R–
KR4! (20 ... P–B3?! 21 P–N4!) 21
Q–K3 (Idea 22 R–Q5! B×R 23 Q–B5
Q–B3 24 P×B±) 21 ... P–B3 22

Q+P+ Q×Q 23 R×Q+ K–B2 24
R–K7+ K–N3 25 P–R5 QR–Q1 26
B–Q6 KR–K1 27 R×R R×R 28
P–B3 R–K8+ 29 K–B2 R–QR8 30
B–N4 R–QN8 31 B–R3 R–N6 32
B–Q6 R–B6 33 R–Q4 (33 P–B5!?
P–R5 34 P–R3 B–N4) 33 ... R–
B7+ 34 K–N3 B–Q2 35 P–R4 B–K3
36 P–B5 B–B5 37 K–B4 B–N4 38 P–
N4 R–B6 39 R–K4 B–B3 40 R–K3 R–
B5+ 41 K–N3 R–R5 42 B–B7 P×P 43
P×P B–Q2 44 B–B4 K–B2 (44 ...
R×P 45 R–K7 B–B3 46 P–R5+ K–R2
47 P–R6=) 45 R–N3 B–B1 46 P–N5!
P×P 47 P×P R×P 48 B–K3 K–N3 49
R–N6+ K–B4 50 P–B6 P×P 51 R×
BP R–R6 52 R–B5+ K–N3 53 R–B6+
K–R4 54 K–B4 R–R5+ 55 K–N3 ½–½

9) Petrosian-Botvinnik, Catalan 1 P–
QB4 P–K3 2 P–KN3 P–Q4 3 B–N2
N–KB3 4 N–KB3 B–K2 5 0–0 0–0
6 P–Q4 QN–Q2 7 Q–B2 P–B3 8 B–
B4 N–K5 9 N–B3 (9 KN–Q2!? P–
KN4 10 B–K3 P–KB4 11 N×N!
BP×N 12 P–B3±) 9 ... P–KN4! 10
B–B1 P–KB4 11 P–N3 B–B3 12 B–
N2 B–N2 (12 ... Q–K2!? and 13 ...
Q–N2) 13 QR–Q1 R–B2 14 N×N!
BP×N 15 N–K1 N–B1 16 P–B3
P×P (*192*)

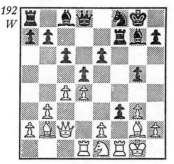

192
W

17 B×P? (17 N×P N–N3 18 P–K4
P–N5 19 N–K5 N×N 20 P×N R×R+
21 R×R±) 17 ... B–Q2 18 N–Q3 B–
K1 19 Q–B1 (19 N–K5!? R–B4 20 P–
K4±) 19 ... R–B1 20 Q–K3 QR–B2

21 N–K5 R–B4 22 B–N2 R×R+ 23
R×R Q–K2 24 B–KR3 P–KR4 25 B–
N2 N–N3 26 N–Q3 B–B2 (26 ... P×P
27 P×P P–B4!) 27 Q–B2 P–N3? (27 ...
P×P 28 P×P P–B4 29 B–QR3 B×P 30
P–K3 N–K4!) 28 P–K4! P×BP 29
P×P P–B4 30 P×P (P–Q5!?) 30 ...
P×P 31 B×B K×B 32 P–K5 N–B1 33
Q–B6+ (33 B–K4!? or 33 Q–K3!?)
33 ... Q×Q 34 P×Q+ K–N1 35 N–
K5 N–Q2 36 N–B3 N×P 37 N×P K–
N2 38 R–K1 R–Q2! (38 ... R–K2?! 39
R–K5 N–Q2 40 N×B!±) 39 N×P+
B×N 40 R×B R–Q8+ 41 B–B1 P–R4
(41 ... N–N5!? 42 P–KR3 N–R7!?)
42 R–K3 N–N5 43 R–R3 P–QR5! 44
P–R3 N–R7 45 K×N R×B 46 R×P
(46 K–N2 R–B8 47 R×P R–B6±)
46 ... R–B7+ 47 K–N1 R–B7 48 R–
R3 R×BP 49 R–KB3 R–B7 50 P–QR4
R–QR7 51 R–B4 R–R6 52 K–B2 R–
R7+ 53 K–K1 R–R6 54 R–B5 P–R5
55 P×P R×QRP ½–½

10) Botvinnik - Petrosian, Queen's
Gambit Accepted 1 P–Q4 P–Q4 2 P–
QB4 P×P 3 N–KB3 N–KB3 4 P–K3
P–K3 5 B×P P–B4 6 0–0 P–QR3
7 P–QR4 N–B3 8 Q–K2 P×P 9 R–Q1
B–K2 10 P×P 0–0 11 N–B3 N–QN5
12 B–KN5 B–Q2 (*193*)

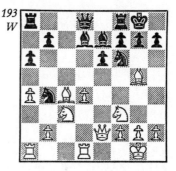

193
W

13 P–Q5! P×P (13 ... KN×P 14 B×B
N×B 15 N–K5 N/5–Q4 16 N×N
P×N 17 B×QP N×B 18 R×N B–N5!
19 Q–K4 B–B4 20 Q–Q4±) 14 N×P

N/5×N (14 ... N/3×N 15 B×B N×B
16 N–K5±) 15 KB×N N×B 16 R×N
B×B 17 N×B P–R3 18 Q–Q2 P×N
19 R×B Q–B3 20 R×NP QR–Q1 21
Q–R5 R–Q3 22 Q–N4 KR–Q1 23 R–
KB1 R–Q5 24 Q–N3 R–Q6 26 Q–B2
R–Q7 26 Q–B7 Q–B5 (26 ... R×BP!?
27 Q×R+ Q×Q 28 R×R P–B3) 27
Q×Q P×Q 28 P–R4 R–QB1 29 R–N4
P–B6! 30 P×P R/B1–B7 31 P–N3 R–
N7 32 K–N2 R–Q6 33 R–N8+ K–R2
34 R–N7 P–B3 35 R–K1 R/Q6×NP
36 R×R (36 R–R7 R–N5 37 R/K1–K7
R×QRP 38 R×P+ K–R3=) 36 ...
R×R 37 R–K6 R–N5 38 R×RP R×
KRP 39 K–N3 P–N4 40 K–N2 K–N3
41 R–R8 R–KB5 42 P–R5 R–QR5
43 P–R6 K–B4 ½–½

11) Petrosian-Botvinnik, Queen's
Gambit Declined, Tarrasch 1 P–QB4
P–QB4 2 N–KB3 N–KB3 3 N–B3
P–K3 4 P–K3 P–Q4 5 P–Q4 N–B3
6 BP×P P×P 7 B–N5 B–Q3!? 8 P×P
B×BP 9 0–0 0–0 10 P–QN3 B–K3
11 B–N2 Q–K2 12 N–K2 QR–B1 13
P–QR3 KR–Q1 14 N/2–Q4 B–KN5
15 B–K2 N–K5 16 Q–Q3 (*194*)

194
B

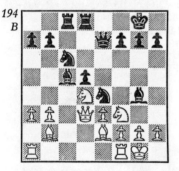

16 ... B–Q3! 17 P–N3 (17 N×N?
R×N 18 N–Q4 B×P+!) 17 ... N–B4
(B–QB4!?) 18 Q–N1 N–K5 19 Q–Q3
N–B4 20 Q–Q1 N–K3 21 R–K1 B–
QB4 22 N×N/B6 P×N 23 P–N4
B–N3 24 Q–R4 Q–K1! 25 QR–Q1
P–B3 26 R–Q2 Q–R4 27 Q–Q1 P–

QB4 28 N–Q4 (28 P×P!? B–R4 29
N–Q4! B×B 30 R/K1×B B×R? 31
N×N R–K1 32 N–B4±) 28 ... B×B
29 Q×B Q×Q 30 N×Q N–N4 31 K–
N2 N–K5 32 R/Q2–Q1 P×P 33 P×P
R–B7 34 B–Q4 B×B 35 R×B R–N7
36 P–R4 R–QB1 (36 ... K–B2!? 37 ...
P–KR4 38 ... P–KN4) 37 R×P R/1–B7
38 K–B3 N–Q7+ 39 K–N2 N–K5 40
K–B3 N–Q7+ 41 K–N2 N–B5 ½–½

12) Botvinnik-Petrosian, Queen's
Gambit Declined 1 P–Q4 P–Q4 2 P–
QB4 P–K3 3 N–QB3 B–K2 4 P×P
P×P 5 B–B4 P–QB3 6 P–K3 B–KB4
7 P–KN4 B–K3 8 B–Q3 N–Q2 9 P–
KR3 P–KR4+! 10 P×P (10 Q–B3!?
P×P 11 P×P B×P) 10 ... QN–B3
11 P–R6 N×P 12 Q–B2 N–R4?!
(12 ... Q–Q2!? 13 ... B–KB4) 13 B–
K5 P–B3 14 B–R2 B–Q3 15 B–N6+
(15 0–0–0!?) 15 ... B–B2 16 N–B3
QB×B 17 Q×B+ N–B2 18 N–KR4
B×B 19 R×B Q–B2 20 N–B3 0–0–0
21 Q–N4+ K–N1 22 P–KR4 N–Q3
23 0–0–0 P–KB4 (23 ... QR–K1!?
24 N–Q2 N–K5∓) 24 Q–N1 P–B5
25 N–K5 N–B2 26 N–N6 (26 N–Q3!?)
26 ... KR–K1 27 R–R3 P×P 28 P×P
N–B3 29 R–B1 P–R3 30 P–R5 N–K5
31 N×N R×N 32 K–N1 N–Q3 33 N–
K5 R–K1 34 R–N3 R–K2 35 R–B8+
K–R2 36 R–B1 N–B5 37 N×N P×N
38 R–B5 Q–Q2 39 R/5–B3 P–B4 (*195*)

195
W

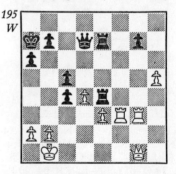

40 R–B1 (P×P? Q–Q6+ 41 K–R1

P–B6∓)   40 . . . P×P   41 P×P Q×P
42 R–Q1 Q×Q   43 R/Q1×Q R/2–K4
44 R–N5 R–K8+   45 K–B2 R/8–K7+
46 K–N1 K–N3   47 R×R R×R   48
R×P R×P   49 K–B2 R–R6   50 P–N3
R–R7+   51 K–B3 R×P   52 K×P
R–B7+   53 K–N4 ½–½

13) Petrosian – Botvinnik, Queen's
Indian 1 P–Q4 N–KB3 2 P–QB4 P–K3
3 N–KB3 P–QN3   4 P–KN3 B–N2
5 B–N2 B–K2 6 0–0 0–0 7 N–B3 N–K5
8 N×N B×N 9 P–Q5 B–B3 10 N–K1
B×B 11 N×B P×P 12 P×P P–B4 13
P×Pep (13 N–K3!?)   13 . . . P×P   14
Q–B2 P–B4 15 R–Q1 Q–K1 16 B–B4
N–B3 17 B–Q6 B–K2 18 P–K3 R–Q1
19 B×B Q×B   20 N–B4 P–N3 (*196*)

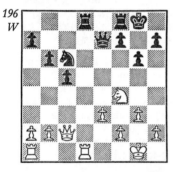

196
W

21 Q–R4 (21 N–Q5?! R×N   22 R×R
N–N5∓) 21 . . . N–K4 22 R×R R R×R
23 R–Q1 P–B5!?   24 P–K4 P–QN4!
25 R×R+ Q×R   26 Q×NP (26 Q–
B2?! N–B6+   27 K–R1 Q–Q5!∓)
26 . . . Q–Q8+   27 K–N2 Q–B6+   28
K–N1 Q–Q8+   29 K–N2 Q–B6+   30
K–N1 Q×KP 31 Q–Q5 Q×Q (31 . . .
Q–N8+   32 K–N2 Q×NP 33 Q–R8+
K–N2 34 Q×P give Black some winning
chances)   32 N×Q N–Q6 33 P–QN4
P×Pep 34 P×P P–B4 35 P–QN4 K–B2
36 P–N5 N–K4 37 P–N6 P–QR4 38
K–B1 K–K3 39 P–N7 N–B3 40 N–B7+
(40 N–N6!? K–Q3   41 P–N8=Q+
draws)   40 . . . K–Q3   41 N–R6 P–R5

42 K–K2 P–R6   43 N–N4! N–N1   44
K–Q3 K–B2   45 K–B2 K×P   46 K–N3
K–N3   47 K×P K–B4   48 K–N3 K–Q5
49 K–B2 K–K5   50 K–Q2 K–B6   51 K–
K1 K–N7   52 P–R4 K–B6   53 N–Q3
N–Q2   54 K–B1 ½–½

14) Botvinnik – Petrosian, Queen's
Gambit Declined 1 P–Q4 P–Q4 2 P–
QB4 P–K3   3 N–QB3 B–K2   4 P×P
P×P 5 B–B4 P–QB3 6 P–K3 B–KB4
7 P–KN4 B–K3 8 P–KR3 N–B3 (8 . . .
P–KR4!?   9 P×P N–Q2 10 B–K2 QN–
B3∓) 9 B–Q3 P–B4 10 N–B3 N–B3
11 K–B1 0–0   12 K–N2 P×P (12 . . .
R–K1!?) 13 N×P N×N   14 P×N N–
Q2? (14 . . . R–K1! or 14 . . . R–B1!?)
Q–B2 N–B3! 16 P–B3 R–B1 17 B–K5
B–Q3 18 QR–K1 B×B   19 R×B! P–
KN3   20 Q–B2 N–Q2 (20 . . . Q–
Q3!?)   21 R–K2 N–N3 (*197*)

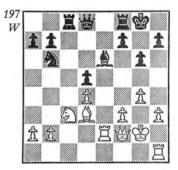

197
W

22 KR–K1 (22 P–KR4 Q–B3 23 P–R5
N–B5!)   22 . . . N–B5   23 B×N R×B
(23 . . . P×B?   24 P–Q5!)   24 R–Q2
R–K1 25 R–K3 P–QR3 26 P–N3 (26
R/2–K2 Q–N3   27 P–B4 R–Q1   28
P–B5 B–Q2 29 P×P Q×KNP 30 R–
K5±)   26 . . . R–B3   27 N–R4 P–N3
28 N–N2 P–QR4 29 N–Q3 P–B3   30
P–KR4 B–B2   31 R×R+ B×R   32
Q–K3 B–B2 33 P–N5 B–K3 34 N–B4
B–B2 35 N–Q3 B–K3 36 P×P! Q×P
37 Q–N5 Q×Q (37 . . . K–N2 38 N–
B4 K–B2 39 R–K2 Q×P? 40 Q–R6
Q–R1 41 N–Q3±)   38 P×Q P–R5

(38 . . . P–R3!?) 39 P×P R–B5 40 P–
R5! P×P 41 N–B5 B–B4 42 K–N3 P–
R5 (No better is 42 . . . P–R3 43 P×P
P–N4 44 R–K2 R×P 45 R–K5 R–KB5
46 N–K6! or 42 . . . K–N2 43 K–B4
P–R3 44 P×P+ K–B3 45 R–QN2!)
43 K–B4 P–R6 44 K–K5 R–N5 (44 . . .
R–B8!) 45 N–Q3 R–N4 46 K–Q6
K–B2 47 K–B6 B×N 48 R×B R–N7!
49 R×P R–N7 50 K×P R×P+ 51
K–B6 P–R4 52 P–Q5 R–N7 53 P–Q6
R–QB7+ 54 K–Q7 P–R5 55 P–B4
R–B7 56 K–B8 R×BP 57 R–R7+ 1–0

15) Petrosian-Botvinnik, Grünfeld
1 P–Q4 N–KB3 2 P–QB4 P–KN3 3 N–
QB3 P–Q4 4 Q–N3 P×P 5 Q×BP
B–N2 6 P–K4 0–0 7 B–K2 N–B3 8 N–
B3 N–Q2 9 B–K3 N–N3 10 Q–B5
(10 Q–Q3 P–B4!?) 10 . . . B–N5 11
P–Q5 (11 R–Q1!?) 11 . . . N–Q2 12
Q–R3 (12 Q–B4!?) 12 . . . QB×N 13
B×B N–Q5 14 0–0–0 N×B 15 P×N
N–N3 (15 . . . P–QB3 16 P×P P×P
17 B–Q4±) 16 Q–N3 Q–Q2 (16 . . .
Q–B1!? 17 P–KR4 P–QB3 18 P–Q6
P×P 19 R×P Q–B2 20 B–B4 B–R3!)
17 P–KR4! P–KR4 18 P–B4! P–K3 19
P×P Q×P 20 Q×Q P×Q 21 KR–N1
K–R2 22 N–N5 R–B2 23 N–Q4 R–K1
(23 . . . B×N!? 24 R×B R–K1! is
better) 24 N–B3 B–R3 25 N–N5+
B×N 26 R×B N–B5 (26 . . . N–B1!?)
(198)

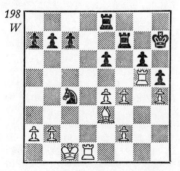

198
W

27 QR–N1? (27 P–B5!! KP×P 28

P×P R×P 29 R–Q7+ K–R1 30 B–
Q4+ N–K4 31 P–B4 wins) 27 . . . R–
KN1 28 K–B2! P–N3 (28 . . . N–Q3!?
29 P–B3 P–R3, then R–Q2 and N–B2)
29 P–N3 N–Q3 30 P–B3 R–Q2 31
R/5–N2 R/2–Q1 32 P–R4! N–B2 33
B–B1 P–K4 34 B–K3 P×P?! (34 . . .
QR–KB1) 35 B×BP R–Q2 36 R–Q2
R×R+ 37 K×R R–Q1+ 38 K–K2
P–B4 39 P–R5! R–Q2 (39 . . . P×P
40 R–QR1 R–Q2 41 R×P R–N2 42
R×BP R×P 43 R–B7±) 40 P×P P×P
41 R–QR1 K–N2 42 R–R6 (42 R–R8!)
42 . . . R–N2 43 R–R8 K–B3 (43 . . .
P–QN4 44 R–QB8 P–B5 45 P–N4±)
44 R–QB8 N–K4 45 K–K3 N–Q2 46
R–B6+ K–B2 47 P–K5 N–B1 48 R–
B6+ K–N2 49 K–K4 P–QN4 50 R–
B6 K–B2 51 R×BP N–K3 52 R–Q5
K–K2 53 B–K3 R–N1 54 R–Q6 P–N5
55 R–R6 R–N4 56 R–R7+ K–K1 57
P–B4 K–B1 58 P–B5 1–0

16) Botvinnik – Petrosian, Queen's
Gambit Accepted 1 P–Q4 P–Q4 2 P–
QB4 P×P 3 N–KB3 N–KB3 4 P–K3
P–K3 5 B×P P–B4 6 0–0 P–QR3
7 P–QR4 N–B3 8 Q–K2 P×P 9 R–
Q1 B–K2 10 P×P 0–0 11 N–B3 N–Q4
12 B–Q3! N/3–N5 13 B–N1 B–Q2
14 Q–K4 P–KN3 *(199)*

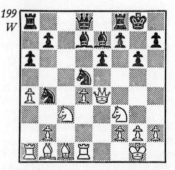

199
W

(14 . . . N–KB3 15 Q–R4 P–R3 16 B×
RP P×B 17 Q×P±) 15 N–K5! B–
KB3 16 Q–B3 B–N2 17 Q–N3 (17
N–K4!? R–B1 18 B–N5 P–B3 19 N×B

Q×N 20 B–R4 Tal) 17...B–K1 18
P–R4! N–QB3 19 N–B3 P–B3 20 N×N
P×N? (20...Q×N!? 21 B–R2 Q–Q2
22 P–Q5 N–N5!=) 21 P–KR5! N–K2
22 P×P B×NP 23 N–R4 B×B 24 R×B
Q–Q2 25 P–N3 R–B2 26 Q–KB3 P–
B4 27 Q–N3 N–B3 28 N–B3 R–K2!
29 B–B4 R–K5 30 N–K5 N×N (Better
30...Q–K3 31 N×N Q×N 32 P–B3
R–K7 33 QR–B1 Q–KN3 34 Q×Q P×
Q 35 R–B7 P–N4!) 31 P×N R–K1 32
P–B3 R–K7 33 R–K1 R–R7 34 B–N5
(34 QR–B1!?) 34...P–Q5 35 B–B6 Q–
KB2 36 QR–Q1 Q–N3 37 Q×Q P×Q
38 B×B K×B 39 P–K6? (39 R×P!
R–QB1 40 R–Q7+±) 39...R–QB1!
40 K–R2 (40 P–K7 R/1–B7!=) 40...
R/1–B7 41 R–KN1 R–Q7 42 R/Q1–K1
K–B1 43 P–K7+ K–K1 44 K–N3 P–
Q6 45 R–K3! R/R7–N7 46 K–B4
R×KNP 47 R–Q1 R/QN7–Q7 48
R×R R×R 49 K–N5 R–Q8! (40...R–
N7+? 50 K–B6 P–Q7? 51 R–Q3±)
50 K–B6 (50 K×P? R–N8+ 51 K–B6
P–Q7 52 R–B3 R–N3+ wins) 50...
P–B5 51 R–K4 R–QB8 52 R–Q4 R–
B3+ 53 K–N5 R–B6 54 K–B6 ½–½

17) Petrosian - Botvinnik, Queen's
Indian 1 P–Q4 N–KB3 2 P–QB4 P–
K3 3 N–KB3 P–QN3 4 P–K3 B–N2
5 P–QR3 P–Q4 6 P–QN4 P×P 7 B×P
B–K2 8 QN–Q2 0–0 9 R–QN1!?
QN–Q2 10 0–0 R–N1 11 P–N5 P–B4
12 P×Pep B×BP 13 P–QR4 Q–B2 14
B–N2 Q–N2 15 R–B1 P–QR3 (N–
K5!?) 16 R–K1 (16 B×RP? B×N!∓)
16...P–QN4 17 P×P P×P 18 B–Q3
KR–B1 19 P–K4 N–N3 20 Q–K2±
(20 P–Q5?! P×P 21 P–K5 N–K5=)
20...N–R5 21 B–R1 B–K1 22 R×R
R×R (200)
23 P–Q5!? N–R4? (23...N–B6!? 24
B×N R×B 25 P–Q6 B–Q1 26 P–K5
N–Q4) 24 P–N3 N–B4 (24...N–B6?!
25 B×N R×B 26 N–Q4±) 25 N–Q4
N×B 26 Q×N/Q3 Q–N3? (26...R–
Q1 27 Q–KB3 N–B3 28 P×P P×P 29

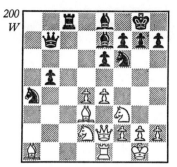

P–K5±) 27 P×P? (27 P–K5! and 28
P–K6!±) 27...P×P 28 P–K5 B–
N5 29 R–N1? (29 R–Q1!?) 29...
B–N3 30 N–K4 Q–N2 (30...R–B5!?)
31 P–B3 B×N 32 Q×B (32 P×B R–
B5!?) 32...Q×Q 33 P×Q B–B4
34 R×P P–N4 35 K–B1 B×N 36 B×B
R–B8+ 37 K–N2 P–N5! 38 B–K3
R–B7+ 39 K–N1 R–B5 ½–½

18) Botvinnik - Petrosian, Queen's
Gambit Declined 1 P–Q4 P–Q4 2 P–
QB4 P–K3 3 N–QB3 B–K2 4 P×P
P×P 5 B–B4 P–QB3 6 P–K3 B–KB4
7 P–KN4 B–K3 8 P–KR3 N–B3 9 N–
B3 QN–Q2 10 B–Q3 N–N3 11 Q–B2
N–B5 12 K–B1 (Sharper 12 B×N!?
P×B 13 P–K4) 12...N–Q3 13 N–Q2
(13 N–KN5 B–Q2 14 P–K4!) 13...
Q–B1 14 K–N2 N–Q2 15 P–B3 P–
KN3 16 QR–QB1 N–N3 17 P–N3
Q–Q2 18 N–K2 (18 P–K4!) 18...
N/Q3–B1 19 P–QR4 P–QR4 20 B–
N3 B–Q3 21 N–KB4 N–K2 22 N–B1
P–R4! 23 B–K2 P–R5 24 B–R2
(B–K1!?) (201)
24...P–N4 25 N–Q3 (25 N–R5!?
R×N? 26 P×R B×P+ is insufficient)
25...Q–B2 26 Q–Q2 N–Q2 27 B–N1
N–KN3 (27...P–KB4!) 28 B–R2 N–
K2 29 B–Q1 P–N3 30 K–N1 P–B3 31
P–K4 B×B+ 32 Q×B (32 R×B!)
32...Q×Q+ 33 R×Q R–Q1 34 K–
B2?! (34 R–Q2!?) 34...K–B2 35 K–
K3 KR–K1 36 R–Q2 K–N2 37 K–B2

P×P 38 P×P N–KB1 39 N–K1 N/1–
N3 40 N–N2 R–Q2 41 B–B2 (41 N–
R2!? R/K1–Q1 42 N–B3 N–K4 43 N/
2–K1!) 41 ... B–B2 42 N/1–K3?? (42
R/B1–Q1 R/K1–Q1 43 N/1–K3 P–
QB4 44 P–Q5 N–K4 45 N–B4 N×N

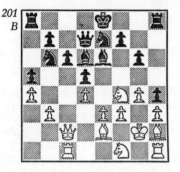

201
B

46 P×N and 47 P–K5) 42 ... P–QB4
43 P–Q5 N–K4 44 R–B1? (44 N–B4!?)
44 ... B–N3 45 K–K1 (45 K–N1!?)
45 ... N–B1 46 R/2–B2 R–KB2 47
K–Q2 N–Q3 48 N–B5+ B×N 49
KP×B P–B5! 50 R–QN1 P–N4 51 P–
N4 (51 NP×P N/4×P+∓) 51 ... P–
B6+! 52 K×P (52 K–Q1 N/4–B5 53
NP×P N–N7+   54 K–B1 P–N5∓)
52 ... R–B2+ 53 K–Q2 N/4–B5 54
K–Q1 N–R6 55 R–N2 N/3–B5 56 R–
R2 RP×P 57 P×P N×P 58 R–R6 N–
B6+ 59 K–B1 N×P 60 B–R4 R/K1–
QB1 61 N–K1 N–B5 0–1

19) Petrosian – Botvinnik, Queen's
Indian 1 P–QB4 N–KB3 2 N–QB3
P–K3 3 N–B3 P–QN3 4 P–KN3 B–N2
5 B–N2 B–K2 6 0–0 0–0 7 P–Q4 N–
K5 8 Q–B2 N×N 9 Q×N P–KB4
10 P–N3 B–KB3 11 B–N2 P–Q3 12
QR–Q1 N–Q2 13 N–K1 B×B 14 N×B
B–N4 (14 ... Q–K2!?) 15 Q–B2 B–R3
16 P–K4 P–B5 17 N–K1 Q–K2? (17 ...
Q–N4!?) 18 P–K5! P×P 19 P×P QR–
Q1 (19 ... R–B2 then N–B1–N3 Tal)
20 Q–K2 Q–N4 (20 ... N–B4!?) 21
K–N2 P–R4 22 N–B3 Q–R4 (22 ...

Q–B4 and P–KN4) 23 B–R3 KR–K1
(23 ... R–B2 24 Q–K4 P–KN4!?) 24
R–Q4 N–N1 25 KR–Q1 R×R 26
R×R P×P 27 RP×P Q–B2 28 Q–K4
P–N3 29 Q–N7 (29 Q–R4! K–N2 30
P–KN4 P–B4 31 R–Q6 R–KB1 32 Q–
B6!±) 29 ... B–N2 30 P–B5! P×P
(30 ... B–B1 31 P×P! P×P 32 Q×Q+
K×Q 33 B×B K×B 34 R–Q6±) 31
B×P N–Q2 32 Q×P N×P 33 Q×Q+
N×Q 34 R–QR4 B–B6 (202)

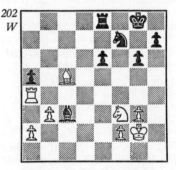

202
W

35 R–QB4? (35 B–Q4!±) 35 ... B–B3
36 B–N6 R–R1 37 R–QR4 B–B6 38
B–Q4 B–N5 39 P–R3 B–Q3? (39 ...
B–K2!? 40 P–QN4 B–Q1 41 B–B3 R–
QB1 gives better resistance) 40 P–QN4
B–B2 41 B–B3 K–B1 42 P–N5 (42 P×
P!?) 42 ... K–K1 43 R–QB4 K–Q2
44 P–R4 R–QB1 45 N–Q2 N–Q3 46
R–Q4 K–K2 47 R–Q3 N–N2 48 N–
K4 P–K4 49 B–N2 B–N3 50 B–R3+
K–K3 51 N–N5+ K–B4 52 N×P
P–K5 53 P–N4+? (53 R–Q7!) 53 ...
K–B5! 54 R–Q7 R–B2 55 R×R B×R
56 N–B6 B–Q1 57 N–Q7 K×P 58 P–
N6 B–N4? (58 ... K–B4!? 59 N–B5
B×P 60 N×N P–K6! 61 P×P B×P
62 N×P K–K3) 59 N–B5 N×N 60
B×N B–B5 61 P–N7 B–N1 62 B–K3
P–N4 (62 ... K–B4 63 K–R3 P–N4
64 B–Q2 K–K3 65 K–N4 K–Q2 66
B×NP K–B2 67 B–B4+±) 63 B–Q2
K–B4 64 K–R3 B–Q3 64 P×RP P–
N5+ 66 K–N2 1–0

20) Botvinnik - Petrosian, Queen's Gambit Accepted 1 P–Q4 P–Q4 2 P–QB4 P×P 3 N–KB3 N–KB3 4 P–K3 P–B4 5 B×P P–K3 6 0–0 P–QR3 7 B–N3 N–B3 8 Q–K2 P×P 9 R–Q1 B–K2 10 P×P N–QR4! 11 B–B2 P–QN4 12 N–B3 B–N2 13 B–N5 0–0 (*203*)

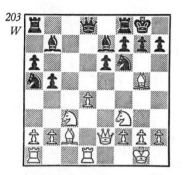

203
W

14 QR–B1 R–B1   15 B–N1 N–B5 16 N–K5 N–N3 17 Q–Q3 P–N3 18 B–R6 R–K1 19 Q–R3 N–B5 20 N×N (20 R–K1!? threatening 21 N×BP) 20 ... R×N 21 N–K2 Q–N3 ½–½

21) Petrosian-Botvinnik, English 1 P–QB4 N–KB3 2 N–KB3 P–KN3 3 N–B3 P–Q4 4 P×P N×P 5 P–K4 N×N 6 QP×N Q×Q+ 7 K×Q B–N5 8 B–K2 N–Q2 9 B–K3 P–K4 10 N–Q2 ½–½

22) Botvinnik - Petrosian, Queen's Gambit Accepted 1 P–Q4 P–Q4 2 P–QB4 P×P 3 N–KB3 N–KB3 4 Q–R4+ N–B3 5 N–B3 N–Q4 6 P–K4 N–N3 7 Q–Q1 B–N5 8 P–Q5 N–K4 9 B–KB4 N–N3 10 B–K3 P–K3 ½–½

9 Petrosian–Spassky

Moscow April 10 1966–June 9 1966

	1	2	3	4	5	6	7	8	9	10	11	12
Petrosian	½	½	½	½	½	½	1	½	½	1	½	½
Spassky	½	½	½	½	½	½	0	½	½	0	½	½

	13	14	15	16	17	18	19	20	21	22	23	24	**Total**
Petrosian	0	½	½	½	½	½	0	1	½	1	0	½	**12½**
Spassky	1	½	½	½	½	½	1	0	½	0	1	½	**11½**

1) Spassky-Petrosian, Caro-Kann 1 P–K4 P–QB3 2 P–Q4 P–Q4 3 N–QB3 P×P 4 N×P B–B4 5 N–N3 B–N3 6 P–KR4 P–KR3 7 N–B3 N–Q2 8 B–Q3 B×B 9 Q×B Q–B2 10 B–Q2 P–K3 11 0–0–0 0–0–0 12 P–B4 KN–B3 13 K–N1 P–B4 14 B–B3 P×P 15 N×P P–R3 (*204*)

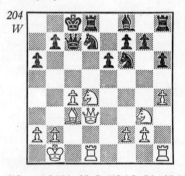

204
W

(15 . . . N–K4 15 Q–K2 N×P? 17 N–N5±) 16 N–B3! B–B4 17 Q–K2 B–Q3 18 N–K4 B–K2! (18 . . . N×N 19 Q×N N–B3 20 Q–K2 Q–B3 21 QR–K1 B–B2 21 N–Q4±) 19 N×N B×N 20 B×B N×B 21 N–K5 R×R+ 22 R×R R–Q1 23 R×R+ (23 R–QB1 R–Q5 24 P–B3 R×RP 25 P–B5!; 24 P–B3 N–K5!) 23 . . . K×R 24 Q–Q3+ K–K2 25 Q–Q4 P–KR4! 26 P–

R3 (26 Q–B4 K–B1 27 P–B3!?) 26 . . . N–Q2! 27 N×N Q×N 28 Q–B5+ (28 Q×P?! Q–Q6+; 28 Q×Q+ K×Q 29 K–B2 K–Q3 30 K–Q3 P–QN3! 31 P–QN4 P–B3=) 28 . . . Q–Q3 29 Q–N5+ (29 Q–K3!?) 29 . . . K–K1 30 Q–K3 Q–B3 (30 . . . Q–Q8+ 31 K–R2 Q–N5! 32 Q–B5! Q×NP 33 Q–QB8+ K–K2 34 Q–B7+ K–B3 35 Q–B4+ K–N3 36 P–B3!=) 31 Q–KN3! P–KN3 32 P–N3 Q–K5+ 33 K–N2 P–K4 34 Q–K3! Q×NP 35 Q×P+ K–B1 (35 . . . K–Q2? 36 Q–B6) 36 Q–R8+ K–K2 37 Q–K5+ ½–½

2) Petrosian-Spassky, Queen's Gambit Declined 1 P–QB4 P–K3 2 N–QB3 P–Q4 3 P–Q4 B–K2 4 N–B3 N–KB3 5 B–N5 0–0 6 P–K3 P–KR3 7 B–R4 P–QN3 8 P×P N×P 9 B×B Q×B 10 N×N P×N 11 R–B1 B–K3 12 Q–R4 P–QB4 13 Q–R3 R–B1 14 B–K2 P–QR4 (14 . . . Q–B1 15 P×P P×P 16 0–0 N–Q2 17 N–Q2 QR–N1 18 P–K4 P–Q5=) 15 0–0 N–R3?! (15 . . . K–B1!?) 16 P×P (16 B–N5 N–N5 17 N–K5 P–B5 18 Q–R4±) 16 . . . P×P 17 N–Q4! B–Q2 (17 . . . N–N5 18 N×B and 19 Q–R4±) 18 B×N R×B 19 N–K2 P–R5? (*205*)
(19 . . . B–N4! 20 KR–K1 B×N 21

160

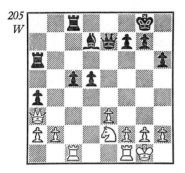

205
W

R×B P-Q5 22 QR-K1 Q-Q3±) 20
KR-Q1 Q-Q3 21 R-Q2! (21 N-B3
P-Q5 22 N-K4 Q-KN3!) 21...B-K3
22 P-R3 R-B2 23 N-B4 P-B5 24
Q×Q R×Q 25 N-K2 P-R6!? (25...
R-N3! 26 N-B3 R-R2 27 R/B1-B2
R-R4!) 26 P×P B-B4 (26...R-R2
27 N-B3!) 27 N-B3 R/B2-Q2 28 R-
Q4 K-B1 29 P-B3 K-K2 30 R/B1-Q1
B-K3 31 R-N1 (31 K-B2!±) 31...
R-R3 32 P-QR4 K-Q3! 33 K-B2
(33 P-K4?! K-B4! 34 QR-Q1 K-N5!)
33...K-B4 34 R-Q2 R-R4 35 K-
K2?! (35 R-N5+ R×R 36 P×R K-N5!
35 P-N4!) 35...B-B4! 36 P-K4
(36 R-N8 B-Q6+ 37 K-B2 P-Q5!∓)
36...P×P 37 P×P R×R+ 38 K×R
B-Q2 39 R-N7 K-B3 40 R-N8 K-B4
41 R-KB8 B-K3 42 R-QN8 B-Q2
43 R-N7 K-B3 44 R-N2 K-B4 45
K-K3 R-R2! (45...B×QRP? 46 R-
N7 B-K1 47 R-B7++±) 46 R-Q2 B-
B3! (46...B×QRP? 47 R-Q5+ K-
N5 48 K-Q4±) 47 P-N4 R-N2 48
R-KB2! R-Q2! 49 R-Q2 (49 R-B5+
K-N5 50 N-Q5+ B×N 51 P×B P-
N3 52 R-K5 P-B3 53 R-K6 R×P=)
49...R-N2 50 P-R4 P-B3! ½-½

3) Spassky-Petrosian, Caro-Kann 1 P-
K4 P-QB3 2 P-Q4 P-Q4 3 P×P P×P
4 P-QB4 N-KB3 5 N-QB3 P-K3
6 N-B3 B-K2 7 P×P N×P 8 B-QB4
N-KB3 9 0-0 0-0 10 Q-K2 N-B3
11 B-K3 N-QR4 12 B-Q3 P-QN3

13 B-KN5 B-N2 14 QR-Q1 R-B1
15 KR-K1 P-KR3 16 B-B1 (16 B-R4!?
N-Q4 17 Q-K4 N-KB3 18 Q-B4)
16...B-N5! 17 B-Q2 KB×N! (17...
QB×N? 18 Q×B Q×P 19 N-QN5!)
18 P×B Q-Q4!= 19 Q-B1! (19 B-
N1!?) 19...Q×RP 20 N-K5 N-N6
21 R-K2 (21 B-QB4? N×B 21 B×P?!
P×B 22 R-K3) 21...N×B (21...
Q-R6! 22 B-K1 N-B8!) 22 R/K2×N
Q-Q4 23 P-QB4 Q-Q3 24 Q-K2
KR-Q1 25 P-R3 N-Q2 26 N-N4
P-KR4 (26...Q-B5!) 27 N-K3 (27
N-K5!? P-KN3; 27...N×N? 28 P×
N Q-B3 29 B-R7+!) 27...P-KN3 28
R-R2 R-R1 29 Q-B2 K-N2 30 B-K4
(30 P-B5!? P×P 31 P×P N×P? 32
B×P; 31...Q×P? 32 Q-N2+; 30
P-B5 Q-B2!) 30...B×B 31 Q×B
N-B3 32 Q-R4 R-Q2 (32...Q-B3!)
33 R/R2-Q2 QR-Q1 34 R-Q3 P-R3
35 Q-N5 N-K5 36 Q-R4 N-B3 (36...
P-B4! 37 P-Q5 P-K4; 36...P-B4
37 P-B3 Q-N6!∓) 37 R-N3 Q-B2
(37...R-QB1!?) 38 P-Q5 (*206*)

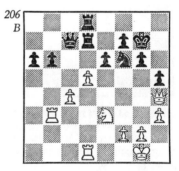

206
B

Q-K4 (38...P×P? 39 N-B5 P×N
40 Q-N5+ K-B1 41 Q×N; 38...
P-QN4! 39 BP×P N×P 40 R-KB1 –
40 N×N R×N 41 R×R R×R threat R-
Q8+ – 40...P×P 41 R×P N-B6 42
R-N2 R-Q5∓; 38...P-QN4! 39 R-
QB1?! NP×P 40 R×P Q-K4! 41
P×P? R-Q8+) 39 R×P P×P 40 N×P
N×N 41 P×N R×P 42 Q×R! R×Q

43 R×R Q–K8+ (sealed) (44 K–R2
Q×P 45 R×P Q–B5+ 46 K–N1=) ½–½

4) Petrosian-Spassky, Catalan 1 P–
QB4 P–K3 2 P–KN3 P–Q4 3 B–N2
N–KB3 4 N–KB3 B–K2 5 0–0 0–0
6 P–Q4 P–B3 7 P–N3 P–QN3 8 B–
N2 B–N2 9 N–B3 QN–Q2 10 Q–
B2 R–B1 11 QR–Q1 P–QN4 12 P–B5
P–N5 13 N–QR4 B–R3 (13 . . . P–
QR4!?) 14 N–K1! B–N4 15 N–Q3
P–QR4 16 P–QR3 P×P 17 QB×P
R–N1 18 R–N1 R–K1 19 N–B3 B–R3
20 KR–Q1 B–KB1 21 P–K4! P×P 22
N×P B×N! 23 Q×B N–Q4! 24 KR–
QB1 N/Q2–B3 25 N–Q6 B×N 26
P×B Q–Q2 27 Q–R6± KR–QB1
28 Q×RP N–K1! 29 Q–B5 R–N4 30
Q–B4 R/N4–N1 (30 . . . N×P? 31
QB×N Q×B 32 Q×R!±) 31 Q–B5
R–N4 32 Q–B4 P–R3 (207)

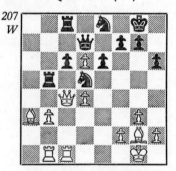

207
W

(32 . . . R–R4 33 B–N4 N×P 34 QB×N
Q×B 35 P–QN4±) 33 R–B2 R/N4–
N1 34 R/N1–QB1 N×P 35 QB×N
Q×B 36 B×N KP×B 37 Q–R4 R–N3
38 R–B5 Q–K3 39 P–QN4 R/B1–N1
40 R×BP R×R   41 Q×R (sealed)
41 . . . Q×Q 42 R×Q R×P 43 K–B1
R×P 44 K–K2 ½–½

5) Spassky-Petrosian, Caro-Kann 1 P–
K4 P–QB3 2 P–Q4 P–Q4 3 P×P P×P
4 P–QB4 N–KB3 5 N–QB3 P–KN3
6 Q–N3 B–N2 7 P×P 0–0 8 P–N3
N–R3 (8 . . . QN–Q2!? 9 B–N2 N–
N3; 8 . . . P–K3 9 B–N2 N×P 10 KN–

K2 N–QB3 11 0–0 N–N3 12 R–Q1±)
9 B–N2 Q–N3 10 Q×Q P×Q 11 KN–
K2 N–QN5 12 0–0 R–Q1 13 P–Q6!
(13 B–N5 QN×QP 14 N×N N×N
15 KR–K1 P–R3 16 B–Q2 B–K3∓)
13 . . . R×QP (13 . . . P×P 14 B–N5±)
14 B–B4 R–Q2 15 KR–Q1 QN–Q4
(15 . . . KN–Q4 16 P–QR3 N×B 17
N×N N–B7 18 QR–B1 N×QP 19
KN–Q5±) 16 B–K5± B–R3? (16 . . .
R–Q1!?) 17 P–QR3 P–K3 (17 . . . R–Q1
18 N×N N×N 19 N–B3 N×N 20
P×N) 18 N×N N×N 19 R–Q3
B–N4 (208)

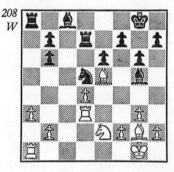

208
W

(19 . . . P–B3? 20 B×N) 20 B×N!
P×B (20 . . . R×B 21 N–B3 R/Q4–R4
22 B–B7 R/R4–R3 23 P–Q5±) 21 P–
KR4 B–Q1 22 R–QB1 R–K2 23 N–B4
B–K3 24 R/Q3–QB3! B–Q2 (24 . . .
R–K1 25 N×B P×N 26 R–B7!±)
25 N×QP R–K3 26 B–B7 K–N2 27
B×B R×B 28 N–K3 P–QN4 29 P–
Q5 R–N3 30 N–B2 (30 R–N3 and 31
R–N4!?) 30 . . . P–R3 31 N–N4 P–N4
32 P×P P×P 33 K–N2 R–KB3 34 R–
K3 (34 R–B7 B–N5! 35 R/B1–B3 R–
K1) 34 . . . R–KR1 35 N–Q3 (35 R–B7?
B–R6+ 36 K–N1 B–N5 37 N–Q3 R3–
KR3 38 R×P K–N1!∓) 35 . . . R–Q3
(35 . . . B–R6+? 36 K–N1 B–N5 37 P–
B4!∓) 36 N–K5 B–R6+ 37 K–B3
R×P 38 R–B7 B–K3 39 R×NP R–B4
(39 . . . K–B3!) 40 R–R7 (40 P–QN4
B–Q4+ 41 K–N4) 40 . . . B–Q4+ (40
. . . R–R7!) 41 K–N4 R–B7 (sealed) 42

K×P R×BP 43 N–Q3 R–B6 44 R/7–
K7 R×R 45 R×R P–B3+ 46 K–B4
K–B2 47 N–N4 B–B5 48 R–QB3
R–R7 49 P–N3 B–K3 50 N–Q3 (50
N–B6 B–Q4 51 N–Q4 R–B7+! 52
K–K3 R–N7 53 N×P B×P!; 50 . . .
R–R7 51 N–Q4 B–Q2 52 P–QN4±)
50 . . . R–R7 51 R–B7+ K–N3 52 N–
B5 B–B2 53 R–N7 (53 R–R7 P–N5!
54 P–R4 R–R6) 53 . . . R×P 54 R×P
R–R8! 55 N–K4 R–KB8+ 56 K–K3
R–K8+ 57 K–B3 R–KB8+ 58 K–K2
R–QN8 59 N–Q2 R–N8 60 K–B2
R–QB8 61 P–QN4 R–B7 62 K–K3
R–B6+ 63 K–B4 R–Q6 64 N–B3 (64
N–K4 B–Q4!=) 64 . . . B–Q4 65 N–
R4+ K–B2 66 R–N8 R–Q5+ 67 K–
K3 R–K5+ 68 K–B2 K–K2 69 N–N6+
K–Q2 70 N–B4 B–B3 71 N–Q3 K–
B2 72 R–KB8 B–N4 73 N–B4 K–Q2
74 R–B7+ K–K1 75 R–QN7 R×P 76
N–Q5 R–N7+ 77 K–K3 R–N6+ 78
K–B4 B–B5 79 N×P+ K–B1 ½–½

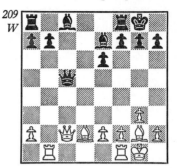
209
W

6) **Petrosian–Spassky,** Queen's Gambit
Declined 1 P–QB4 P–K3 2 P–Q4 N–
KB3 3 N–KB3 P–Q4 4 N–B3 P–B4
5 BP×P N×P 6 P–KN3 N–QB3
(6 . . . P×P 7 N×N Q×N 8 Q×P Q–
QN4! (8 . . . Q×Q 9 N×Q B–N5+ 10
B–Q2 B×B+ 11 K×B±) 9 P–K3 B–
N5+=) 7 B–N2 N×N (7 . . . P×P
8 N×P KN×N 9 P×N N×N 10
Q×N B–K2=) 8 P×N P×P 9 P×P
B–N5+ 10 B–Q2 B–K2 (10 . . . B×B+
11 Q×B±) 11 0–0 0–0 (11 . . . N×P?
12 Q–R4+ N–B3 13 N–K5± B–Q2 14
B×N P×B 15 Q–R5 or 13 . . . Q×B
14 N×N B–Q2 15 QR–Q1 and 16
R×B) 12 R–N1 (12 B–B3!; 12 P–K3!)
12 . . . N×P 13 N×N Q×N 14 Q–B2
Q–B4 (*209*)
15 Q×Q (15 Q–R4 B–Q2 16 Q×B
QR–Q1=; 15 Q–K4 Q–R6 16 Q–B2
Q–B4=) 15 . . . B×Q ½–½

7) **Spassky–Petrosian,** Queen's Pawn
1 P–Q4 N–KB3 2 N–KB3 P–K3 3 B–
N5 P–Q4 4 QN–Q2 B–K2 5 P–K3

QN–Q2 6 B–Q3 P–B4 7 P–B3 P–
QN3 8 0–0 B–N2 9 N–K5 (9 P–QR4!?)
9 . . . N×N 10 P×N N–Q2 11 B–KB4
(11 B×B Q×B 12 P–KB4 0–0 13
P–K4=) 11 . . . Q–B2 (11 . . . P–KN4?!
12 B–N3 P–KR4 13 P–KR3) 12 N–B3
(12 Q–N4? P–KN4 13 B×NP R–KN1
14 P–KR4 P–KR3) 12 . . . P–KR3!
13 P–QN4 P–KN4! 14 B–N3 P–KR4
(14 . . . P×P? 15 P×P B×P 16 N–Q4)
15 P–KR4 NP×P! (15 . . . P–N5 16
N–K1 N×P 17 B–N5+ K–B1 18 P×P
P×P 19 Q–R4±) 16 B–KB4 (16 N×P?
P×B5 17 B–B2 B×N 18 B×B Q×P∓)
16 . . . 0–0–0 17 P–R4? (17 P×P P×P
18 R–N1 unclear) 17 . . . P–B5! 18 B–
K2 (18 B–B5!? if 18 . . . P×B 19 P–K6
B–Q3 20 P×N+ R×P 21 Q–Q4) 18 . . .
P–R3! 19 K–R1 QR–N1 20 R–KN1
R–N5 21 Q–Q2 (21 N–R2!? R–N3
22 N–B3 KR–N1 23 Q–Q2) 21 . . .
KR–N1 22 P–R5 P–N4 23 QR–Q1
B–B1! (threatening 24 . . . P–B3 25
P×P P–K4) 24 N–R2 N×P! 25 N×R
P×N 26 P–K4 B–Q3 (26 . . . P×P??
27 B×N±) 27 Q–K3 N–Q2 (27 . . .
P–N6!? 28 P–B3!) 28 B×B Q×B 29
R–Q4? (29 P–B4! P–B4 30 P–K5 Q–
B2) 29 . . . P–K4! 30 R–Q2 (30 R×
QP!? B×R 31 R–Q1 N–B3 32 P×B∓)
30 . . . P–B4! 31 P×QP (31 P×BP P–
R6!∓; 31 P×BP N–B3! 32 P–B3 N–
R4! 33 P×P N–N6+ 34 K–R2 P–Q5!∓)
31 . . . P–B5 32 Q–K4 (32 Q–R7 P–
K5∓) 32 . . . N–B3 33 Q–B5+ K–N1

34 P–B3 (34 Q–K6 Q×Q 35 P×Q
N–K5!) 34...B–B1 35 Q–N1 P–N6
36 R–K1 P–R6 37 B–B1 (37 P×P P–
N7+ 38 K–N1 Q–Q2!∓) 37...R–R1
38 P×P B×P 39 K–N1 (39 B×B Q–
Q2!) 39...B×B 40 K×B (40 R×B
Q–Q2 intending 41...Q–R6 or 41...
Q–QR2+) 40 ... P–K5! 41 Q–Q1
(*210*)

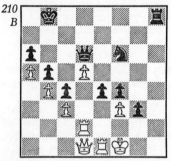

210
B

(41 P×P P–B6!) 41...N–N5 (sealed)
42 P×N P–B6 43 R–KN2 P×R+ (44
K×P Q–B5!) 0–1

8) Petrosian-Spassky, English 1 P–
QB4 P–QB4 2 N–KB3 N–QB3 4 N–
B3 N–B3 4 P–Q4 P×P 5 N×P P–K3
6 P–K3 (6 P–K4 B–N5=) 6...B–K2
(6...P–Q4 7 P×P P×P 8 B–K2
B–Q3=) 7 B–K2 0–0 8 0–0 P–Q3
9 P–QN3 P–QR3 10 B–N2 B–Q2 11
Q–Q2 Q–B2 12 QR–B1 QR–B1 13
KR–Q1 Q–N1 14 N–B3 KR–Q1=
15 B–Q3 (15 N–KN5 B–K1 16 QN–K4
N×N 17 N×N P–Q4 18 P×P R×P
19 Q–B3 N–Q5! 20 Q×R N×B+ 21
K–B1 R×R+ 22 K×N Q×Q 23 R×Q
R–Q1 24 R–B7 B–B1∓) 15...B–K1
16 Q–K2 (16 P–K4 P–Q4!=) 16...
P–Q4! 17 P×P N×P 18 N×N R×N
(*211*)
19 P–QR3 (19 Q–B2!? P–R3 20 B–R7+
K–R1 21 R×R P×R 22 B–B5±;
19 Q–B2!? P–KN3 20 Q–B3!; 19 Q–
B2 R–QB4 20 B×P+ K–R1 21 Q–
N1! R×R 22 R×R P–B4 23 B×BP;
19 Q–B2 R–KR4! 20 P–KR3 P–R3

threatening 21...R–QB4) 19...
R/B1–Q1 20 B–K4 R×R+ 21 R×R
R×R+ 22 Q×R Q–Q1 23 Q×Q
B×Q ½–½

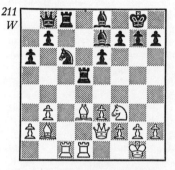

211
W

9) Spassky-Petrosian, Caro-Kann 1 P–
K4 P–QB3 2 P–Q4 P–Q4 3 P×P P×P
4 P–QB4 N–KB3 5 N–QB3 P–K3 6
N–B3 B–K2 7 P×P N×P 8 B–Q3 N–
QB3 9 0–0 0–0 10 R–K1 B–B3 11 B–
K4 N/B3–K2 12 Q–B2 (12 N–K5
B–Q2 13 Q–Q3 P–KN3 14 B–R6 B–
N2 15 B×B K×B 16 B×N!±) 12...
P–KN3 13 B–R6 B–N2 14 B–N5 (*212*)

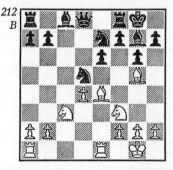

212
B

(14 Q–Q2!?) 14...P–B3! 15 B–Q2
B–Q2 16 Q–N3 (16 P–KR4 B–B3 17
P–R5 N–B4 18 P×P P×P 19 P–KN4
N/B4–K2=) 16...B–B3 17 B×N
(17 R–K2 Q–Q2=) 17...P×B 18
N–K4 R–B2 19 N–B5 N–B4 20 P–
KR3 B–B1 21 N–K6 Q–Q2 22 N×B
R/2×N 23 B–N4 KR–K1 24 R×R+
R×R 25 R–K1 R×R+ 26 B×R ½–½

10) Petrosian-Spassky, King's Indian
1 N–KB3 N–KB3 2 P–KN3 P–KN3
3 P–B4 B–N2 4 B–N2 0–0 5 0–0 N–B3
6 N–B3 P–Q3 7 P–Q4 P–QR3 8 P–Q5
N–QR4 9 N–Q2 P–B4 10 Q–B2 P–K4
11 P–N3 N–N5 12 P–K4 (12 B–N2
P–B4 13 QR–K1!?) 12 ... P–B4 13
P×P P×P 14 N–Q1!? (14 B–N2! B–Q2
15 QR–K1 P–N4 16 N–Q1±) 14 ...
P–N4 15 P–B3?! (15 B–N2 R–N1 16
P–B3 N–KB3 17 B–B3! B–R3 18 R–
K1) 15 ... P–K5! 16 B–N2 KP×P
17 B×P B×B 18 Q×B N–K4 19 B–K2
P–B5!? (19 ... R–R2!?) 20 NP×P
(213)

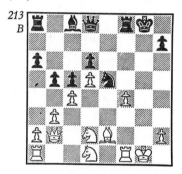

213
B

(20 R×P R×R 21 P×R N–N3 22 N–
K4 KN×P 23 N–B2 R–R2) 20 ...
B–R6? (20 ... R×P! 21 N–K3 Q–N4+
22 K–R1 R×R+ 23 N/Q2×R R–R2∓)
21 N–K3!! B×R (21 ... R×P? 22 R×R
Q–N4+ 23 R–N4 – 23 K–R1 Q×R 24
R–N1+∓ - 23 ... N×R 24 N×N
B×N 25 B×B Q×B+ 26 K–R1
Q–Q5 27 R–N1+ K–R1 28 Q×Q
P×Q 29 R–N4±) 22 R×B N–N3 23
B–N4 N×P? (23 ... R×P? 24 B–K6+
K–B1 25 R×R+; 23 ... Q–B3! 24
B–K6+ K–R1 25 Q×Q+ R×Q 26
P–B5 N–K4 27 N–K4!±) 24 R×N!
R×R 25 B–K6+ R–B2 26 N–K4
Q–R5 (26 ... R1–R2 27 N–KB5! Q–
KB1 28 Q–B6!+) 27 N×QP Q–N4+
28 K–R1 R–R2 (28 ... Q×N 29 B×R+
K–B1) 29 B×R+ R×B 30 Q–R8+!
1–0

M

11) Spassky-Petrosian, French 1 P–K4
P–K3 2 P–Q4 P–Q4 3 N–QB3 P×P
4 N×P N–Q2 5 N–KB3 KN–B3 6 N×
N+ N×N 7 B–KN5 B–K2 8 B–Q3
P–B4 9 P×P Q–R4+ 10 P–B3 Q×P
(B4) 11 Q–K2 B–Q2 (11 ... 0–0 12
0–0–0 R–Q1 (12 ... B–Q2? 13 B×N
B×B 14 B×P+) 13 N–K5 Q–B2 14
P–KB4 and if 14 ... P–KR3 15 P–
KR4±) 12 N–K5! B–B3 (12 ... N–
N5!? 13 N×P! K×N 14 B×B Q×
KBP+ 15 Q×Q N×Q 16 K×N
K×B±) 13 P–KR4! R–Q1 (13 ...
B×P?! 14 R–KN1 B–B3 15 0–0–0!±)
14 0–0–0 N–Q2 15 N×B!? (15 B×B!
Q×B 16 N×B P×N 17 B–K4±)
15 ... B×B+ 16 P×B Q×NP+ 17
K–B2 P×N 18 R–R5 (18 B–K4 Q–
QB4 19 R–R5 Q–N3 20 Q–B3±)
18 ... Q–B5 19 B–K4 (19 B–N6?!?
Q–R5+ 20 K–B1 P×B 21 Q×P K–B1
22 Q–Q6 K–B2 23 R–R3 KR–K1)
19 ... Q–B2! *(214)*

214
W

20 Q–B4 (20 Q–N4!? P–N3 21 B×NP
BP×B 22 Q×KP+ K–B1 23 R–R3;
20 Q–N4 N–B3 21 Q×NP K–K2
22 B–N6!; 20 Q–N4 K–K2!? 21 Q×NP
KR–N1) 20 ... P–QB4 21 Q–N5
(21 R×RP!?=) 21 ... P–N3 22 R–R4
(22 R×N?! R×R 23 R×BP Q–Q3∓)
22 ... 0–0 (22 ... K–K2 23 B–B6
N–K4 24 Q×P+=) 23 Q–B6!? Q×Q
24 B×Q N–K4 25 R×R R×R 26
B–N5 (26 ... R–N1 27 P–R4 P–KR4

28 R–K4 N–N5   **29** P–B3 N–B3   **30** R–QB4 N–Q4!) ½–½

12) Petrosian-Spassky, King's Fianchetto 1 N–KB3 P–KN3 2 P–B4 B–N2 3 P–Q4 P–Q3 4 N–B3 N–Q2 5 P–K4 P–K3 6 B–K2 P–N3 7 0–0 B–N2 8 B–K3 N–K2 9 Q–B2 P–KR3 10 QR–Q1 0–0 11 P–Q5! (Preventing 11 . . . P–KB4) 11 . . . P–K4 12 Q–B1 K–R2 13 P–KN3 P–KB4!? (13 . . . P–QR4!? 14 N–KR4 N–QB4 and 15 . . . B–B1) 14 P×P N×BP (14 . . . P×P 15 N–KR4! and 16 P–B4±) 15 B–Q3 B–B1 16 K–N2 N–B3 17 N–K4 N–R4!? (17 . . . N×N 18 B×N N N×B 19 P×N! B–N5! 20 Q–B2 Q–K1) 18 B–Q2 B–Q2 19 K–R1 (19 P–KN4 N–R5 20 N×N Q×N 21 P×N Q–R6+±) 19 . . . N–K2 20 N–R4! B–R6 (20 . . . P–B3 21 P–B3 P×P 22 P×P R–B1 23 Q–N1±) 21 R–N1 B–Q2 (21 . . . Q–Q2 22 P–KN4!) 22 B–K3 (22 P–B3!? and 23 QR–B1) 22 . . . Q–K1 (22 . . . N–B4 23 N×NP! K×N 24 P–KN4) 23 QR–K1 Q–B2 24 Q–B2 K–R1 25 N–Q2 N–B4 26 N×N! (26 N×P+? Q×N 27 P–KN4 N/R4–N6+ 28 P×N Q×P∓) 26 . . . P×N 27 P–KN4! P–K5!? (27 . . . P–B5?! 28 B–N6 Q–B3 29 B×NP – 29 P×N P×B 30 P×P P–K5! – 29 . . . RP×B 30 B–K4±) 28 P×N P–B5!? (28 . . . P×B 29 Q×P QR–K1!) 29 R×B!! Q×R 30 R–KN1 Q–K4 (30 . . . KP×B 31 Q×P Q×R+ 32 K× Q R–N1+ 33 K–R1 P×B 34 Q×P R–N4 35 N–K4! R–K1 36 P–KR4! R×RP 37 Q–Q4 R/1–K4 38 N–B6! wins; 30 . . . B–N5 31 R×B! Q×R 32 B–Q4 K–N1 33 B×KP R–B2 34 P–B3 Q–N4 35 B–N6 R–K2 36 N–K4) 31 N–B3!! (*215*) KP×B (31 . . . P×N 32 B–Q2! wins) 32 N×Q? (32 Q×P! B–B4 33 N×Q B×Q 34 B–Q4! P×N (34 . . . B–K5+ 35 P–B3!) 35 B×P+ K–R2 36 R–N7+ K–R1 37 R×P+ and 41 R×B should win) 32 . . . P×Q 33 B–Q4! P×N 34 B×P+ K–R2 35 R–N7+ K–R1 36 R–

215 B

B7+ K–N1 37 R–N7+ K–R1 38 R–N6+ (38 R×B+ K–N1 39 R–N7+ K–R1 40 R×P+ K–N1 41 R–N7+ K–R1 42 R–N1+ K–R2 43 R–QB1 QR–K1 44 B–Q4 R–K7 is satisfactory for Black) 38 . . . K–R2 39 R–N7+ ½–½

13) Spassky-Petrosian, Caro-Kann 1 P–K4 P–QB3 2 P–Q4 P–Q4 3 N–QB3 P×P 4 N×P B–B4 5 N–N3 B–N3 6 P–KR4 P–KR3 7 N–B3 N–Q2 8 P–R5 B–R2 9 B–Q3 B×B 10 Q×B Q–B2 11 B–Q2 P–K3 12 Q–K2! KN–B3 13 0–0–0 0–0–0 14 N–K5 N×N (15 . . . N–N3 16 B–R5 P–B4 17 Q–N5!±) 15 P×N N–Q2 16 P–KB4 B–K2 17 N–K4 N–B4 18 N–B3 P–B3! (18 . . . R–Q5 19 B–K3 R×R+ 20 R×R R–Q1 21 Q–N4!±; 18 . . . KR–K1 19 P–KN4! B–B1 20 P–N5±) 19 P×P B×P 20 Q–B4 (20 P–QN4? B×N 21 B×B Q×P 22 K–N1 – 22 B–Q2 Q–B3! or 22 . . . Q–K5! – 22 . . . N–K5 23 B×P KR–N1∓) 20 . . . Q–N3 21 P–QN4! (21 B–K3? N–N6+) 21 . . . N–R3 22 N–K4! (22 Q×P+? K–N1 23 P–R3 – 23 N–K4 KR–K1 24 Q–B5 Q–Q5 – 23 . . . R×B! 24 K×R Q–Q5+) 22 . . . N–B2 23 KR–K1 R–Q5 (23 . . . B–K2!? 24 B–B3 N–Q4 25 B×P B×P) 24 Q–N3 Q–N4 25 P–B3! R×N!? (25 . . . R/5–Q1 26 N–B5!±) 26 R×R Q×RP 27 Q–B4 Q–KB4 28 Q–K2 P–KR4 29 B–K1 R–K1 30 P–N3 P–R4 31 P×P Q×RP 32 Q–QB2 (32 P–B4 Q–R6+ 33 K–N1 and 34 R–Q3; 32 P–B4?!

B–B6 33 B×B (33 R–Q3 Q–R6+ and
34 ... Q–N5+) Q×B+ 34 K–N1
Q×NP 35 Q×P R–B1) 32 ... Q–KB4
33 R–R4 P–KN4?! (33 ... P–QN4!?)
34 P×P B×P+ 35 K–N1 Q×Q+ 36
K×Q P–K4 (36 ... P–N4!? 37 R–K4
N–Q4) 37 R–K4 N–Q4 38 B–B2 N–
B3 39 R–QR4 K–B2 40 B–B5 N–Q4
41 R–K4 (*216*)

216
B

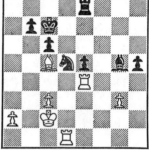

P–N3 (sealed) 42 B–N1 (42 P–B4 P×B
(42 ... N moves 43 R×P! R×R 44 B–
Q6+) 43 P×N K–Q3! 44 R–QR4
B–K6! 45 R–R6 B–Q5 46 P×P R–KB1
with counterplay) 42 ... B–Q1 43
R–KB1 N–B3 44 R–K2 P–B4 45 R–
B5 K–Q3 46 P–R4! K–Q4 47 K–Q3
N–N5 48 R–QN2 (48 R×RP R–B1!)
48 ... R–R1 49 P–R5! P–B5+ (49 ...
P×P 50 R–QN5!) 50 K–K2 K–K5
51 R–B7 P×P 52 R–N8 P–QR5 53 R–
QB8 (53 R–Q7 P–R6!) 53 ... B–B3
54 R×P+? (54 R×R B×R 55 R–B7!
wins) 54 ... K–B4 55 R–QR7 (55 R×P
R–QB1! 56 P–B4 R–QN1 57 R–R2
R–N6 with counterplay) 55 ... P–R6
(55 ... R–Q1!? 56 R/7×P B–N4!) 56
R×P R–QN1 57 R–N4 R–QB1 58 P–
B4 B–K2 59 P–B5! P–K5 (59 ... B×P??
60 R–B3) 60 R–R7 B–B3 (60 ... B×P??
61 R–R5) 61 R–R7(?) (61 R/7–R4!)
61 ... K–N3 62 R–Q7 K–B4 63 R–Q5+
B–K4 64 R–N6 P–K6! (64 ... R–QR1
65 B–Q4! R–R7 66 B–N2! R–R1 67
B×B N×B 68 R–KR6 wins) 65 K–B3
65 B×P K–K5 66 R–Q3 B×P) 65 ...

N–B3 66 R–Q3 R×P 67 B×P R–B7
68 R–Q8 R–B6 68 K–K2 R–B7+ 70
K–Q1 R–B6 71 B–B2 N–K5? (71 ...
N–N5!?; 71 ... R–R6) 72 R–B8+ K–
N4 (72 ... N–B3!? 73 R/8×N+ B×R
74 R×B+! K×R 75 B–Q4+ K–N4!
76 B×R P–R5!; 72 ... K–N5? 73 R–
N4!) 73 R–N5! R–Q6+ (73 ... N×B+
74 R×N R–K6 75 R–K2! wins) 74 K–
K2 R–Q4 75 R×R N–B6+ 76 K–B3
N×R 77 R–QR8 (77 K–K4 N–B3+ 78
K×B? N–Q2+) 77 ... K–B4 78 R–R5
K–K3 79 B–K1 N–B3 80 R–N5 N–Q4
81 B–Q2 B–N2 82 B–B1 B–K4 83 B–
N2 B–B2 84 R–B5 B–Q3 85 R–B1
N–K2 86 R–K1+! (86 R–KR1? N–B4!
87 R–R3 N×P=) 86 ... K–B4 87 R–
QR1 N–B3 88 R–R6 B–K4 89 R×N
B×B 90 R–B5+ K–N3 91 K–B4
B–N2 (sealed) 1–0

14) Petrosian-Spassky, King's Indian
Attack 1 N–KB3 N–KB3 2 P–KN3
P–QN4 3 P–QR4 P–N5 4 P–Q3 B–N2
5 P–K4 P–Q3 6 B–N2 QN–Q2 7 0–0
P–K3 8 P–R5 R–QN1 9 QN–Q2 B–K2
10 N–B4 0–0 11 R–K1 P–QR3= 12
B–B4 B–R1 13 Q–K2 R–K1 14 P–R3
B–B1 15 N/4–Q2 (15 P–K5 P×P 16
KN×P N×N 17 N×N B×B 18 K×B
Q–Q4+!=) 15 ... P–N3 16 B–N5 P–
R3 17 B–K3 B–KN2 18 K–R2 Q–K2
19 R–R2? (19 N–KN1!? and 20 P–KB4)
19 ... K–R2 20 N–KN1 P–Q4! 21 P–
KB4 P–K4! 22 BP×P Q×P (22 ...
QN×P!? 23 P–Q4 N–B5! 24 N×N
P×N 25 P–K5 N–Q4) 23 P–Q4 (23 B–
B4 Q–K2 24 B×BP QR–B1∓) 23 ...
Q–K3 24 P–K5 N–K5 25 R/2–R1
P–QB4! 26 N×N P×N 27 P–B3
NP×P 28 NP×P P×P (28 ... R–N6!)
29 P×P P–B3! 30 P×P N×P 31 QR–
N1 N–Q4! 32 Q–Q2 R×R 33 R×R
Q–Q3! 34 N–K2 Q–R6 35 B–N1
Q–Q6! 36 Q–K1 (*217*)
(36 Q×Q? P×Q 37 N–B4 N–B6
wins) 36 ... B–QB3?! (36 ... R–
QB1 37 R–Q1 R–B7! 38 R×Q P×R

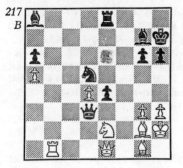

217
B

39 B–B3 N–B2! but not 39 . . . N–B5
40 P×N B×B 41 K–N3 R×N 42
Q–Q1 B–K5 43 P–R4!; 37 R–B1 R×R
38 N×R Q–B7 39 N–K2 P–K6∓;
38 . . . Q–QB6 39 Q×Q N×Q 40
N–N3∓) 37 R–Q1? (37 R–B1 B–N4
38 N–B3!=) 37 . . . Q–R6 (37 . . . B–
N4!? 38 R×Q P×R 39 B×N R×N+
40 Q×R P×Q 41 B–B2 B×P 42 B–K1
37 . . . B–N4!? 38 N–B4!?) 38 N–B4!
N×N 39 P×N B–N4 (39 . . . Q–Q3!
40 B–K3 B–Q2 and 41 . . . B–B4∓)
40 B–K3 B–Q6 41 P–R4! (sealed)
41 . . . Q–Q3 42 P–R5 P–N4 (42 . . .
P×P 43 Q–B2 R–Q1 44 B–R3!) 43
Q–N3 B×P 44 B×B (44 B×P?! R×B
45 R×B R–K6!∓) 44 . . . Q×B 45
P×P Q–K4 (45 . . . Q–B4 46 Q–B4!)
46 Q×Q R×Q 47 P×P R×QRP
(47 . . . P–K6 48 B–B3 P–K7 49 R–K1
R×QRP 50 K–N3 R–R7 51 K–B2 P–
R4 52 K–K3!=) 48 K–N3 R–N4+
49 K–B2 P–R4 50 R–QR1 K×P 51
B–R1 R×P 52 K–K3 B–B7 53 R–QB1
R–R6+ 54 K–Q4 P–R5 55 B×P B×B
56 K×B P–R6 57 K–Q4 ½–½

15) **Spassky-Petrosian,** Sicilian 1 P–K4
P–QB4 2 N–QB3 N–QB3 3 P–KN3
P–KN3 4 B–N2 B–N2 5 P–Q3 P–Q3
6 N–R3 N–B3 7 0–0 B–N5 8 P–B3
B×N 9 B×B 0–0 10 B–K3 N–K1! 11
Q–Q2 N–B2 12 QR–K1 P–N3 13 N–
Q1 P–Q4 14 Q–K2 P–K3 15 P–KB4
P–B4= 16 B–B1 R–B2 17 B–N2 Q–

Q2 18 N–B2 R–Q1 19 P–B3 P–QN4
20 P×QP P×P 21 B–Q2 P–B5 22 Q–
B3 N–K2 23 P×P NP×P (23 . . . QP×P
24 B–K3!) 24 P–N3! N–B1 25 P×P
P×P   26 B–B1 Q–R5   27 R–Q1!
R/1–B1 (27 . . . R×R?! 28 R×R 27 . . .
R/2–Q2?! 28 R×R R×R 29 R–K1)
28 B–K3! N–N3 (28 . . . Q×P?! 29 B–
B5 R–K1 30 Q–B6 threatening 31 B–
Q5) 29 B–B5 (29 N–R3!? P–KR3 30
R–Q6) 29 . . . R–B1 30 B–N4 N–R3
(30 . . . P–QR4?! 31 B–B5) 31 B–Q6
Q–R4 32 P–N4 Q×BP 33 Q–K2! Q–
B3?! (33 . . . N–B4!?) 34 KR–K1! R–Q2
35 B–K7! R×B (35 . . . Q–B2? 36 R×R
N×R 37 B–N7 wins) 36 Q×R Q×Q
37 R×Q N–B4 38 P×P P–B6! (38 . . .
P×P 39 B–R3!) 39 P×P P P×P 40 R–
K2 (40 R×P B–Q5! 41 R×B P–B7
42 R–Q1 N–Q6!!) 40 . . . R–B2 (*218*)

218
W

41 N–K4 (41 N–N4!?) 41 . . . N–K3!
42 N×P! (sealed) (42 N–N5 N×P 43
R–K8+ B–B1 44 B–K4 P–B7 45
B×BP R×B 46 R/1–Q8 N–Q2) 42 . . .
N–Q5! (42 . . . N×P 43 R–K8+ K–B2
44 N–N5!) 43 R–K5! (43 R/2–Q2 R×N
44 R×N B×R 45 R×B R–B7!) 43 . . .
B×R 44 P×B R×N 45 R×N K–B2
46 R–Q6 R–B4 47 R–B6+ K–N2 48
B–K4 R×P 49 R×P+ K–B2 50 B–B2
(50 R–N4! and 51 B–B2) 50 . . . R–K8+
51 K–B2 R–QR8 52 R–QB6 R×P 53
P–R4 N–Q4 54 K–B3 R–R6+ 55 K–
K4 R–QB6 ½–½

16) Petrosian-Spassky, King's Fianchetto 1 P–Q4 P–KN3 2 P–K4 B–N2 3 N–KB3 P–Q3 4 B–K2 P–K3 5 P–B3 N–Q2 6 0–0 N–K2 7 QN–Q2 P–N3 8 P–QR4 P–QR3 (8 . . . B–N2 9 P–R5!) 9 R–K1 B–N2 10 B–Q3 0–0 11 N–B4 Q–K1 12 B–Q2 (12 P–K5!? P–Q4 13 N–K3; 12 P–K5 P×P 13 KN× P±) 12 . . . P–KB3 13 Q–K2 K–R1 14 K–R1 Q–B2 15 N–N1 P–K4! (15 . . . P–KB4?! 16 P×P N×P 17 Q×P N–R5 18 P–B3) 16 P×P BP×P 17 P–B3 N–QB4 18 N–K3 Q–K1! (18 . . . N×B?!) 19 B–B2 P–QR4 20 N–R3 B–B1 (21 . . . B–QR3!?) 21 N–B2 B–K3 22 Q–Q1 Q–B2 23 R–R3 B–Q2 24 N–Q3 N×N 25 B×N B–R3 26 B–B4 Q–N2 27 R–K2 N–N1 *(219)*

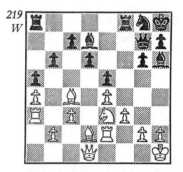

219
W

28 B×N! R×B 29 N–Q5 B×B 30 R×B B–K3 31 P–QN4 Q–B2 32 Q–K2 R–R2! 33 R–R1 R–KB1 (33 . . . P×P!? 34 P×P R/1–R1 35 Q–Q1 K–N2) 34 P–N5 R/2–R1 35 Q–K3 QR–N1 36 R–KB1 Q–N2 37 Q–Q3 R–B2 38 K–N1 R/1–KB1 39 N–K3 P–N4 40 R/2–KB2 P–R4 41 P–QB4 (sealed) 41 . . . Q–N3 42 N–Q5! R–KN1 (42 . . . B×N 43 BP×B P–N5 44 P×P R×R 45 R×R R×R 46 K×R Q×NP) 43 Q–K3 K–R2 44 Q–Q2 R/1–N2 45 Q–K3 K–N1 46 R–Q2 K–R2 47 R/2–KB2 R–B1 48 Q–Q2 R/2–B2 49 Q–K3 ½–½

17) Spassky-Petrosian, Sicilian 1 P–K4 P–QB4 2 N–KB3 N–QB3 3 N–B3 P–KN3 4 P–KN3 B–N2 5 B–N2 N–B3 6 P–Q3 0–0 7 N–KR4 R–N1 8 P–B4 P–Q3 9 0–0 B–Q2 10 P–B5! P–QN4 11 B–N5 P–N5 12 N–Q5 P–QR4 (12 . . . N×N 13 P×N N–K4 14 Q–Q2±) 13 K–R1 (13 Q–Q2!?) 13 K–R1 N–K4 14 Q–Q2 B–B3 15 QR–K1± P–R5 16 Q–K2 (16 B–R6!?; 16 P–KR3!? and 17 P–N4) 16 . . . Q–Q2 17 B–B1 Q–N2 18 N–K3 P–K3 *(220)*

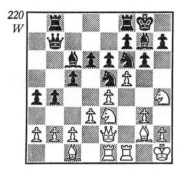

220
W

19 P×KP?! (19 P–N4 KP×P 20 KN× BP!?) 19 . . . P×P 20 N–B3 N×N 21 R×N P–Q4! 22 P×P P×P 23 N–N4 QR–K1 24 N×N+ B×N 25 R–K3 R×R 26 Q×R R–K1 27 Q–B2 R×R+ 28 Q×R K–B2 29 Q–K2 Q–K2 ½–½

18) Petrosian-Spassky, Queen's Indian 1 P–Q4 N–KB3 2 P–QB4 P–K3 3 N–KB3 P–QN3 4 N–B3 B–N2 5 P–QR3 B×N? (5 . . . B–K2 6 P–Q5!±; 5 . . . P–Q4=) 6 NP×B B–K2 7 P–B4 P–Q4 8 P–KB5! KP×P 9 B–N2 0–0!? 10 P×P (10 N×P?! N×N 11 B×N P–B3 12 B–N2 B–Q3 and 13 . . . Q–R5 with counterplay) 10 . . . B–Q3 (10 . . . QN–Q2 11 Q–Q3! (11 P–Q6 B×P 12 B×R Q×B with compensation) 11 Q–Q3 P–N3 12 B–N5 R–K1 13 P–KR4 (13 0–0–0! QN–Q2 (13 . . . P–KR3 14 B–Q2! but not 14 B×P N–N5!) 14 P–B3

(14 P–K4? P×P 15 N×P B–K2 16 P–Q6 P×P 17 N×N+ B×N 18 B×B R–B1+!) 14 . . . P–B5 15 B–R3 R–K6 16 Q–N5 Q–K1 17 N–K4±) 13 . . . QN–Q2 14 P–R5 R–N1 15 P×P?! (15 Q–R3 Q–K2! 16 K–B1 Q–B1 17 B–B3 P–N4 18 P–K3 Q–N2 19 N–K2±) 15 . . . BP×P 16 0–0–0 P–N4! 17 N×P (17 P–K4 P×P 18 B×P (18 N×KP B–K2 19 B–R3 N–B1) 18 . . . N–B1! 19 Q–R3 B–B5! but not 19 . . . B–K2 20 B×P P×B 21 Q–R8+ K–B2 22 B–R6!) 17 . . . Q–B1 18 R–Q2 Q–N2 (18 . . . Q–R3 19 N×B Q×N 20 R–B2 N×P±; 20 . . . N–K5 21 B×N P×B 22 Q–R3 N–B1 23 R–B6 Q×QP 24 R×P+ P×R 25 Q–R8+ K–B2 26 Q–B6+ K–N1 27 R–R8 mate) 19 N–B3 Q–N6 20 Q–B2 K–N2! (20 . . . B×P? 21 Q×Q R×Q 22 P×B R×N+ 23 K–N2 R–B5 24 K–N3) 21 B–B3 (21 Q×Q R×Q 22 K–B2 KR–QN1 23 N–R4±; 23 . . . N–K5 24 B×N P×B 25 R–R4 or 23 . . . R/6–N4 24 P–N4 N×P 25 B×N R×B 26 N–B3) 21 . . . P–KR4! 22 Q×Q R×Q 23 R–B2 KR–QN1 24 P–K3 K–B2 25 R–Q1 (25 B–K2? R×N 26 R×R N–K5; 25 N–N1!? intending 26 N–Q2 and 27 N–B4) 25 . . . N–N3 26 B×N K×B 27 B–K2 P–R5 28 P–B4 R–K1 29 K–Q2 (*221*)

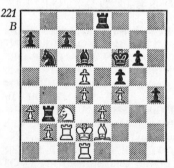

221
B

R×N! 30 R×R! (30 P×R N×P 31 B–N5 R×P 32 P–B4 B×BP 33 P×N R–QN6+ and 34 . . . R×B∓) 30 . . .

N×P 31 B–N5! (31 R–B6 N×KP 32 R–KR1 N–N7; 31 R–N3 N×KP 32 R×N B×BP) 31 . . . N×R (31 . . . R×P?! 32 R×R B×BP 33 R–K1 P–N4 34 K–Q3 N×R 35 R×N B×R 36 K×B±) 32 B×R N×R 33 K×N ½–½

19) Spassky–Petrosian, French 1 P–K4 P–K3 2 P–Q4 P–Q4 3 N–QB3 N–KB3 4 P–K5 KN–Q2 5 N–B3 P–QB4 6 P×P N–QB3 7 B–KB4 B×P 8 B–Q3 P–B3 9 P×P N×P 10 0–0 0–0 11 N–K5 (11 B–N3!?) 11 . . . B–Q2 (11 . . . N–K5? 12 B×N R×B 13 N–Q3!) 12 N×N B×N 13 Q–K2 Q–K2 14 QR–K1 QR–K1 15 B–N3 P–QR3 16 P–QR3 Q–KB2 (16 . . . N–Q2!?) 17 P–N4 B–Q5 18 B–K5 (18 N–Q1 P–K4! 19 P–QB3 B–R2 20 B×KP? N–Q2! wins) 18 . . . B×B 19 Q×B N–Q2 20 Q–N3 P–K4! 21 P–B3 Q–B5?! (*222*)

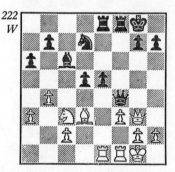

222
W

(21 . . . Q–B3!? 22 N–Q1 P–QN4 23 N–K3 Q–B5) 22 Q×Q R×Q 23 R–B2 P–KN3 24 R–Q2 N–N3 25 R/2–K2 N–Q2 26 N–Q1 P–QN4 27 P–B3 R–B2 28 B–B2 K–N2 29 B–N3 P–KR4 30 N–K3 N–N3 31 N–B2 N–Q2? (31 . . . R/2–K2 32 P–KB4 P–K5 33 N–Q4 B–Q2) 32 R–K3! P–R5 33 P–R3 R–B3 34 N–Q4! B–N2 35 P–R4 R–Q1 36 N–K2 P×P?! (36 . . . K–R3!?) 37 B×RP N–N3 38 B–N3 P–K5

(38 . . . R–K1 39 N–Q4 N–Q2 40 B–
R4) 39 N–Q4 K–R3 40 R–Q1 R–QB1?
(40 . . . R–Q2!?) 41 P×P! (sealed) (41
R–R1 R–K1 42 R–R5 R–Q3 43 R–B5)
41 . . . P×P 42 N–K6! N–B5 (42 . . .
P–R4 43 P×P N–B5 44 B×N R×B
45 N–Q4 R–R5!; 43 N–B5 B–R1 44
N×P B×N 45 R×B R×P 46 R×P+
K–N2; 43 R–Q6! N–B5 44 B×N
R×B 45 N–Q8! R×R 46 N–B7+
K–R4 47 N×R R–B2 48 P–N5 wins)
42 . . . N–R5 43 R–QB1 N–N7 44
N–B5 R×N 45 P×R N–Q6; 43 R–Q7
B–R1 44 R–QB7 R–QN1 45 P–N4!)
43 B×N R×B 44 N–B5 R–B2 45 R–R1
K–N4 46 R–R5! (46 N×RP B×N 47
R×B R–Q2!) 46 . . . K–B5 (46 . . . K–
R3 47 N×B R×N 48 R×RP R/2–
QB2 49 R–K6 R×BP 50 R×R R×R
51 R×P wins) 47 K–B2 B–Q4 48 N–
N3! K–K4 49 K–K2 R–QB3 50 N–Q2
K–K3 (50 . . . R–KB5? 51 P–B4!) 51
N×P B–B5+ 52 K–Q2 R–Q2 53 K–
B2 K–B2 54 R–K5 K–N2 55 N–Q2
B–N4 56 N–B3 B–R5+ 57 K–N2 R–
Q8 58 R/5–K4 R–KB8 59 R–K1 R×R
60 R×R R–B3 61 R–K4 P–N4 62
N×NP R–B7 63 K–R3 B–B3 64 R×P
B×P 65 N–K4 R–K7 66 N–B5 B–B8
67 R–KB4 R–K8 68 P–R4 1–0

20) Petrosian–Spassky, Nimzo-Indian
1 P–Q4 N–KB3 2 P–QB4 P–K3 3 N–
QB3 B–N5 4 P–K3 0–0 5 B–Q3 P–B4
6 N–B3 P–Q4 7 0–0 N–B3 8 P–QR3
B×N 9 P×B QP×P 10 B×BP Q–B2
11 B–Q3 P–K4 12 Q–B2 B–N5?!
(12 . . . R–K1!? 13 N×P N×N 14
P×N Q×P 15 P–B3 B–Q2 16 P–QR4
B–B3 17 P–K4 QR–Q1 18 B–QB4
P–QN3=) 13 N×P N×N 14 P×N
Q×P 15 P–B3 B–Q2 (223)
16 P–QR4! (16 R–K1 B–R5! 17 Q–N2
QR–Q1 18 B–B1 P–QN3 19 P–QB4
KR–K1 20 Q×Q R×Q=) 16 . . . KR–
K1 (16 . . . P–B5!? 17 B×P QR–B1!)
17 P–K4 P–B5 18 B–K2 B–K3 (18 . . .
+!?) 19 B–K3 Q–B2 20 QR–N1

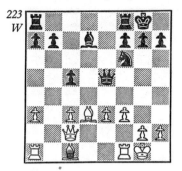

223
W

N–Q2 21 R–N5!± P–QN3 22 KR–N1
Q–B3 23 B–Q4 P–B3 24 Q–R2 K–R1
25 B–B1 P–KR3 26 P–R3 QR–N1 27
P–R5 R–N2 (27 . . . P–R3 28 R×P!
N×R 29 P×N Q–N2 30 Q–R5±)
28 P×P P×P 29 Q–KB2?! (29 Q–N2!
R–R1 30 Q–N4 R/2–R2 31 B×NP R–
R6 32 B–Q4 R–N6 33 R×R P×R 34
P–QB4!) 29 . . . R–R1 30 Q–N2 R/2–
R2! (30 . . . R–R3 31 Q–N4!±) 31
B×NP R–R7 (31 . . . R–R6!? 32 B–B2
R–N6 33 R×R P×R 34 P–QB4 R–
QN1) 32 Q–N4 R–QB7? (32 . . . R/R7–
R5 33 Q–K7 R–QN1 34 R/5–N2
R/5–R1 35 B–B7±; 32 . . . R/1–R6!
33 B–Q4 R–N6 34 R×R P×R 35 P–
QB4 R–QB7 36 Q×P R–B8! 37 R–
Q5! unclear) 33 B–B2 Q–B2 (33 . . .
R/1–R7 34 B–N3!) 34 Q–K7 B×P?
(34 . . . Q–B3 35 B–Q4±) 35 P×B
R×B 36 K×R Q–R7+ 37 B–N2 N–K4
38 R–N8+ R×R 39 R×R+ K–R2
40 R–Q8 N–N3 (40 . . . N–Q6+ 41
R×N wins) 41 Q–K6 1–0

21) Spassky–Petrosian, French 1 P–K4
P–K3 2 P–Q4 P–Q4 3 N–QB3 N–KB3
4 B–KN5 P×P 5 N×P B–K2 6 B×N
B×B 7 P–QB3 N–Q2 8 N–B3 0–0
9 B–Q3 P–K4! 10 Q–B2 (10 Q–Q2!?)
10 . . . P×P 11 P×P P–KN3 12 P–
KR4! B–N2! 13 P–R5 N–B3 14 P×P
RP×P (224)
15 0–0–0 (15 N/4–N5 Q–K2+ 16 K–
B1! N–Q4 17 R–K1; 15 N/4–N5!

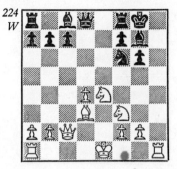

224
W

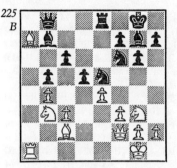

225
B

N–Q4)   15 . . . N × N!   16 B × N B–
N5 = 17 Q–N3 (17 B × QNP? R–N1
18 B–K4 B × N   19 B × B B × P∓)
17 . . . Q–QN3 18 R–R4 (18 Q × NP?
QR–N1 19 Q–Q5 Q–B5+ 20 K–N1
KR–Q1; 18 K–N1!?) 18 . . . Q–B5+

19 Q–K3 Q × Q+ 20 P × Q B × N 21
P × B P–QB3 22 K–Q2 KR–K1 23 P–
N4 B–B3 24 R–N4 R–K2 25 B–Q3
QR–K1 26 R–K1 P–R3 27 B–B4 K–N2
28 R/4–N1 R–KR1   29 R–KR1 R × R
30 R × R R–Q2 31 B–N3 B–Q1 32 P–
B4 P–KB4 33 K–Q3 P–R4 34 P × P
B × P 35 R–QB1 K–B3 36 R–B4 R–Q1
37 K–K2 B–B2   38 R–R4 P–KN4
39 P × P+ K × P ½–½

22) **Petrosian–Spassky,** Polish 1 P–Q4
P–QN4 2 P–K4 B–N2 3 P–KB3 P–
QR3 4 B–K3 P–K3 5 N–Q2 N–KB3
6 P–B3 B–K2 7 B–Q3 P–Q3 8 P–QR4
P–B3 9 N–K2 QN–Q2 10 0–0 0–0
11 N–KN3 R–K1   12 P × P RP × P
(12 . . . BP × P?!   13 N–N3 and N–
QR5±) 13 R × R Q × R 14 Q–B2 B–
KB1 15 P–N4!± Q–N1 16 N–N3
P–N3 17 R–R1 P–K4 18 Q–B2 P–Q4
19 QP × P QN × P 20 B–B2 B–N2?
(20 . . . P–R4! 21 P × P P–R5! 22 N–K4
N × N 23 B × N P × P 24 B–B2 P–R6!)
21 B–R7 Q–B2 22 B–N6 Q–N1 23 B–
R7 Q–B2 24 B–N6 Q–N1 25 B–R7
(225)
Q–B1? 26 B–Q4! P–R4 27 P–R3 P–R5
28 N–KB1 P × P   29 P × P N/K4–Q2

30 N/B1–Q2 (30 P–K5!? N × P 31 N–
B5!?) 30 . . . P–B4 31 N × P N × N 32
P × N B × P 33 B–N3! (33 B × N wins)
33 . . . B–B4   34 R–R7 N–Q2 (34 . . .
R–B1 35 Q × P wins) 35 N–B3 Q–N1
(36 P–B6) 1–0

23) **Spassky–Petrosian,** French 1 P–K4
P–K3 2 P–Q4 P–Q4 3 N–QB3 N–KB3
4 B–KN5 P × P 5 N × P B–K2 6 B × N
B × B   7 N–KB3 B–Q2!? 8 Q–Q2
(8 B–Q3 B–B3 9 P–B3 N–Q2 10 Q–
K2 B–K2 11 0–0 0–0 12 QR–Q1 N–
B3=) 8 . . . B–B3 9 N × B+ Q × N 10
N–K5 0–0 11 0–0–0 N–Q2?! (11 . . .
R–Q1!? 12 P–KR4 B–K1 13 R–R3
N–B3) 12 N × B P × N 13 P–KR4!
QR–N1 14 R–R3 P–B4 (14 . . . R–N3!?
15 Q–N5 KR–N1) 15 Q–N5!± (226)

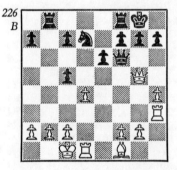

226
B

P × P (15 . . . Q × BP? 16 R–KB3 Q–N8
17 B–N5 wins; 15 . . . KR–Q1 16 KR–
Q3±) 16 Q × Q N × Q 17 R × P R–N2

18 R–QN3! R×R 19 RP×R R–R1 20
R–QB4 N–K1 (20 . . . N–Q4 21 P–N3
or 21 R–B5±) 21 R–R4 N–Q3 22 P–
N3 K–B1 (22 . . . N–B1 23 R–QB4;
22 . . . P–QR4 23 P–QN4) 23 B–N2
R–B1 24 R×P K–K2 25 K–Q2 P–R3
26 P–QB4 P–N4 27 P×P P×P 28 K–
B3 K–Q2 29 P–QN4 R–KR1 30 P–
N5 R–R7 (30 . . . N–B1 31 B–B6+ K–
Q1 32 R–R8 wins) 31 B–B6+ K–Q1
(32 P–B5 N–B4 33 P–N6 wins; 32 P–
N6?! P×P 33 R–Q7+ K–B1 34 R×N
K–B2 35 R–Q7+ K×B 36 R×P∓) 1–0

24) Petrosian-Spassky, King's Indian
1 P–Q4 N–KB3 2 P–QB4 P–KN3
3 P–KN3 B–N2 4 B–N2 0–0 5 N–
QB3 P–Q3 6 P–K3 QN–Q2 7 KN–
K2 P–QR3 (7 . . . P–B3!?) 8 P–N3
R–N1 9 P–QR4! P–QR4 10 B–QR3
P–B3 11 0–0 Q–B2 12 Q–Q2 R–K1
13 QR–B1 R–R1 14 KR–Q1∓ N–N1
15 P–R3 N–R3 16 K–R2 P–R4 17 P–
B4! N–QN5 18 R–B1 P–K4 19 BP×P
P×P 20 P–Q5 R–Q1 (20 . . . P–K5?
21 P–Q6! Q–Q1 22 QR–Q1∓) 21 P–
K4 N–Q2 (21 . . . P–R5 22 P–N4
B×P?!) 22 R–QN1 N–B4 23 N–R2
N/5–R3 24 Q–K3 Q–N3 (24 . . . P–N3
25 N/K2–B3∓) 25 N/K2–B1 Q–R2
(25 . . . N×RP 26 Q–KB3! P–B3 27 N–
Q3 N/R5–B4 28 Q–K3 N–Q2 29 P–
B5∓) 26 N–Q3 N×N 27 Q×N R–K1
28 R–N2 N–B4 29 Q–K3 N–Q2 30
Q–B1 (30 Q–N5!?) 30 . . . Q–N3 31
R/2–KB2 P–B3 (31 . . . Q×P? 32
R×P! Q×N? 33 Q–N5! K–R2 33 B–
B1 wins) 32 R–B3 Q–Q1 33 N–B3
N–B1 34 Q–B2 (34 R–Q1!) N–R2 35
R–Q3 Q–B2 36 Q–K2 B–R3 37 P–R4

B–B1 38 P–Q6?! (38 B×B) 38 . . .
Q–B2 39 B–R3 B×B 40 K×B KR–Q1
227)

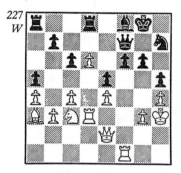

227
W

(40 . . . P–N3!?) 41 P–B5 (sealed) Q–
K3+ 42 K–N2 B–R3 43 N–Q1 N–B1
44 N–N2 N–Q2! 45 R/3–KB3 Q–N5
46 Q–B4+ K–N2 47 N–Q3 R–K1 48
R–QN1 (48 B–N2!? P–KN4!? (48 . . .
Q–K3 49 N×P! N×N 50 Q×Q R×Q
51 R×P) 48 . . . Q–K3 49 Q×Q R×Q
50 P–QN4 P×P 51 R×NP R–R2 52
R–N2 (52 R–B2!? or 52 R–B1!?)
52 . . . R–K1 53 R–B1 K–B2! (53 . . .
R×P? 54 R×NP R–Q1 55 N–N4!
wins) 54 P–R5 K–K3 55 B–N4 B–K6!
56 R–K2 B–Q5 57 K–R3 R–KB1
58 R–B1 R/2–R1 59 K–N2 R–KN1
(59 . . . P–KN4!?) 60 N–K1 P–KN4
61 N–B3 P×P 62 N×RP R–N5 63
N–B5 R1–KN1 64 K–R3 R/1–N4
(64 . . . P–R5! 65 P×P R–B5∓) 65
R–QN1 R×KP 66 R×R R×N 67
R–K2 R–B6! 68 K–N2 R–Q6 69 R–Q2
R–K6 70 R–R2 P–B4 71 B–K1 N×P
72 B–B2 R–N6 73 R×R N×R 74
R–R3 N–B4 75 B×B P×B 76 R–KB3
P–Q6 77 K–B2 ½–½

10 Petrosian–Spassky

Moscow 14 April–17 June 1969

	1	2	3	4	5	6	7	8	9	10	11	12
Petrosian	1	½	½	0	0	½	½	0	½	1	1	½
Spassky	0	½	½	1	1	½	½	1	½	0	0	½

	13	14	15	16	17	18	19	20	21	22	23	**Total**
Petrosian	½	½	½	½	0	½	0	1	0	½	½	**10½**
Spassky	½	½	½	½	1	½	1	0	1	½	½	**12½**

1) Spassky–Petrosian, Sicilian 1 P–K4
P–QB4 2 N–KB3 P–K3 3 P–Q4 P×P
4 N×P P–QR3 5 B–Q3 N–QB3 6
N×N NP×N 7 0–0 P–Q4 8 N–Q2
N–B3 9 Q–K2 B–K2 10 P–QN3 0–0
11 B–N2 P–QR4 12 P–KB4! P–N3
(12 ... N–Q2!?) 13 QR–Q1 (13 P×P
BP×P 14 Q–K5 B–R3; 13 QR–K1!)
13 ... N–Q2 14 P–B4 P–R5 15 P–
KB5! KP×P 16 P×BP B–B3 17 B×B
(17 P×NP!?) 17 ... N×B 18 Q–B2
RP×P 19 RP×P R–R7 20 P×NP (20
B–N1) 20 ... BP×P 21 P–R3 Q–K2!
22 Q–Q4 P–B4 23 Q–B4 B–N2! 24
QR–K1 Q–N2 25 Q–K3 P–Q5! 26 Q–
K6+ Q–B2 27 Q–K2 R–K1 28 Q–B2
R×R 29 Q×R (29 R×R N–N5!) 29 ...
Q–K1! 30 Q×Q+ N×Q 31 B–K4
R×N 32 B×B N–Q3 33 B–Q5+ K–
N2 34 P–QN4! P×P 35 P–B5 N–B4
36 P–B6 (36 R–N1) 36 ... R–QB7 37
P–N4? (37 R–N1!) 37 ... N–Q3?
(37 ... N–K6 38 R–B7+ K–R3 39
B–K4 P–N6 40 P–B7 R–B6; 40 R–Q7
R–B5 and 41 ... K–N4; 40 R–QN7 N–
B5 41 P–B7 N–Q3) 38 R–B4 P–Q6
39 R–Q4 P–Q7 40 B–N3 R×P 41
R×QP N–K5 42 R–Q7+ K–B3 43
R×P R–B8+ 44 K–N2 N–B4 45 B–B7
(45 B–Q5 P–N6 46 B×P N×B 47 P–
R4 N–Q5! 48 P–N5+ K–B4 49 P–R5

P×P 50 R×P K–N5) 45 ... P–N6
46 P–N5+ K×P 47 P–R4+ K–B3 48
P–R5 R–B7+ (48 ... P×P 49 B×NP!;
48 ... P–N4 49 B–N6!) 49 K–B3 P–N7
50 B–R2 P×P (50 ... P–N4 51 R–B7+
K–K4 52 P–R6) 51 R×P R–B8 (228)

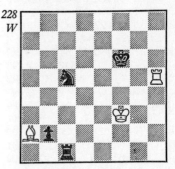

228
W

52 R–R6+? (52 K–K3 N–R5 53 R–R4
N–B6 54 R–QN4) 52 ... K–K4 53
R–QN6 N–R5 54 R–K6+ (54 R–N4
R–QR8 55 R×N R×B 56 R–QN4
K–Q4) 54 ... K–Q5 55 R–K4+ K–B4
56 R×N R–QR8 0–1

2) Petrosian–Spassky, Tarrasch 1 P–
QB4 P–K3 2 P–Q4 P–Q4 3 N–QB3
P–QB4 4 BP×P KP×P 5 N–B3 N–
QB3 6 P–KN3 N–B3 7 B–N2 B–K2
8 0–0 0–0 9 B–N5 P×P 10 KN×P

174

P–KR3 11 B–K3 B–KN5 12 N–N3 B–K3 13 R–B1 (13 N–B5 P–Q5!) 13 . . . R–K1 14 N–N5 (14 N–B5 B×N 15 B×B N–K5) 14 . . . Q–Q2 15 N/N5–Q4 B–KR6 16 N×N P×N 17 Q–Q3 B×B 18 K×B P–QR4! 19 R–B2 P–R5 20 N–Q2? (20 N–B5) 20 . . . Q–N2! 21 K–N1 QR–B1! 22 KR–B1 N–Q2 23 N–B3 P–QB4 24 P–N3 P×P? (24 . . . B–B1) 25 P×P B–B1 26 R–R1 N–B3 27 R/B2–R2 R–R1 28 R×R R×R 29 R×R Q×R 30 Q–B2 N–K5 31 N–Q2 N×N 32 B×N Q–R3 33 K–B1 (33 P–K4? Q–K7 34 P×P P–B5 35 P×P B–N5) 33 . . . Q–N4 34 B–B3 P–N3 35 Q–Q1 Q- B3 36 P–B3 Q- K3 37 K–N2 P–R4 38 P–R3 B–Q3 (38 . . . P–R5 39 P×P!) 39 Q–Q3 B–K4 40 B×B Q×B (*229*)

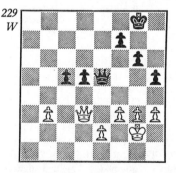

229
W

41 P–R4! K–B1 42 K–B1 K–K2 43 K–B2 Q–K3 44 Q–N5 Q–Q3 45 Q–N7+ K–B3 46 Q–N5 Q–B2 47 Q–Q3 P–B5 48 P×P P×P 49 Q–B3+ K–K3 50 K–K3! Q–B4+ (50 . . . Q–K4+ 51 K–Q2 Q×Q+? 52 K×Q K–Q4 53 P–K4+!) 51 Q–Q4 Q–R6+ 52 K–Q2 Q–R4+ 53 K–B2 Q–QN4 54 K–B3 Q–N6+ 55 K–Q2 Q–N5+ 56 K–B2 Q–R5+ 57 K–B3 Q–R4+ 58 K×P Q–B2+ 59 K–Q3 Q×P 60 Q–K4+ K-B3 61 Q–Q4+ K–K2 ½–½

3) Spassky-Petrosian, Sicilian 1 P–K4 P–QB4 2 N–KB3 N–QB3 3 P–Q4 P×P 4 N×P P–KN3 5 P–QB4 N–B3

6 N–QB3 N×N 7 Q×N P–Q3 8 B–K3 B–N2 9 P–B3 0-0 10 Q–Q2 B–K3 (10 . . . Q–R4 11 N–N5!) 11 R–B1 Q–R4 12 B–K2 (12 N–Q5!) 12 . . . KR–B1 13 P–QN3 P–QR3 14 N–Q5 (14 0-0 P–QN4) 14 . . . Q×Q+ 15 K×Q N×N 16 BP×N B–Q2 17 R×R+ R×R 18 R–QB1 R×R 19 K×R (*230*)

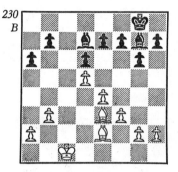

230
B

19 . . . K–B1 20 K–B2 P–K3 21 P–QR4 P×P 22 P×P K–K2 23 B–Q3 B–K4 24 P–N3 K–K1 25 K–Q2 K–K2 26 B–N6 B–K1 27 P–B4 B–N2 28 P–KN4 B–Q2 29 P–R3 P–KR4 30 B–K2 P×P 31 P×P B–N7 32 K–K3 B–B8+ 33 K–B3 B–N7 34 B–Q3 B–B6 35 P–B5 P×P 36 B×BP B×B 37 P×B K–Q2 38 K–K4 B–K8 39 K–Q3 K–B1 40 K–B4 B–Q7 41 P–N4 B–K8 42 P–N5 B–Q7 43 B–Q4 B–K8 ½–½

4) Petrosian-Spassky, Tarrasch 1 P–QB4 P–K3 2 P–Q4 P–Q4 3 N–QB3 P–QB4 4 BP×P KP×P 5 N–B3 N–QB3 6 P–KN3 N–B3 7 B–N2 B–K2 8 0-0 0-0 9 B–N5 P×P 10 KN×P P–KR3 11 B–K3 B–KN5 12 N–N3 B–K3 13 R–B1 R–K1 14 R–K1 Q–Q2 15 B–B5! QR–B1 16 B×B Q×B 17 P–K3 KR–Q1 18 Q–K2 B–N5! (18 . . . P–Q5 19 N×P N×N 20 P×N R×P 21 N–N5 R×R 22 N×R!) 19 P–B3 (19 Q–B1 N–K5 20 N–K2) 19 . . . B–B4 20 QR–Q1 N–K4 21 N–Q4 (21 N×P R×N 22 R×R N×R 23 P–

K4 N–Q6!) 21 . . . B–N3 (21 . . . B–Q2
22 P–B4 B–N5 23 P×N!) 22 B–R3
R–B5!? 23 P–KN4 (23 P–B4 B–R4 24
Q–B1 N–B3! 25 P–KN4 N×NP 26
N×P R1×N 27 Q×R Q–R5!; 23 Q–B1
Q–N5) 23 . . . R–N5 24 P–N3 (24
P–B4 N–B5–Q3) 24 . . . N–B3 25 Q–
Q2 R–N3 26 N/B3–K2? (26 N–R4)
26 . . . B–R2 27 B–N2 R–K1 28 N–
N3 N×N 29 P×N R–K3 30 R×R
Q×R 31 R–QB1 B–N3 32 B–B1?
(32 K–B2!) 32 . . . N–R2! 33 Q–B4
N–B1 (33 . . . Q–N3 34 R–B5 N–N4!)
34 R–B5 (34 Q–K5!) 34 . . . B–N8! 35
P–QR4 N–N3 36 Q–Q2 Q–KB3 37
K–B2 (37 R–B1 N–R5) 37 . . . N–B5
38 P–R5 (38 R–B3 N–K3) (*231*)

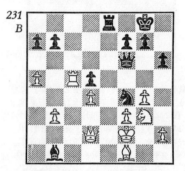

231
B

38 . . . B–Q6! 39 N–B5 (39 Q–B3 Q–R5
40 K–N1 B×B 41 R–B8 B–N4!) 39 . . .
Q–N4! (threatens 40 . . . N–R6+) 40
N–K3 Q–R5+ 41 K–N1 B×B (42
N×B R–K7; 42 K×B Q–R6+ 43 K–
B2 Q×RP+ 44 K–K1 R×N+) 0–1

5) Spassky-Petrosian, Semi-Tarrasch
1 P–QB4 N–KB3 2 N–QB3 P–K3 3 N–
B3 P–Q4 4 P–Q4 P–B4 5 BP×P N×P
6 P–K4 N×N 7 P×N P×P 8 P×P
B–N5+ 9 B–Q2 B×B+ 10 Q×B 0–0
11 B–B4 N–B3 12 0–0 P–QN3 13
QR–Q1 B–N2 (13 . . . N–R4 14 B–
Q3 B–N2 15 KR–K1 R–B1? – 15 . . .
Q–Q3 – 16 P–Q5 P×P 17 P–K5!) 14
KR–K1 (14 P–Q5 N–R4 15 B–Q3 – 15
P×P!? – 15 . . . P×P 16 P–K5 B–B1!)

14 . . . R–B1 (14 . . . N–R4 15 B–Q3
Q–Q3) (*232*)

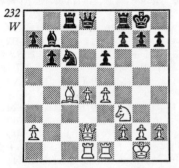

232
W

15 P–Q5! P×P (15 . . . N–R4! 16 P×P
Q×Q 17 P×P+ K–R1 18 N×Q N×B
19 N×N R×N 20 P–K5 B–B1 21 P–
K6 B×P 22 R×B P–N3=; 16 B–Q3
P×P 17 P–K5!?) 16 B×P (16 P×P
N–R4 17 B–B1 Q–Q3 18 N–N5 Q–
R3!) 16 . . . N–R4 (16 . . . Q–K2 17
Q–B4 R–B2 18 N–R4 Q–K4) 17 Q–
B4 Q–B2 18 Q–B5 B×B 19 P×B Q–
B7 (19 . . . N–B5 20 N–N5 P–N3 21
Q–R3 P–KR4 22 N–K4!; 19 . . . Q–Q3
20 N–N5 Q–N3 21 Q×Q RP×Q 22
P–Q6!) 20 Q–B4! Q×RP 21 P–Q6
QR–Q1 22 P–Q7 Q–B5 23 Q–B5
P–KR3 (23 . . . Q–B3 24 N–K5 Q–K3
25 Q–B2) 24 R–QB1 Q–R3 25 R–B7
P–QN4 26 N–Q4 Q–QN3 (better
26 . . . Q–Q3 27 N×P Q–Q7 28 R–
KB1 N–N6!) 27 R–B8 N–N2 (27 . . .
P–N5 28 R–K8 Q×N 29 R×R+
R×R 30 R×R+ K×R 31 Q–B5+!;
27 . . . P–N3 28 R×R Q×R 29 Q×
QNP) 28 N–B6 N–Q3 29 N×R!
N×Q 30 N–B6 1–0

6) Petrosian-Spassky, Queen's Gambit
1 P–QB4 P–K3 2 P–Q4 P–Q4 3 N–
QB3 B–K2 4 N–B3 N–KB3 5 B–N5
P–KR3 6 B–R4 0–0 7 R–B1 N–K5 8
B×B Q×B 9 P–K3 P–QB3 10 Q–B2
N×N 11 Q×N N–Q2 12 P–QR3
P×P 13 B×P P–QN3 14 0–0 B–N2
15 KR–Q1 KR–Q1 16 B–K2 QR–B1

17 P–QN4 R–B2 (17 . . . P–QB4 18 NP×P P×P 19 Q–R5) 18 R–B2 R–R1 19 N–Q2 P–QR4 (19 . . . P–K4 20 P–Q5) 20 B–B3 (20 P×P R×P 21 N–B4 R–R1 22 R–N1 P–QB4) 20 . . . R–R2 21 R–N1 P×P 22 P×P Q–B1 23 P–R3 Q–K2 (23 . . . Q–R1) 24 R/2–B1 (24 N–B4 P–QB4) 24 . . . B–R3 25 Q–N3 B–N4 26 N–K4 N–B3 (*223*)

233
W

27 N×N+ (27 N–B3 B–Q6 28 R–R1 R×R 29 R×R P–K4) 27 . . . Q×N 28 Q–N2 Q–K2 29 R–R1 R×R 30 R×R R–R2 31 R×R Q×R 32 B–K4 Q–K2 33 Q–R3 P–N4 34 Q–B3 Q–Q3 35 B–B3 K–B1 36 P–K4 K–N2 37 P–K5 Q–K2 38 B–K4 Q–Q1 39 Q–R1 Q–K2 40 Q–R3 Q–Q1 41 Q–R1 Q–K2 42 Q–B3 Q–R2 43 K–R2 Q–R7 44 Q–B3 Q–Q7 35 Q–B6+ K–N1 46 Q–Q8+ K–N2 47 Q–B6+ K–N1 ½–½

7) Spassky–Petrosian, Slav 1 P–Q4 P–Q4 2 P–QB4 P–QB3 3 N–KB3 N–B3 4 N–B3 P×P 5 P–QR4 B–B4 6 P–K3 P–K3 7 B×P B–QN5 8 0–0 QN–Q2 9 Q–K2 0–0 (9 . . . N–K5 10 B–Q3!) 10 P–K4 B–N3 11 B–Q3 R–K1 (11 . . . B–KR4) 12 P–K5 (also 12 N–K5 N×N 13 P×N N–Q2 14 P–B4) 12 . . . N–Q4 (12 . . . B×B 13 Q×B N–Q4 14 N–KN5!) 13 B×B (13 N×N KP×N 14 N–K1 B×N!) 13 . . . BP×B! 14 B–Q2 B–K2 15 Q–K4 N–B1 16 P–R5 R–B1 17 KR–B1 P–QR3 (17 . . .

P–B4 18 P×P B×P 19 R–Q1; 18 . . . R×P 19 N–QR4) 18 Q–N4 P–R3 19 N–K4 Q–Q2! 20 P–R4 (*234*)

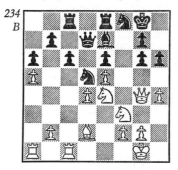

234
B

20 . . . KR–Q1 21 R–B4 Q–K1 22 QR–QB1 (22 P–QN3 followed by B–B1–R3) 22 . . . R–B2 23 N–N3 Q–B2 24 N–K1 R2–Q2 25 N–B3 R–B2 26 Q–K4 R2–Q2 27 Q–N4 ½–½

8) Petrosian–Spassky, Queen's Gambit 1 P–QB4 P–K3 2 P–Q4 P–Q4 3 N–QB3 B–K2 4 N–B3 N–KB3 5 B–B4 P–B4 6 QP×P N–R3 7 P–K3 N×P 8 P×P P×P 9 B–K2 0–0 10 0–0 B–K3 11 B–K5 R–B1 12 R–B1 P–QR3 13 P–KR3 P–QN4 (*235*)

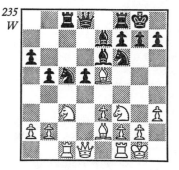

235
W

14 B–Q3? (14 N–Q4) 14 . . . P–Q5! 15 B×QP (15 N×P N×B 16 N×B? P×N; 15 N–K2 P×P) 15 . . . N×B 16 Q×N B–B5 17 Q–N1 B×R 18 R×B N–Q4 19 N–K2 (19 N–K4 Q–B2–B7) 19 . . . B–B3 20 R–Q1 Q–B2 21 B×B N×B 22 N3–Q4 Q–K4 23 Q–Q3

KR–Q1   24 P–QR4! P×P   25 R–R1
N–K5!   26 Q×P R–R1   27 Q–Q3 (27
Q–B4 Q–B3   28 N–B4 Q–QN3!;   27
... KR–QB1   28 R×P!)   27 ... R–
K1   28 N–B4 P–N3   29 Q–R3 Q–B3
(threatens 30 ... N×P)   30 N–Q3 (30
R–QB1 KR–QB1   31 R×R+ R×R
32 Q×P R–B8+   33 K–R2 N×P   34
Q–R8+ K–N2   35 Q–B3 R–R8+   36
K–N3 R–KB8!)   30 ... KR–QB1   31
R–Q1 R–B5   32 P–QN4 (32 P–B3 N–
N6   33 P–N3 R–B6   34 Q–N4 R1–
QB1 35 P×P Q–N4 36 P–B4 Q–KR4!)
32 ... R1–QB1   33 P–N5 R–B6   34
Q–R1 (34 Q×P R×N!;   34 Q–N2 P–
R6   25 Q–N1 P–R7!)   34 ... R×N!
35 R×R Q×P+   36 K–R2 Q–N6+
37 K–N1 Q–B7+   38 K–R2 Q–N6+
39 K–N1 N–B7   40 N–B6 (40 R–B3
N×P+   41 K–R1 N–B7+   42 K–N1
R×R   43 Q×R N–N5)   40 ... N×P+
41 K–R1 N–B7+   42 K–N1 N×R   43
N–K7+ K–B1   44 N×R Q×KP+
(45 K–R2 Q–K4+;   45 K–R1 N–B7+
46 K–N1 N–N5+   47 K–R1 Q–R3+)
0–1

9) **Spassky-Petrosian**, King's Indian
1 P–Q4 N–KB3   2 P–QB4 P–B4   3 P–
Q5 P–K4   4 N–QB3 P–Q3   5 P–K4 P–
KN3   6 B–Q3 N–R3   7 KN–K2 N–
QN5!   8 B–N1 B–N2   9 P–KR3 B–Q2
10 B–K3 0–0   11 Q–Q2 N–R3   12 B–Q3
N–QN5   13 B–N1 N–R3   14 P–R3 N–
B2   15 B–Q3 R–N1 (15 ... P–QN4!?)
16 P–QN4 P–N3   17 P–N4 P–KR4
18 P–KN5 (18 P–B3 N–R2)   18 ...
N–R2   19 P–KR4 P–B3   20 0–0–0 (20
P–B4 KP×P   21 N×P Q–K1   22 P–K5
KBP×P   23 N×NP R–B4!)   20 ..
KBP×P   21 RP×P B–N5!   22 QR–N1
Q–K1 (22 ... R–B6   23 N–N3 R×B!?;
22 ... P×P   23 P×P Q–Q2)   23 P–N5!
R–R1   24 K–B2 R–B6   25 N–N3 P–R3
(25 ... R×B   26 Q×R Q–Q1   27 B–K2
B–Q2   28 B×P!)   26 P–R4 P×P   27
BP×P! Q–B2? (27 ... Q–KB1 28 B–K2
R–B5) (*236*)

236
W

28 B–K2 R–B5   29 P–B3 R×BP (29 ...
B×P   30 B×B R×B   31 N×P!)   30
B×R Q×B   31 R–R2 Q–B1   32 R–B2
Q–B1   33 N–B1 R–R2   34 Q–Q3 Q–R1
35 Q–B4 Q–Q1   36 N–KR2 B–Q2   37
N–B3 B–N5   38 Q–B1! B–Q2   39 K–
N3 B–K1   40 N–Q2 N–B1   41 N–B4
N–R2   42 Q–N2 (42 N×NP N×QNP)
42 ... B–B1   43 **R**–R2 R–N2 (43 ...
N–R1   44 P–R5 and 45 R/1–QR1)   44
K–B2 B–K2   45 R–N1 Q–N1   46 R/2–
N2? (46 P–R5! P×P   47 P–N6 or 47
N×RP; 46 ... N–R1 47 P×P N/R1×P
48 N–R5)   46 ... N–R1   47 R–R2?
(47 P–R5)   47 ... B–Q1!   48 K–Q3 B–
Q2   49 R/N1–QR1 N–B1   50 K–B2
B–K1   51 Q–K2 B–QB2   52 R–KB1
B–Q1   53 R/R2–R1 N–R2   54 R–KN1
N–B1   55 B–Q2 N–R2   56 R–R3 N–B1
57 R1–QR1 N–R2   58 P–R5 P×P   59
N×RP B×N   60 R×B N–B2   61 R–
QN1 N–B1   62 B–K3 N–Q2   63 Q–B2
K–N2   64 K–Q3 K–N1   65 Q–QR2
N–N3 ½–½

10) **Petrosian-Spassky**, Nimzo-Indian
1 P–Q4 N–KB3   2 P–QB4 P–K3   3 N–
QB3 B–N5   4 P–K3 0–0   5 B–Q3 P–
QN3 6 KN–K2 P–Q4 7 0–0 P×P (7 ...
P–B4; 7 ... B–N2)   8 B×P B–N2   9 P–
B3! P–B4   10 P–QR3 P×P   11 P×B
P×N   12 N×P N–B3 (12 ... N–Q4
or 12 ... P–QR3)   13 P–N5 N–K4
(13 ... N–QR4 14 B–K2!)   14 B–K2 Q–
B2 (14 ... N–Q4 15 Q–Q4)   15 P–K4
KR–Q1   16 Q–K1! Q–B4+   17 Q–B2!

Q–K2 (17...Q×Q+ 18 K×Q N–Q6+ 19 B×N R×B 20 B–K3!) 18 R–R3 N–K1 19 B–KB4 N–N3 20 B–K3 N–Q3 (20...Q–N5 21 R–N1 N–K4 22 B–KB1 N–Q6 23 B×N R×B 24 R1–R1) 21 KR–R1 N–QB1 (*237*)

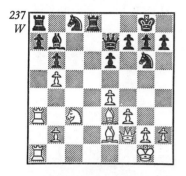

22 B–KB1 (intending N–K2–Q4) 22... P–B4 23 P×P P×P 24 R–R4 R–K1 25 B–Q2 Q–B4 26 Q×Q P×Q 27 R–QB4 R–K4 28 N–R4 P–QR3 (28... N–N3 29 R×P) 29 N×P P×P 30 N×B R×R 31 R×N+ K–B2 32 N–Q8+ K–K2 33 N–B6+ K–Q2 34 N×R+ K×R 35 N×N P×N 36 B–B3 R–N8 37 K–B2 P–N5 38 B×KNP 1–0

11) Spassky-Petrosian, Queen's Indian 1 P–Q4 N–KB3 2 P–QB4 P–K3 3 N–KB3 P–QN3 4 P–QR3 B–N2 5 N–B3 P–Q4 6 P–K3 QN–Q2 7 P×P P×P 8 B–K2 B–Q3 9 P–QN4 0–0 10 0–0 P–QR3 11 Q–N3 Q–K2 12 R–N1 (12 P–N5 P×P 13 N×NP P–B4 14 N×B Q×N 15 P×P P×P!) 12... N–K5! 13 P–QR4 (13 N×P B×N 14 Q×B N–B6) 13...N/2–B3 (13... B×NP 14 N×N! P×N 15 Q×B P–QB4 16 P×P P×N 17 B×P) 14 P–N5 N×N 15 Q×N N–K5 16 Q–B2 KR–B1 17 B–N2 (17 N–Q2 P×P 18 P×P P–QB4!) 17...P–QB3 18 P×BP B×BP 19 Q–N3 Q–Q2 20 R–R1 P–QN4 21 P–R5? (21 P×P) 21...B–N2 (also 21...P–N5 and 22...B–N4) 22 N–K5 Q–Q1 (22...Q–K2!; 22...

B×N 23 P×B N–Q7 24 Q–N4 N×R 25 B–N4) 23 KR–Q1 (23 B–Q3! N–Q7 24 B×P+!) 23...Q–R5 24 P–N3 Q–K2 25 P–B3 N–N4 26 P–R4 N–K3 27 P–B4 P–B3 28 N–B3 N–Q1! 29 K–B2 N–B2 30 N–Q2 (*238*)

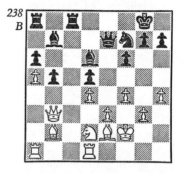

30...R–B5! 31 Q–Q3 (31 N×R QP×N) 31...R–K1 32 B–KB3 B–N5 33 B–R3 B×B 34 R×B N–Q3 35 R–K1 P–B4 36 R3–R1 N–K5+ (36... R1–QB1!) 37 B×N BP×B 38 Q–N1 Q–Q2 39 R–R2 R/K1–QB1 40 N×R (40 N–N3 Q–R6! 41 R–KR1 R–B7+; 41 R–N1 R–B6 42 N–B5 R/1×N 43 P×R P–Q5) 40...QP×N 41 P–Q5 (41 Q–N4 P–B6 42 R–B2 R–B5 43 Q–N3 Q–N5) 41...B×P 42 R–Q1 P–B6 43 R–B2 Q–R6 44 R–N1 Q–N5 45 K–N2 Q–B6+ 46 K–R2 Q×KP 47 P–B5 (47 Q–Q1 Q–Q6 48 Q–N4 Q×R+ 49 R–N2 Q×R+!) 47...Q–B4 48 R–KB1 P–N5 49 P–B6 P–N6 50 R2–B2 P–B7 51 Q–B1 P–K6 52 P–B7+ K–B1 53 R–B5 P–N7 54 Q×NP P–B8(Q) 55 Q×P+ K×Q 56 R–N5+ 0–1

12) Petrosian-Spassky, Tarrasch 1 P–QB4 P–K3 2 P–Q4 P–Q4 3 N–KB3 P–QB4 4 BP×P KP×P 5 P–KN3 N–QB3 6 B–N2 N–B3 7 0–0 B–K2 8 N–B3 0–0 9 B–N5 P×P 10 KN×P P–KR3 11 B–K3 B–KN5 12 Q–R4! N–QR4 (12...Q–Q2 13 N×P!) 13 QR–Q1 N–B5 14 B–B1 Q–B1! 15

Q–B2 (15 N×P N×N 16 B×N N–N3 17 Q–N3 N×B 18 Q×N B–B3; 15 Q–N5 N–N3 16 Q–Q3 B–N5) 15 . . . R–Q1 16 P–N3 N–K4 17 B–N2 Q–Q2 18 P–B3! B–R4 (18 . . . B–K3 19 P–B4; 18 . . . B–KR6 19 B×B Q×B 20 Q–B5!) 19 Q–B5! N–B3 (19 . . . Q–B2 20 N/3–N5 Q–N1 21 N–K6!) 20 Q×Q R×Q 21 N×N P×N 22 N–R4 (239)

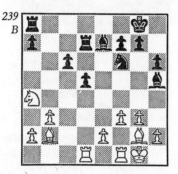

239
B

22 . . . N–K1 (22 . . . P–B4 23 B×N; 22 . . . B–Q3 23 B–KR3 R/2–Q1 24 R–B1) 23 R–B1 (23 B–KR3 R–B2 24 B–K5 B–Q3 25 B×B N×B 26 P–K4 N×P!?) 23 . . . R–B2 24 B–K5! B–Q3 (24 . . . N–Q3 25 P–KN4 B–N3 26 P–B4!) 25 B×B N×B 26 KR–Q1 N–N4 27 K–B2 (27 P–KN4 B–N3 28 P–B4 P–B3? 29 R×BP!) 27 . . . P–B3 28 P–K3 (28 N–B5! R–K2 29 N–R6 B–K1 30 P–QR4 N–Q3 31 P–K4) 28 . . . B–B2 29 B–B1 N–Q3 30 R–B3 (30 B–R6) 30 . . . K–B1? (30 . . . P–N4) 31 N–B5 P–QR4 32 R1–B1 R–K2 33 B–R3 R1–R2 34 P–R4 (34 N–Q3 B–K1 35 N–B4) 34 . . . P–N4! 35 R–Q1 K–N2 36 N–Q3 B–K1 37 N–B1 P–KB4 38 N–K2? (38 B–N2 P–N5 39 P–B4) 38 . . . P–N5! 39 B–N2 P×P 40 B×P N–K5+ 41 B×N BP×B 42 N–Q4 R–B2+ 43 K–N2 R–B3 44 R–KB1 R×R 45 K×R P–R4 46 K–N2 B–Q2 47 R–B2! R–R3 48 P–KN4! (Black threatened K–B2–K2–Q3 and P–QB4) 48 . . . P×P 49 K–N3 ½–½

13) Spassky-Petrosian, Petroff 1 P–K4 P–K4 2 N–KB3 N–KB3 3 N×P P–Q3 4 N–KB3 N×P 5 Q–K2 Q–K2 6 P–Q3 N–KB3 7 B–N5 Q×Q+ 8 B×Q B–K2 9 N–B3 P–B3 10 0–0–0 N–R3 11 N–K4 N×N 12 P×N N–B4 13 KR–K1 B×B 14 N×B K–K2 (240)

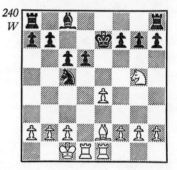

240
W

15 N–B3 R–Q1 16 N–Q4 P–KN3 17 B–B1 K–B1 18 P–QN4 N–K3 19 N–N3 P–N3 20 R–K3 B–N2 21 P–QR3 R–Q2 22 P–N3 R–K1 23 P–KR4 R/Q2–Q1 24 B–B4 N–B2 25 R/Q1–K1 ½–½

14) Petrosian-Spassky, Queen's Gambit 1 P–QB4 P–K3 2 P–Q4 P–Q4 3 N–KB3 N–KB3 4 B–N5 B–K2 5 P–K3 0–0 6 P×P P×P 7 N–B3 QN–Q2 8 B–Q3 P–QN3 9 0–0 B–N2 10 R–B1 P–B4 11 B–B5 (threatens 12 B×N/7 Q×B 13 B×N B×B 14 P×P P×P 15 N–K4) 11 . . . R–K1 12 R–K1 (12 B×N/7 Q×B 13 P×P P×P 14 B×N B×B 15 N–QR4 P–B5 16 R×P B–R3) 12 . . . N–B1 13 P×P P×P 14 N–QR4 N–K5 15 B×B Q×B 16 N–Q2 N–Q3 17 B–N4? (17 B–R3) 17 . . . P–B5 18 N–KB3? P–B4! 19 B–R3 N–Q2? (19 . . . P–N4 20 P–KN4 P–KR4 21 P×BP P–N5) 20 P–KN3 N–B3 21 N–Q4 P–N3 22 N–QB3 N/Q3–K5 23 B–B1 QR–B1 24 R–B2 Q–N5 25 N×N N×N 26 Q–K2 N–B4 27 Q–Q2 P–QR4 28 P–N3! Q×Q 29 R×Q B–R3 30 R1–Q1 R/K1–Q1 31 R–N1 K–B2 32 B–K2 (32 P×P P×P 33 R–N6;

32 ... B×P   33 R–B2)   32 ... N–Q6!
33 R/2–Q1 (33 P×P P×P 34 R–N6 P–
B6! 35 R×N P–B7 36 N×QBP B×R)
33 ... K–K2 34 K–B1 N–N5 35 P–
QR3 N–R7! 36 P×P! N–B6 37 R–N6!
R–Q3 (37 ... N×R 38 R×B; 37 ...
B×P 38 B×B) 38 R×R K×R 39 R–B1
N×B 40 K×N P×P 41 K–Q2 R–QN1
42 K–B3 K–Q4 43 R–Q1 K–K5?
(43 ... K–B4) (*241*)

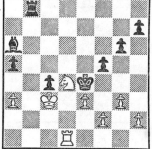

241
W

44 P–B3+ K×KP (44 ... K–Q4 45
N×P+; 44 ... K–K4 45 N–B6+) 45
R–Q2! (threatens mate) 45 ... R–N6+
46 N×R P×N 47 R–Q7 (47 P–B4!)
47 ... P–R4 (47 ... K×P 48 R×P K–
N7 49 R–R6) 48 R–QR7 (48 R–Q6
B–K7 49 P–B4 K–B7 50 R×P K–N7)
48 ... B–B8! 49 P–B4 P–KR5! 50
P×P (50 R×P P–R6!) 50 ... K×P 51
R×P K–K5 (51 ... K–N5 52 R–R4+
P–B5 53 R–N4) 52 K×P? (52 R–R8
P–B5 53 R–K8+ K–B6 54 R–K6!;
53 ... K–Q4 54 R–KN8) 52 ... P–B5
53 R–KN5 P–B6 54 R×P B–R6!
(54 ... P–B7 55 R–KB6 K–K6 56 P–
R5 B–K7 57 R×P!) 55 R–N1 (55 R–
KB6 B–B4 56 R–B6 P–B7 57 R–B1
B–R6 58 P–R5 K–B4!) 55 ... P–B7
56 R–QB1 ½–½

15) Spassky-Petrosian, Petroff 1 P–K4
P–K4 2 N–KB3 N–KB3 3 N×P P–Q3
4 N–KB3 N×P 5 Q–K2 Q–K2 6 P–Q3
N–KB3 7 B–N5 Q×Q+ 8 B×Q B–
K2 9 N–B3 P–B3 10 0–0–0 N–R3 11

KR–K1 N–B2 12 B–B1 N–K3 13 B–Q2
B–Q2 14 P–Q4 P–KR3 15 B–Q3 P–
Q4 16 P–KR3 R–Q1 17 P–R3 0–0
18 B–K3 B–B1 19 N–KR4 KR–K1 ½–½

16) Petrosian-Spassky, Tarrasch 1 P–
QB4 P–K3 2 P–Q4 P–Q4 3 N–KB3
P–QB4 4 BP×P KP×P 5 P–KN3 N–
QB3 6 B–N2 N–B3 7 0–0 B–K2 8 N–
B3 0–0 9 B–N5 B–K3 10 P×P B×P
11 B×N (11 N–QR4) 11 ... Q×B
12 N×P Q×P 13 N–B7 QR–Q1 14
Q–B1 Q×Q 15 QR×Q P–QN3
(15 ... B–N3) 16 N×B P×N (*242*)

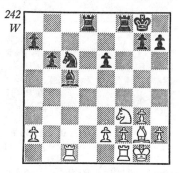

242
W

17 R–B4 (17 B–R3 R–B3 18 N–N5 N–
Q5 19 K–R1!?) 17 ... N–Q5 18 N×N
R×N 19 R×R B×R 20 P–K3 B–B4
21 R–Q1 R–B2 22 B–K4 P–N3 23
P–KR4 (23 B–B2–N3) 23 ... R–B2
24 K–N2 B–K2 25 K–B3 K–N2 26 R–
Q2 B–N5 27 R–B2 R×R 28 B×R
K–B3 29 B–Q3 P–KR3 30 B–K4 P–
KN4 31 P–R5 B–K8 ½–½

17) Spassky-Petrosian, Sicilian 1 P–K4
P–QB4 2 N–KB3 P–K3 3 P–Q4 P×P
4 N×P P–QR3 5 B–Q3 N–QB3 6 N×
N NP×N 7 0–0 P–Q4 8 N–Q2 N–B3
9 P–QN3 B–N5! 10 B–N2! P–QR4
(10 ... B×N 11 Q×B P×P 12 Q–N5)
11 P–QB3 B–K2 12 P–QB4 0–0 13
Q–B2 P–R3 14 P–QR3 B–R3! 15
KR–K1 Q–N3 16 KP×P (16 Q–B3
P–Q5!) 16 ... BP×P 17 P×P B×B
18 Q×B KR–Q1! 19 N–B4 Q–R3 20

Q–KB3 R×P 21 QR–Q1 R–KB4 22
Q–N3 R–KN4 23 Q–B7!? (Q–KB3)
(*243*)

243
B

23 ... R–K1 (23 ... N–Q4 24 Q–Q7
R–Q1 25 Q–R4 N–B5; 24 R×N P×R
25 R×B P×N 26 R×P R×P+!; 25
P–KR4!?) 24 B×N P×B (24 ... B×B
25 N–Q6 R–KB1 26 N–K4) 25 R–Q7
R–QB1 26 Q–N7 Q×Q 27 R×Q
K–B1 28 P–QR4 B–N5 29 R–K3
(29 R–Q1 R–Q4!) 29 ... R–Q1 30 P–
N3 R–Q8+ 31 K–N2 R–QB4 32
R–KB3 P–B4? (32 ... K–N2) 33 P–
N4 R–Q5 34 P×P P×P 35 R–N8+
K–K2 (35 ... K–N2 36 R–N3+ R–N5
37 R–N5) 36 R–K3+ K–B3 37 R–N6+
K–N2 38 R–N3+ K–B1 39 R–QN8+
K–K2 40 R–K3+ K–B3 41 R–N6+
K–N2 42 R–N3+ K–B1 43 R×P P–B5
44 R/N3–R3 (44 R–N4 P–B6+!; 44
R–KB3 R–N4+ 45 K–R3 K–N2 46 R–
R4 R/N4–Q4) 44 ... K–N2? (44 ...
R–N4+ 45 K–B3 K–K2) 45 R/R6–
R5! P–B6+ 46 K–N3 R×R 47 R×R
R–Q6 48 N×P K–N3 49 R–QN5 B×N
50 R×B R×P 51 R–R8 R–R6 52 P–R5
K–N4 53 P–R6 K–N3 54 P–R7 K–N2
55 P–R4 K–R2 56 P–R5 K–N2 57 P–
R6+ K–R2 58 K–B4 1–0

18) Petrosian–Spassky, Tarrasch 1 P–
QB4 P–K3 2 P–Q4 P–Q4 3 N–QB3
P–QB4 4 BP×P KP×P 5 N–B3 N–
QB3 6 P–KN3 N–B3 7 B–N2 B–K2
8 0–0 0–0 9 B–N5 P×P 10 KN×P

P–KR3 11 B–K3 R–K1 12 R–B1 B–B1
13 N–N3 B–K3 14 N–N5 B–KN5
15 P–KR3 B–KB4 16 N/N5–Q4 N×N
17 N×N B–Q2! 18 Q–N3 Q–R4 19
P–R3 B–Q3 20 Q–Q3 Q–Q1 21 KR–
Q1 Q–K2 22 B–Q2 N–K5 23 B–K1
(23 Q–N3 QR–Q1 24 Q×NP B×NP!)
23 ... B–K4! 24 Q–N3 (*244*)

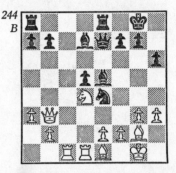

244
B

24 ... B×N (24 ... QR–Q1! 25 Q×
NP N×NP!; 25 Q×QP B–R5 26 Q×N
B×R 27 R×B Q–B3) 25 R×B B–B3
26 P–KR4 Q–K4 27 Q–K3? (27 P–K3)
27 ... Q–B3 (threatens 28 ... N×NP)
28 B×N R×B 29 R×R P×R 30 B–B3
Q–B4 31 R–Q1 R–K1 32 R–Q6 (32
Q×QRP P–K6!) 32 ... P–B3 33 R–Q4
(33 Q–B4!? Q–KR4 34 R×P!) 33 ...
P–R3 34 K–R2 Q–N5 35 P–R4 K–B2
36 K–N1 R–K4 37 R–Q6 R–KB4
(37 ... R–KR4!?) 38 P–N3 Q–R6 39
B–K1 Q–N5 40 B–B3 Q–R6 41 B–Q4
P–KR4 (41 ... R–B6 42 P×R P×P
43 Q–K6+) 42 B–B3 K–N1 43 R–
Q8+ K–R2 44 R–Q6 Q–N5 45 P–
R5 Q–N3 46 P–QN4 Q–B2 47 B–Q4
Q–B5 48 B–B5 R–K4 49 B–Q4 R–KB4
50 B–B5 Q–B7 51 Q–Q2 Q–N6 52
Q–Q1 Q–N7 53 Q–Q2 Q–R8+ 54
Q–Q1 Q–K4 55 Q–Q4 Q–K1 56 Q–
B4 B–N4 57 Q–K6 Q×Q 58 R×Q
R–Q4 59 R–Q6! (59 R×KP R–Q8+
60 K–R2 B–B3) ½–½

19) Spassky–Petrosian, Sicilian 1 P–K4
P–QB4 2 N–KB3 P–Q3 3 P–Q4 P×

4 N×P N-KB3   5 N-QB3 P-QR3
6 B-KN5 QN-Q2   7 B-QB4 Q-R4
8 Q-Q2 P-R3   9 B×N N×B   10 O-O-O
P-K3   11 KR-K1 B-K2? (11 ... B-Q2
12 P-B4 O-O-O)   12 P-B4 O-O   13 B-
N3 R-K1   14 K-N1 B-B1   15 P-N4!
N×NP (15 ... P-QN4   16 P-N5 P×P
17 P×P N-R4   18 P-N6)   16 Q-N2
N-B3 (16 ... P-K4   17 N-B5)   17
R-N1 B-Q2   18 P-B5! (threatens 19
P×P P×P   20 N-B5)   18 ... K-R1
19 QR-KB1 Q-Q1 (19 ... P-K4   20
N-K6!; 19 ... Q-K4   20 N-B3)   20
P×P P×P (245)

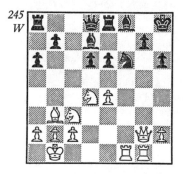

245
W

21 P-K5! P×P   22 N-K4 N-R4 (22 ...
P×N   23 N×N P-KN4   24 Q-R3
R-K2   25 R×P B-N2   26 R×B!)   23
Q-N6! P×N (23 ... N-B5   24 R×N
P×R   25 N-KB3 Q-N3   26 N-K5!)
24 N-N5 (24 ... P×N   25 Q×N+
K-N1   26 Q-B7+ K-R1   27 R-B3) 1-0

20) Petrosian-Spassky, Queen's Gambit
1 P-QB4 P-K3   2 P-Q4 P-Q4   3 N-
KB3 B-K2   4 N-B3 N-KB3   5 B-N5
O-O   6 P-K3 P-KR3   7 B×N B×B   8
Q-Q2 P-QN3   9 P×P P×P   10 P-QN4
B-N2   11 R-QN1 P-B3   12 B-Q3
N-Q2   13 O-O R-K1   14 KR-B1 P-
QR4   15 P×P! (15 P-QR3 P×P   16 P×P
P-QN4!)   15 ... R×RP   16 B-B5 R-R3
(16 ... P-QN4?   17 B×N)   17 R-N3
P-N3   18 B-Q3 R-R2   19 K1-N1 B-N2
20 P-QR4 Q-K2   21 B-B1 B-R3   22
P-R4 B×B   23 R×B P-R4 (23 ...

Q-K3   24 P-N3 Q-R6   25 R-B1 R-
K3!)   24 R-K1 R2-R1   25 P-N3 Q-Q3
26 K-N2 K-B1   27 R1-QN1 K-N1
28 Q-Q1 B-B1   29 R/N3-N2 B-N2
30 R-B2 R-R2   31 R/N1-B1 N-N1
32 N-K2 R-B2 (32 ... R×P   33 R×P!)
33 Q-Q3 R-R2   34 Q-N3 R-R3   35
N-B4 R-Q1   36 N-Q3 B-B1 (36 ...
R-QB1   37 N-N4 R-R4   38 N×BP!)
37 N/B3-K5 R-B1   38 R-B3 B-K2   39
N-KB4 B-B3   40 N/K5-Q3 R-R4
(246)

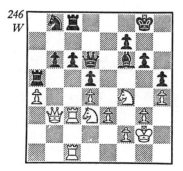

246
W

41 Q×NP R×P   42 R-B5! R-R3
(42 ... N-Q2   43 R×BP!)   43 R×QP!
Q×N (43 ... Q-B1   44 Q-N7)   44
Q×R Q-K5+   45 P-B3 Q-K3   46
Q-B4 Q×P (46 ... R-K1   47 R-K5!)
47 N-K5 R-B1   48 R-B5! B-K2   49
R-QN1! B×R (49 ... K-N2   50 R-N7;
49 ... B-Q3   50 R-N2)   50 R×N
(50 ... K-R1   51 N×BP+ K-N2   52
N-N5) 1-0

21) Spassky-Petrosian, Ruy Lopez
1 P-K4 P-K4   2 N-KB3 N-QB3   3 B-
N5 P-QR3   4 B-R4 N-B3   5 O-O B-K2
6 R-K1 P-QN4   7 B-N3 O-O   8 P-B3
P-Q3   9 P-KR3 N-Q2   10 P-Q4 B-B3
11 B-K3 N-R4   12 B-B2 N-N5   13 B-
B1 B-N2   14 P-QN3 N5-N3   15 B-K3
R-K1   16 P-Q5 R-QB1 (16 ... B-K2)
17 QN-Q2 P-B3   18 P-B4 BP×P   19
BP×QP Q-B2   20 R-QB1 Q-N1   21
P-QR4! N-B4   22 P×P P×P   23 R-R1
P-N5   24 Q-K2 N/N3-Q2 (247)

247
W

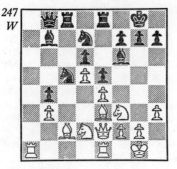

248
B

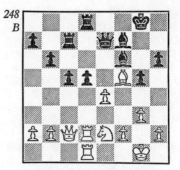

25 B–Q3!? (25 N–B4 B–R3 26 N3–Q2)
25 ... N × B? (25 ... B × P!?) 26 Q × N
B–R1 27 N–B4 N–B4 28 B × N! R × B
29 R–R4 P–R3 30 Q–Q2 B–K2 31
R1–R1 B–N2 32 Q × NP P–B4 33 R–
R7! R–B2 34 P × P Q–B1 35 N–K3
P–K5 36 N–Q4 B–KB3 37 R–KB1
B–R3 38 R × R Q × R 39 Q–R4 R–R1
40 R–Q1 Q–N1 41 N–B6 Q–N2 42
Q × P Q × P 43 R–K1 B–B6 44 R–N1
Q–R7 45 N–QN4 Q–R5 46 Q–K6+
K–R1 47 Q × QP B–K7 48 N–B6 Q–R7
49 R–N8+ R × R 50 Q × R+ K–R2
51 Q–KN3 B–KR4 52 K–R2 B–K8
53 P–B6! (53 ... P × P 54 N–B5 B–N3
55 N/6–K7) 1–0

22) Petrosian–Spassky, Queen's Gambit
1 P–QB4 P–K3 2 P–Q4 P–Q4 3 N–
QB3 B–K2 4 N–B3 N–KB3 5 B–N5
0–0 6 P–K3 P–KR3 7 B × N B × B
8 Q–Q2 P–QN3 9 P × P P × P 10 R–Q1
B–K3 11 P–KN3 N–Q2 12 B–N2
B–K2 13 0–0 P–QB3 14 Q–B2 R–B1
15 N–K5! N × N 16 P × N P–B3 17
P × P (17 Q–N3 B–B2!; 17 ... P × P?
18 P–K4!) 17 ... B × P 18 N–K2 Q–Q3
19 R–Q2 (19 P–K4 Q–N5) 19 ...
KR–Q1 20 KR–Q1 Q–K2 21 N–B4
B–B2 22 B–R3 R–B2 23 B–B5 (23
N–N6 Q–K1 24 B–B5 B × P) 23 ...
P–KN4! 24 N–K2 P–B4 25 P–K4!?
(*248*)
25 ... B–Q5! (25 ... P–Q5 26 P–B4)
26 N × B (26 Q–R4 P–QN4! 27 Q × NP

P × P) 26 ... P × N 27 Q–Q3 P × P
28 B × P K–N2 29 Q–KB3 Q–B3 30
Q × Q+ K × Q 31 P–N3 P–QR4 (32
R × P? R × R 33 R × R K–K4) ½–½
23) Spassky–Petrosian, Sicilian 1 P–K4
P–QB4 2 N–KB3 N–QB3 3 P–Q4
P × P 4 N × P Q–B2 5 N–QB3 P–K3
6 B–K3 P–QR3 7 B–Q3 N–B3 8 0–0
N–K4 9 P–KR3 B–B4 10 Q–K2 P–Q3
11 P–B4 N4–Q2 12 N–N3 B × B+
13 Q × B P–QN3 14 QR–K1 B–N2
(14 ... P–K4 15 P × P P × P 16 N–Q5)
(*249*)

249
W

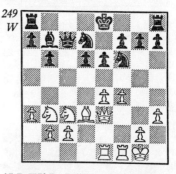

15 P–K5! P × P (15 ... N–Q4 16 N × N
B × N 17 P × P Q × P 18 Q–Q4) 16
P × P N–Q4 17 N × N B × N 18 R–B4
P–QN4 19 N–Q4 R–QN1 (19 ... 0–0
20 R–R4; 19 ... P–KN3 20 B × QNP!)
20 P–B3 P–N3 21 P–R3 0–0 22 R–R4
P–B4 (22 ... KR–Q1 23 Q–R6 N–B1
24 R–B4 and P–KR4–5) 23 P × Pep
R × P 24 B–K4 N–B4 25 B × B P × B

26 Q–K7 Q×Q 27 R×Q P–KR4 28
N–B3 N–K5 29 R–Q7 R–Q3 30 R×R
N×R 31 R–Q4 N–B5 32 R×P N×NP
33 R–Q6 P–R4 34 R×P+ K–R2 35

R–QB5! N–B5 (35 . . . P–QR5 36 N–K7
R–K1 37 R–B5) 36 P–QR4 N–N5
37 P×P R×P 38 P–B4 R–N2 39 P–B5
R–R2 40 R–Q6 K–N2 ½–½

INDEXES

1 People

2 Events

3. General

4. Openings

5. Games